Praise for Completing Vyasa's Mahabharata

In *Completing Vyasa's Mahabharata*, Abhinav Agarwal puts together lesser-known stories, the upakhyaanas, that feed into Ved Vyasa's grand saga. Each of the 67 tributaries in this collection flows into The Mahabharata, also known as the fifth Veda. They offer complex and diverse windows with which to examine the text, and interrogate the tenets and the typal structures that give body to a constantly-evolving, ever-elusive, always-dominant ethos of ancient India—Dharma. With this book, Abhinav also makes his mark as an Indic scholar-storyteller on three counts. First, he is steeped in the Indian tradition, where the hermeneutics of faith underline the writing, even as he captures the several philosophical contestations that define Bharat. Second, he conforms to the rigour of modern scholarship that is necessary to power his retellings with intellectual credibility, the use of the V.S. Sukthankar-edited Critical Edition, for instance. And third, he does these with the skill of a contemporary writer who grasps you from the first line to the last. I enjoyed reading this book; you will too.

—Gautam Chikermane,
Vice President, Observer Research Foundation, and Author

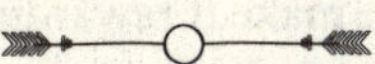

Abhinav introduces some of the main characters and also some of the forgotten characters from The Mahabharata with such lucid narration, it evokes the feelings and memories of hearing the verses in Sanskrit. The writing is simple and elegant, with regular anecdotes for contemporary readers to connect better in case they are not thoroughly aware of all the stories and the characters. The emotions displayed are uncomplicated and blatant, connecting with the magic, mystery and history of Indian culture with astute details and great pride.

—Koral Dasgupta,
Author, Entrepreneur, Professor, Painter

Over the last many years, Abhinav Agarwal has carved a niche for himself as a writer wholly in tune with the rich civilizational heritage of this land. A technology professional, he has effectively created a parallel, independent career by his keen pursuit of Indic studies. His numerous, carefully researched articles on personages of the Epics, like Krishna in the Mahabharata, have established him as a writer accessible to a young audience eager to re-connect with our legacy.

Abhinav Agarwal has addressed complex issues like Dharma, with a sensitivity that is rare to find. His account of the dilemmas that confronted Yudhishthira after the great war makes poignant reading.

He now ventures to write a full-fledged book on 67 Upakathas (sub-tales) that complete the Mahabharata. The Upakathas were identified by Alf Hiltebeitel, renowned scholar, whose books on the Epic are mandatory reading.

Abhinav Agarwal tells stories of Shakuntala, Nala–Damayanti, Savitri, Yayati, Amba, and so many more in a style that would engross bibliophiles across generations. Questions that arise naturally while reading about certain personalities and incidents in the Epic have been elaborately discussed.

Each Upakatha has been situated within the larger narrative of the Epic. Citations from the original text, and translations where required, add gravitas to the work. Detailed footnotes which provide explanations of technical terms, and biographical details of the dramatis persona, make it rewarding reading. The extent of research involved in writing this book can be gauged from the fact that the footnotes number over one thousand!

All in all, *Completing Vyasa's Mahabharata* holds the promise of emerging as the definitive text for the general reader.

—Meenakshi Jain, Senior Fellow,
Nehru Memorial Museum and Library,
awarded Padma Shri by the President of India

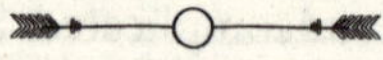

The tale of Mahabharata is simple at one end and extremely complex on the other, with thousands of characters. Abhinav weaves together the various threads of the magnum opus, moving from one yuga to another, to connect and narrate engaging tales. Like the weaves and motifs of a complex carpet, which appears impossible to unravel, Abhinav takes the reader through the stories creating a tapestry which is not only beautiful but easy to understand.

With brevity at its core, yet not missing out on important facts of the tale, the engaging pace keeps the reader hooked as she reads stories of Shakuntala, Nala, Damayanti, Saavitri, Yayati, Ambaa, or Ashtavakra.

The reader would not only emerge educated but get a far better sense of the various sub-tales, upakathas of Mahabharata, and how they link to the main narrative.

True to its name *Completing Vyasa's Mahabharata,* completes the story of the great epic for the lay reader.

—Vikrant Pande,
Translator and Author

An absolutely brilliant exposition on how to tell and retell the world's greatest epic. Just when one thinks enough has been said and written on the Mahabharata, comes along this masterpiece. Wonderfully evocative, from the first page to the last.

—Anand Ranganathan,
Author and Scientist

Completing Vyasa's Mahabharata by Abhinav Agarwal is a must read that deserves a place in your bookshelf for this unique compilation of Upakhyanas of Mahabharata.

Upakathas are ancillary stories invoked in the Mahabharata in the course of conversations between various people. Upakathas make the itihasa richer by adding a unique sense of context and perspective to the continuous deliberation on Dharma.

Abhinav Agarwal makes an erudite attempt to present this contextual knowledge corpus to the modern reader. Abhinav makes a crucial addition to the literature on Mahabharata, especially to the readers of various abridged editions. Read it and make everyone you know read it. The book leaves the reader enriched by a wealth of perspectives and nuances.

—Saiswaroopa Iyer, Author

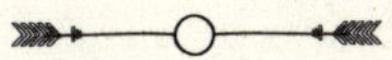

A wonderfully readable retelling of the many sub-plots of the Mahabharata. Writer Abhinav Agarwal gives them the independent life they deserve while maintaining the style and tenor of the original. Reading it gives the joy of wandering through the meandering lanes of an old city without bothering about the grand palaces and famous sites.

—Sanjeev Sanyal,
Economist and Writer

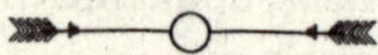

This book will be an invaluable resource in the growing corpus of English literature on the Mahabharata. The upakhyaanas are woefully ignored nowadays, but it is impossible to fully appreciate and understand the narrative of the epic without delving into these stories within the story. Many are wisdom tales in their own right that provide their own unique gloss on Dharma and the other themes underpinning the Mahabharata. Agarwal's book makes these stories easily accessible to the lay reader—it has the flow of an eminently readable novel, while providing all of the necessary background information and cross-references necessary for deeper research. I also appreciate that there is no deviation from the text or unnecessarily editorializing or embellishment, just a commendable and successful effort to streamline the narrative in a way that it resonates for the modern reader in English. The footnotes are a treasure trove of information. This book is a must-have for any collection in English on the Mahabharata.

—Aditi Banerjee, Author

COMPLETING VYASA'S MAHABHARATA

67 Upakathas for the Modern Reader

COMPLETING VYASA'S MAHABHARATA

67 Upakathas for the Modern Reader

ABHINAV AGARWAL

Title: Completing Vyasa's Mahabharata: 67 Upakathas for the Modern Reader
Author: Abhinav Agarwal

ISBN: 978-93-92209-45-1

First published in India 2023
This edition published 2023

Published by:
BluOne Ink LLP
306, Tower-I, Assotech Business Cresterra,
Plot No. 22, Sector 135, Noida.

Website: www.bluone.ink
Email: publisher@bluone.ink

Printed in India

ॐ

नारायणं नमस्कृत्य नरं चैव नरोत्तमम् ।
देवीं सरस्वतीं व्यासं ततो जयमुदीरयेत् ॥

nārāyaṇaṁ namaskṛtya naraṁ caiva narottamam
devīṁ sarasvatīṁ vyāsaṃ tato jayam udīrayet

To

Bibek Debroy*, without whose translations, support, and encouragement, this book would not have been possible.*

This is for you, sir.

To

Rick Dehring, without whose translations, support and encouragement, this book would not have been possible.

This is for you, sir.

CONTENTS

FOREWORD

Who has the time to read the entire Mahabharata? 100,000 *shlokas* by some accounts, roughly 80,000 *shlokas* with the Critical Edition of BORI (Bhandarkar Oriental Research Institute). With say 20 words per *shloka*, that's 2 million words for the former and 1.6 million words for the latter. In this day and age, when time is at a premium and social media presence beckons, few lack the patience and perseverance. In an earlier era, these stories were heard from grandparents, passed down verbally. With the inevitable breakdown in the joint family system, a generation of grandchildren missed hearing these stories from their grandparents and those grandchildren have now become grandparents. Who doesn't know about the Mahabharata, and the Ramayana? Most have a passing degree of familiarity with both, or think they do.

The Mahabharata is a vast compendium. It is an encyclopaedia. It isn't only about stories. There is geography, history and extensive sections on *dharma* of various types, *raja dharma* included. Approximately, two-thirds of the Mahabharata is in the form of this other material. If one focuses on stories (*dharma* is also taught through stories) alone, and doesn't possess the time and inclination to read the unabridged Mahabharata, in whatever language, one will miss out on this material. Abridgement means some material is suppressed. It's like reading the executive summary or abstract of a paper. Most people have read some abridged version of the Mahabharata. Anyone who has done the exercise of drafting an executive summary knows that one should focus on key points. For the Mahabharata, this means stories, leaving out the other material as boring and extraneous. Hence, people will often not know that this other material exists in the Mahabharata.

But the sampling bias becomes worse. The selected stories are reduced to those that concern the Kurus (Duryodhana and his brothers) and the Pandavas (Yudhishthira and his brothers) and the battle in Dharmakshetra Kurukshetra. Other accounts are left out. A Mahabharata-based quiz will reveal this gap in awareness. Who was Animaandavya? Who was Vriddha Kumari? Who was Srinjaya? These three are random selections from the 67 in Abhinav Agarwal's book. There will be a flicker of recognition at some of the names chosen. Who has not heard of Shakuntala, Nala and Damayani, Agastya or Rama? Some care is needed though. Which Shakuntala are we familiar with, the one from the Mahabharata, or the one made famous by Kalidasa? Which Rama story, from the Valmiki Ramayana or some other Ramayana, or from the Mahabharata? Yes, indeed, there are differences between the versions.

In Sanskrit, there are two different words, *akhyana* and *upakhyana*. The words are allied, but with slightly different nuances. An *akhyana* is a narrative. An *upakhayana*, with the pre-fix added, is a narrative or account that is repeatedly told and retold. As composed by Krishna Dvaipayana Vedavyasa, Mahabharata was originally an *akhyana*, taught to Romaharshana or Lomaharshana. However, retold again and again through oral transmission, and embellishments added to the original, over a period of time, it has become *upakhyana*. Today, it is impossible to sift out the original from the present text. For example, many years ago, M. R. Yardi did a statistical analysis of different styles used in Mahabharata *shloka*s to decide whether there were multiple authors.[1] He concluded that there were five different authors—Vaishampayana, Suta, Sauti (Suta's son), the author of Harivamsha and the author who classified the Mahabharata into different *parva*s. All such exercises are inherently subjective and arbitrary. There is no objective method of knowing what the original Mahabharata looked like. Clearly, today's text wasn't yesterday's text. For example, most of us will automatically say Mahabharata has 18 *parva*s. Yes, that's true. But there is internal evidence to suggest Mahabharata also possessed a 100-*parva* classification once. BORI's Critical Edition (CE) was a phenomenal exercise. Taking some fifty years to complete, using the criterion of a *shloka* occurring in multiple manuscripts, it sought to identify what might have been the oldest version. As the introduction to CE makes abundantly clear, BORI made no claims that CE is the original Mahabharata. CE has been criticized, primarily on grounds of excision and omission of *shloka*s. No one has criticized CE on grounds of commission of *shloka*s, that is, not excising them. Abhinav Agarwal's book is based on CE.

I know few people who are as steeped in Mahabharata, and Puranas, as Abhinav is. That obsession and knowledge has led to this collection of 67 upakhyanas, retold in a very reader-friendly and attractive fashion, as befits an author who has written fiction. Given the etymological meaning of *upakhyana*, the author has authored an upakhyana himself. The Mahabharata is a text that deserves to be treated better than Mahabharata for dummies. Abhinav Agarwal is too young to be described as a traditional grandparent. However, he has done what grandparents would have done once upon a time, retold stories from the Mahabharata, that too, relatively unfamiliar ones. Once upon a time, grandparents retold the stories in non-English languages. In this day and age, English has become important, and the stories have to be communicated not only to an Indian audience, but also to a global one. To that end, this is an excellent book and every reader will be much better informed about anecdotes and episodes. The Mahabharata deserves this. I commend Abhinav and hope this upakhyana runs into several reprints.

Bibek Debroy
March 2023

ACKNOWLEDGMENTS

Writing a book is mostly a solitary task; having it see the light of day is not. Many people helped make this book possible. First, without Shri Bibek Debroy's translations, guidance, and suggestions—always forthcoming, always insightful—this book would not have been possible. Gautam Chikermane, whose enthusiasm for this book and its idea surpassed even mine. Anirudh Chakravartty, who accepted my book proposal in one day, and which then left me scrambling to finish the editing. Hari Kiran Vadlamani, whose patience, support, and vision is exceeded only by his unstinted support. To the extended family of Indica and the authors whose knowledge and passion for the Mahabharata serves as a constant inspiration—Saiswaroopa Iyer, Deepak M.R., Bharathi V., Pranshu Saxena, Shivakumar G.V., and others.

To Alf Hiltebeitel, who passed away before this book could see the light of day, and whose paper, *Not Without Subtales*, sparked the idea for this book. Profs Vishwa Adluri and Joydeep Bagchee, and their pathbreaking books on the Mahabharata and Hiltebeitel's work.

Mini Narayanan, whose editing skills and sharp eye for spotting inconsistencies immeasurably improved this book and caught bloopers that would otherwise have caused me no little amount of embarrassment. Any remaining errors are, of course, mine alone. Syed Dilshad Ali, for the wonderful cover. Praveen Tiwari, who has worked closely and guided the book through every step.

My wife, Bhavana, who was born in Kurukshetra; nothing more need be said. Anvita and Anika, who have waited patiently while I have stolen precious minutes and hours on weekends to spend with Vyaasa.

I know I have forgotten some names, and I hope they will excuse my lapse.

Abhinav
31 May 2023
Jyestha Shukla Ekadashi, VS 2080

Introduction

In the corpus of texts on Hinduism, 'shruti' texts are the most revered. The word shruti means 'that which is heard', and shruti texts are considered divine in origin and authorless. The Vedas are shruti texts. Then come 'smriti' texts. Smriti means 'that which is remembered' and were composed by authors. This is the reason Vyaasa is known as the compiler of the Vedas but the author of the Mahabharata. Among smriti literature, you have Puranas, Itihaasa, and other texts. Itihaasa, which means 'that is indeed as it was', can also be translated as history, and includes only two texts—Ramayana and Mahabharata.

The Mahabharata was written by Krishna Dvaipaayana, also known as Ved Vyaasa. After composing it over a period of three years, he taught it to five of his disciples. One of them, Vaishampaayana, then retold it to King Janamejaya, himself a descendant of the Pandavas and the grandson of Abhimanyu. This was the first public recital of the epic. Ugrashrava, a soota (bard, storyteller) who was one of the auditors of this recital, travelled to Sage Shaunaka's hermitage in Naimisharanya, where he then retold it to the sages assembled there. From there, the text travelled to other parts of India, Asia, and the world.

The Mahabharata itself tells us that Vyaasa first composed this account in 24,000 verses and which was known as Bhaarata. No traces of this original text have survived, and conjectures—sometimes informed but mostly otherwise—by academicians and amateurs alike have yielded neither consensus nor insights on what this original text may have looked like. The Mahabharata also tells us that there is a 150-verse summary, which can be found in the Parvasamgraha Parva. When expanded into 100,000 verses, it came to be known as Mahabharata—this much is also told to us in the Mahabharata itself.

The Mahabharata is divided into 18 major books, or Parvas. Another classification, described in the Mahabharata itself, divides it into one-hundred minor Parvas. Minor Parvas, or upa parvas, are entirely contained within the major parvas. Within each Parva and upa parva, you have chapters, and within chapters you have verses.

In 1919, the Bhandarkar Oriental Research Institute (BORI), in Pune (then called Poona), embarked on a mammoth project to analyse all available versions and recensions of the epic and to constitute a Critical Edition. This project completed in 1966, arriving at a final constituted version of 73,000 verses. With the addition of Harivamsha, considered an appendix to the Mahabharata, another 6,000 verses were added to this Critical Edition.

Interspersed within the Mahabharata's main narrative, there are many sub-tales. Of those, there are some that are called upakhyaanas, or upakathas, and they number 67 according to one enumeration by scholar, Alf Hiltebeitel. His criteria were simple—an upakhyaana is one where the text itself mentions it as such, or where the Parvasamgraha parva cites it as such, or is called an upakhyaana in the Critical Edition. 67 fit this definition.

These upakhyaanas may appear to be digressions, but they often provide a crucial connective tissue that not only binds the text together, but also answers those nagging questions that a reader would have. For example, why did Ambaa, the Kaashi princess, in a later life become the cause of death of Bheeshma, the redoubtable warrior whom even Parashuraama could not defeat? The Ambaa upakhyaana has the answers. Take the case of Sage Parashuraama; why was a brahmana like him imbued with the attributes of a warrior? Two upakhyaanas answer this question. Why did the Kurus descend from Puru, the youngest son of Yayaati, and not the eldest? The Yayaati upakhyaana answers that question, and much more. What did Duryodhana tell Shalya to convince him to become Karna's charioteer? Turn to the Tripuraa upakhyaana to know why. What had detained Krishna that he couldn't be with the Paandavas when they took part in those fateful games of dice? Krishna himself answers in the Shaalva-vadha upakhyaana. Why was Vidura, the wisest of the three brothers, fated to spend his life serving and not ruling? The Animaandavya upakatha sheds light. And the list goes on. These upakathas, in a way, complete the Mahabharata, and hence the title of this book.

Taken together, these 67 upakhyaanas total 10,091 verses, which is a shade under 14 per cent of the Mahabharata. Not all these upakathas are the same length, however. Not even close. The shortest one comes in at 21 verses; there are two that are only 22 verses long. On the other hand, Nala Damayanti is 901 verses long, Raama is 727 verses long, Ambaa is 673 verses long. Not all are narrated by the same person. Hiltebeitel breaks down the narrators thus:

> As to upākhyāna *narrators*, Vaiśampāyana addresses ten to Janamejaya (1–4, 11, 32, 39–40, 66–67); Bhīṣma narrates twenty-three: 21 (44–52, 54–65) to Yudhiṣṭhira and the Pāṇḍavas and two (35–36) to Duryodhana; Lomaśa Ṛṣi tells eight of nine (from numbers 14–22) to the Pāṇḍavas, Mārkaṇḍeya Ṛsi also tells them eight (23–28 and 30–31), and Kṛṣṇa three (12, 41–42); Citraratha narrates three (6–8) to Arjuna and the Pāṇḍavas; Śalya tells two: one (33) to Yudhiṣṭhira, the other (38) to Karṇa and Duryodhana; Vyāsa tells one to Draupadī's father Drupada (9) and another to the Pāṇḍavas (29); and six are told by single-time speakers: Kuntī to Pāṇḍu (5; the only upākhyāna spoken by a woman), Nārada to the Pāṇḍavas (10); Bṛhadaśva to the Pāṇḍavas (13); Akṛtavraṇa to the Pāṇḍavas (15; interrupting Lomaśa's skein); Rāma Jāmadagnya to the Kauravas (34); and Duryodhana to Karṇa and Śalya (47).[1]

The 67 upakathas you will read in this book are not verse translations; for that you have unabridged translations. Rather, these are retellings written with two objectives in mind. Three, if you count the sheer joy of retelling these stories. First, to retell these immortal stories in a manner that will strike a chord with the reader of the 21st century. This means adopting a style that makes these upakathas read more like a thriller. Yes, the Mahabharata is an aakhyaana (narrative), itihaasa (history), purana (ancient lore), katha (story), samhita (collection), fifth Veda, shaastra (treatise), dharma shaastra, artha shaastra, moksha shaastra, charita (biography), jaya (victory), and even an upakhyaana![2] But what the Mahabharata also is arguably the greatest thriller ever written.

Second, to provide enough additional information by way of footnotes to the reader who is intrigued to want to know more, to read up the original, or an unabridged translation, for themselves. If you read a quoted verse that goes, '*I rejected the gods and chose you.*' or '*Hope vanished like breath on a mirror.*' then a certain curiosity may lead the reader, via these footnotes, to the text. This verse citation is a three-part number. For example, the first quoted verse above is 3.75.1, and it is from the Nala Damayanti upakhyaana; it refers to the third parva—Aranyaka Parva, seventy-fifth chapter, first verse.

There is also a fourth reason—to retell these stories without introducing creative distortions, misrepresentations, and worse, and which serve little purpose. For example, you will not read in this book that Karna was not allowed to compete in Draupadi's swayamvara—for the simple reason that the Vyaasa Mahabharata says nothing of the sort. Rather, Vyaasa tells us, in 1.179.4 (that would be the first parva, Adi, 179th chapter, fourth verse), that Karna participated, but failed to pierce the target. That Draupadi stopped Karna is a fabrication, a later interpolation, a distortion. Why it was inserted, why it became a popular misconception, and why it has been used by authors to rationalize their own prejudices, ideological agendas, and creative failings are all fascinating questions that I do not get into.

There are several translations of the Mahabharata available in the English language, starting with Ganguly's mammoth effort more than a century ago. The one I have used as my basic source is Shri Bibek Debroy's unabridged English translation of the BORI Critical Edition, published by Penguin from 2010 to 2014. For the Sanskrit verses, I relied on John Smith's online transcription of the Critical Edition.

There were three choices I faced in spelling names. I could have gone for spellings with diacritical marks. That meant writing Vaiśampāyana, Pāṇḍava, Śalya, Nārada, Bhīṣma, and so on. However, outside of an academic setting, they add an inevitable turgidity to the reader's experience. They distract. On the other hand, outside of popular names whose pronunciations are well-known, not using these marks can lead to some phonetic ambiguity. For example, writing Kalmashapada instead of Kalmāṣapāda may lead to a wrong pronunciation. What is one to do? I chose a middle-ground. I have written Kalmāṣapāda as Kalmaashapaada, Vātāpi as Vaataapi, Bhīṣma as Bheeshma, Nārada as Naarada, and so on.

For those not familiar with the Mahabaharata, I leave you with two summarizations—one that is 50 words long, the second that is 500 words long.

The Mahabharata, in 50 words

The Mahabharata is an account of the descendants of the Kuru lineage; the Paandavas and Kauravas. A lifelong rivalry between the cousins culminated in an 18-day battle in Kurukshetra where the Paandavas emerged victorious. Only three warriors from the Kaurava side and eight from the Paandava side walked away alive.

The Mahabharata, in 500 words

King Shaantanu of Hastinapura married Ganga, the river goddess. They had one son named Devavrata. After Ganga left Shaantanu, he married Satyavati, the daughter of a fisherman who insisted that Satyavati's son be made king after him as a pre-condition. Devavrata not only agreed to renounce his claim to the throne but also took a vow of lifelong celibacy. For this fierce vow, he came to be known as Bheeshma. Satyavati gave birth to two sons. The elder one died before ascending the throne, while the younger son died heirless. Satyavati then summoned her son, Vyaasa, born from a union with Sage Paraashara before her marriage to Shaantanu, to father sons on the two widowed queens of her younger son. Dhritaraashtra was born to the elder queen, but blind. Paandu was born to the younger queen, but weak in health. A third son, Vidura, also fathered by Vyaasa but born to a maid, was the wisest of the three.

Dhritaraashtra, on account of his blindness, could not become king. His younger brother, Paandu, ascended the throne. After accidentally killing a sage, Paandu renounced the throne and left for the forest with his two wives, Kunti and Maadri. In the forest, after he had become father to five sons, begat by invoking the gods, Paandu and Maadri died. Kunti returned to Hastinapura, where her five sons, the Paandavas, grew up with the hundred sons of Dhritaraashtra and his wife, Gandhaari, known as the Kauravas. Goaded by their maternal uncle, Shakuni, Duryodhana, the eldest Kaurava, nursed a lifelong envy and hatred towards his cousins and which saw him try to kill the Paandavas many times.

The Paandavas survived, and in a swayamvara held by King Drupada of Paanchala, married the king's daughter, Draupadi. The kingdom of Hastinapura was partitioned and the Paandavas given suzerainty over Indraprastha. Disgruntled over losing half the kingdom and the rising popularity and prosperity of his cousins, Duryodhana and Shakuni goaded Dhritaraashtra into inviting the Paandavas for a game of dice. Yudhishthira, the eldest Paandava, accepted, and ended up losing his wealth, kingdom, his brothers, and even his wife. Draupadi was insulted and humiliated in the court. A second round of dice saw the Paandavas lose again and had to accept a thirteen-year period of exile.

When the thirteen-year exile ended, the Kauravas refused to hand over Indraprastha to the Paandavas. After several rounds of futile negotiations, the last of which was conducted by Krishna, war was waged. On the plains of Kurukshetra, seven divisions of the Paandava army and eleven divisions of the Kaurava army faced off against each other. Led by Draupadi's brother and guided by Krishna, the Paandavas emerged victorious after 18 days.

Saddened by the colossal loss of life, Yudhishthira considered becoming a renunciate. He was persuaded by Krishna to listen to Bheeshma, who lay on a bed of arrows in Kurukshetra, awaiting death. A lengthy counsel by Bheeshma convinced Yudhishthira to ascend the throne. Thirty-six years after the war, the Paandavas ascended heaven.

Within the universe of this account, all that exists in this world can be found in the Mahabharata—love and hate, intrigue and innocence, war and peace, designs and accidents, curses and boons, beauty and hideousness, and much, much more. With this, I urge, request, invite you to dive into the world of the Mahabharata, as seen through its 67 sub-tales, upakhyaanas, upakathas.

1 SHAKUNTALA

Soft as Steel

Parva: Adi (1) **Upa parva: Sambhava (7)**
Chapters: 62-69 **Shlokas: 305**

The eighteen-day war at Kurukshetra ended. Countless died—eighteen akshauhinis[1] were decimated, and probably a billion casualties.[2] The grief-stricken mother of the Kaurava princes, Gandhaari, had walked the battlefield that was now strewn with countless corpses—of soldiers, her relatives, of her sons. Gandhaari had cursed Krishna and his clan for allowing this senseless war to take place, a war that her son had been willing to wage rather than return half the kingdom to his cousins, or even as much land as covered by the tip of a needle. Thirty-six years later, the curse came true, bound by Gandhaari's words, brought to an inevitability by the added curse of sages Vishwaamitra, Kanva, and Naarada.[3] It was what Gandhaari had cursed and what Krishna himself had willed.

The Yaadavas,[4] Vrishnis[5] and the Andhakas,[6] numbering 5,00,000, all killed themselves in a fratricidal war. The city of Dwaarka sank into the ocean, returning to the ocean what had once been borrowed from the ocean.[7] Krishna and Balaraama departed from the material world. The Paandavas decided to renounce the world after being told rather bluntly by Vyaasa that their time on earth had come to an end.

> Know that the time for your departure has arrived.[8]

The Paandavas and Draupadi departed for the heavens. Only Yudhishthira would enter heaven in his mortal body. Before they departed, they instated Arjuna's grandson, Pareekshit, as the king. After Pareekshit's death, his son, Janamejaya, became king. Pareekshit's death, however, had not been from natural causes, nor had he died fighting on the battlefield. For someone who had been still-born and revived by none other than Krishna, Pareekshit's end had been quite gruesome. Takshaka, the king of serpents, had crept up Pareekshit's heavily guarded tower and bitten the king to death. Such had been the potency of his venom that the king's body was set aflame. It was much later that Janamejaya learned the details of how his father had died—from Sage Uttanka.[9]

Janamejaya held Takshaka responsible for his father's death, and he resolved to put an end to Takshaka. A death for a death. A death by fire for a death by fire. A grand sarpa-satra—snake sacrifice—was held. The power of the chants would draw the king of serpents into those sacrificial flames and to its deserving end.

Thus, the sarpa-satra was initiated. Serpents—young, old, large, small, of all shapes, colours, and types were consigned to the flames. Soon enough Takshaka would also follow. But he didn't. The wait continued. Janamejaya grew impatient. He didn't know that Takshaka, the king of serpents, was friends with Indra, the king of the gods.

> 'O Brahmanas! why hasn't Takshaka been pulled into this flame yet?' Janamejaya demanded.
> 'O King! Indra protects him. Our mantras cannot overcome Indra's sheath that protects Takshaka,' the priests replied.
> 'Is that so? Then chant your mantras to bring Indra to this sacrifice.'
> 'And, err…, what then?' asked the nonplussed priests.
> 'As goes Indra, so will Takshaka. If not without Indra, then with Indra,' Janamejaya ordered.
> 'We don't understand, O King,' the priests uttered. Yes, they had heard the king, yes, they had understood, but they couldn't believe their ears.
> 'O Priests! it must be exactly as I said. If Takshaka won't come because of Indra, then let Indra too be consigned to the flames along with Takshaka, because of Takshaka,' Janamejaya said.

> O Brahmanas! If Takshaka is in Indra's palace, hurl him into the fire with Indra himself.[10]

The priests looked at each other. The king's order was inviolable. They started their chants afresh. The skies darkened. A snake, the grandest they had seen, started to descend. It was Takshaka. But there was no Indra. Offerings at sacrifices were for the gods. The gods themselves weren't meant to be the offerings. Even friendship had its limits; even one with the king of the gods. Takshaka descended, resisting futilely the pull of the mantras.

But the grand, gruesome, and gory sarpa-satra ended prematurely. Aasteeka, a young brahmin's words had a calming effect on Janamejaya. He paused the sacrifice that had been fated and cursed to fail.[11] This cycle of jinxed sacrifices had followed Janamejaya's ancestors, whether it was Yudhishthira's Rajsuya sacrifice, which was marred by Shishupala's death at the hands of Krishna or his Ashwamedha sacrifice, which was marred by the appearance of a skeptical mongoose.[12] Aasteeka, himself the son of a serpent, had been conceived to save his mother and relatives from their mother's curse.[13] The words of Aasteeka were persuasive enough to persuade the king to order a pause to the snake sacrifice. Takshaka remained suspended mid-air while the king decided whether the sacrifice would end or resume. When King Janamejaya finally called for the snake sacrifice to be ended, there was much joy, for generations of enmity had finally come to an end.

Janamejaya now wanted to understand what had sparked this feud between Takshaka and his ancestors. Why had Takshaka killed his father, King Pareekshit?[14] He wanted to learn his own history; he wanted to hear what had happened, as it had happened; in other words, he wanted *Itihaasa*—this is indeed what happened. For the first time, the events of the Mahabharata were recited in public, by Sage Vaishampaayana,[15] on the instructions of Krishna Dvaipaayana Vedvyaasa.[16]

Vaishampaayana started off with a summary of the main events,[17] telling Janamejaya about the lifelong enmity Duryodhana and his maternal uncle, Shakuni, harboured against the Paandavas, and which had ultimately led to the eighteen-day war in Kurukshetra. This all-too brief precis, however, led to only more questions from Janamejaya. It could not have been a mere trifle over which such a great destruction had been wrought. Cousins didn't go to war and annihilate each other on the battlefield over mere jealousies.

Vaishampaayana decided that a summary was not sufficient; the entire history of the Kuru clan would need to be told, for much would otherwise be lost in the summary, for the subtleties of dharma could only be gleaned from the details. So comprehensive would the account be that it would become an all-encompassing tome of knowledge.

> Whatever is found here on dharma, artha, kama and moksha, may be found elsewhere. But whatever is not in it, cannot be found anywhere else.[18]

Thus far, Vaishampaayana had walked Janamejaya through the origins of Vedvyaasa himself, Vidura, the other Kurus, Drona, Kripa, and others. Janamejaya now asked Vaishampaayana to tell him how his lineage had come to be.

Thus starts the account of Shakuntala.

King Dushyanta was the founder of the Paurava dynasty, named after King Puru. We will learn more about Puru in the upakhyaana on Yayaati. For now, let's stay with Dushyanta. He was a strong and just ruler; peace and prosperity reigned in his kingdom, people adhered to dharma, and the king was much loved by his people—whether in cities or in the countryside.

As was the wont of kings, Dushyanta too was fond of hunting. Many such hunts would result in many an adventure, every single one of them unexpected. On this day, on one such hunt, Dushyanta went to the forest, accompanied by many soldiers, cavalry, and elephants. Marching deeper and deeper into the forest, he and his soldiers hunted many animals there—literally, thousands. The day progressed, the sun grew hotter and hotter, and soon enough the king found himself both hungry and thirsty. The king saw dry leaves, twigs, a parched earth, but no ponds, lakes, or water bodies.

If Janamejaya got a feeling of déjà vu when listening to Vaishampayaana, we are not told. Was it not his father, Pareekshit, who had also found himself in a forest after a long day of hunting on a hot day, and ended up getting himself cursed? Had history first occurred with Dushyanta, and merely repeated many generations later, with Pareekshit, Janamejaya may have wondered.

In search of water, Dushyanta went deeper and deeper into the forest, eventually coming across a grove by a river, where a cool breeze blew, the grass was green, and where verdant trees offered plenty of shade. Entering it, he saw a hermitage with sages milling about. Chants of mantras from the Rig Veda being recited could be heard from the riverbank, and most surprisingly, the king saw deer and predators coexisting.

Dushyanta realized that this was Sage Kanva's[19] hermitage. The proper thing to do was to introduce himself to the sage and pay his respects. Getting down from his chariot, he entered the hermitage and looked around for the sage, calling out his name. Not the sage, but a young maiden approached him and offered him grass, water, and fruits—the traditional form of welcome to a guest. She also told Dushyanta that Sage Kanva had gone out to collect fruit and would be back shortly.

> She was dazzling in her beauty, austerities and humility and endowed with beauty and youth.[20]

Dushyanta may have expected to encounter any number of things in the hermitage, both expected and unexpected, but certainly not a maiden as young, with as sweet a smile as hers, and as pretty as her. She introduced herself as Shakuntala, Sage Kanva's daughter. Dushyanta was now surprised yet again—how could the sage, as firm in his vows of brahmacharya as Kanva was, have fathered a daughter? Yes, she was daughter of Kanva, Shakuntala told Dushyanta, but not his biological daughter. Seeing the look of bewilderment on Dushyanta's face, she told him the story of her birth which she had heard her father tell a sage.

This was a time when Sage Vishwaamitra was deep in meditation, acquiring austerities that would elevate him to the status of a brahmarshi to rival Vasishtha.[21] Brahmarshi Vasishtha was not perturbed by this, but it certainly alarmed Indra, the king of the gods, who was always apprehensive about potential rivals—imagined or real—to his throne. The surest way to halt Vishwaamitra's mission was by, well, interrupting his meditations. Indra summoned Menaka, an apsaraa[22] in Indra's court and beautiful beyond compare, and told her to seduce the sage and to turn him away from his rigid austerities.

> Menaka went white.
> 'O King of the gods!' she let out a whimper.
> 'Yes, the most beautiful of apsaraas, what ails you?' asked Indra.
> 'I can't do this!'

'You have to.'

'He is Vishwaamitra! He who killed Brahmarshi Vasishtha's sons.'

'I know.'

'He created an entire river[23] for his ablutions.'

'Yes, he is a formidable sage.'

'He is now powerful enough to make the earth tremble with a kick, who can uproot Mount Meru like a toy.'

'And if he is not stopped, he will one day uproot me from my throne!' Indra said.

'Do you remember Sage Matanga's sacrifice, where even you had to present yourself? You know why, don't you?'

'Please don't remind me,' Indra frowned. Fear of Vishwaamitra, it had been.

'So how do you think, what makes you think, how could you think I can succeed where even you didn't?' Menaka asked.

'Because I am a mere king of the gods.'

'Then what am I? What chance do I stand?' Menaka pleaded.

'You are the most beautiful of apsaraas there is. Tilottamma may be the most perfect, but yours is a beauty which no mortal has been able to resist.'

There it was. The die was cast.

The king of the gods' command could not be defied. What had to be done had to be done. Menaka requested Indra to have Manmatha[24] and Marut[25] help in making her task easier. She shared her plan with Indra, who agreed, putting the wind god and the god of love at her disposal.

Armed with a smidgeon of confidence now, Menaka entered the hermitage where Vishwaamitra was deep in meditation. There she started her celestial dance, hoping to sway and distract the sage with her moves that had the grace and allure to tempt both humans and gods. Manmatha and Marut watched, mesmerized. Both waited for an opportune moment. Somewhere deep within the recesses of his meditation, Vishwaamitra heard, or perhaps felt, the apsaraa's dance steps. The rhythms of her steps, the cadence of her moves, all permeated some part of Vishwaamitra's consciousness.

His eyes opened. Manmatha and Marut seized the moment, for it would be now or never. Moving with a perfection that only gods could achieve, the wind god gusted; the god of love shot his amorous arrow. That whiff blew off Menaka's garment at the instant Vishwaaamitra eyes fell on her, the same instant that the arrow found its mark, timed to cosmic perfection. No human could have detected the celestial interference. In another world, another time, Shiva would, and his gaze would reduce the god of love to ashes,[26] but for now, today, Vishwaamitra was no god, but today was his lucky day.

Not for nothing was Menaka known for her beauty in all the words. Vishwaamitra was but a human, a man of strengths and weaknesses, of anger and love, of detachment and desire. The sage was captivated by Menaka's beauty and form; desire awoke inside him; his penance broken, forgotten. Indra smiled, relieved. His throne was safe once more.

The sage and the apsaraa were lost in the bliss of their union. Time passed. A daughter was born to Menaka on the banks of the Malini River. Her task completed, the celestial apsaraa departed for the heavens. Vishwaamitra realized he had been distracted from his penances by Indra and Menaka. The fault had been his. Dejected at this lapse, he too left, returning to his penances.

The daughter of the most beautiful of apsaraas and the most fearsome of sages lay in the desolate forest, abandoned. Lions and tigers infested the forest. Only *shakuna*[27] birds sheltered her, forming a protective ring around her, letting no harm come to the infant. Her cries attracted the attention of Sage Kanva. It was there, in that state, that the sage found her. He adopted her and named her Shakuntala in honour of the birds that had protected her. Since the dharma texts define a father as someone who provides either the body, protection, or food, Kanva became her father. This, Shakuntala told Dushyanata, was the history of her birth.

Shakuntala had grown to be a beautiful young maiden; Menaka's daughter could not be but a stunning beauty. As to the question whether she had inherited Vishwaamitra's temper, there should not have been any doubt. Dushyanta was now smitten by Shakuntala. He proposed to her, and since her father was not present, requested her to marry him as per Gandharva rites. Why the Gandharva form of marriage? Dushyanta explained that there were eight forms of marriage,[28] and that six of those were sanctioned for kshatriyas and kings.

Shakuntala's heart had also been captivated by Dushyanta; she agreed to his proposal for a Gandharva marriage. She did put forth two conditions, however. The first was that this marriage remain a secret, and the second condition was that their son be the king to succeed Dushyanta. Several generations later, the latter condition would repeat itself, when Satyavati's father would put the same condition in front of Shaantanu, but with rather different consequences. But we digress. Dushyanta agreed to both conditions and the two married. It was soon time for Dushyanta to return to his capital. Before departing, he reiterated his vows to Shakuntala, promising to send an army with horses, foot-soldiers, chariots, and elephants to escort her to the capital. She was his queen, and she would be accorded that status, he promised.

> It is what you deserve and I promise you truthfully.[29]

Eventually Sage Kanva returned to the hermitage. When Shakuntala did not go and meet him, embarrassed as she was, the sage divined what had transpired. Kanva sat down and had a talk with his daughter. While the marriage had been without his consent, he did not consider the marriage itself to be against dharma. A Gandharva marriage, after all, did have dharmic sanction. Much later, Arjuna would adopt the same method to marry Krishna's sister, Subhadra, and no less a person than Krishna himself would defend it in the assembly hall of the Yaadavas.[30] Moreover, Dushyanta was a great king and a follower of dharma. Kanva prophesized that Dushyanta and Shakuntala's son would be an even greater king. Yes, a son was on the way.

In due course of time, Shakuntala gave birth to a son. As befitting a prince born to such illustrious parents, even at the tender age of six, he was fearless and strong. Such was his fearlessness that he rode tigers and lions and had no fear of elephants, boars, or buffaloes. Seeing these qualities, Kanva named him Sarvadamana.[31] He also decided that it was time for Sarvadamana to be anointed the heir apparent and for Shakuntala to be reunited with Dushyanta. More than six years had passed, but Dushyanta had still not sent the army he had promised to escort Shakuntala to his kingdom.

> Born from the father, the son is the father himself.[32]

Accompanied by Kanva's disciples, Shakuntala set off with her son to Hastinapura. Arriving at Dushyanta's court, she reminded the king of his promise to instate their son as the heir apparent. Dushyanta looked, surprised.

Dushyanta knew everything—that Shakuntala was his wife, that he made certain promises to her, but he answered with words that hit her like a thunderbolt. He exclaimed that he remembered neither her nor any promise, leave alone having had any relation with her.

> I do not remember having had any relation with you for dharma, artha or kama.[33]

While her beauty came from Menaka the apsaraa, Shakuntala's temper was her genetic father, Vishwaamitra's gift. First stunned, then flustered, embarrassed, and finally incensed, Shakuntala collected herself and chided the king for lying like a commoner. When he, the king, himself was the witness to his promise, how could he lie to himself? Shakuntala said the husband himself is reborn as his son through his wife, which is why the wife was also known as jaya.[34] Disowning her was a repugnant act in itself, but how could Dushyanta forsake his own son, she asked. It was the son who saved the ancestors from the hell known as *put*, and hence a son was called a putra.[35] A wife conferred on a husband the right to perform rites, to live the life of a householder. How could he even think of forsaking his wife, she asked.

> A wife is half the man. A wife is the best of friends. A wife is the source of the three objectives. A wife is a friend at the very end.[36]

> The wise have said that a man is himself born as his son.[37]

There was no greater joy than the embrace of one's son, and yet Dushyanata was forsaking his own son. Shakuntala reminded him that it was he who had come to her father's hermitage; it was he who had asked her hand in marriage; and it was he who had agreed to her two demands and vowed to honour them. Only knaves went back on their word. She was Menaka's daughter, the best among the six foremost apsaraas;[38] yet this man sitting in front of her, Dushyanta, had abandoned her without a second thought. The least Dushyanta could do was to not abandon his son.

> The wife is the sacred ground in which the husband is born again.[39]

Dushyanta listened to Shakuntala, his ears turning red at the tongue-lashing he was receiving, but he did not cede. No, he instead chose to double down with even harsher words. Shakuntala, Dushyanta alleged, was a liar; Shakuntala's parents, Menaka and Vishwaamitra, Dushyanta averred, were worthless. He, on the other hand, was a king, he proclaimed.

If Shakuntala had only been annoyed, she was now furious. Her anger, kept in reasonable check so far, now erupted. If Dushyanta wanted to compare births, then so be it—for her birth was far nobler than his, Shakuntala retorted.

> O Dushyanta! My birth is nobler than your own. O Lord of Kings! You are established on earth. But I roam the sky. Know that the difference between you and me is that between a mustard seed and Mount Meru.[40]

Shakuntala chided, berated, lambasted Dushyanta—it behoved him to do better than to behave like a fool, like a pig searching for filth—for only fools looked for evil in the words of the good, just as a pig searched out filth.

> Until he sees his face in a mirror, the ugly man thinks himself to be more handsome than others.[41]

If the truth was dear to Dushyanta, if the Vedas were sacred to him, then the truth was equal to all the Vedas, superior to a hundred sons and a thousand sacrifices, and yet he was forsaking his son, not willing to even acknowledge him.

If Dushyanta would not accept their son, Shakuntala said she wouldn't distress over the fact. She would leave this assembly, to never return. As for her son, she wouldn't worry. When Dushyanta was dead, her son would rule the entire earth. No one was going to deny her son his right, least of all his reprobate of a father.

> Like a pig searches out filth, the fool seeks out evil words when he hears good and evil in men's speech. But the swan always searches out milk from the water. Like that, the wise one seeks out words of quality when he hears good and evil in men's speech.[42]

As she prepared to depart, a celestial voice spoke, proclaiming that Shakuntala's son was indeed Dushyanta's own son, and exhorted him to recognize both of them. Before fading, the voice also prophesized that because Dushyanta would maintain both, his son would also be known as Bharata.

Dushyanta relented, and in front of the entire assembly accepted Shakuntala as his wife and Bharata as their son. The astral validation was important to Dushyanta, lest people cast aspersions on Shakuntala or Bharata. The celestial voice would not be questioned or doubted. The people would accept Shakuntala as Dushyanta's wife and Bharata as his son.

In due course of time, Bharata grew to become a great king, conquering all before him.

Life and time would play out their roles over several generations. It was Sage Vishwaamitra who fathered Shakuntala; it was Sage Kanva who found, sheltered, and raised Shakuntala as his daughter. Many, many generations later, it would be the same sages Vishwaamitra and Kanva, accompanied by Naarada, who would collectively pronounce a curse[43] on the entire Yaadava race, dooming them to destruction. The circle of time always turns, sometimes slowly, taking generations.

2

YAYAATI

The Roots of Desire; The Fruits of Temptation

Parva: Adi (1) **Upa parva: Sambhava (7)**
Chapters: 70-80 **Shlokas: 360**

Sage Vaishampaayana had told Janamejaya that his ancestor, Dushyanta, was the founder of the Paurava dynasty. But who was Paurava? How was he related to Dushyanta? Why was the dynasty named after Paurava? Weren't the Paandavas and Kauravas also called Bharat-vanshaja (descendants of Bharata)? This was confusing to Janamejaya, and he put forth his doubts to the sage.

Vaishampaayana started from the very beginning of the family tree to clarify.[1] The very beginning meant, literally, the very beginning—Vaishampaayana started with Brahma. Daksha was one of Brahma's ten sons. Daakshaayani was one of Daksha's daughters,[2] and she married Sage Kashyapa. Vivasvat[3] was one of Kashyapa's sons. Yama was Vivasvata's son. From Yama was born Maartanda.[4] Manu[5] was Maartanda's son. Among Manu's ten sons, two were Ikshvaaku[6] and Ila.[7] Yes, Raama, son of Dashratha, was Ikshvaaku's descendant, but that is a different story for a different time. Ila had six sons through Urvashi, of which Aayus was one. Nahusha was one of Aayus' sons, and Yayaati was one of Nahusha's six sons.

The account had come to Yayaati. And Puru was one of Yayaati's five sons. Not the eldest; Puru was the youngest son of Sharmishtha. Vaishampaayana paused.

'O Sage, who was Sharmishtha?' asked Janamejaya.

'She was Vrishaparva's daughter,' replied Vaishampaayana.

'Who was Vrishaparva?'

'He was the king of the asuras.'

'An asura? Have I descended from an asura? O Sage, am I an asura because I am Vrishaparva's descendant?' asked the aghast Janamejaya.

'Are you an Aditya because you are descended from Vivasvat?' answered the sage by way of question.

'I am a Survavanshi because I am Vivasvat's descendant,' proffered Janamejaya.

'You certainly are a Maanava because you have descended from Manu, and I think that will do for now,' Vaishampaayana said.

'Yes, that will do for now, I think,' Janamejaya fell silent. 'But why did Puru get to be heir and not any other of Yayaati's elder sons?' he asked after a moment.

'Yes, why Puru and why not his elder siblings. Listen on,' said Vaishampaayana.

Yayaati had two wives—Devayaani and Sharmishtha. From Devayaani were born Yadu and Turvasu; while Druhyu, Anu, and Puru were Sharmishtha's sons. Because of a curse, Yayaati lost his youth. Desperate to regain it, he requested his sons to give him their youth. All but Puru refused. Yayaati cursed all but Puru. Puru became Yayaati's chosen heir, and his descendants were known as Purus, or the Pauravas.

'This is Itihaasa—what had happened,' concluded Vaishampyaanaa.

'Is that it, O Sage?'

'This is indeed what happened,' Vaishampaayana said.

'But who cursed Yayaati, my ancestor? What had he done to deserve such an agonizing curse? And why a curse that dispossessed him of his youth? Why did four of his sons refuse their father?' Janamejaya let loose a volley of questions.

'These are all questions that deserve a detailed response. Hear who Devayaani, the strong-willed woman was; who Sharmishtha, the quiet but determined woman was; hear about Kacha, Yayaati, and the devas and the asuras,' Vaishampayaana smiled. He had Vyaasa's blessings and teachings, and he was ready with the answers.

Devayaani—Kacha

Vaishampaayana went back to a time when a fierce war raged between the gods and the asuras. While the gods had Brihaspati[8] as their officiating priest, the demons had Shukracharya[9] as theirs. These battles were brutal, and a great number of gods and asuras were killed in every such encounter. However, Shukra possessed the knowledge of sanjivani, with which he was able to revive the asuras killed in battle. Brihaspati didn't, and thus the gods that died in battle against the asuras fell, never to rise again.

With their numbers depleting after every confrontation with the asuras, the despairing gods racked their brains for a solution. After much deliberation, they contrived a most audacious stratagem. They approached Kacha, Brihaspati's son, and requested him to head down to the asuras. No, they weren't asking Kacha to wage a lone battle against the Asuras.

Kacha was to become Shukra's disciple and gain from the sage the knowledge of sanjivani. That would even the scales like nothing else. One day the asuras and the gods would come together to churn the ocean and obtain nectar, which the gods would keep for themselves, but that was far away as only a possibility. For now, the gods had to stop falling to the asuras.

> He always protects the demons, but does not protect those who are not demons.[10]

The gods also suggested that Kacha could woo Kaavya's daughter, Devayaani, if that helped. All was fair in love and war, after all.

> You are certain to obtain the knowledge by propitiating Devayani with your conduct, magnanimity, sweetness, action and self-control.[11]

Kacha agreed to the Gods' entreaties and proceeded to asuraloka where Shukracharya resided.

Once in asuraloka, Kacha introduced himself as the son of Brihaspati and grandson of Angirasa. He requested Shukra to accept him as his disciple and student. Shukra agreed, for there was no reason for the learned preceptor of the asuras to deny knowledge to a student as distinguished as Kacha. The son of the guru of the gods thus became a student of the guru of the asuras.

Kacha was a multi-talented person. He was not only a good student but also a good singer, dancer, and also adept at playing musical instruments. A young Devayaani couldn't help but grow attracted to Kacha, and the two would often spend time talking to each other in the hermitage. Acquaintance turned to friendship;

friendship morphed into love. Devayaani had lost her heart to Kacha.

The new student's identity did not remain hidden from the asuras for long. They found out that Kacha, the bright new student in their preceptor's hermitage, was none other than Brihaspati's son. The son of their sworn enemy's preceptor could be here for one and only one reason. The asuras reached a conclusion—Kacha had to die.

The asuras watched. They would bide their time. When the opportunity came, they would seize it. They would have to act outside the hermitage. There could not be any violence in their guru's hermitage.

One day Kacha went to the forest to graze cattle. The asuras followed him. Once deep inside the forest, far away from sight and sound of the hermitage, they waylaid and killed him. Their task was not done, yet. They proceeded to chop Kacha up into small pieces. The asuras were still not done. They fed those pieces to jackals and wolves. The threat had been eliminated. The triumphant asuras returned. Their preceptor's secret of the sanjivani had been saved from falling into the hands of the agent of the gods.

If there was one flaw in the asuras' plan, however, it was their very own preceptor. Dusk fell, the cattle returned to the hermitage, but Kacha didn't. Devayaani suspected some calamity had befallen him. Love had sharpened her sixth sense. She went up to her father, Shukra, and beseeched him to bring Kacha back to life. A doting father would not refuse. After all, he had his knowledge of sanjivani. Kacha was brought back to life—from the stomachs of the animals that had eaten his chopped up remains. Kacha stood before Shukra and Devayaani—alive and intact. Kacha had heard of the miraculous powers of the sanjivani, but this demonstration was more than he had ever imagined. In this war between the gods and asuras, love had brought one person from the gods' side back from the dead. Kacha and Devayaani's budding romance had already paid dividends.

When the asuras heard that Kacha had been brought back to life and was back in their guru's hermitage, with both body and soul intact, they were glum, but not for long. They had at least learned something from this escapade. Their preceptor could bring their plans to nought. Something had to be done about Shukra's penchant for bringing their enemy back to life, they decided. Plans were remade afresh; surveillance of Kacha resumed. Soon enough, opportunity came knocking again.

Kacha ventured out into the forest to pick flowers for Devayaani. The asuras waylaid Kacha a second time. They killed him, like they had before. Their guru could still bring him back to life. Then they burned Kacha's body up. Their guru could still resurrect Kacha from the ashes. Then they mixed the ashes with sura (wine). Their guru could still bring back Kacha to life from the ashes mixed with sura. But this time they had thought of everything. The asuras took the sura to their guru, Shukra. An unsuspecting Shukra accepted the sura the asuras had brought and drank the wine. The asuras returned, triumphant. Even their guru could not revive Kacha now.

When Kacha didn't return from the forest, Devayaani suspected, again, that the asuras had killed him, again. She went a second time to her father with the same request—bring back Kacha to life. This time, however, the sage demurred. The asuras, he realized, were not going to relent. Every time he brought Kacha back to life, they would just kill him again. Perhaps it was best to accept what had happened and move on.

That was unacceptable to Devayaani. She loved Kacha and could not bear to lose her beloved Kacha. Moved by her daughter's lamentations, Shukra first decided to find out where Kacha was. He called out to his disciple. Promptly came the disciple's reply. Shukra looked left, he looked right, he looked up, he looked down, and then he looked no more. The voice had come from within. Kacha was inside Shukra. The asuras had truly won. Kacha was not coming out alive.

> 'Are you inside my stomach, Kacha?' Shukra asked
> 'Yes, O Shukra, I am inside you,' Kacha replied.
> 'This is impossible! Just how did you end up inside me?'
> 'I remember, O Sage, I remember now. Thanks to your powers, I have retained my memory. They killed me.'
> 'Who killed you?' demanded Shukra.
> 'The asuras,' Kacha replied.
> 'Again?' asked Shukra.
> 'Again.'
> 'And then?'
> 'Then they burned me to ashes.'
> 'But...but...,' exclaimed Shukra. *How did you end up in my stomach?*

But he now knew. He sat down.

'Then they mixed the ashes in wine,' Kacha continued.

'And then they offered me the wine,' Shukra held his head in his hands.

'And you drank the wine.'

'The wine which contained your ashes,' Shukra completed, shutting his eyes. 'Yes, I drank it.'

'Yes, O Sage.'

Shukra stood up and walked over to Devayaani. Seeing her father's gait and demeanour, her heart sank. Shukra shook his head.

'What do you mean, Father? You have the knowledge; you alone know how to bring the dead back to life. Bring back Kacha to life. Please!' Devayaani pleaded.

'Yes, I can bring him back to life, my child. I will chant the mantras. Kacha will come to life.'

'So why are you hesitating, Father?'

'He will emerge from my stomach, rending it asunder as he does,' Shukra said.

'But that means…,' Devayaani gasped in horror.

'Yes, Kacha's life will mean my death. That is how it must be.'

'It cannot be. I will not be the cause of your death. No daughter will, Father,' Devayaani cried.

'Then forget about Kacha, my child.'

'That I cannot do, either, Father,' Devayaani sobbed.

Shukra sighed. The gods had won. The asuras had lost. Kacha's mission would be successful, thanks to the asuras: the stupid, thoughtless, reckless, too clever-by-half asuras, Shukra fumed.

> Kacha can only be brought to life through my death.[12]

There was a way out, Shukra concluded. He spoke to Kacha once more. Kacha listened, and then acquiesced. Shukra imparted the knowledge of sanjivani to Kacha. He then brought Kacha back to life. As Kacha emerged from Shukra's stomach, alive once more, the sage fell, dead, his stomach ripped open by that act of giving life. Once outside, and alive, Kacha used his newly acquired knowledge to bring Shukra back to life.

> No one can emerge alive from my stomach, but a Brahmana cannot be killed.[13]

Once back from the dead, Shukra's anger turned to the asuras, for they had deceived him, their preceptor. Shukra summoned the daanavas and berated them. Their actions had ended up achieving exactly what they had tried to stop.

> 'You are fools,' Shukra shouted at the asuras.
>
> 'But, O Guru…,' one started. They had heard that Kacha had come back to life. Which meant they had failed again. But it also meant that their preceptor, Shukra, had come up with a way to bring Kacha back to life from within his own stomach. Seeing Shukra's demeanour, hearing him berate them, they stood, their heads bowed.
>
> 'Don't call me your guru. A guru dispels darkness, but no light of my knowledge can ever dispel the darkness of stupidity inside your brains,' Shukra shut him up. They waited for their preceptor to announce a suitable punishment. Not a curse, they hoped.
>
> 'No, there is no point in cursing someone as foolish as you. Your actions are your own curse,' Shukra said.
>
> 'What do you mean, O Sage?" the asuras were nonplussed.
>
> 'Kacha now knows the secret of the sanjivani, you fools. Because you fed his ashes to me in a drink. To bring him back to life, I had to first impart that knowledge of sanjivani to him. When he came out, I died. He brought me back to life. He knows the secret,' Shukra let out a hollow laugh, 'and he tested it on me first. Are you happy? Are you still smug? Isn't this what you wanted?'
>
> 'No, O Shukra, we didn't think…,' mumbled an asura.
>
> 'No, of course not, you didn't,' Shukra said. 'You didn't think, for you cannot. I am the real fool here, for I can think, but I didn't,' he sighed. 'I succumbed to the temptation of liquor. The fault is mine.'

Shukra laid out an injunction from that day onwards—any brahmana who drank wine would be committing the sin of killing a brahmana.

Kacha continued to stay in the hermitage till such time as he had completed his studies under Shukra. The asuras left him alone. Devayaani waited for the day when Kacha would no longer be her father's disciple. The day arrived, and Kacha got ready to depart. Devayaani opened her heart to Kacha. While he had been a student of her father's, she had respected his status of a student. But now that his studies were completed, she expressed her love for him. She asked that that he marry her. Kacha said no. Devayaani looked at him, stunned.

Kacha's reasoning was that since she was his guru's daughter, a matrimonial bond between them was inappropriate. Devayanai disagreed, for love was love. Furthermore, he was no longer her father's student. There would be no act of impropriety if he married her.

Kacha finally put forth the point that both had originated from Shukra's body, and by that measure, dharma mandated that the two were siblings. A marriage between siblings was, therefore, out of the question.

Devayaani knew that Kacha was right. However, he had deceived her. He had come there to learn the secret of the sanjivani. Perhaps his affections towards her had also been a subterfuge. Betrayed, furious, she cursed Kacha that his knowledge would never achieve success. He would never be able to use the knowledge he had gained from his father.

> O Kacha! If you spurn me for the sake of dharma, artha or kama, despite my asking, your knowledge will never achieve success.[14]

Kacha accepted her curse. He told Devayaani that while her curse meant his knowledge would be fruitless, the ones he taught that knowledge to would nonetheless attain success.

Devayaani's curse had been uttered not out of a sense of dharma, but kaama. Kacha had a prophecy for Devayaani too—not only would she not marry Kacha, but no sage's son either. Her desire of marrying a sage's son[15] would never come true. In that state of discord and heartbreak the two parted. Kacha left for the heavens, to the land of the gods, from where he had come; Devayaani stayed back, heartbroken.

Devayaani—Sharmishtha

Kacha returned to heaven to a hero's welcome. Armed with the knowledge of the sanjivani, the resurgent gods, led by Indra,[16] set out to battle the asuras once more. On the way, in a forest, Indra saw several women playing in a lake. On a whim, Indra momentarily transformed into a gust of wind. It ended up mixing up everyone's garments. His mischief done; Indra departed.

The actions of the gods affect humans in many ways. Even a small act, done in jest, but by the king of the gods, would have far reaching consequences. The clothes, that Indra had scattered, belonged to Devayaani, Sharmishtha, and others. Devayaani was

Shukra's daughter. Sharmishtha was the daughter of Vrishaparva,[17] the king of the asuras. When Sharmishtha and Devayaani emerged from the waters, their garments were not where they had left them. The wind had strewn them all over. After a short but futile attempt at sorting out their garments, they did the next best thing—they picked up the garment closest to them. In this mix-up, Sharmishtha ended up putting on Devayaani's garments.

Devayaani saw Sharmishtha wearing her clothes, and she lost her temper.

> 'How dare you?' Devayaani shouted at Sharmishtha.
> 'What did I do?' asked Sharmishtha.
> 'How dare you wear my clothes? Remember your place, Sharmishtha.'
> 'My place? Just where and what is that place, Devayaani?'
> 'Your father is my father's student. He is beneath my father, and so are you. That is your place. This conduct is unbecoming of you, Sharmishtha.'
> 'Really, Devayaani? Look at your father; what is he?" asked Sharmishtha.
> 'What do you mean?'
> 'He is nothing but a beggar. Nothing beyond, nothing more than an ordinary beggar that roams the streets. Look at him, always going around begging, with a begging bowl in his hand, waylaying anyone and everyone to beg for alms. On the other hand, my father gives—never receives. The world trembles before him, just as your father does, too. If I have put on your clothes, I have done you a favour. We are not equals, Devayaani. Don't talk of conduct to me. Begone.'

> You are defenceless and deserted. You are a beggar who trembles before me, who is armed. Find an equal. I do not regard you as one.[18]

Sharmishtha stepped forward to snatch back the clothes; Devayaani clung to them. Sharmishtha shoved Devayaani, who staggered back and fell into a well. Sharmishtha walked off without a second look.

Devayaani may have been rescued from the well sooner or later, but the person who pulled her out was not one of her maids, or friends, but King Yayaati, who happened to pass by that part of the forest. Yayaati, as was common with kings, had come to hunt deer. So engrossed had he been that he had forgotten about food and water, and now he found himself thirsty.

Hunts and their unintended consequences were a common theme in the Mahabharata. Dushyanta had ended up marrying Shakuntala after one such sojourn into the forest;[19] Pareekshit ended up getting cursed;[20] Bhangaashwaana ended up changing his gender;[21] so had Shikhandi;[22] Pareekshit[23] fell in love with a princess who turned out to be a frog;[24] Shaantanu had followed a deer he had shot and ended up meeting Satyavati;[25] Paandu had shot a deer, that turned out to be a sage, and had been cursed as a result;[26] Samvarna had ventured into the forest for a hunt and met Tapati;[27] King Vishwaamitra had turned to the path of the brahmana after his encounter with Sage Vasishtha. The list was long.

In search of water for himself and his two horses, Yayaati found himself in that part of the forest where Sharmishtha and Devayaani had been not long ago. Peering down, Yayaati didn't find water but did see a young lady down in the well. The obvious question that arose in his mind was—who the lady was. He posed his question to Devayaani, who told Yayaati who she was.

Devayaani was still in the well. She offered her right hand and asked Yayaati to pull her out. Yayaati obliged. Devayaani emerged from the well. Yayaati bade her farewell and departed. There the matter rested. Now there was the matter of the spat between Devayaani and Sharmishtha. What the daughters had begun would have to be settled by the fathers.

Devayaani did not return home, to Shukra's hermitage. She stayed put. She turned to her companion, Ghurnika, who had come looking for her, to go back and tell her father what had happened. She was to tell Shukra that Devayaani would not enter Vrishaparva's city.

> It is through their own faults that people reap happiness and sorrow.[28]

Ghurnika hurried to Kaavya[29] and gave him an account of what had transpired—the spat that had ended with Sharmishtha shoving Devayaani into a well. A distraught father rushed to the forest. A doting father wrapped his arms around his daughter, comforted and consoled her, and asked what had happened, for he still couldn't believe that her friend, Sharmishtha, could have pushed Devayaani down a well. Devayaani repeated the words that the asura king's daughter had said to her, that she had called Shukra a beggar whose hands were always outstretched for alms and who always sang the praises of the king.

> The learned regard as a true charioteer he who reins in his anger like horses, not he who hangs onto the reins tightly.[30]

> A man who restrains his anger through forgiveness is compared to a snake that casts off its old skin.[31]

Perhaps those were words of anger said in the heat of the moment. Perhaps Sharmishtha didn't mean those words. Vrishaparva respected him, Shukra said, and would never use such harsh words or harbour such thoughts about his preceptor. Shukra tried to pacify his daughter, to let bygones be bygones, to not let anger cloud her judgment. Devayaani was implacable.

> Young boys and girls are not always sensible and quarrel with each other. They do not know true strength or weakness. The wise never imitate them.[32]

Devayaani held that disrespect towards a teacher and bad conduct were not to be tolerated. She would not budge. She would not return. Shukra could not refuse his daughter. He made his way to the capital and to Vrishaparva's court. There he declared to the king that he was forsaking him. He could no longer live in the kingdom after the disrespect shown to his daughter.

> A wise man who desires welfare should not live among people with evil intent, who speak ill of high birth and good conduct.[33]

A kingdom without a preceptor, a king without a guru was unthinkable. An aghast king apologized for any misconduct his daughter may have committed. The insult had been of Devayaani, the apology needed to be addressed to her, Shukra maintained. Devayaani would hear this apology from the king himself and no one else.

Vrishaparva, desperate to stop his preceptor from abandoning him and the asuras, hurried to the forest. There, in front of Devayaani and all present, the king of the asuras apologized to his guru's daughter. Devayaani accepted his apology. But…

But her anger still boiled. There was one more matter that needed to be resolved—that of Sharmishtha. Her barbs had been like jagged arrows dipped in venom. It was not enough that Sharmishtha's father had apologized. Devayaani wanted more. Sharmishtha would have to pay for her words and deed. Devayaani demanded that Sharmishtha, along with 1000 other women, become her servants. Who served and who was the master needed to be settled and shown to the world.

This was communicated to Sharmishtha. She agreed. She did not want to be the cause of Shukra abandoning the asuras. Hers had been the deed, hers had been the words, the atonement too would have to be hers. Sharmishtha departed for the forest along with a thousand maids. The princess had become a maid servant. In another time, in another world, another queen, Draupadi, would find herself a sairandhari (maid) of another queen, Sudeshna.[34] As would another queen, Damayanti, serve King Subahu's queen and daughter, as a sairandhari.[35]

Sharmishtha was now Devayaani's maid. Devayaani had won and got what she had asked for. But slivers of vengeance still sliced through her heart. Her triumph over Sharmishtha had to be rubbed in.

> 'Dear Sharmishtha, this is appalling,' Devayaani said sweetly, smiling.
>
> Sharmishtha stayed silent.
>
> 'Look at me,' Devayaani ordered.
>
> Sharmishtha looked at Devayaani.
>
> 'Look at me, the daughter of a beggar. Look at you, the daughter of one who gives alms. Gosh! How can you be my servant?'
>
> 'I will do what I have to do to save my family from a calamity,' Sharmishtha said quietly, softly.
>
> 'I guess someone now knows her place, doesn't she?'
>
> 'Yes, and I will go wherever you go.'
>
> 'Yes, you will, won't you? You will have to. And now, we will go to my father's hermitage.'
>
> 'Yes, and when you are married, even then I will come with you and serve you.'
>
> 'Of course, you will. You are now my indentured servant. Don't you forget it,' Devayaani snapped.
>
> 'No, Devayaani, I won't forget that whatever I have now belongs to you,' Sharmishtha said.
>
> 'But you will always be my friend, dear Sharmishtha,' Devayaani smiled sweetly, the smile not reaching her eyes.

Kaalchakra—the wheel of time would turn; it always did.

Devayaani—Yayaati—Sharmishtha

But where was Puru? Yayaati had made an all-too brief appearance. Where was his story? He had left after pulling Devayaani out of the well. Where was he? Hadn't Janamejaya's question to Vaishampaayana been why his was called the Paurava dynasty?

Time passed. Sharmishtha continued to serve as Devayaani's maid. Fate, one day, brought Devayaani to the same forest where this saga had begun, with Sharmishtha and her thousand maids in tow. Devayaani sat. Sharmishtha massaged her feet. A thousand maids waited in attendance.

Fate, that same day, brought Yayaati too to the same forest on a hunt. Again, he came to the same spot, thirsty. He saw both Devayaani and Sharmishtha. Devayaani sat, Sharmishtha by her side, on the ground. He was intrigued by this incongruous sight. Sharmishtha looked a noble woman, of a noble lineage, and yet she sat there like a maid, serving Devayaani. Puzzled, he stepped up and asked them who they were.

Sharmishtha stayed silent. Devayaani spoke. She introduced herself, again, and then introduced Sharmishtha—as her servant. Sharmishtha sat, quiet. Yayaati was taken aback. How could the daughter of the king of the daanavas, Vrishaparva, have become a maidservant? He asked, but Devayaani brushed him off, and instead asked Yayaati to introduce himself.

Yayaati told Devayaani that he was the son of a king, Nahusha, and now a king himself. Devayaani came straight to the point and asked him to marry her. If Yayaati was taken aback, he didn't say so. He did, however, demur. Sages usually married their daughters to sons of sages. A marriage between a kshatriya and a brahmana may not be appropriate, Yayaati maintained.

Devayaani reminded Yayaati that kshatriyas and brahamanas had united earlier, and the kshatriyas of the day had descended from sages, so by that reckoning, Yayaati too was the son of a rishi. Furthermore, it was she who had offered her hand to Yayaati, and Yayaati had accepted it when he had pulled her out of the well. She had taken the decision then, that Yayaati would be her husband. Yayaati had no objections in that case. Dushyanta had proposed the gandharva form of marriage to Shakuntala, but Yayaati wanted Shukra's prior approval.

> The snake kills only one. The sharpest weapon kills only one. But if angry, a Brahmana can destroy many cities and kingdoms.[36]

A message was sent to Shukra, who rushed to meet the king. Devayaani asked her father to bestow her upon Yayaati, for she had made up her mind to accept Yayaati, and no one else, as her husband. If Kacha's words echoed somewhere in Devayaani's mind and heart, we don't know, but his prophecy was coming true—she would marry, but not the son of a sage, notwithstanding her reasoning about kshatriyas and brahmanas being one. The dictates of destiny had everyone dancing to its tunes.

Shukra acceded to his daughter's demand. Devayaani would marry Yayaati. Sharmishtha would accompany Devayaani, as she would have to, being Devayaani's maid. Shukra took Yayaati aside.

'Yayaati, my soon-to-be son-in-law,' Shukra said.

'Yes, O Sage,' Yayaati answered.

'Devayaani will be your wife. Live with her as per dharma.'

'I will, O Sage.'

'Sharmishtha will accompany Devayaani.'

'I see,' Yayaati said.

'She is the daughter of a king.'

'I know, O Sage.'

'Accord her the respect she deserves.'

'I will, O Sage.'

'Do not call her to your bed,' Shukra said, looking Yayaati in the eyes.

For a minute no one spoke. Yayaati stared at Shukra. He finally accepted that Shukra was serious.

'I won't, O Sage,' Yayaati said. Of course, he wouldn't. Why would he? No, he wouldn't, he reminded himself.

Shukra nodded.

Devayaani married Yayaati and they went to his kingdom. As was the proper thing to do for the daughter of the king of the asuras, Yayaati had a house built in a grove near the palace for Sharmishtha and her thousand maids. The days came and the weeks and months passed. Life moved along. The wheels of time continued to spin.

In due course, a son—Yadu—was born to Devayaani. The news reached Sharmishtha. She became aware of the passage of time. She too was a woman. She too was young. She too desired a husband. She too wanted children of her own. But time was passing by. It was passing her by. The passage of time, she could do nothing about. But as time went by, so would her youth. There was nothing she could do about that, either. But was there hope and a solution close at hand to the other problem—of a husband and children? Where would she find a husband from? She was a servant in Devayaani's palace. But what was good for Devayaani would be equally good for Sharmishtha, the asuri thought.

> I can also see your beauty. I do not even see a blemish that is as small as the point of a needle.[37]

It was not long afterwards that Yayaati came out into the grove. Sauntering around, he found himself face-to-face with Sharmishtha. The young, pretty, and single Sharmishtha greeted Yayaati. He greeted her.

'My wishes on your becoming a father, O King,' Sharmishtha said.

'Thank you, O Sharmishtha,' Yayaati said.

'How time passes.'

'Yes, it does, doesn't it?'

'Time is passing me by, O King.'

Yayaati stayed silent.

'Please help me.'

'How?' Perhaps he could help her find a suitable husband, he thought.

'You can do me a favour.'

"Yes, please tell me."

'Bestow upon me the same favour as you did on Devayaani,' Sharmishtha told Yayaati.

For a minute the silence screamed between them. Yayaati stared at Sharmishtha. She looked back at Yayaati. She was serious. This was no joke. Words failed Yayaati.

'You don't mean..., do you?' Yayaati stuttered.

'I mean exactly what you think I mean, O King.'

'But....'

'I also know you have thought the same, haven't you?' Sharmishtha kept her gaze on Yayaati.

'Yes, I mean...,' Yayaati stumbled for words. 'Sharmishtha, there is no doubt that you are beautiful. No, you are flawless.'

'So what is the hesitation?'

'Devayaani's father, Shukra. I gave the sage my word.'
'But I am also your wife, am I not?' Sharmishtha asked.
'What? How? I don't understand,' Yayaati said.
'I am Devayaani's slave, and thus I belong to you, the king.'
'Yes, but I cannot lie to Devayaani...'
'Yes, you can. No sin accrues if you lie under five circumstances. If you lie to Devayaani about me, no sin will befall you.'
'But you are, were, her friend, Sharmishtha.'
'But I am still her friend. There is not much difference between one's own husband and one's friend's husband,' Sharmishtha smiled. 'What is hers is yours and what is hers is mine, isn't it?'

It is no sin to commit a falsehood in five cases—in jest, to women, at the time of marriage, when confronting death and when all one's riches are liable to be lost.[38]

Sharmishtha's beauty, brains, and presence of mind won the day. Yayaati acceded to Sharmishtha. In due course, a son—Druhyu—was born to Sharmishtha.

It is held that one's husband and one's friend's husband are closely related. A friend's marriage is equal to one's own. I have chosen my friend's husband as mine.[39]

The news of the birth of a son to Sharmishtha reached the palace and Devayaani. Whether it was curiosity or suspicion, she asked Sharmishtha who the son's father was. Sharmishtha replied that it was a sage who had given her a boon, which resulted in this son. Devayaani persisted and asked Shamishtha for the sage's name and lineage.

'What was the sage's name, Sharmishtha?' asked Devayaani. 'What was his gotra?'
'Don't' ask me all these trifling details, O Devayaani. That sage, oh, how do I begin to describe him? His radiance overpowered me. In the presence of his effulgence I had no room for either thought or speech. No words were necessary, no questions were needed. Nothing was asked, nothing was spoken. It was just him and me and sheer bliss,' Sharmishtha said, smiling sweetly.

If that was the case, then so be it. Devayaani's curiosity and suspicions allayed, she returned home, happy.

In due course, another son was born to Devayaani—Turvasu. In due course, two more sons were born to Sharmishtha—Anu and Puru. Puru! That name, after whom their lineage was named! The dots were starting to fall in line.

One day, Devayaani and Yayaati went to a forest. There she saw three children playing around. Yayaati's heart skipped a beat and then sank. They were no ordinary children, for they were dressed regally and had a royal demeanour about them. He knew their father. He also knew their mother. Curious, Devayaani asked the children who they were, who their mother was, who their father was. Yayaati stood, mute, dumb, frozen with fear. His heart heard the countdown to his downfall.

The children looked at Yayaati and pointed to him—of course, he was their father!

Three.

They then shared their mother's name—Sharmishtha.

Two.

The children ran up to their father. Yayaati stood there, immobile with fear and foreboding. He would neither look at them nor acknowledge them. The heartbroken children ran crying to their mother. Devayaani followed close behind. Sharmishtha stood, quietly.

> 'You vile woman, you treacherous serpent, you ungrateful wench!' Devayaani screamed at Sharmishtha.
>
> 'Who, me?' Sharmishtha asked sweetly.
>
> 'Yes, you. How dare you? You had said these were the children of a sage.'
>
> 'Yes, Devayaani, but they are. After all, hadn't you said that Yayaati too was a sage, being the descendant of one?'
>
> Devayaani stared, speechless. 'How could you cast your eyes on my husband?' she asked.
>
> 'But my friend, Devayaani, whatever belongs to me is yours, isn't it? Yayaati is yours. You chose Yayaati as your husband, didn't you? So did I. Simple and practical, wasn't it?'

Sharmishtha now had three children. Devayaani had two. She was now in a relatively inferior position vis-à-vis Devayaani.

One.

A despairing and devastated Devayaani left and went straight to her father. She poured out her woes. She lamented that not only had she been deceived by Sharmishtha, but since Sharmishtha now had three sons, while she had only two, she now had the upper hand in this situation.

> You chose the king as your husband. So did I. According to dharma, a friend's husband is one's own husband.[40]

Sages, when angered, cursed; when crossed, they cursed. Kaavya Ushanaas[41] did the same. He cursed Yayaati that he would lose his youth since it was his youth that had made him so licentious. Yayaati pleaded for clemency. He made one last, desperate, attempt to stave off this most cruel of curses. To refuse a woman who solicited a man was a terrible sin, equivalent to the killing of an embryo. To no avail. The curse took immediate effect. Yayaati became old, decrepit, unable to enjoy life, unable to partake in any pleasures of life.

Even then, Yayaati lamented that he still desired the pleasures of youth. Taking just a smidgeon of pity on Yayaati, Shukra granted him one concession—the king could take the youth of anyone who was willing to this exchange.

An eager, desperate Yayaati went to each of his sons, starting with the eldest—Yadu, Turvasu, Druhyu, and Anu. Each of the four sons refused. To drool like infants, to be unclean, unable to speak clearly, able to enjoy neither riding horses nor the company of women, to be wrinkled, ugly, and thin, to be weak and suffer defeat at the hands of the young—no, this was not acceptable to Yadu, Turvasu, Druhyu, or Anu.

> White hair and beard, cheerlessness, flabbiness, wrinkles on the body, ugliness, weakness, thinness, incapacity to work, defeat by the young and forsaking by those who depend on you—I do not wish for this old age.[42]

Yayaati cursed each of them, and to each of them went a different curse. Yadu's sons, the Yaadavas, would have no share in the kingdom; Turvasu's lineage, the Yavanas, would go extinct; Druhyu's desires would never come true, his descendants would be known as the Bhojas; and Anu's offspring, the Mlecchas, would perish of old age immediately on attaining youth.

Only the youngest, Puru, the fifth son, agreed to his father's wish. He would take his old age and pass his youth to his father. Yayaati blessed him that his children would be the heirs to the kingdom and be known as the Pauravas.

Yayaati became young. Puru took his father's wrinkles, infirmities, and old age. For a long, long time, Yayaati enjoyed the pleasures that a newfound youth brought. This time, however, he stayed within the confines of dharma. Every good thing comes to an end, and when it did, Yayaati handed back to Puru his youth. His time was coming to an end, and he decided to crown Puru the king.

Much later, when on his deathbed, Bheeshma would share with Yudhishthira words on the futility of desires and the mirage of pleasures:

> When the body ages, the hair also ages. When the body ages, the teeth age. The eyes and ears also age. However, thirst is not destroyed.[43]

When Puru was crowned king, all four varnas—brahmanas, kshatriyas, vaishyas, and shudras—in his kingdom rose in protest. How could the rights of the elder sons be ignored, and the youngest son crowned king? Yayaati quieted those questions. Just being the eldest did not confer an inalienable right to the throne. Qualities too, mattered.

> It is the opinion of the learned that a son who acts counter to the father's wishes is no son at all.[44]

This, thus, was the tale of Yayaati, whose love for life and a search for gratification of desires was never satiated, and which ended up earning him a curse from Shukra, and who passed his throne to his youngest son, Puru, and decreed that his descendants would be known as Pauravas.

Thence was Janamejaya also called a Paurava.

Much later, a similar saga would play out. Devavrata would willingly renounce his claim to the throne so that his father could marry Satyavati and her son become king. Neither son would live to become king, and the saga of fate would roll its dice once more.

Even the case of Paandu was similar. His wife, Kunti, invoked the Gods and got three sons. His second wife, Maadri, invoked the mantra to summon a God once, but got two sons. Kunti stopped her from using the boon a second time, and the count of sons stayed in favour of Kunti. History almost repeated itself.

In all that transpired between Devayaani, Sharmishtha, and Yayaati, whose fault was it, at whose door would one lay the blame, pin the label of guilt on? Were matters black-and-white?

Was it Sharmishtha's fault, for reacting as violently as she did over a trifle? Did she need to push Devayaani into a well? Or was it Devayaani's, for flying into a rage over a mere mix-up of clothes? Did Devayaani take her revenge to extremes by having Sharmishtha serve as her servant even after marriage; was that humiliation necessary? Didn't she realize Yayaati's hedonistic nature after marriage? What about Shukra, who gave in to his daughter's temper and demands, despite being the one to advise her to let bygones be bygones? What about Yayaati, who gave in to Sharmishtha's enticements with little resistance? Once is understandable, but twice, and then thrice—he fathered three children with Sharmishtha; surely not an act of accidence. Was seducing Devayaani's husband the most apt retribution that Sharmishtha could have chosen to inflict?

Finally, what about the king of the gods, Indra, who started this saga? A mere wind that blew a maelstrom spanning generations and sealing the fate of entire lineages? Simple cause-and-effect is rarely that simple, is it?

The ways of dharma were truly subtle.

3

MAHAABHEESHA

Long Lived the Curse

Parva: Adi (1) **Upa parva: Sambhava (7)**
Chapter: 91 **Shlokas: 22**

Why Puru became king and not any of his elder brothers, and why Janamejaya was called a Paurava, Janamejaya now understood. Vaishampaayana had continued his account of the lineages of Puru and Paandu, ending with Janamejaya's sons and grandson.[1]

Puru was Yayaati's youngest son and he had been appointed heir. Why that had happened, Janamejaya had heard from Vaishampaayana. Another of Janamejaya's ancestors, Shaantanu, had not been the eldest, and yet become king.[2] Shaantanu's eldest son, Devavrata, also had not become king. He had lived a long life and displayed immense valour on the battlefield in Kurukshetra and elsewhere. Clearly, Devavrata had been capable and eligible. Yet he had not become king. In fact, he had himself renounced his claim to the throne. Why was that, asked Janamejaya.

Who was Shaantanu? He was a descendant of Puru. But if we were to trace the entire lineage, which is what Vaishampaayana did, and if we list only the sons in the lineage, it would look like this[3]: Puru → Pravira (m. Shuraseni) → Manasyu (m. Souviri) → Subhru (via apsaraa Anadhrishti) → Richepu → Matinaara → Tamsu → Ilina (m. Rathantari) → Dusyhanta (m. Shakuntala) → Bharata.

Let's pause for a minute at Bharata. Though he had nine sons through three wives, he found none of them qualified enough to succeed him. So, through the grace of Sage Bharadwaaja, he got a child named Bhumanyu. He adopted Bhumanyu as his son and anointed him king.

Resuming the family tree, we get Bharata → Bhumanyu (m. Pushkarini) → Suhotra (m. Aikshvaki) → Ajameedha (m. Dhumini) → Riksha → Samvarana[4] (m. Tapati) → Kuru (m. Vahini) → Abhishyanta (one of his brothers was Janamejaya[5]) → Pareekshit[6] → Dhritaraashtra[7] (his other brothers were Paandu[8], Baahlika, Hasti and others; Hastinapura, the capital of the Kurus, was named after Hasti) → Prateepa → Shaantanu (Prateepa's eldest son was Devaapi, but he became a renunciate early in life; the other sibling was Bahlika, who fought in the Kurukshetra war).

This is how we arrive at King Shaantanu. Devavrata was the youngest of eight sons that Shaantanu had with Ganga.

'O Sage, did any of the first seven sons of Shaantanu become king?' asked Janamejaya.

'No, they were drowned by their mother, Ganga, shortly after birth,' replied Vaishampaayana.

'What a horrible death,' exclaimed Janamejaya.

'All eight had been cursed.'

'No wonder they all died so soon.'

'No. The early deaths of the first seven was not because of the curse. Rather, their death was the redemption of the curse. It is what they had asked for.'

'I see. So does that mean that Devavrata was not cursed, and therefore he lived a long life?'

'No.'

'Does that mean he was also cursed?'

'Yes. In fact, his was the most severe of curses.'

'I see. So that means his long life on earth was the curse that he had to bear?'

'Yes. It was also what his mother, Ganga, wanted.'

'I don't understand, O Sage. Why was Devavrata cursed? Why were his seven brothers cursed? Why did Ganga drown her first seven sons and not the eighth?'

King Mahabheesha was a great king of the Ikshvaaku dynasty, Vaishampaayana began. As per the laws of time he died; and when he did, he attained heaven. One day, while in heaven, Mahabheesha went to pay homage to Brahma. In that congregation, Ganga also happened to arrive. In that same gathering, a gust of wind disturbed Ganga's clothes. While all the gods lowered their eyes out of a sense of decorum, Mahabheesha did not. He stared, gaped, gazed at Ganga. This was not the behaviour expected of gentlemen, least of all of someone in heaven, and did not go down well with Brahma. The king was undeserving of heaven, Brahma fumed. He would be reborn on earth, Brahma pronounced his curse. Mahabheesha accepted the curse; he had no choice, after all. He had been, after all, guilty of an indiscretion in heaven. But if he was going to be reborn, perhaps he could choose who his father would be, what lineage he would be born into. People with stores of merit and in heaven had that much prerogative. After some deliberation, he decided to be born as King Prateepa's son.

Ganga had witnessed Brahma curse Mahabheesha. Whatever his indiscretion, Ganga had also felt some attraction towards Mahabheesha. Brahma's curse had left her saddened. As she walked, lost in thought, she came across the eight divine vasus,[9] looking even more dejected. She asked them the reason for their moroseness. They revealed that Sage Vasishtha had cursed them for what they believed had been a minor transgression.

Had the Vasus' been a minor transgression? One of the vasus was Dyou.[10] Once his wife took a liking to Sage Vasishtha's cow. This cow was no ordinary cow, either. It was divine and could fulfil any wishes one had. This is the cow that Dyou's wife wanted for her friend, and she goaded her husband into stealing it from the sage. No, not borrow, but steal. Dyou did just that, with the help of his seven other vasu brothers. If the vasus thought their identity would remain a secret, they were mistaken. The moment Vasishtha returned to the hermitage and found the cow missing, he divined who the thieves were. He pronounced a curse on all eight of them—to be born as men. Relenting only after the vasus beseeched the sage to soften the curse, Vasishtha maintained that while seven of them would be redeemed from the curse within a year, the eighth one—Dyou—who had been the principal perpetrator of the theft, would have to live a long and cursed life on earth. He would be brave, but he would live without fathering any children.

Now, seeing Ganga, a thought struck the vasus. Then another. And then a third. They put forth their requests to her. They requested Ganga, the holiest of all rivers, to bear them on earth. She agreed. She would, in a personified form, bear all the vasus on earth. Their second request was that King Prateepa's son be their father. Ganga agreed to this too. She would unite with Mahabheesha on earth (Mriytulok).

Vasishtha had cursed all of them to be born on earth. Ganga had agreed to bear them on earth. But Vasishtha had not specified how much time they would have to spend in Mrityulok before they could return to the heavens. They requested Ganga to redeem them from their earthly existence at the earliest. As soon as they were born, Ganga should convey them to the heavens, they requested.

Ganga acquiesced, but with one condition. She wished that at least one of her mortal sons live a long life on earth. The Vasus agreed and proposed that this eighth one would possess one-eighth of the energies of each of the vasus. This eight Vasu was Devavrata.

Thus, Mahabheesha was born on earth as Shaantanu; Ganga appeared on earth in a human form and married Shaantanu and bore the eight vasus as her sons. Seven of those vasus attained heaven shortly after birth at the hands of Ganga. The eighth Vasu lived on as Devavrata and became known to the world as Bheeshma, living a very, very long life, till the age of the curse had exhausted itself, attaining salvation with the blessings of Krishna, on the battlefield of Kurukshetra.

4

ANIMAANDAVYA

Justice Impaled

Parva: Adi (1) **Upa parva: Sambhava (7)**
Chapter: 101 **Shlokas: 34**

At the time that Yudhishthira, the incarnation of Dharma, lived on earth, there lived another incarnation of Dharma. One had been the result of an express wish of his earthly father that his eldest son be the embodiment of Dharma. The other had been the curse of a sage. One was Yudhishthira, also known as Ajameedha,[1] Paartha,[2] Kaunteya, Ajaatshatru,[3] or mostly as Dharmaputra.[4] The other was Vidura.

There was once a famous sage called Maandavya. During one of his penances, he had taken a vow of silence.[5] Maandavya stood under a tree near the entrance of his hermitage, silent, praying, hands raised. Close by, some thieves were on the run. Chasing them were the king's guards. Fleeing from the royal sentries, the robbers came to and rushed into Maandavya's hermitage, their loot in tow. Moments later the king's guards arrived. They suspected the thieves had taken refuge in the sage's hermitage. They asked Maandavya about the robbers' whereabouts. The sage didn't answer. He was observing a vow of silence.

Not getting an answer from the sage, the guards entered the hermitage and found both the robbers and the stolen goods there. The sage had been quiet because, of course, he was in cahoots with the robbers; his silence had been one of convenience, not of a penance. Surely the sage was the thieves' accomplice, the guards concluded. Off they marched to the king, with the sage and robbers in tow. The king, eager to pronounce judgment and verdict, wasted no time in declaring the entire lot guilty. The sentence? Bandits and their accomplices deserved only one sentence—death. The means? To be impaled on a stake. Maandavya kept quiet.

The punishment was carried out. Maandavya was impaled on a stake. But he lived. He stayed there, impaled, without food or water. Wondering what sin he had committed to deserve such a gruesome fate, he summoned other sages. They came, but in the form of vultures. They also asked him what sin he had committed, for he must have done something to deserve this fate. Nothing happened without reason. Maandavya could think of none. Perhaps this was fate, Maandavya mused.

Meanwhile word reached the king that among those he had pronounced guilty and sentenced to death was one who was a brahmana. The king was appalled. Aghast at what he had just done—imposed a death sentence on a brahmana, the king rushed to Maandavya. He apologized to the sage and had him brought down from the stake. The king himself set upon extracting the stake from Maandavya's body. The sage's tribulations didn't end, however. To everyone's horror, the king was unable to fully extract the pole. Part of it remained embedded inside the sage and wouldn't come out. The king did the next best thing—he cut the shaft at both ends. The sage could now walk, but with a stake still inside him. He came to be known as Animaandavya[6] from that day onwards—Maandavya with the tip (Ani) of the stake.

For as long as Animaandavya lived, he thought about his fate. Sages who were steadfast and adhered to their dharma were not falsely accused, much less impaled. Eventually he died and went to heaven. He posed the question that had haunted all his life to Dharma—what sin had he committed, especially one that warranted a punishment as grisly as his? Dharma replied that Maandavya, as a child, had pierced an insect's tail with a blade of grass. For that act of cruelty, he had been subjected to punishment similar in nature.

Was that fair? For a lapse committed as a child, this sentence was grossly disproportionate, Animaandavya maintained. This was neither justified nor expected from Dharma, the god of justice. Animaandavya cursed Dharma. The punishment—to be born as a man to a shudra woman. Second, he decreed that an act performed by a child under the age of fourteen years would not be a sin.

Dharma took birth as Vidura, born to Sage Vyaasa and the Kuru Queen Ambika's maid. Despite being the most learned, the most qualified, the wisest of the three brothers—Dhritaraashtra, Paandu, and Vidura—he lived his life serving them, never considered as a legitimate heir to the throne, serving a king blinded by the love for his son.

Yudhishthira was born from Dharma because Paandu had been cursed to die if he united with his wife. Vidura was born from Dharma because Dharma himself had been cursed.

It was only natural, therefore, that when Vidura died, his soul merged with another manifestation of Dharma on earth, Yudhishthira.[7]

5

VYUSHITASHVA

A Precedence to the Paandavas

Parva: Adi (1) **Upa parva: Sambhava (7)**
Chapters: 112-113 **Shlokas: 34**

The five Paandavas were Paandu's sons, but fathered by the gods, not by him. Yudhishthira was Dharma's son, Bheema Vayu's, Arjun Indra's, and the twins—Nakula and Sahadeva—the Ashwin twins'. That is how the Paandavas had come to be born, Sage Vaishampaayana replied to Janamejaya's question on the origins of the Paandavas. Why was Paandu unable to father children, asked Janamejaya? Yes, it was because of a curse; and it was because of a thoughtless action on his part during a hunt.

Because Dhritaraashtra was blind, he was not seen as fit to ascend the throne. Paandu was crowned king. Deciding to take a break from his royal affairs, he once went to the forest on a hunt.[1] He prowled around, looking for deer. Soon enough, he spotted a stag mating with a doe. Taking out five arrows from his quiver, he shot them at the couple. The arrows found their mark. But the arrows had killed not a deer and a doe, but a sage and his wife. Yet another king had killed a brahmana. There would be consequences.

The deer and doe were Sage Kimdama and his wife. As the dying sage revealed his identity, Paandu remained uncontrite. Kimdama asked Paandu what had driven him to shoot them down in so callous a manner. In Paandu's view, however, what he had shot were animals, and animals could be killed as and when he pleased. Killing animals was the right of kings. Whether waking or asleep, walking or running, it was irrelevant. He had not shot his arrows at a brahmana, but a deer.

> Deer can be killed openly and through trickery. That is the dharma of kings. Since you know that, why are you blaming me?[2]

Kimdama lamented that because of Paandu's act, his lineage was going to end; a lineage that was famous for its sages. Paandu's addiction to hunting had brought about this calamity. As Paandu had acted out of unbridled kaama, snuffing out a life, so would his end be, cursed the sage. Passion had begun this saga, and passion would end it.

> It is known that killing occurs, whether prepared or unprepared, through different means—strength and sharp arrows. O deer! Why are you blaming me?[3]

The only consolation for Paandu was that since he had killed Kimdama unintentionally, he would be spared the sin of killing a brahmana. However, Paandu would die the moment he mated with his wife, cursed Kimdama. Furthermore, the sage said, since the king had killed a couple—the sage and his wife—the same fate would befall the one he mated with. With that curse, Kimdama died, leaving Paandu to ponder over the rashness of his actions.

> Overcome by desire, when you unite with your loved one, at that very instant, you will depart for the land of the dead. The woman with whom you unite in your last moments will also go to the land of the king of the dead, inescapable for all beings.[4]

The act had been done. The consequences would follow. As Paandu reflected on the events, he realized that just as his father, Vichitravirya,[5] had been a victim of drinking,[6] so too had he fallen to an addiction—hunting. Even his great-grandson's, Pareekshit, end would come because of an addiction to hunting.

Paandu decided that he would henceforth lead the life of a hermit. He would beg for food and restrain his senses. There would be no more hunting, no more wanton killing of animals, and there would be no more kaama of any kind.

> I will not mock anyone, nor will I furrow my brow at anyone.[7]

When Paandu shared this news with his wives, Kunti and Maadri, both insisted on accompanying him. The three set out for the forest. True to his word, Paandu immersed himself in austerities and gained the status of a brahmarshi (the highest attainment for a sage).

Life would have continued in that vein, but for one thought that gnawed at Paandu. There was one debt that he had not yet repaid. He was without a son, and Kimdama's curse meant he couldn't father a child.

> According to dharma, men are born on this earth with four debts—to ancestors, gods, rishis and men. The man who does not discharge them at the right time has no worlds. This has been established by those who know dharma. The gods are pleased through sacrifices, the sages through studying and austerities, the ancestors through sons and shraddhas and men through kindness.[8]

Paandu confided in Kunti. He could no longer procreate, but he still wanted to become a father to pay off his mortal debt. There was a way out, he told her. The texts had suggested a solution. They spoke of six types of sons—'*the son born from one's own self, the son presented, the son purchased, the son born from one's widow, the son born through one's wife before marriage and the son born through a loose wife*'.[9] Therefore, Paandu suggested that Kunti mate with a brahmana and beget sons. Such sons would be Paandu's, as per dharma, and his debt to his ancestors would be repaid. He even cited the example of Sharadandaayani, the wife of a warrior, who had sired sons this way.

This was a way, but it unacceptable to Kunti. She had been faithful to Paandu and she was not going to change now. Curse or no curse, she was confident that she would become the mother of Paandu's sons. Paandu remained unconvinced. Kunti's words reflected more hope than reality, Paandu believed. Kunti stayed adamant. To convince Paandu that the course of action he was recommending was not a wise one, Kunti told him the account of Vyushitashva, a king born in the Puru lineage and a rajarshi. Vyushitashva had performed several yagnas (sacrifices), including the ashwamedha (horse) and somasanstha (from soma juice).

Vyushitashva had been married to Bhadra, the beautiful daughter of Kakshivat. However, the king died before he could have had a child with Bhadra. His death was caused by consumption, in much the same way as Vichitravirya had died childless, a victim of consumption. Bhadra was heartbroken and lamented piteously.

It was then that a heavenly voice spoke and granted her the boon of children. It was through this route that Bhadra gave birth to the three Shaalvas and four Madras. There would be some heavenly solution that would surely present itself, Kunti said.

Paandu concurred that the gods could help, but Vyushitashva had been no ordinary king, he reminded Kunti. Vyushitashva's status had been godlike, and Paandu was no god. On the other hand, if Kunti's concern was performing an act of adharma, Paandu told her that there was once a time when women were independent and had freedom in their choice of partners, even after marriage. This was not considered against dharma for such was the dharma of those times.

The present system of monogamy as was followed in society was set down, Paandu said, by Sage Shwetaketu, son of Sage Uddalaka. Once a person came over to their hermitage and taking Shwetaketu's mother by her hand, the two walked away. She would return after having spent time with the man. Shwetaketu was aghast. This act rebelled against his sense of morality. But such had been the dharma of the times, and this was acceptable to his father. But not to Shwetaketu, however. His authority as a learned sage, respected in society, gave him powers to decree new rules for society that would govern the bond of marriage. One of those was an injunction against infidelity.

Paandu cited another example of Kalmaashpaada and his wife Madayanti, who gave birth to Ashmaka through Vasishtha.[10] Also, Paandu reminded Kunti, hadn't he also been born this way, from Ambaalika and Sage Vedvyaasa?

Paandu persisted. Seeing her husband's resoluteness, Kunti shared a secret that she had kept with her all these years. She possessed a boon obtained from the fearsome Sage Durvaasa. The boon gave her the power to summon any god. When summoned, the god would bestow a son on her. That boon could enable both Paandu to obtain a son via Kunti as well as let Kunti preserve her fidelity.

What Kunti did not tell Paandu was she had already used that boon once. In a moment of distraction and youthful indiscretion, she had summoned Surya, the sun god.[11] The son born was growing up as the adopted son of Adhiratha, the suta, and his wife, Radha. His parents named him Vasushena; the world would know him as Karna.

Paandu agreed to Kunti's suggestion. The first God that Paandu asked Kunti to summon was Dharma himself. The first Paandava—Yudhishthira, the son of Dharma, the human embodiment of righteousness—was born.

Four more sons were born this way. Bheema, through Vayu, the wind god; Arjuna through Indra, the king of the gods; Nakula and Sahadeva, through the Ashwin twins. Nakula and Sahadeva were Maadri's sons, who asked Paandu to request Kunti to let her use the boon to also become a mother. She used one boon to summon the Ashwin twins and gained two sons.

6

TAPATI

The Suryavanshi

Parva: Adi (1) **Upa parva: Chaitraratha (11)**
Chapters: 160-163 **Shlokas: 102**

Shortly after the birth of the five Paandavas, Paandu succumbed to desire. One day he tried to unite with his wife, Maadri. Sage Kimdama's curse took effect and his life. Maadri too followed her husband in death, just as Kimdama has cursed.[1] The Paandavas and Kunti returned to Hastinapura. On Dhritaraashtra's instructions, Vidura and Bheeshma performed Paandu's last rites. The subjects grieved the death of their king and the widowing of the queen. Vyaasa also arrived. He saw the grieving folks, but he also saw the dark clouds that loomed in the years to come. He advised his mother and her daughters-in-law to leave the palace and retire to the forest. Satyavati, Ambika, and Ambaalika[2] set out for the forest.

> Happy times are over. Terrible times lie ahead.[3] You will not be able to witness the destruction of your sons and lineage.[4]

The young Paandava princes grew up in Hastinapura. Drona was Sage Bharadwaaja's son and had acquired the knowledge of weapons from Sage Parashuraama. Bheeshma appointed Drona teacher of the Kuru princes. The sons of both Paandu and Dhritaraashtra learned under the same teacher.

Bheema's superhuman strength came to be widely known. So did Duryodhana's resentment and hostility towards Bheema, specifically, and the Paandavas, in general, become well-known.

Duryodhana's hatred was implacable. He tried to drown, and then poison, Bheema.[5]

When their education was complete, Drona had the Kuru princes display their skills to the public. Karna also made his appearance at that event, and a new enmity was cemented—between Arjuna and Karna.[6] Duryodhana seized the moment to crown Karna the king of Anga, earning his lifelong friendship and loyalty, as well as a skilled rival against his cousins.[7]

Duryodhana never abandoned his attempts to do away with the Paandavas. With Vidura's timely warnings, however, they survived every single attempt on their lives. Duryodhana and the Kaurava princes had a mentor in the wicked Shakuni, their maternal uncle. They also had a reluctant ally in their father, Dhritaraashtra. The blind king, however, was cognizant that public opinion was with the Paandavas, as were the loyalties of kings who had once been allied with Paandu. He, despite being king, could not exile the Paandavas, much to Duryodhana's frustrations.

> How can we forcibly exile him, especially since he has allies, from the kingdom of his father and grandfather?[8]

'So, we cannot exile my cousins—is that what you are saying, O Father?' Duryodhana asked Dhritaraashtra.

'Yes, son.' Dhritaraashtra replied.

'Why, Father, why? You are king, are you not? And yet you can't,' Duryodhana threw up his arms in frustration, frustrated even more that his father could not see the anger and hate he had for his cousins.

'Paandu took good care of his allies. Even after his death, they remember him fondly. They will not tolerate us exiling the Paandavas,' Dhritaraashtra replied.

'Okay, so we don't exile them. Let us send them away,' Duryodhana smiled.

'It's all the same thing, Duryodhana. It won't work.'

'Oh yes, it will work, O Father.'

'How?' Dhritaraashtra perked up.

'Once you send them away, I will use the treasury to win over the people. The Paandavas may have their father's allies, but they will also need the people's support. Once the people are with us, the Paandavas will be unable to raise a claim to the throne.'

'Yes, it would work,' smiled the blind king.

'Do you like the plan then?' asked Duryodhana.

'Yes, I do. Your words echo what my heart too desires.'

> 'Then why didn't you say something earlier, O Father?' asked Duryodhana.
>
> 'Because I feared the elders—Bheeshma, Drona, Kripa, and Vidura. They would never approve of the Paandavas' banishment; and if they rebel, my throne won't stand,' Dhritaraashtra sighed.
>
> 'But they don't matter, O Father.'
>
> 'What do you mean? Do Bheeshma, Drona, Kripa, and Vidura count for nothing?'
>
> 'Let's see where they stand, each one of them. The grand old warrior, Bheeshma, will stay neutral,' Duryodhana said.
>
> 'I see. What about Drona?' asked Dhritaraashtra.
>
> 'Where Ashwatthaama goes, so will his father, our beloved guru, Drona. And Ashwatthaaama is my friend.'
>
> 'Kripa?'
>
> 'Kripa does not have a mind of his own. Where Bheeshma is; where his sister, Kripi, is; where Drona is, so will Kripa be. Rest assured, O Father, for your son is smart enough to have figured all this out.'
>
> 'And what about Vidura?' asked Dhritaraashtra.
>
> 'Yes, he is partial towards the Paandavas. He has made no secret of that. He always favours them. But he can do nothing without the support of Bheeshma, Drona, and Kripa. He can rant all he wants.'
>
> 'In that case, go ahead. I will ask the Paandavas to go visit Vaarnavata. Use the time and opportunity wisely,' Dhritaraashtra said.

Duryodhana didn't tell his father he intended to do more than use the time wisely. He summoned his trusted advisor, Purochana, and gave him a task.[9] Purochana would build a grand house for the Paandavas in Vaarnavata. It would be no ordinary house. Generations to come would remember and talk about the house. It would be built of the most inflammable substances that could be found. A single spark would turn that mansion into a raging inferno. The Paandavas would perish there. It would be the house of lac.

Vidura may have been powerless on his own, but he had a trusted network of spies who brought him information good and bad, from far and wide, of mundane events, of conspiracies and happenings. Through one of those spies, he came to know of the conspiracy to burn the Paandavas in the house of lac in Vaarnavata. He warned the Paandavas,[10] who escaped into the forest.

The advisers and the treasury are now under our control.[11]

In the forest, they encountered the raakshasa, Hidimba.[12] Bheema dispatched Hidimba to the other world and married his sister,

Hidimbaa, who had grown besotted with Bheema. She gave birth to a son, Ghatotakacha, who stayed back with his mother. On Vyaasa's advice, the Paandavas moved to a small town called Ekachakra. There, Bheema rid the town of the menace of another raakshasa, Bakasura.[13]

After leaving Ekachakra, the Paandavas moved on. Along the way, they learned about the upcoming swayamvara ceremony of Draupadi, daughter of King Drupada, to be held in the king's capital of Kaampilya. On Vyaasa's advice, they set out for Drupada's kingdom, still in disguise as brahmanas.

It was night by the time the Paandavas and Kunti arrived at the banks of the Ganga. The king of the gandharvas, Chitraratha, was also there, along with his wives. The Paandavas' presence annoyed him no end. They were travelling at night—it was frowned upon for humans to travel after dusk. Frowned upon or not, Arjuna didn't take kindly to being challenged thus. If he, Arjuna, and the Paandavas decided to travel at night, they would. No one dared bar their path. Chitraratha challenged them and Arjuna took the challenge up. In short order, Arjuna defeated him.

> Whether it is night or day or twilight, how can the ocean, the Himalayas or this river be barred to anyone?[14]

A vanquished Chitraratha was disconsolate. No man would put up with insults with his wife present.[15] Neither had Chitraratha. Ego had driven him to challenge Arjuna. Now he sat defeated, his pride humbled, his chariot reduced to ashes. From that day on, the morose Chitraratha declared he would call himself not Chitraratha, but Dagdaratha. Why? Chitraratha meant someone adorned with a chariot. But now there was no chariot. Arjuna's divine weapon, Agneya, had charred his chariot. Dagdaratha—someone whose chariot has been reduced to ashes—was a more befitting name for him.

His pride humbled, Chitraratha sat and talked with Arjuna. The gandharva king said that he was surprised to see the Paandavas in this state of penury. The Kurus were known for their prosperity. And yet, here they were, the Paandavas, descendants of Kuru—walking alone, without the company of learned brahmanas, without the fire of a householder. Such were the vicissitudes of fate.

In their discussions Chitraratha referred to Arjuna as the descendant of Tapati.[16] He and the other Paandavas knew themselves as belonging to the Kuru lineage, as sons of Paandu, as sons of Kunti, but not of Tapati. Who was Tapati, asked Arjuna?

The gandharva replied that Tapati was Surya's daughter and Saavitri's[17] young sister. If one went by Chitraratha's description, then Tapati was a beauty par excellence. When the time came, Surya decided that she should be married to King Samvarana, the son of King Riksha,[18] who was handsome, righteous, and steadfast in the pursuit of dharma.

Once Samvarana went out to the forest on a hunt. This time too, both the king and his horse were overcome with thirst and hunger. His horse could not bear the thirst and died. Leaving him behind, Samvarana went ahead, searching for water and food. He found neither but did come across Tapati. Forgetting his thirst, he was smitten by her beauty. Remember, she was very, very beautiful.

He asked her who she was, for he was convinced she was either a goddess, asuri, yakshi, raakshasi, nagini, or gandharvi. No human could be as beautiful as her, he maintained. Perhaps she was Shri, personified. Perhaps her dazzling beauty was a manifestation of the sun's brilliance itself. Tapati didn't utter a word. Worse, she vanished in the twinkling of an eye, leaving a hungry, thirsty, and now love-stricken king behind.

Samvarana wandered around the forest, looking for her, calling out to her. Exhausted, despondent, he collapsed. Tapati appeared again and Samvarana's outpourings of love started afresh. He knew he loved her, and he proposed the gandharva marriage to her, for he could not wait to marry her.

Tapati reciprocated his feelings, but unlike Shakuntala, asked that the king first seek her hand in marriage from her father. Saying so, she vanished, yet again; and Samvarana collapsed to the ground, yet again. It was in this state that the ministers and attendants found their king. They revived him with a generous sprinkling of water. Samvarana sent away the attendants, keeping beside him only his wise and old minister.

Samvarana needed to seek Tapati's father's blessings and approval. For twelve days, Samvarana prayed to Surya. The twelve days passed, but Tapan[19] did not manifest. The king's priest, Vasishtha, meanwhile recognized the king's desire and the appropriateness of such a union if it were to fructify. He took Samvarana's approval to intercede on the king's behalf with

Surya.[20] Vasishtha then went to Surya[21] and asked for Tapati's hand on behalf of Samvarana. Vasishtha was a brahmarshi, respected in all the worlds. Samvarana was a brave and honourable king. Surya agreed to Vasishtha's proposal.

Vasishtha led Tapati to the mountain where Samvarana was praying. Endless was the king's delight on seeing Vasishtha return with Surya's[22] daughter. After their marriage, Samvarana and Tapati decided to spend time in the mountain, leaving the running of the kingdom to his minister.

For twelve years the married couple stayed in the forest. For twelve years it didn't rain in the kingdom. That caused much pain, misery, and death. Finally, Vasishtha went to the mountain and reminded the king that he had been neglecting his duties. He needed to return to the capital. Samvarana agreed. As Samvarana stepped foot in the city, so did the rains.

Samvarana and Tapati eventually had a son named Kuru. Because Arjuna was a descendant of Tapati, the gandharva had addressed Arjuna as Taapatya, one born from Tapati.

VASISHTHA

Deadly Sagacity

Parva: Adi (1) Upa parva: Chaitraratha (7)
Chapters: 164-168 Shlokas: 173

Vasishtha was the guru to Arjuna's ancestors. Vasishtha was a brahmarshi who had conquered anger. Vasishtha had had a long-running feud with Vishwaamitra. Who was Vasishtha, Arjuna wanted to understand from Chitraratha.

Vasishtha could have killed Vishwaamitra and his entire clan, but he hadn't. For his pacificism, to which he had remained committed in the face of extreme provocations, Vasishtha had to pay a heavy price. Vishwaamitra had been responsible for Vasishtha's sons' deaths, and he would have been justified in retaliating against the Kushikas,[1] but he hadn't. He had conquered both anger and desire, difficult even for the gods. Such a person—and guru—was Vasishtha. The Paandavas needed a preceptor like Vasishtha, Chitraratha counselled.

Yes, the Paandavas would heed Chitraratha's advice and ask a sage to become their preceptor, Arjuna accepted. But who was Vishwaamitra? He had been a king. But wait, wasn't he a brahmana? A king could be a rajarshi, like Janaka was, and many other wise kings, but Vishwaamitra was a brahmarshi. Even multiple births could prove insufficient for such an elevation. Yet Vishwaamitra had managed that in one life. The fire to become a brahmarshi had been sparked by a visit to Vasishtha's hermitage.

Vishwamitra was the son of Gaadhi, the king of Kanyakubja. As a king, Vishwamitra would often head to the forest with his army on hunts. On one such hunt, he came by Vasishtha's hermitage.

The sage greeted him and offered him food and water, not only for the king but his entire retinue. The retinue that consisted of thousands of soldiers.

Vasishtha was not serious, thought Vishwaamitra. Or perhaps he expected the king to refuse this offer. How could a sage living in the middle of a forest have the means to feed a king's escort? No, Vasishtha was earnest. The secret lay in a cow named Nandini[2] that Vasishtha had. Because of her, Vasishtha was able to feed the king, his ministers, and entourage.

Vishwaamitra had everything a king could have, but he didn't have a cow like Nandini.

> 'I am not an unreasonable man, O Sage. Name your price,' asked Vishwaamitra.
>
> 'O King, Nandini is not just for me. She is for the gods, she is for guests, she is for the sacrifices I conduct,' replied Vasishtha.
>
> 'I see. I don't doubt Nandini's powers. She is truly remarkable. Nor do I question your wanting to keep such a valuable cow for yourself. But I will give you not just one cow in exchange for Nandini; not even ten, or a hundred. Ten thousand—that is how many cows are yours in exchange for Nandini. That is more than enough, and then some more, to fulfil all your needs. What do you say?'
>
> 'O King, Nandini is not an item to be traded away. Please understand me.'
>
> 'You are truly one tough negotiator, O Sage. Have it your way then—Nandini for my entire kingdom. Even in your wildest dreams you could not have thought that a cow would one day bring you so much fortune,' laughed Vishwaamitra.
>
> 'O King, I am most humbled by your offer. I cannot, however, part with Nandini; not for thousands of cows, not for your entire kingdom,' Vasishtha said with a tone of finality.
>
> 'You do know that you are a brahmana, don't you?' asked an incredulous Vishwaamitra.
>
> 'Yes, I do, O King.'
>
> 'Brahmanas are no match for kings. Have you forgotten this simple fact of life?' a hardness crept into Vishwaamitra's voice.
>
> Vasishtha stayed silent.
>
> 'I can take by force what you do not fork out. I don't want to do that because I respect you. But your stubbornness has diminished that respect I had. Such covetousness does not behoove a brahmana.'
>
> Vasishtha stayed silent.
>
> 'O Sage. I will ask you again. I will ask you one last time—will you hand Nandini over?'

> 'I cannot, O King,' Vasishtha spoke.
>
> 'You cannot, but I can. I will take her with me,' exclaimed Vishwaamitra. 'I have been patient, respectful, and deferential; but to no avail. I tried to reason with you in a soft, sweet, conciliatory language; but to no avail. I will now speak to you in the language that you understand.'
>
> 'I cannot stop you from doing what you must,' Vasishtha said.

Vishwaamitra stepped back and ordered his soldiers to secure Nandini and take her to the capital. The soldiers walked up to Nandini and they pushed. They pushed, they pulled, they shoved, they dragged; but could not budge Nandini an inch. The soldiers then took sticks and hit, caned, and whipped the mute, defenceless cow. Nandini bellowed, cried, and howled. But neither did she leave the hermitage, nor did Vasishtha help her.

Nandini dragged herself loose of the soldiers and their nooses and ropes and trotted to Vasishtha. Tears flowing, she asked how he could stand there and watch the king's soldiers illtreat her so. Vasishtha replied that he could not forsake the path of patience and forgiveness. Was there nothing the sage would do? That was no reason for Nandini to not put a stop to this persecution at the hands of the soldiers, Vasishtha said. She had the means within her—if she could provide for others' sustenance, she could also create the means to protect herself.

Nandini's eyes signalled comprehension and a resolve. She turned around, no longer the docile, gentle cow. A fearsome look in her eyes, she turned on the king's soldiers. From different parts of her body, she created an entire army of soldiers—pahlavas, barbaras, mlecchas, yavanas, shabaras, shakas, Simhalas, kiratas, dramidas, and daradas. This army of soldiers routed Vishwamitra's soldiers, every single one of them. They fled in all directions but found no refuge.

> Vishvamitra's army was driven 3 yojanas away and though it cried out in panic, there was no saviour to be found.[3]

Vishwaamitra saw all this happen in front of his eyes. He couldn't believe the sight, must less fathom it. One solitary cow, belonging to one powerless brahmana, had annihilated his entire army. Vishwamitra stood there, his pride pricked, his vanity vanquished, his army routed. He, his kingdom, his might, his wealth, his soldiers, were nothing compared to a brahmana's powers. There and then, Vishwaamitra decided he wanted the powers of a brahmana. If he remained a king, he could at best become a rajarshi—a king with the qualities of a sage. Perhaps even a maharshi. No, that is not what he wanted. He wanted to be a brahmarshi—the highest level of enlightenment there was.

Vishwaamitra gave up his throne. He immersed himself in austerities. Slowly, surely, he would acquire the same powers that Vasishtha possessed, and then there would be a battle between equals, and he would finally take his revenge.

Time passed. One particularly nasty dispute had arisen between the two sages—Vasishtha and Vishwaamitra—over who would be the officiating priest for King Kalmaashpaada.[4] This only added to the rancour between the two sages.

King Kalmaashpaada once went on a hunt in the forest and found himself on a narrow path. The path could allow only one person to pass through at a time. From the other side the king saw Vasishtha's son, Shakti, walking up. Either the sage could pass first, for which the king's chariot would have to retrace its steps; or the chariot could pass, for which the sage would have to step back. Obviously, neither budged. The sage spoke in soft words, but the king didn't yield. The king shouted and berated Shakti, but the sage didn't yield. Arrogant, frustrated, angry, the king lost all control of his senses and whipped Shakti.

Shakti was enraged at the king's misconduct. This was not the conduct of kings, the sage said, but that of a raakshasa. Therefore, Kalmaashpaada would become one, a maneater, cursed Shakti.

Watching this altercation, hidden from both, unknown to both, was Vishwaamitra. This was, he realized, an opportunity he could use to his advantage. Vishwamitra ordered a raakshasa, Kimkara, to enter Kalmaashpaada's body. The king wandered around, tormented by both Shakti's curse and the presence of raakshasa Kimkara inside him that he knew nothing about.

Wandering in the forest in a daze, Kalmaashpaada came across a brahmana who wanted some food. Kalmaashpaada smiled at the irony. A brahmana had just cursed him to become a maneater, and here was a brahmana asking him for food. Kalmaashpaada, however, desisted. He still had a vestige of self-control left in him. He would not become a cannibal, not for as long as he could. If it is food the brahmana wanted, he would give him food.

The brahmana had a most unusual request—he wanted food with meat in it. Why a brahmana wanted meat, the king didn't ask. He told the brahmana to wait while he went to his palace to fetch the food.

Kalmaashpaada returned to his palace but forgot about his promise to the brahmana. Much later, at midnight, he remembered. He summoned his cook and asked him to prepare some food with meat and take it to the brahmana in the forest. The cook bowed and rushed to the kitchen.

It was midnight. All food in the royal kitchen had been prepared, cooked, and eaten. The cycle of preparation of food would begin afresh in a few hours, at dawn. But the king had ordered the cook to take the food immediately. The cook scoured the kitchens but could find no meat. He went back to the king.

> 'O King, there is no meat left in the royal kitchens. What should I do?' the cook bowed before Kalmaashpaada.
>
> 'Are there no animals left? No sheep, goat?' asked Kalmaashpaada.
>
> 'No. O King,' replied the cook.
>
> 'No meat is no problem,' growled Kalmaashpaada.
>
> The cook looked up at the king.
>
> 'Meat is meat, isn't it?' the king continued.
>
> 'I don't follow you, O King.'
>
> 'Humans are meat, aren't they?' the king smiled.
>
> The cook shivered involuntary, his eyes widening in horror.
>
> 'Oh, don't look so alarmed. Go on, go ahead. Find some human flesh, cook it, and take it to the brahmana,' a mad grin dancing on Kalmaashpaada's lips.
>
> 'But O King…,' the words choked in the cook's throat.
>
> 'If you won't tell anyone, neither will I,' Kalmaashpaada started laughing. A mad, demented laugh.
>
> The cook could swear it was the laugh of a raakshasa, not a king. He nodded, his lips unable to mouth acquiescence. He turned around and walked back to the kitchens on trembling legs, trying to regain his composure, lost in thought on where to procure human flesh from.

The king had been right, the cook rationalized. Wasn't human flesh also meat, after all? The one place where the cook knew he could find human flesh was with the executioner, who was rarely without criminals sentenced to death. He placed his request before the executioner. Yes, sure, a convict had been executed not long back.

The executioner cut off some flesh off the corpse and brought it to the cook. The cook took the human flesh, cooked it, mixed it with rice, and took off for the forest to hand it over to the brahmana.

The brahmana had waited and waited. He was ravenous by midnight but had chosen to wait. The king would not go back on his word. The longer the wait, the tastier the meat prepared in the royal kitchens would be, he knew. The cook walked up to the brahmana and handed over the food to him. The brahmana's brows furrowed. His ascetic powers told him that this was human meat that the cook had brought to him.

The enraged brahmana cursed that Kalmaashpaada, so evidently fond of human flesh, would himself turn into a man-eating monster. Once cursed by Shakti, and a second time by the brahmana, the curse acquired immense potency. Whatever restraint and control over his senses Kalmaashpaada may have possessed, he now lost.

Setting out once again for the forest, wandering about, crazed, dazed, cursed, Kalmaashpaada came across Shakti. Who better to begin his cannibalistic journey than by eating the person who had first cursed him, wondered Kalmaashpaada. Like a tiger devouring its preferred prey, Kalmaashpaada made a meal of Vasishtha's son. Vishwamitra had witnessed all this. He egged Kalmaashpaada on to devour Vasishtha's other sons too, which the king-turned-cannibal did.

> Because you have imposed this unparalleled curse on me, I shall begin my man-eating predicament by eating you first.[5]

News reached Vasishtha that all his sons had been killed by Kalmaashpaada at Vishwaamitra's behest. He would not take revenge on Vishwaamitra. Devastated, grief-stricken, he lost the will to live. He would not take anyone's life; he would give his own up.

Vasishtha trudged to the top of Mount Meru and threw himself off the peak. His body, now light as a feather, landed on a stone. Vasishtha got up, undeterred. If the earth would not help him, he would seek fire. He lit a blaze in the forest and entered the inferno. The fire didn't even singe him, much less burn him. Vasishtha made his way to the ocean. He tied a stone around his neck and walked into the waters. The waves washed him back ashore. The elements would not be a part in the sage's death.

Dejected by these failures, he returned to his hermitage. That place reminded him even more of his dead sons. He left once again, even more determined to end his life. The rains had been plentiful. The river was in spate. The current would wash him away, take him under. He tied himself up with ropes and jumped into the river. The river however tossed him, tore loose those ropes, and washed him back to its banks.[6] He tried once more to drown himself in a different river. The river, taking the brahmana to be fire, scattered helter-skelter, and came to be known as Shatadru.[7]

Dejected once more, despondent even more, Vasishtha once again made way to his hermitage.

Lost in his thoughts, he hadn't heard someone else's footsteps. When he did, he turned around. It was his daughter-in-law, Adrishyanti. She was Shakti's widow and had been pregnant with his child. In his grief, he had forgotten all about her. Vasishtha went up to her. Standing next to her, he heard the divine sound of the Vedas being chanted. He looked down. The Vedic chants were emanating from her womb. It was his grandson. The sounds calmed Vasishtha. Clarity returned to his mind. He abandoned any thoughts of ending his life. He would live, for his daughter-in-law and grandson. The two returned to their hermitage. Standing, waiting for them was Kalmaashpaada.

The cursed maneater, possessed by the raakshasa Kimkara, having already eaten Shakti, his brothers, and the brahmana, lumbered towards them, a club swinging in his hand. A shriek escaped Adrishyanti's lips. A calm Vasishtha assured Adrishyanti that he was really King Kalmaashpaada. Adrishyanti remained terrified. Kalmaashpaada was now almost within reach.

As Kalmaashpaada took another step forward, Vasishtha let out a roar. That stopped Kalmaashpaada in his tracks, frozen midstep, unable to move. Vasishtha stepped forward and sprinkled holy water, sanctified with mantras, on Kalmaashpaada.

For twelve long years Kalmaashpaada had lived a cursed life of a man-eating raakshasa. His existence had been one unending hell of torment and darkness. As the holy water freed him from the curse, and the raakshasa exited him, the energy and brightness of a king reborn lit up the entire forest. Free, purified, restored, he bowed down before Vasishtha in gratitude.

A short while later, Kalmaashpaada requested Vasishtha for a favour. He wanted to continue his lineage. Could the sage oblige?

Vasishtha agreed, went to Ayodhya, and fathered a son to the queen[8], who grew up to be King Ashmaka.

If Kalmaashpaada[9] had been freed from the curse, then why couldn't he have gone back to his queen and fathered a child, asked Arjuna? Yes, Kalmaashpaada should have, said the gandharva Chitraratha, but he couldn't. When the king had been under the twin curses and wandering around in the forest, he had happened upon a brahman and his wife. Terrified of the raakshasa that Kalmaashpaada was, the couple ran away but the king pursued them and caught hold of the brahmana.

Despite the brahmani's[10] entreaties, Kalmaashpaada gobbled up the brahmana. With tears of rage flowing from the brahmani's eyes, she cursed Kalmaashpaada to die the moment he united with his wife. If a son was in his fate, then a son would be born, but not through him, but through Vasishtha, the brahmana's wife pronounced.

Kalmaashpaada was now free of the curse. But he had also forgotten much of what he had done as a raakshasa. He had hastened to his palace to embrace his queen. Madayanti, however, wouldn't let him close. An embrace could turn into a passionate union. Kalmaashpaada may have forgotten the brahmani's curse, but Madayanti hadn't. This rebuke triggered a stroke of recollection in Kalmaashpaada's mind. He now remembered. He also knew what he had to do—he went back to Vasishtha.

When fate conspired with circumstances, when the missteps of karma collided with destiny, a path had to be forged. Kalmaashpaada had to live with the consequences of his actions and continue his lineage through Vasishtha. So would Paandu, but through the gods.[11]

8

AURVA

Blinding Rage

Parva: Adi (1) **Upa parva:** Chaitraratha (7)
Chapters: 169–172 **Shlokas:** 86

Life continued with a semblance of normalcy in Sage Vasishtha's hermitage. His daughter-in-law and his departed son, Shakti's, wife, Adrishyanti, gave birth to a son named Paraashara. The man who would one day become Vyaasa's father grew up in the hermitage under Vasishtha's tutelage. It was but natural for him to believe that Vasishtha was his father. Once he was grown up, his mother, Adrishyanti, told him that his father, Shakti, had been killed by Kalmaashpaada, and that Vasishtha was his grandfather. Paraashara was beside himself with rage. So great was his anger that he wanted to burn the whole world down. Vasishtha called him to his side and started to tell an ancient account.

In the Haihaya[1] lineage there was once a great king named Kritaveerya. Soon after Kritaveerya's death, his descendants found themselves in need of wealth. They pondered over the problem till one of them remembered that the Bhrigus[2] were affluent. Surely the sages could share some of their riches with them. However, the Haihayas were kshatriyas. Kshatriyas never asked; they gave.

If they went as mendicants, however, that would not be beneath their dignity to ask, Kritaveerya's sons decided. They changed from mighty warriors into penurious mendicants and trudged to the Bhrigus. Word reached the Bhrigus that the Haihayas were coming.

The Bhrigus were not keen on sharing their riches with Kritaveerya's descendants. With the Haihayas coming disguised as mendicants to ask, beg, for wealth, they would be unable to refuse. But what if they had no wealth to give? The Bhrigus decided to bury whatever riches they had. Some gave their riches away to other brahmanas. They would now not be uttering an untruth if they said they didn't have any wealth, they reasoned.

The Haihayas came, disguised as mendicants, and begged for wealth. The Bhrigus shrugged; they didn't have any. The Haihayas did not believe the Bhrigus. That a clan known for their wealth was now penurious was preposterous. Their suspicions lingered. They skulked about. One day, on a hunch, or on a whim, these kshatriyas dug up the earth in and around the Brigus' hermitage. Lo and behold, they struck gold—the same treasure that the Bhrigus had buried to keep these kshatriyas from discovering. The same wealth that the Haihayas had begged for and the same wealth the Bhrigus had claimed they didn't have.

Infinite was the rage of these kshatriyas. This was an act of betrayal. The Bhrigus had dared to lie to the king's successors. Retribution was called for. Proportional or not, just or not, they didn't care. Bloodlust took over. Out came arrows from their quivers, swords were unsheathed. No quarter was given, no mercy shown, no discrimination between the aged and the children was exercised, neither men nor women were spared. Not even pregnant women were spared. An utter and complete destruction of the Bhrigus loomed. Those who could flee, fled; those who couldn't, were killed.

Very few survived. Among them was a pregnant woman. Desperate to save her unborn child, she kept her embryo in her thigh, hiding it from the Haihayas. Not for long, though. One day, the kshatriyas spotted her, and after her they came, swords out, arrows drawn, ready to kill. The child, and the gods, chose that moment for its birth. The unborn was born, and the moment he was, a great, dazzling, blinding light shone from him. So bright that it blinded the kshatriyas.

Blinded, fearful, in pain, the Haihayas fled. They wandered around the Himalayas. Unable to find a cure, they found their way back to the brahmani. There they pled with her, begged for forgiveness. They implored her to restore their eyesight. But they were requesting the wrong person, the brahmana lady replied. It was not she, but her son who was responsible for their loss of sight. The Bhaargava[3] was wrathful at the senseless slaughter they had perpetrated. If there was anyone who could restore their eyesight, forgive them, it was that child, Aurva, her son, the brahmana lady said.

The child's wrath had crested. Aurva forgave the kshatriyas. They got their eyesight back. They returned to their kingdoms. But Aurva kept thinking about the matter.

A world where such a senseless carnage could take place, where his ancestors had been slaughtered without mercy, was not one worth preserving. Aurva would burn down the worlds—not just of men, but also of the gods and the asuras. Aurva possessed the knowledge and the power of austerities to do so. Even before he had been born, he had spent a long time in his mother's womb listening to the sages, imbibing all the knowledge of the Vedas and the Vedaangas[4] from the Bhrigus. Armed with this knowledge, he began to perform penances. The destruction of the three worlds loomed.

Aurva's ancestors, the Bhrigus, appeared before him and requested him to desist from his penances. What was done was done. Their deaths were no one's responsibility but theirs. Aurva was taken aback. Hadn't the Haihayas slaughtered them, one and all, without discrimination, without mercy? Bhrigus revealed that this was what they had wanted, and it is what they had contrived to cause.

As highly learned sages, they had lived long lives. Death wouldn't come to them. They could not commit the sin of taking their own lives, either. Neither were they immortal nor did they desire infinitely long lives. The course of nature had to be allowed to take itself. Hence, they came up with this design to instigate the kshatriyas. What could these sages do to inflame the tempers of kshatriyas to such an extent? By burying treasure that these kshatriyas would come begging for in the guise of mendicants.

> **Anger has the purpose of restraining the evil and protecting the good.[5]**

Aurva listened. It made sense. However, the killing of the Bhrigus had been indiscriminate and senseless. It had been an act of sin, evil. On the other hand, he could not disregard his ancestors. He was faced with a dilemma. If he held on to his anger, it would destroy him. If he unleashed this anger outward, it would destroy the three worlds. His ancestors suggested an alternative—Aurva could cast the fire of his rage into the ocean.

Aurva did as instructed. The fire still rages inside the ocean, as evident from submarine volcanoes erupting from time to time.

If Aurva could find an outlet for his rage, so could Paraashara, Vasishtha advised.

Paraashara acceded to his grandfather's advice. However, it had been a raakshasa that had killed his father. Paraashara would kill all raakshasas. Just as Janamejaya had decided to hold a sarpa-satra to kill all serpents, so too did Paraashara decide to perform a raakshasa satra[6] and destroy all the raakshasas in the world.

Vasishtha did not stop Paraashara this time. Three sacrificial fires were lit, Paraashara's energy blazed like a fourth fire. Raakshasas started being consumed in the sacrificial fires—young and old alike. The killing was indiscriminate.

Vasishtha had dissuaded Paraashara from destroying the worlds. To stop him from this sacrifice of raakshasas would have to fall on other sages. Sage Atri came there, along with Pulastya, Pulaha, and Kratu. Atri wanted to know why Parashara was killing even those raakshasas who had nothing to do with his father Shakti's death. Would the innocent also have to perish along with the guilty one? Kalmaashpaada, who had been responsible for Shakti's death, was already about to ascend to heaven. Nothing would be served by killing him now.

Paraashara listened to Atri and the sages. He found wisdom in their words. Yes, the sacrifice had to come to an end. He ended the sacrifice and threw the fire that still burned into a forest that lay to the north of the Himalayas.

> If there is one who punishes crimes in the worlds, no one in the worlds will dare to commit a crime. But if a crime doesn't find a punisher, many in the worlds will commit crimes. A man who has the power to punish a crime and doesn't do so, despite knowing that a crime has been committed, is himself tainted by the deed, even if he is the lord.[7]

9

PANCHENDRA

Five Gods for One

Parva: Adi (1) Upa parva: Vaivahika (13)
Chapter: 189 Shlokas: 40

The strength of the kshatriyas needed to be tempered and guided by the wisdom of brahmanas. The gandharva king, Chitraratha, advised Arjuna that they, the Paandavas, appoint Sage Dhaumya[1] as their priest. They found the suggestion most agreeable. The Paandavas departed from River Ganga and made their way to the Utkochaka forest where Dhaumya resided. Dhaumya agreed to the Paandavas' request. Dhaumya became their priest and advisor.[2]

The Paandavas, along with Kunti, and now Dhaumya, set out once again. They had escaped the fiery death that Duryodhna had planned for them at Vaarnavata. They had resided in Ekachakra and Bheema had rid the village of the raakshasa, Bakasura. They had met the gandharva King Chitraratha and the Paandavas had learned something more about their lineage. Now they walked more. They would have to make their way back to Hastinapura and announce to the world that they, the Paandavas, were alive. But now was not the time. Along the way, they met some brahmanas who were also travelling, but who had a specific destination they were making their way to.

The Paandavas asked where the brahmanas were going. They were on their way to King Drupada's kingdom, the brahmanas replied. Drupada was holding a grand swayamvara for his daughter, Draupadi. The Paandavas that the world knew about had perished in the house of lac at Vaarnavata. Brahmanas were not going to participate in the swayamvara. But they were still curious about the grand spectacle the brahmanas had said had been put up. Lavish gifts would be distributed. The brahmanas hoped to receive this largesse. This is what was driving them to the south of Paanchala.[3]

They would also do well to go there and partake in the gifts, the brahmanas told the Paandavas. Oh, and since one of those poor brahmanas, viz., Arjuna, looked like a handsome god, perhaps Draupadi would choose him as her husband, the brahmanas thought out aloud, perhaps half in jest. If nothing else, Bheema could win a few wrestling bouts and get some more wealth.

To wrestle or not, to receive gifts or not, Yudhishthira concurred that they, the Paandavas, should also make their way to Drupada's kingdom. To the world, they were dead, having been burnt up in the fire at Vaarnavata. They were also, at this point, without powerful allies. Hence, discretion was the need of the hour. They would find it easier to mingle with the hundreds and thousands of brahmanas who would already be there. Taking part in Draupadi's swayamvara was not on their minds, yet.

Reaching Kaampilya,[4] the Paandavas and their mother, Kunti, stayed in a potter's house.

As it turned out, they met Vyaasa on their way. He, obviously, recognized the Paandavas. As they sat talking, Vyaasa shared with the Paandavas that Drupada[5] had always desired to have his daughter, Draupadi, marry Arjuna. Draupadi had a twin brother, Dhrishtadyumna, and one other sibling, who had been a woman.[6]

To ensure that only Arjuna—the most skilled archer in the land—would win the contest, and thus the swayamvara, and therefore Draupadi's hand in marriage, Drupada had gone to great lengths to design the challenge. But now Arjuna, along with the other Paandavas, was dead. If the contest was such that only Arjuna could have won it, and if Arjuna was now dead, who would Draupadi marry? Anyone? No one? Drupada was a worried man.

> On seeing Droupadi, Pritha's mighty-armed sons and the brave and great-natured twins were struck with the arrows of the god of love.[7]

The day of the swayamvara arrived. Along with the Paandavas, the gods, daityas, vasus, maruts, and others[8] came to watch, as did kings from far and wide to participate.[9] Among those who arrived were chiefs from the Vrishnis and Andhakas. Among them were Balaraama and Krishna. Krishna spotted the Paandavas and pointed them out to Balaraama.

The kings had all assembled. Dhrishtadyumna had set out the rules of the swayamvara and told the kings what they had to do to win the contest, and Draupadi's hand. Through the hole of the contraption constructed they had to shoot five arrows in succession.[10] The kings looked at the contraption, apprehension in their minds. The kings looked at Draupadi, longing and desire in their hearts. The kings looked at each other, feelings of rivalry and jealousy in their eyes.

> Then they all looked at the illustrious Krishna who was standing there. They looked at each other and sat down, her image in their hearts.[11]

Draupadi's swayamvara commenced. Kings stepped up to the bow; some couldn't even lift the bow. Those who could, couldn't string it. The recoil of the string lacerated their bodies. Some of the kings who tried and failed were Duryodhana, Vikarna, Duhshasana, Yuyutsu, and Karna.[12]

> Mentally struck with desire, they suddenly stood up from their royal seats and exclaimed, 'Krishna will be mine.'[13]

Now that the kshatriyas had failed, Arjuna stepped forward, strung the bow, and with the five arrows provided, pierced the target. He had won the swaymavara, just as Drupada had hoped. To the kings assembled, this was a double insult. Their pride had been pricked; their egos deflated. Their anger mounted at being bested by a mere brahmana. They demanded that Drupada select one of them as the suitor instead; else they would dispatch Drupada to the other world and Draupadi to the same fire from which she had emerged.

Bheema and Arjuna stood, ready to protect Draupadi and repulse any king who dared advance towards her. Yudhishthira left along with Nakula and Sahadeva.

> The ways of dharma are always subtle and, therefore, we do not know the ways in entirety.[14]

A brief skirmish occurred between the kings assembled on the one hand and Bheema and Arjuna on the other. Even the redoubtable

Shalya got into a brief scrimmage with Bheema, only to be lifted off the ground and thrown off by the Paandava.[15] While Bheema used a tree trunk to fend off the kings,[16] Karna was repulsed by Arjuna. He retreated from the battle, unable to face Arjuna.

> At these words, Radheya Karna withdrew from the battle, because the maharatha thought that Brahmana strength was invincible.[17]

The kings accepted defeat. They retreated. Not many generations ago, Bheeshma had returned from Kashi with three princesses. Now, Bheema and Arjuna returned with Draupadi to the potter's house where Kunti sat. They announced, perhaps in jest, perhaps in a moment of flippancy, certainly driven by destiny, that they had brought alms—the 'alms' being Draupadi. Kunti asked them to share the alms together; 'together' being the five Paandavas.

> When those immensely radiant ones looked at Droupadi, their love for her arose and put their senses into turmoil.[18]

There stood Draupadi, a princess more beautiful than any other in the land. There stood Kunti, having just asked the Paandavas to 'share' her. There stood the Paandavas, stupefied by their mother's words but also besotted by Draupadi's beauty. Draupadi's allure would drive many to behaviour most foul in the years to come. Keechaka and Jayadratha would unleash their nefarious designs. Envy among brothers over a beautiful maiden would be their downfall, as Sage Naarada would warn the Paandavas later.

Arjuna alone could marry Draupadi; or all the Paandavas could. Doing the former was what the rules of the swaymavara had dictated. Doing the latter would be what their mother's instructions demanded.

Drupada meanwhile learned from Dhristadyumna the identity of the brahmanas—they were none other than the Paandavas. He was elated. He heard from Dhristadyumna that all five had been asked to marry her. He was now on the horns of a dilemma.

> The knot tied by destiny cannot be untied.[19]

Drupada invited all the Paandavas to his palace. The debate moved to the palace. How could one woman marry five men, Drupada asked out aloud? Yudhishthira insisted that all five would have to marry Draupadi, for that had been her mother's instructions. But such a thing was just not done, it was not proper, it was against dharma, it was unprecedented, maintained Drupada. Yudhishthira recalled that Jatilaa[20] had been the wife to seven sages. The situation was not that unprecedented, it seemed. Drupada remained unconvinced.

Vyaasa, who had been present in Kaampilya, had also accompanied the Paandavas to Drupada's palace. Vyaasa knew what Drupada didn't; he knew what no one else knew. The question of dharma now fell upon him to resolve. He knew why Draupadi was destined to have five husbands. But Vyaasa would share this with only Drupada, for it could embarrass the king were it to become public knowledge. Vyaasa took Drupada inside; the Paandavas, Dhristadyumna, Kunti, everyone waited.

Vyaasa spoke and Drupada listened. Vyaasa spoke about a time when a great satra (sacrifice) had been performed where Yama was the officiating priest. So busy was Yama with his duties at the sacrifice that he could not attend to his other duty of being the god of Death. Without Yama in control, no deaths occurred. This was against the course of nature; one born had to die. Indra, Kubera, Varuna, and other gods and sages approached Brahma for guidance.

Death was what separated the gods from the mortals, the gods reasoned. If the mortals stopped dying, where would that leave the gods, they wondered. If mortals became gods without trying, no one would aspire to become gods. Yama had not forgotten his duties, Brahma assured the gods. Once the satra was completed, Yama would resume his duty, renewed. Death would catch up with the mortals, Brahma pacified the gods. Relieved, the gods took leave of Brahma and proceeded to the site of the satra.

There the gods saw a lotus in the Bhagirathi (Ganga). Intrigued, Indra went to look more closely. He saw a resplendent lady there. She was half immersed in the waters of the Ganga, evidently to fetch water. However, the lady was weeping. Each tear, as it fell, turned into a lotus. Bewildered and inquisitive, Indra asked her who she was and why she was crying. The lady simply asked Indra to follow her. She led the way, and Indra followed. They soon reached the Himalayas.

There sat a young man on a throne, surrounded by women. They all were playing dice. Indra, king of the gods, introduced himself. He, Indra said, was the one who ruled over the universe. The young man neither paid attention nor looked up from his game. Indra, king of the gods, was angered. Who would ignore, not pay attention and respect, when the king of the gods spoke? A lesson needed to be taught to the impertinent person, Indra decided. Before he could decide on an appropriate next step, the young man finally turned and looked at Indra. The next moment, Indra stood rooted to the spot, paralyzed, unable to move. The young man turned his attention back to the game. Indra stood there, immobile. He stayed that way till the game was over.

The game over, the man turned his attention to Indra. Indra had too much pride and arrogance, said the man. Who was this person? He was Shiva, and he had decided that Indra needed a lesson in humility. He took Indra to the peak of a mountain and asked him to move the peak aside. Indra did as told and then peered inside. He recoiled in horror. There were four other Indras inside. Four gods who looked like him. Shiva told him they were also Indras. Indra would have to join these four Indras.

Indra was penitent. If he had known the person he was being arrogant with was Shiva, he wouldn't have dared. Perhaps Shiva could forgive him. A curse, once pronounced, could not be revoked. That was not the nature of curses. These five would have to remain in the cave. But the effects of curses could be diminished. These Indras would eventually return to heaven. But not before being born as humans—a common form of punishment for gods. Yama, the vasus had been so cursed, as had been Mahabheesha, among many others. These four Indras requested Shiva that the gods Dharma, Vayu, and the Ashvin twins be their fathers. As for the present, newly cursed Indra, he decided he would create a version of himself that would be born on earth—as Arjuna.

Shiva then ordained that Shri (Lakshmi) would be their wife on earth. But they first needed Narayana's approval. Narayaana gave his permission. A manifestation of Shri would be born on earth to be the Paandavas' wife. But Narayana also plucked two hairs from his body, one white and the other black. From the white hair was born Balaraama as Rohini's son, while from the black hair was born Keshava as Devaki's son.

The five Paandavas were one, Vyaasa told Drupada. Arjuna was none other than Indra himself, while the other four Paandavas were also manifestations of Indra. In case Drupada had any lingering doubts, Vyaasa bestowed divine sight upon Drupada. With this vision, Drupada was able to see the Paandavas in their divine forms, each one an Indra.

This explained why the five Paandavas were none other than Indra. Draupadi would not be marrying five different men, but one. But the question now was why Draupadi had been the chosen one for the five Indras, now the five Paandavas? Why had Shri selected her to manifest herself as Draupadi?

The answer lay in Draupadi's previous birth, where she had been the daughter of a sage. The sage was unable to find a suitable a husband who she liked. Taking matters into her own hands, the girl prayed to Shiva.[21] Pleased, Shiva appeared before her to grant a boon. Pleased, she asked for a husband accomplished in all qualities, but in her eagerness, repeated this five times. Gods, when pleased, listen. So did Shiva. He granted her the boon that she would have five such husbands,[22] for she had asked Shiva five times.[23] To give less than what she had asked for would have been inappropriate. After all, she had not asked for immortality. She had only asked for something more impossible than even everlasting life—a perfect husband.

Thus was the sage's daughter born as Drupada's daughter. The decision was now Drupada's, Vyaasa said. Draupadi was none other than a reincarnation of Shri, created by none other than Brahma, ordained by none other than Shiva, with the blessings of none other than Vishnu, destined to be wife to the five Indras as wished for by none other than Draupadi herself in an earlier life.

Drupada gave his consent, and the marriage was solemnized.

> The god himself knows what is best. Since Shankara has ordained it to be thus, dharma or adharma, I will commit no sin.[24]

10
SUNDA AND UPASUNDA

Desire Destroys the Daityas

Parva: Adi (1)
Upa parva: Arjuna-vanvaasa (16)
Chapters: 201-204
Shlokas: 119

The Paandavas' marriage to Draupadi triggered a renewal of alliances between kings and the Paandavas that had been dormant since Paandu's death. New ones would be forged. Drupada's existing allies would now become the Paandavas' allies by extension. A dejected and despondent Duryodhana, Duhshaasana, Shakuni, and Karna returned to Hastinapura. Vidura too got to know that the Paandavas had succeeded in winning Draupadi's hand. The time had come to inform King Dhritaraashtra.

'O King, I have some wonderful news,' exclaimed Vidura.

'Don't keep it to yourself, O Vidura. Share this good news with your blind brother, too,' replied Dhritaraashtra, perking up.

'The Kurus are prospering,' gushed Vidura.[1]

'The Kurus? I knew it. This is the best news you could have brought me,' Dhritaraashtra said, beaming. The only event of note, of late, had been his sons' sojourn to Kaampilya to take part in Draupadi's swayamvara. The only good news about the Kurus, therefore, had to be their success. A beautiful wife for his son, a powerful king as an ally—Dhritaraashtra was ecstatic.

'I cannot contain my joy, O Vidura!' Dhritaraashtra continued. 'A princess like Draupadi deserved someone as brave and valorous like my son. Send the best of ornaments and the finest of clothes for my daughter-in-law. Tell my son, Duryodhana, to come meet me with Draupadi.'

> 'O King, you are mistaken. The Kurus are indeed prospering, but it is not your son who won Draupadi's swayamvara.'
>
> 'Then, who? What do you mean, Vidura?'
>
> 'The Kurus have succeeded. The Paandavas have married Draupadi.'
>
> Dhritaraashtra sat stunned, stupefied, for a moment. The smile vanished from his face, but only for a moment. The king knew that while he was blind, Vidura wasn't.
>
> 'O Vidura, this is more than good news that you have brought me. Whether Duryodhana or the Paandavas won the swayamvara, it doesn't matter, they are all equally dear to me. Much as Paandu was close to my heart, the Paandavas are even dearer.[2] That they are alive brings me even more joy. Oh, my heart cannot contain its happiness,' the blind king, broken-hearted, raved.

Vidura went away, pleased. His brother, the king, had acted in a just and noble manner. Perhaps there was hope for unity and amity in the house of the Kurus.

When the Kuru elders assembled the next day, however, there was much debate and acrimony over the next course of action. Duryodhana, Duhshaasana, Shakuni, and Karna were on one side, arguing against giving the Paandavas their due; Bheeshma, Drona, Vidura, and others on the other.

> Nor will we succeed in alienating Krishna from them. She chose them in a time of adversity and they are now prosperous.[3]

The Paandavas were alive. Dhritaraashtra, as the Kuru king, could choose to invite the Paandavas back or he could elect to go to war with them. War now meant fighting not only the Paandavas, but also Drupada, the Dasharhas, and their allies. Already, rumours had been swirling about the Yaadava army preparing to march to Hastinpaura to enforce the Paandavas' right to the throne. If the Yaadavas attacked, Drupada's army and his allies too would join in the offensive. But inviting the Paandavas back would mean giving them their rightful share of the kingdom.

Dhritaraashtra finally chose the path of dharma—driven perhaps by the exigencies of the situation—and dispatched Vidura as the royal emissary to invite the Paandavas, Kunti, and Draupadi.

> Therefore, I can never favour a war with them. Have a treaty with those warriors and give them land.[4]

> My views are the same as those of the great-souled Bhishma.
> Let Kunti's sons have a share in the kingdom.[5]

Once the Paandavas returned to Hastinapura, Dhritaraashtra announced the partition of the kingdom, with the Paandavas getting sovereignty over Khaandavprastha.[6]

The Paandavas abided by Dhritaraashtra's compromise and settled in Khaandavaprastha. Soon enough it became a centre of attraction for people from all over the land. Brahmanas and artisans alike flocked to the city.

Janamejaya had listened as Vaishampaayana had described how everyone at Draupadi's swayamvara had been smitten by her beauty. The Paandavas were no exception. Past karma and fate had determined that all five would marry her. Strife was inevitable under such circumstances, unless the wise foresaw the possibility and forestalled it. How did that come about, Janamejaya wished to learn?

Not long after the Paandavas had settled down in Khaandavaprastha, Sage Naarada came visiting. Yudhishthira, along with the other Paandavas and Draupadi, paid their respects to the sage. Naarada then asked Draupadi to leave as he had words that only the Paandavas needed to hear. Once she had departed, Naarada asked the Paandavas to lay down a rule for how they would live and cohabit with Draupadi, wife to all five of them, lest they meet the same fate as Sunda and Upasunda.

'O Sage, what is it you wish to tell us that you couldn't say in front of Draupadi?' asked Yudhishthira.

'It concerns Draupadi,' replied Naarada.

"'Oh,' replied Yudhishthira. 'Should we be concerned on her account?'

'No, it is not she that I am worried about, but you.'

'Why us, O Sage?'

'She is a wife to not one, but all five of you. Dissension is inevitable. Strife will follow.'

'Surely, not!' Yudhishthira exclaimed.

'If it could happen to Sunda and Upasunda, it can happen to you all, too.'

'Who were Sunda and Upasunda?' asked Yudhishthira.

'They were two asura brothers,' replied Naarada.

'What was so special about them that you took their name as a cautionary example? Surely, we are better than those asuras,' Yudhishthira asked.

'Their love for each other was legendary.'

'Like the love we have for each other...'

'Yes. So valorous were they that no one could kill them. Only they were capable of destroying each other.'

'I see.'

'And they did. Both killed each other.'

'Why? What happened that those two turned on each other?'

'Because of Tilottamma, the celestial apsaraa.'

'But why, how?' asked Yudhishthira.

'Listen, O Dharmaraja. Understand the dharma that needs to be followed between all of you and Draupadi. Listen and understand the past to prevent its recurrence in the future,' Naarada thus began.

Hiranyakashyapa was a mighty daitya[7] born to Sage Kashyapa and Diti. One of the five sons of Hiranyakashyapa was Prahlaada. One of Prahlaada's sons was the daitya Nikumbha.[8] Nikumbha had two sons, Sunda and Upasunda. The two siblings were inseparable. When they grew up, as was the wont of asuras, both wanted to conquer the three worlds. That meant appeasing the gods to obtain boons. Both went to the Vindhya mountains and performed great penances. Such was the potency of their fiery austerities that smoke began to emanate from the Vindhyas. The terrified gods tried their best to distract the two daityas, to no avail. The gods even sent beautiful women to distract the daityas. They failed, for the feminine form that could distract them had not yet been created—literally. Yet.

Brahma finally relented, as he had to for anyone who meditated on him long enough, and appeared before them. The two could ask Brahma for a boon. Sunda and Upasunda had a long list—the knowledge of how to create illusions, which was granted; the knowledge of weapons, which was granted; immense strength, which was granted; and immortality—naturally, which was denied, naturally.

It was not that Brahma had never granted immortality before. Raavana's younger brother, Vibheeshana, had been granted this boon.[9] Brahma's reasoning was clear. Their penance had been for a specific purpose—to conquer the three worlds. This precluded them from the boon of immortality. This was also the reason why Vibheeshana had been granted immortality—his penances had been without any specific wish.

If they could not get immortality from Brahma, then they would get as close to immortality as possible, reasoned Sunda and

Upasunda. They asked for the boon that they have no fear from anything or anyone, except themselves. Brahma granted the boon and returned to his celestial abode. The two brothers ended their penances. They had what they had wanted from Brahma, even immortality—or so they thought.

> 'We did it, Sunda, we did it,' exulted Upasunda.
> 'Yes, we did it, didn't we?' winked Upasunda.
> 'Lord Brahma gave us what we wanted, and I don't think even he realizes it,' guffawed Sunda.
> 'No fear from anyone, anything,' chimed in Upasunda.
> 'Except us,' interjected Sunda.
> 'Except us,' echoed Upasunda. Both burst out into peals of laughter.
> 'You and I, turning on each other. The mere thought is preposterous.'

The two returned, hugging each other in celebration, love. The two together would rule the world for all eternity now.

Eternity was destined to end sooner than they expected.

Armed with the boons from Brahma, the two daityas returned to their kingdom and made merry for many years, drinking and partying. Once they were done with their carousing, they set out to conquer the three worlds. They first invaded the abode of the gods and drove them out. They then invaded the nether world and forced out the naagas from there. Two worlds conquered, only one more remained. They set their eyes on earth after that, and specifically targeted the brahmanas. Because of Brahma's boon, the brahmanas' curses had no effect on the daityas and hence they did not fear the brahmanas. When the brahmanas fled and hid themselves, Sunda and Upasunda changed their form into elephants and lions and tigers and killed brahmanas where they could find them. Having subjugated the three worlds, the two daityas settled down and lived in Kurukshetra.

> Sacrifices and studying ceased and the brahmanas were exterminated. The earth bereft of festivals and sacrifices cried out in fear. All buying and selling ended. The worship of the gods was stopped.[10]

Unable to bear this torment, the gods, sages, and other semi-divine beings went to Brahma. Upon hearing their accounts of the destruction wrought by Sunda and Upasunda, Brahma pondered over the situation. After all, it had been his boons that had empowered these two daityas. Coming up with solution was his responsibility, therefore. After much thought, Brahma summoned Vishwakarma, the celestial architect. The creator tasked the celestial architect with creating a woman who would be the ultimate, universal, and irresistible object of desire.

Whatever Vishwakarma created was perfect, whether a building or a person. The tiniest part of such a person would be perfect. From perfection would arise perfection. Vishwakarma set about collecting all that was perfect and desirable in all the three worlds. From this he crafted and perfected a flawless being and presented her to Brahma. One look at her and Brahma gave her the name Tilottama.[11] She bowed before Brahma. He tasked her with one and only one assignment—go to Kurukshetra, seduce the two brothers, and create dissension among them.

What Brahma's boon had done, Tilottama would undo.

Before departing, Tilottama circumambulated all the gods assembled there. The gods could not keep their composure and self-control. None except Brahma. Indra couldn't resist staring at her as she walked around the gods. As she did, a thousand eyes popped on his body, each eye taking in Tilottama's form and figure. Even Shiva could not stop from wanting to catch a glimpse as she passed by his side. A face popped up as she moved to his side, behind him, and then to his other side. Thus did Shiva come to have four faces.

Brahma smiled; what even Mahaadeva could not resist, what even the king of the gods had surrendered to, Sunda and Upasunda stood no chance against.

Sunda and Upasunda, in the meantime, having conquered all three worlds and with nothing else left to win, spent their time in making merry, eating, drinking, and in the company of women. One day they went to the Vindhya mountains with some women to continue their revelries.

Tilottama happened to—by sheer accident, providence, destiny—arrive there, dressed in a red garment, plucking flowers.

> 'She is my wife and your superior,' said Sunda. 'She is my wife and your sister-in-law,' replied Upasunda. In their anger, they shouted at each other, 'She is mine, not yours.'[12]

Tilottama had the desired effect on Sunda and Upasunda. Each was more driven by desire than the other. One grabbed her left hand, the other her right hand; Sunda insisted she would be his wife, Upasunda insisted she would be Sunda's sister-in-law. Each lay claim to Tilottama; neither willing to concede the other's assertion. They were brothers, but in place of filial love there were now new emotions between—lust and anger. Verbal jousts turned into physical blows. They lay into each other with their clubs. Each was as strong as the other, each invulnerable to all but the other. Two brothers as attached and devoted to each other as Sunda and Upasunda turned on each other.

The Paandavas sat in silence. Naarada finished with words of advice for Yudhishthira. Lest there be friction and fights between the Paandavas over Draupadi, the brothers would have to take appropriate steps. It was not for Naarada to lay down those rules. The brothers, in Narada's presence, decided then and there that if any brother saw Draupadi when she was with another Paandava, he would have to leave for the forest and spend twelve years in exile.

Inevitable dissension and ignominy had been averted. The wheels of fate and time would turn and churn out a new itihaasa. A lesson had been learned from the end of two daityas who lived in Kurukshetra. The infinite forks of destiny and karma would, however, still lead the Paandavas to the plains of Kurukshetra. But that was several years in the future.

11

SHAARANGAKAS

Trust, but Verify

Parva: Adi (1)	Upa parva: Khaandava-daha (19)
Chapters: 220–225	Shlokas: 147

Sage Naarada had advised the Paandavas and they had decided on a code of conduct they would all follow when with Draupadi. Fate willed otherwise. Arjuna had to enter the chamber where Yudhishthira and Draupadi sat. As had been agreed upon, Arjuna left for the forest.[1] He went to several pilgrimage sites, holy rivers, and met and married Uloopi, the daughter of the king of the Nagas, Kouravya.[2]

In the kingdom of Manalura, there ruled King Chitravaahana. He had one daughter, Chitraangada.[3] Arjuna married her, and per the king's wishes, agreed that the son born would stay back in the kingdom and be king after him. Many, many years later, their son, Babruvaahana, and Arjuna would meet in battle. One would die.[4]

Arjuna also redeemed Vargaa[5] and her four friends from a curse. The last period of Arjuna's exile was spent in Dwaarka, with his dear friend and relative, Krishna. Arjuna, on Krishna's urging, carried Subhadra off on his chariot and married her.[6] With much difficulty did Arjuna persuade Draupadi to accept Subhadra as a co-wife.

A second load always loosens the first tie, however strong.[7]

On one warm summer day, Krishna and Arjuna decided to go to the banks of the Yamuna along with other friends. Relaxing there, they were approached by a brahmana with a request both most usual and unusual.

The brahmana said he was hungry, but he wanted neither alms nor a cow. He also did not want wealth. He wanted food, but his diet was not the normal diet of humans. The brahmana said that he wanted to devour the Khaandava forest. That was unusual. But he was no ordinary mortal. The brahmana revealed himself to be Agni.

'Sure, O Agni,' began Arjuna, 'but you don't need our help to devour the forest.'

'No, I certainly wouldn't,' smiled Agni. 'But there is a hitch.'

'What is that?'

'Indra.'

'The king of the gods?' asked Arjuna.

'Yes. Your celestial father.'

'What interest does he have in the Khaandava forest that he would want to obstruct you?'

'His friend, Takshaka, lives in this forest,' replied Agni. 'Every time I have tried to consume Khaandava, Indra rains down. All I get is steam and smoke, but no food. No sooner do I start the fire than Indra extinguishes it.'

'In that case, we can certainly help you, O Brahmana. But there is a hitch,' replied Arjuna.

'What is that?' asked Agni, smiling.

'I can string an arrow to the bow, pull back the bowstring, and release them faster than anyone. But my bow is not strong enough to match my speed. Nor is my chariot sturdy enough to hold all the arrows in all the quivers I would place on it. My horses need to be fast. Even Krishna needs a weapon to match his valour.'

'Consider it done,' replied Agni.

On Agni's instructions, Varuna, the god of the waters, fetched from the ocean and handed to Arjuna the Gandeeva bow, quivers of inexhaustible arrows, and a chariot with four horses and with a monkey on its banner. To Krishna he gave the chakra that had been created by none other than Vishwakarma, the celestial architect. Armed with these weapons, Krishna and Arjuna mounted their respective chariots. The Khaandava forest burned, along with those inside it.

Indra tried but failed to deter Arjuna and Krishna. The gods rallied around Indra in their offensive but were repulsed. Even a peak from the Mandara mountain that Indra hurled at them was ineffectual; Arjuna's arrows shattered it to pieces. The falling debris did end up killing even more animals that lived in the Khaandava forest.

Although Indra, Arjuna's celestial father, was pleased with his son's valour, his efforts to deter Arjuna and Krishna, and protect his friend, Takshaka, continued.

Takshaka, as fate would have it, was not in the forest at the time; he was in Kurukshetra. But Takshaka's wife was there, and she died saving her son, Ashvasena, from the inferno. Ashvasena escaped, and he bided his time waiting to take revenge. He would get his chance on the seventeenth day of the battle at Kurukshetra.[8]

It was only when Indra learned, from a heavenly voice, that Takshaka was not in the Khaandava forest, and that defeating the duo of Krishna and Arjuna was not possible even for the king of the gods, and that the destruction of the Khaandava forest was fated, did Indra withdraw from the battle. In the fire that consumed the Khaandava forest, only six beings escaped alive—Ashvasena, Maaya,[9] and the four Shaarangakas. Maaya sought Arjuna's protection and thus saved his life.

But who were these Shaarangakas, Janamejaya inquired of Vaishampaayana.

There was once a great sage by the name Mandapaala, said Vaishampaayana. After a life of penances on earth, when he attained heaven, he did not find the fruits of his life of asceticism that he expected. Surprised, he asked the gods present why that was so. The gods replied that the brahmana had not paid one debt as a human—that of having offspring, and thus the fruits of heaven were closed to him. This was also why Paandu had been so insistent on having children,[10] to repay the four debts that men were born with; and the debt to one's ancestors could only be repaid by having children. The gods told pretty much the same thing to Mandapaala.

> Hear about the debts men are undoubtedly born with – to rituals, brahmacharya and offspring, and these are respectively discharged through sacrifices, austerities and progeny.[11]

This set Mandapaala thinking on how he could have children, and fast. The thought of spending another human life in repaying this debt didn't appeal to Mandapaala. A speedier alternative was needed. Birds—was the answer that came to him, and thus he took the form of a Shaarangaka bird and married a female bird named Jarita. Through her, he had four sons—Jaritaari, Saarisrikva,

Stambamitra, and Drona[12]—in the form of birds. His debt repaid, he went away to be with his human wife, Lapita. Heaven could wait.

Time passed and Khaandava's destruction was nigh. To a sage like Mandapaala the signs were visible. He saw Agni advancing towards Khaandava. He also knew his children lived in that forest. Neither could he enter the forest to extract them to safety, nor were they old enough to fly to safety. Naturally, he worried. With Arjuna and Krishna arrayed against Indra and all the gods, there would be no stopping Agni. Mandapaala prayed to the one and only god who could save his children—Agni. Agni was pleased and granted him the boon that his children would be safe from the fire that would burn down Khaandava. Neither Mandapaala's wife nor his young children knew this, however.

Inside Khaandava, the fire now raged like an inferno. Jarita, the mother of the four Shaarangaka birds, was beside herself with worry. Her sons were too small to escape on their own, nor she strong enough to carry them off to safety. She could not abandon them to the fire, either. If their death was fated, they would die together. She enveloped her kids as best as she could under her wings. Her sons, young though they were, nonetheless urged their mother to escape to safety. If she lived, the lineage could be continued even if all four of them perished in the blaze, they urged Jarita.

Meanwhile, outside the forest, even though Mandapaala had obtained a boon from Agni assuring his kids' safety, he still worried. Even when with Lapita, his human wife, he remained pensive.

Back in the forest, Jarita kept thinking of ways to save her children. A new hope arose. She recalled espying a rat hole nearby. Such a burrow could be a lifesaver. One such tunnel, hole, burrow had saved the Paandavas at Vaarnavata. It had been Vidura who had cautioned Yudhishthira to escape a forest fire by taking refuge underground, like a rat does—*The burner of grass and the drier of dew do not kill animals in holes.*[13] What had worked for the Paandavas would work just as well for the Shaarangaka birds. Their mother, Jarita, pointed out the rat hole to her sons and urged them to take refuge there. They would be safe from the fire.

An uncertain death is superior to one that is certain.[14]

This plan had a hitch. A rat hole meant a rat. Rats could eat up birds; especially birds as small and defenceless as the Shaarangakas. Between being burnt alive by the fire and being eaten by the carnivore in the hole, they preferred the former, for there was at least a small chance, even if infinitesimally small, of escaping alive. They confided their doubts to their mother.

Yes, that was a reasonable cause for doubt, Jarita accepted. But she allayed their fears by telling them that a hawk had snatched the rat and flown away with the rodent in its claws. No rat, no risk. But, started the birds, what if the rat had escaped and returned to its burrow? No, Jarita replied; she had seen the hawk fly off with the rat and eat it.

The Shaarangakas remained unconvinced. They again beseeched their mother, Jarita, to leave them and find safety elsewhere. They would take their chances with the fire. If they lived, Jarita could come back to them; if not, it was important that she live and propagate her lineage. Jarita agreed, reluctantly, and left for a safe spot.

Agni advanced inexorably. It was soon near the Sharangaka birds, blazing, thundering, scorching. Seeing the fire advance towards them, all four took turns addressing and praising Agni, just as their father had; Jaritaari first, then Saarisrikva, Stambamitra, and finally Drona. They beseeched Agni to save them, just as the waves of the ocean spare houses on the shore. Pleased with their devotion, Agni[15] told Drona, the youngest, that both his father's and his words were important to him and that he would do as they wished.

Meanwhile, Mandapaala had not stopped worrying about his children, even though Agni had assured him of protecting his children. Lapita, his wife, became envious, suspecting that all this fretting and concern was more on account of affections he still harboured for Jarita and less on account of his four Shaarangaka sons. But hadn't he come back to her after leaving Jarita, Mandapala asked Lapita.

> He who casts off that which he has, for the sake of that which might be there, is stupid and the world disregards him.[16]

Meanwhile, as promised, the fire passed by, sparing the four Shaarangakas. A relieved Jarita rushed back. Seeing them safe and sound, they all embraced each other and wept tears of joy and relief. All was well that had ended well.

Mandapaala also rushed into the forest. He was greeted with silence; neither Jarita nor her sons would speak with him. Jarita finally broke her silence after a spell to tell Mandapala she wanted him to have nothing to do with their children since he had abandoned them at their time of need to go gallivant with another wife. But hadn't he prayed to Agni to save their children, Mandapaala wondered aloud? What more could he have done? After a frank exchange of words between husband and wife, a reconciliation took place between all.

Resuming his account of the Khaandava forest, Vaishampaayana said that Agni completed consuming the Khaandava forest, thanks to the two Krishnas, Vasudeva Krishna and Arjuna. Pleased, he granted them boons. Krishna asked for a lasting friendship with Arjuna. Agni granted that boon.

Arjuna asked for Indra's weapons. He had witnessed their potency and he desired to add them to his arsenal. Agni granted Arjuna's boon, but with a caveat. The time to obtain those weapons was not now. Arjuna would get those divine weapons, but he would first have to please Shiva. Only then would his path to receiving Indra's weapons be cleared. That time and day would arrive, but only after the Paandavas had lost everything in the game of dice.

The fire of Khaandava forged enmities that would last generations. Takshaka would get his revenge by killing not Arjuna, but his grandson, Pareekshit. The same Pareekshit, who was killed while still in his womb by Ashwatthama's divine weapon and granted the boon of life by none other than Krishna. The same Pareekshit, years later, would invite death at the hands of Takshaka out of a misplaced sense of ego. A brahmana's curse would realize itself through Takshaka's venom. The same Takshaka would irk Sage Uttanka by stealing the earrings he was carrying back to his guru's wife. Uttanka would seek his revenge against Takshaka by reminding Pareekshit's son, Janamejaya, of the serpent's murder of his father.

Ashwasena, Takshaka's son, escaped from the fire, but bided his time. Turning himself into an arrowhead, he found his way into Karna's quiver. Karna's first plan, Indra's Shakti, had been used up in killing Ghatotakacha. But on the seventeenth day of the battle at Kurukshetra, Ashwasena would become Karna's Plan B in his quest to kill Arjuna. No Plan B would work for Karna on that fateful day, however.

> Though Kounteya loves dice, he has no knowledge. If challenged, he will certainly come.[17]

What about Maaya, the celestial architect? He would construct for the Paandavas the finest palace ever known—where Yudhishthira would conduct his Rajasuya yagna, signalling his unchallenged supremacy as emperor of Bharatvarsha; where Duryodhana's envy at the wealth, prosperity, pomp, and power that the Paandavas had acquired would break all restraints. An invitation would be wrangled out of Dhritaraashtra—blind to his son's faults, blinded by love for his son—to be sent to the Paandavas to come for a game of dice, to be delivered by none other than a hapless Vidura. Just one harmless game of dice. To be played between Yudhishthira, who was fond of gambling and could never refuse a round; and Shakuni, who was good at gambling and who had never lost.

What Krishna and Arjuna had destroyed in Khaandava would eventually destroy what they would build at Indraprastha.

> It has been said that a man who does not feel envy is a wretch. O Indra among kings! O Lord! This ordinary prosperity does not please me. I am miserable on seeing the blazing prosperity of Kunti's son.[18]

Thus ended Adi Parva.

12

SHAALVA-VADHA

Unforeseen Consequences?

Parva: Aranyaka (3) **Upa parva: Kairata (31)**
Chapters: 15-23 **Shlokas: 281**

Maaya, the architect of the asuras, designed and built a grand palace at Indraprastha. He went to Lake Bindu and Mount Mainaka to fetch jewels, gold, and other ornaments to adorn the palace with. In addition, Maaya also fetched a conch named Devadutta, which he handed to Arjuna;[1] and a club that he handed to Bheema.[2] In fourteen months, the sabha was built.[3]

The Paandavas moved into their palace on an auspicious day after ten thousand brahmanas had been fed and given gifts, and after sages and kings been honoured. Among those present were Asit, Devala, Dhaumya, Naachiketa, Shunaka, Krishna Dvaipaayana and his disciples—Shuka, Sumantu, Jaimini, Paila, and Vaishampaayana.

Shortly thereafter Sage Naarada came calling on the Paandavas. This time he asked Yudhishthira a series of questions to help the newly crowned king navigate the right course in governance.[4] In response to Yudhishthira's question on the grandeur of their palace, Naarada compared it with Indra, Yama, Varuna, and Kubera's palaces and found them coming up short against the Paandavas' palace. Before leaving for Dwaarka, Naarada suggested that Yudhishthira conduct the famed Rajsuya sacrifice, but only after due deliberations and consultations.

The thought of holding the Rajasuya sacrifice and the prestige it carried drove Yudhishthira to distraction. The only person he could turn to advice was in Dwaarka. A messenger was dispatched, and Krishna travelled back to Indraprastha. Yudhishthira confessed that he desired to perform the yagna, but merely wishing would not turn it to reality.

> O Krishna! I wish to perform rajasuya. But it cannot be performed merely through my wishing it.[5]

Yes, Yudhishthira had the capability of performing the Rajasuya, but as long as a king named Jarasandha stood in his way, the Rajasuya would not be successful, Krishna told Yudhishthira. Jarasandha had dethroned kings who stood in his way and imprisoned them. Eighty-six were already languishing in his prisons; once the tally reached a hundred, he would slay them in a grand sacrifice and proclaim himself as the undisputed ruler of the land. Yudhishthira's window of opportunity was fast closing.

To go against such a mighty and ruthless king was not to Yudhishthira's liking, especially since it would mean putting Bheema, Arjuna, and Krishna in harm's way. Yudhishthira balked. Arjuna, however, argued against giving up. Krishna's advice was to use brains more than brawn against an opponent as invincible in battle as Jarasandha. Rather than march against the king of Magadha with an army, Krishna suggested a wrestling bout between Jarasandha and Bheema.

> The wise always enter the house of a well-wisher through a gate, but use that which is not a gate for the house of an enemy.[6]

Krishna, Bheema, and Arjuna went alone to Magadha. Krishna gambled in giving Jarasandha a choice; the Magadha king's ego drove him to choose Bheema as his sparring opponent. Arjuna was too puny in Jarasandha's opinion, and he didn't consider Krishna his equal. Many years later, the same Krishna would berate Yudhishthira for offering the same choice to Duryodhana.[7] Duryodhana too would choose Bheema as his opponent among all five Paandavas.

Bheema and Jarasandha fought for fourteen days. The duel ended with Jarasandha's death, after which the eighty-six kings imprisoned by Jarasandha were set free. The last hurdle to Yudhishthira's Rajsuya sacrifice was cleared.

Yudhishthira went ahead with the Rajsuya yagya. It proclaimed his undisputed suzerainty over the entire land. The grand event was marred, however, by Shishupala's death at Krishna's hands.[8]

After the yagna, Duryodhana toured the great palace that Maaya had built for the Paandavas,[9] gawking at its opulence, wonderstruck by the marvels in the palace. Gaping, envy gnawing at him, Duryodhana mistook a crystal platform for a pool and drew up his clothes to walk over it, only to be laughed at by Bheema. Moments later, he mistook a pool for a crystal platform, walked into it, fell into the water, and was laughed at again by the Paandavas and others. Duryodhana was livid.

While all this was happening at Indraprastha, Krishna was away at Dwaarka. Shishupala's death had ignited a chain of events that had drawn Krishna away from Indraprastha.

> Enemies must be killed through every means possible, before they cause harm through war or force.[10]

Consumed by envy, rage, embarrassment, Duryodhana left for Hastinapura. On the journey back to Hastinapura, Shakuni fed his nephew's anger and resentment. He advised Duryodhana to get Dhritaraashtra to invite Yudhishthira for a game of dice—which the blind king did, much against Vidura's counsel. In the game of dice that took place, Yudhishthira lost everything—gems,[11] the gold in his treasury,[12] his royal chariot,[13] his stable of elephants,[14] one hundred thousand servant girls,[15] thousands of male servants,[16] chariots, along with their horses, charioteers, and accompanying warriors,[17] the gandharva horses Chitraratha had given to Arjuna,[18,19] thousands of soldiers,[20] four-hundred chests containing gold,[21] all remaining wealth,[22] all his cattle,[23] his city and kingdom,[24] his four brothers, himself,[25] and then Draupadi.[26] As he sat silent, a mute spectator to the wiles of fate and the consequences of his addiction, the queen of Indraprastha was dragged by the hair into the court by Duhshaasana, declared a slave by Duryodhana, and insulted as a prostitute by Karna. The Kuru elders watched. Only Vidura and Vikarna spoke out.

> However, she submits to many and it is therefore certain that she is a courtesan. It is my view that there is nothing surprising in her being brought into the sabha in a single garment, or even if she is naked.[27]

When a semblance of shame dawned on Dhritaraashtra, he granted the Paandavas back their freedom and kingdom. Krishna was not at Hastinapura when all this took place. The Paandavas left for Indraprastha, angry and determined to seek revenge for the humiliation.[28] An equally determined Duryodhana stomped to Dhritaraashtra's chamber, with Karna, and Shakuni in tow, and demanded that the king recall the Paandavas for a rematch. All others present—including Vidura, Drona, Ashwatthaama, Somadutta, Bahlika, Bhurishrava, Bheeshma, Vikarna, and Gandhaari—vehemently disagreed. The king overruled all of them.

> It is a great misery that the world is full of contradictions. The evil find satisfaction in that which scares the good.[29]

A messenger was dispatched and Dhritaraashtra's missive conveyed to the Paandavas. Yudhishthira agreed, yet again, and the Paandavas returned to Hastinapura a second time. There Shakuni announced a new, single stake. There would be a terrible price to be paid by the loser—spend twelve years in exile in the forest, followed by a thirteenth year in an inhabited place, but incognito. If recognized, the twelve-year exile and thirteenth year would be repeated. The dice were rolled, Yudhishthira lost, and the Paandavas were deprived once again of their kingdom and riches. The Paandavas had lost their kingdom for thirteen years. Where was Krishna?

As the Paandavas and Draupadi departed for the forest, the portents of what would happen in the fourteenth year were clear to all who cared to see.

> Kunti's son Yudhishthira is departing, covering his face with his garment. Paandava Bheema is spreading his long arms, as he goes. Savyasachi is following the king, scattering sand. Maadri's son Sahadeva has smeared his face, as he goes. Nakula, the most handsome man in this world, follows the king. His mind is despondent and he has smeared his entire body with dust. The large-eyed and beautiful Krishna follows the king. She is weeping and has covered her face with her hair.[30]

Draupadi's words were a chilling reminder of the fate that awaited Hastinapura, its men and women who had stayed mute spectators to the evil perpetrated under the rule of their blind king. The dice of fate had rolled, time would reveal the stakes. The incarnation of Shri had been insulted and humiliated. The consequences would be severe.

> In the fourteenth year, the wives of those who have caused my present plight, will find their husbands dead, their sons dead, their relatives dead and their beloved ones dead. Their bodies will be covered with the blood of their relatives.[31]

Even before the Paandavas had settled down in the forest, Duryodhana started worrying about what would happen next. Perhaps the Paandavas would not stay the entire duration of their exile. Shakuni's advice to his nephew was to trust in the Paandava's sense of right and wrong, for they would not break the condition of the stake. Duryodhana agreed, though half-heartedly. Seeing his friend and benefactor so dejected, Karna instigated all to go kill the Paandavas where they were.

Fortuitously, word reached Vyaasa. The sage counselled and warned Dhritaraashtra against letting his son indulge in any such misadventure. Maitreya[32] warned Duryodhana that Bheema had already dispatched the raakshasa, Kirmira, to his death.[33] He would not hesitate to kill Duryodhana.

> It has been said that the nature instilled in a man at birth does not leave him before his death.[34]

Maitreya's words had no effect on Duryodhana. With a deliberate display of boredom, he drew circles on the ground with his feet; with visible indifference and defiance, he slapped his thighs with his arms. Maitreya, angered, cursed Duryodhana that those thighs would be shattered by Bheema. Between Bheema's resolution and Maitreya's curse, Duryodhana's fate was sealed.

Where was Krishna? He had left Indraprastha shortly after beheading Shishupala with his chakra. When he finally came to the Kaamyaka forest, along with other Vrishnis, Bhojas, and Andhakas, Draupadi bared her grief and suffering before Krishna.

> When the wife is protected, the offspring are protected. When the offspring are protected, one's own soul is protected.[35]

Yudhishthira had the same questions as Draupadi; specifically, why Krishna had not been with them in their moment of greatest tribulations. Krishna sat and spoke; all others listened.

The events set in motion at Yudhishthira's Rajsuya sacrifice had been more severe and unexpected than anyone may have imagined. The assembly of kings at Indraprastha had been divided in its opinion—was what Krishna did, when he beheaded Shishupala, the right thing or not? One king, Shaalva,[36] decided that Krishna alone was responsible for these events. Krishna and his clan would have to suffer consequences for his actions.

Enraged at Shishupala's death at Krishna's hands, and even while Krishna was at Indraprastha, Shaalva left and marched upon Dwaarka. With his army he started to lay that capital city to waste. When news reached Krishna, he rushed to fight Shaalva, and after a fierce battle, destroyed Soubha,[37] Shaalva's city, and killed Shaalva. It was this attack on Dwaarka and the subsequent battle with Shaalva that had prevented Krishna from being with the Paandavas.

What was this great battle that had so occupied Krishna, Yudhishthira wanted to know?

When news reached the residents of Dwaarka that Shaalva was advancing with an army, preparations were made on war footing. The town was stockaded, fortified, and barricaded; infantry and cavalry guarded it day and night, led by Ugrasena and such warriors as Uddhava, Gada, Saamba, and others.

It was hoped the enemy would not breach the gates of Dwaarka; but if it did, bridges were destroyed to deny easy movement to the enemy. Boats were stopped from plying. Spikes were erected in moats. Contingency plans made in times of peace were now activated in times of war.

In times of distress, the rules of aapad dharma applied. People no longer had the same freedom of movement as in times of peace. If a resident had to move about, prior permission was required. Even then, they had to carry an official seal to confirm the permission. Fortified, forewarned, the town awaited its foe.

Shaalva arrived, with his army led by General Kshemavriddhi, and laid siege to Dwaarka. The Vrishnis marched out to take the army head on, led by Charudeshna,[38] Samba,[39] and Pradyumna.[40] Shaalva's army faced early setbacks. The Vrishnis routed Kshemavriddhi from the battlefield. A daitya named Vegavan took his place, but he too was soon killed by Samba. Charudeshna battled with a daanava named Vivindhya and killed him. Perhaps this would be a short and swift victory for Dwaarka, its army thought. It was mistaken.

Just when it appeared that the cavalry and soldiers of Shaalva's army had been routed, Dwaarka's residents were greeted with a sight that filled them with dread. Shaalva descended on Dwaarka atop his flying citadel, Soubha. The huge city, armed to the teeth, hovered over Dwaarka. They could fight a foe on foot, on horseback, on chariots, on elephants. But a flying citadel? Dwaarka's army started to lose heart.

Pradyumna refused to lose hope or admit defeat. He roused the army with fighting words instilled them with courage. Ascending his golden chariot, with a makara[41] as his flag, he took on Shaalva and his army.

Shaalva's army had fought with weapons so far. Now Shaalva turned to maaya, illusion, to counter Pradyumna. Out of thin air, a barrage of arrows descended from the skies on Pradyumna. Pierced by these arrows, bleeding, Pradyumna nonetheless retaliated with a special arrow. Like missiles that zero in on heat signatures, Pradyumna's arrow could seek the heart out. It found its mark and struck Shaalva. He collapsed in his chariot, unconscious, but not yet dead. The sight of their king falling was enough to scatter Shaalva's army.

Soon enough, Shaalva regained consciousness. The battle resumed. Shaalva counterattacked with the ferocity of someone whose pride had been deflated in battle. He retaliated with an arrow that struck Pradyumna near his collarbone. Pradyumna sank in his chariot, bleeding, unconscious, helpless. Daruki[42] did what a wise charioteer would do. He took the chariot, and his king, to safety. Pradyumna regained consciousness after some time. When he came to, he found himself far away from the battlefield. He was appalled, ashamed. He, Krishna's son, had retreated from the battlefield. He berated Daruki for having done so. Daruki, on the other hand, maintained that it was the dharma of a charioteer to protect his warrior's life, which he had. Dead warriors wouldn't win any battles. Now that Pradyumna had regained consciousness, he would take him back to the battlefield.

The battle between Pradyumna and Shaalva resumed afresh, with each firing arrows and celestial weapons at each other, each becoming more aware of the other's strengths. In response to Shaalva's daitya weapons, Pradyumna fired brahma weapons of his own. Shaalva succumbed once more, falling unconscious. Pradyumna readied a special weapon. The arrow would finish off Shaalva. Shaalva's end seemed near. But someone intervened.

Before Pradyumna could fire the arrow that would kill Shaalva, he was stopped by Sage Naarada. The sage had been sent down by none other than the gods themselves. Shaalva would die, but not at Pradyumna's hands. Brahma had decreed that Shaalva's death would be at Krishna's hands. Pradyumna nodded in understanding, bowed before Naarada in acceptance, and withdrew his weapon. Shaalva regained consciousness, and fled. He would return, stronger, more resolute.

Krishna finally reached Dwaarka. A sight of destruction and waste greeted him. Gone was Dwaarka's splendour. The city presented a desolate picture of ruin. Shaalva had to die, Krishna resolved. He would not return to Dwaarawati without killing Shaalva. He sought the king's[43] permission, took the blessings of the brahmanas, ascended his chariot, and announced his departure.[44] He would not wait for Shaalva to return; Krishna would take the battle to Shaalva. Krishna made way for Marttikavata.[45]

Krishna learned that Shaalva was on his flying fortress, Soubha. Krishna pursued Soubha. From afar, atop Soubha, Shaalva saw Krishna approach. A confident Shaalva challenged Krishna to a battle. Dwaarka could be destroyed later; now was the time to take out Krishna, Shaalva decided. Shishupaala's murderer would die at his hands, Shaalva desired. Krishna's first burst of arrows[46] failed to even reach Soubha. Shaalva's counterstrike, on the other hand, was such that the skies were carpetted with the barrage of arrows that rained down. Krishna retaliated; thousands of danavas fell into the ocean, dead.

Shaalva's barrage of arrows had, however, wounded Krishna's charioteer, Daruka, who resembled a pincushion, covered from head to toe in arrows, blood oozing from the wounds. Krishna tended to Daruka's wounds. He saw a messenger rushing towards his chariot. The messenger had devastating news. While Krishna had been tending to Daruka, Shaalva had launched a new offensive on Dwaarka. This time he had proven successful. Shaalva had claimed a prized foe. Vasudeva, Krishna's father, had fallen to Shaalva. Krishna sat down in shock. His father was Shaalva's prisoner.

With Satyaki, Pradyumna, and Balarama present, how had Shaalva managed to penetrate Dwaarka's defences and get to Vasudeva, Krishna sat, lost in thought. If Shaalva had captured

Vasudeva, it meant that even Pradyumna, Satyaki, and others must have fallen to Shaalva. He had succeeded in overrunning Dwaarka. Krishna sat in his chariot, overwhelmed. But there was worse to come.

Krishna looked up as the flying citadel, Soubha, floated into view. From high above, a corpse fell, hurtled down to the ground, and landed with a thud close to Krishna. It was Vasudeva, his father. Krishna stared at the lifeless corpse. Grief overwhelmed him. He sat, crushed. Composing himself, he looked up again.

There was no city, no flying fortress, no Shaalva; and on the ground, no Vasudeva. Krishna had fallen prey to Shaalva's power of illusions, albeit momentarily.

Aware now that Shaalva would use maaya also, Krishna resumed his battle with Shaalva. The duel raged, with Shaalva using danavas and mountains to strike at Krishna. With time passing, Daruka spoke to Krishna, urging him to kill Shaalva, to show no mercy.

> An enemy should be killed with all one's valour and even a weak enemy should not be disregarded by those who are strong, even if he is at one's feet, not to speak of one who is standing in battle.[47]

The time for fighting Shaalva with normal weapons was past. This was the time for using the invincible weapon, Krishna's chakra, that had been crafted by Vishwakarma, and which had been given by Agni himself. Krishna asked Daruka to hold steady his chariot. Krishna invoked his chakra.

The chakra manifested itself. It awaited instructions. Krishna gave it two tasks—destroy Shaalva's flying fortress, Soubha; and destroy whoever was inside it. Krishna hurled the chakra. It rose, advanced, and sliced the flying city in half. Soubha crashed to the ground, destroyed. It would never rise again. The city destroyed, the first task completed, the chakra returned to Krishna. Krishna unleashed it a second time. The chakra pursued its second target—Shaalva. Like Soubha, Shaalva was also sliced in two.

Krishna completed his account. Shaalva and his assault on Dwaarka was why he could not be with the Paandavas at Hastinapura. By the time he had killed Shaalva, the two games of dice had been completed. The Paandavas had lost, and lost again. The Paandavas and Draupadi would have to spend thirteen years in exile. But the forest was no place for Draupadi's young sons.

A simple dispute, that rose into a raging disagreement and debate, resulted in Shishupaala's death at Krishna's hands. That set off a chain of events most fateful. When Krishna was at Indraprastha, Dwaarka came under assault; when Krishna was at Dwaarka fighting Shaalva, the fateful games of dice took place and the Paandavas lost everything.

Krishna left for Dwaarka with Abhimanyu and his mother, Subhadra. Dhrishtadyumna left with Draupadi's sons—Prativindhya (from Yudhishthira), Sutasoma (from Bheema), Shrutakirti (from Arjuna), Shatanika (from Nakula), and Shrutakarma (from Sahadeva). Dhrishtaketu left with his sister, Karenumati, Nakula's wife. The Paandavas and Draupadi watched their sons depart. They would meet them only after thirteen years.

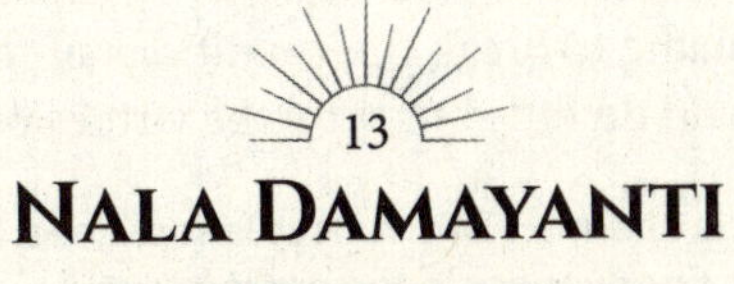

13 NALA DAMAYANTI

The Bonds of Misery

Parva: Aranyaka (3) Upa parva: Indralokabhigamana (32)
Chapters: 50-78 Shlokas: 901

Yudhishthira was the embodiment of dharma; he was the son of Dharma. Dharma, when protected, was supposed to protect; yet it had failed to protect Yudhishthira. A phrase from what Draupadi told Yudhishthira—*dharmo rakSati rakSitaH*—would be repeated, by the wise and otherwise, over the millennia.

> I have heard from aryas that a king protects dharma and dharma in turn protects him. But I think it does not protect you.[1]

Despite being cheated, abused, and insulted by Duryodhana and others, Yudhishthira had chosen to swallow those humiliations. He had not retaliated. Where was his kshatriya dharma? Had he forgiven those who had wronged him? Did he not understand the nature of revenge and remission? Draupadi shared with Yudhishthira what Prahlaada had revealed to Bali on the nature of retribution and forgiveness. The subtext was clear—Yudhishthira would be unwise to forgive the Kauravas. Dharma demanded revenge and retaliation. What held Yudhishthira back, demanded Draupadi?

> Revenge is not always superior. Nor is forgiveness always superior. Learn the nature of both, so that there is no scope for doubt.[2]

Caught in a bind, with no means of retaliating against the Kauravas, and loathe to break the conditions of the game of dice, Yudhishthira could do little but extol the virtues of forgiveness.

> Forgiveness is dharma. Forgiveness is sacrifices. Forgiveness is the Vedas. Forgiveness is the sacred texts.[3]

The same Yudhishthira would, years later, at the end of the Kurukshetra war, spurn Duryodhana's offer of peace and declare that the war would end only when one of them were dead.[4] Time and place dictated strategy; Yudhishthira knew that only too well. Dharma was indeed subtle. So what held him back now?

> If, between the two of us, both of us remain alive, all beings will be uncertain about who has emerged victorious.[5]

Shortly thereafter, Bheema spoke to his elder brother. Forcefully, as only Bheema could, he made the case that under exigent circumstances the texts approved of treating a month to be a year. It was futile to wait thirteen years. Worse, the intervening years would give Duryodhana time and opportunity to further strengthen his position vis-à-vis the Paandavas. If they wanted to reclaim their kingdom, the time was now, Bheema declared. Yudhishthira demurred.

If Yudhishthira had not suggested retaliating against the Kauravas, he had his reasons. He now shared those.

Bheema would have known, but Yudhishthira still reminded his younger brother that the Kauravas boasted of such warriors on their side as Ashwatthama, Bhurishrava, Drona, Duryodhana, Karna, Shalya, and others. The Kauravas' treasury had furthered swelled from the wealth Yudhishthira had lost in the game of dice. The Kaurava army was paid on time. After all, hadn't Naarada offered the same counsel to Yudhishthira when he had visited the Paandavas in Indraprastha—'*Are your soldiers given their rations and wages on time?*[6]' If the army was paid its wages and its generals treated with respect, there was no reason for them to rebel. But what about Bheeshma, the grand patriarch, whose word carried the weight of generations and who stood the tallest among the Kurus?

Painful as it was, Yudhishthira knew, and reminded Bheema, that Bheeshma's loyalties lay with the Kurus. His affections towards the Paandavas lay buried under the largesse of the Kurus. The same was true for Kripa also.

> Though the conduct of Bhishma, the mighty-armed Drona and the great-souled Kripa is equal, they will certainly be driven by the royal morsels.[7]

The reality of his situation was something Bheeshma also knew and would acknowledge the same to the Paandavas on the eve of the war.

> A man is the servant of wealth. But wealth is never anyone's servant... I am tied to the Kouravas because of wealth... The Kouravyas have robbed me through wealth.[8]

Yes, Arjuna's bow was the best there was. Yes, Arjuna was the most skilled archer there was. Yes, Arjuna's quiver would provide an inexhaustible supply of arrows. But that would not be enough. Nor would Bheema's mace suffice when it came to facing the combined might of the Kuru army. Leaving aside the matter of allies, of whom they now had few, they needed to better arm themselves. War may have been a distant prospect, thirteen years into the future, but it was inevitable, he feared. Yes, Yudhishthira knew a war was coming.

> The four parts of *dhanurveda* are today established in Bhishma, Drona, Kripa and Drona's son.[9]

The warrior best suited and skilled to acquire the weapons and their knowledge was Arjuna. Arjuna would have to leave the Paandavas and seek Shiva and Indra's favours and receive celestial weapons. Agni had promised that Arjuna would receive Indra's weapons, but only after propitiating Shiva.[10] That time was now.

With a heavy heart, Arjuna bid the Paandavas farewell and departed on his multi-year quest to acquire the skill and weapons they would need much later to face their kith and kin on the battlefield of Kurukshetra. Apart from celestial weapons, an encounter with Urvashi, the apsaraa, would also yield a curse that would serve as a boon during their thirteenth year of exile.

The Paandavas would have to spend several years of their thirteen years of exile without Arjuna. Yes, their cup of woes was truly full. Yudhishthira was disconsolate. When Sage Brihadashva arrived in Dvaitavana, Yudhishthira welcomed him and paid him homage, and then poured his heart out over his state and fate. Robbed of his kingdom, cheated of his wealth, compelled to be a mute spectator to the public humiliation of his wife, Draupadi, and now deprived of the company of his beloved Arjuna also—was there any person as miserable than him, Yudhishthira lamented?

> I think that there is no man who is more miserable than I am.[11]

What had been, would again be. Yudhishthira was neither the first, nor would be the last, to experience miseries. King Nala had experienced more, worse, than Yudhishthira, Brihadashva told Yudhishthira.

Nala and Damayanti

Nala[12] was the king of the Nishadha[13] kingdom and son of Veerasena. He was learned, brave, virtuous, and a follower of dharma. He was also handsome to the point of inviting comparisons with Kandarpa, the god of love, himself. In other words, he was almost as perfect a king and bachelor as one could imagine.

Meanwhile, as valorous as Nala was the king of Vidarbha, Bheema.[14] Through a boon conferred by Sage Damana, Bheema became the father of four children—a daughter named Damayanti and three sons named Dama, Daanta, and Damana. Damayanti grew up to be a beautiful maiden. So beautiful that it drove the gods to distraction. They could not stop gushing over her stunning looks, her allure, her grace. The gods eulogized Damayanti's beauty in Nala's presence. The gods sang paeans to Nala's beauty in Damayanti's presence. It was but inevitable that both developed an attraction for each other, even before setting eyes on each other.

Nala now wanted more than just to hear of Damayanti's beauty. He wanted her to hear his declaration of affection. But how? One day, when he was in his palace's inner quarters, Nala saw a flock of swans with golden wings descend. Fascinated, he caught hold of one. The swan, desperate to escape with its life, offered to go to Damayanti and sing Nala's praises. That offer was entirely agreeable and completely acceptable to Nala. He let go of the swan and the entire flock, grateful, flew to the capital of Vidarbha, to Damayanti's palace.

Seeing that most unusual flock of golden swans descend in her palace, Damayanti and her friends dashed after the swans. The golden swan, which carried Nala's message, scampered here and there, and led Damayanti to a secluded spot, away from her friends and attendants. There it spoke in a human language. If Damayanti was surprised by the swan's human language, she soon forgot her wonder when it started to talk of Nala's qualities and beauties. Damayanti listened, enraptured. If Nala had sent her a message, she too would send one back. She gave the golden swan a message. The swan departed.

> We have seen gods, gandharvas, men, serpents and rakshasas. But we have never seen one like him.[15]

If the gods had been enraptured by Nala and Damayanti, and Nala's heart stolen by Damayanti, Damayanti's heart was pin-cushioned by Kamadeva's arrows of love. She pined for Nala. Neither the waking nor the sleeping hours gave her any comfort. She found solace in nothing. Food held no allure. All she could do was glance up at the skies, waiting, hoping, praying for the swans to fly down with another message from Nala.

Her friends saw this change come over Damayanti. The princess was unwell. They informed the king. King Bheema, her father, was a wise man. Once upon a time, he too had been a youth. He knew his daughter's ailments were of the heart, not of the body. He decided the time had come for Damayanti to be married. So that the princess may pick her suitor, he announced a swayamvara where Damayanti would garland the suitor of her choice.

As news of Damayanti's swayamvara reached the kingdoms in the land, kings from near and far flocked and descended on Vidarbha, each hoping to be the favoured one that Damayanti would garland. News reached Nala too; he also set out for Vidarbha.

The kings were, one and all, making a beeline for Vidarbha; not to Indra's court. Indra noticed the dip in attendance at his own court. When he saw Sages Naarada and Parvata, he put forth his queries.[16]

> 'O Sage, where have all the kings gone? Is my court no longer important or attractive to them?' Indra asked.
>
> 'No, O Indra, not at all. The kings are all going to, or have already reached, Vidarbha,' Naarada replied.

'Is King Bheema of Vidarbha now a more powerful king than even me?' Indra asked, suspicious, shifting in his throne.

'No, O Indra. It is not King Bheema's power that draws the kings to Vidarbha. It is his daughter, Damayanti.'

'Huh? Princess Damayanti?'

Meanwhile, three other gods, Agni, Varuna, and Yama had also joined Indra in his court. They also listened to Naarada.

'Damayanti is the jewel that all kings desire. Her beauty dazzles with a light that outshines your court, O Indra. Her father is holding a swayamvara for her. She will pick one king; she will garland one king; one king will be crowned the luckiest man on earth,' replied Naarada.

'Oh, I see. What about those she doesn't garland?' Indra asked, smiling as he saw the other gods.

'They will have to return with nothing more than a glimpse of the princess.'

'So fortune will favour only one among those countless kings?' asked Indra.

'Yes, O Indra,' Naarada replied. He and Parvata took their leave.

'What about the gods?' Indra mused out aloud. 'Surely the gods will stand a better chance than mortals, won't they?'

'Yes, they will,' exclaimed the other gods assembled.

'And the king of the gods will stand a better chance than even the gods, won't he?' winked Indra.

'Does that mean…?' asked the gods.

'Yes, we should also attend her swayamvara,' Indra said.

Indra, Agni, Varuna, and Yama departed for earth, each wishing to be the lucky one. At Damayanti's swayamvara, kings, gods, and the king of gods would all try their luck.

The gods descended to earth and made their way to Vidarbha, disguised as humans. Who should they meet there, but Nala. They had already heard that Nala was handsome, that he rivalled the god of love in looks, but those had been mere words. Seeing Nala in person, their confidence faded. With Nala as a suitor, Damayanti wouldn't even glance at the gods, they knew. But the gods would not be deterred.

The gods hit upon a most ingenious ploy to have their way. They approached Nala and asked him to be their messenger. Without asking what the message was, Nala agreed.

'But who are you?' asked Nala.

'We are the immortals. You know us as gods. I am Indra,' Indra replied, and introduced the other gods, Agni, Varuna, and Yama.

'I am blessed to have seen you in person, O Gods!' Nala exclaimed.

'Indeed, you are,' replied Indra.

'Who is the message for? What is the message?' Nala asked.

'For Damayanti.'

'Princess Damayanti, of Vidarbha?' Nala frowned.

'Yes.'

'I see. What is the message, O Gods?' Nala felt uneasy. What message could the gods have for his Damayanti, he wondered. Not *his* yet, he corrected himself.

'She should marry,' Indra started.

'Yes, she will, O Indra. Her father, King Bheema, is holding a swayamvara so she may select a groom of her choice,' Nala replied.

'She should marry one of us,' Indra said. 'One of us gods.'

'Please, O Indra, not that. Ask me anything but that,' Nala replied, horrified. 'I too want to marry her. I am a suitor, not a messenger. I cannot be… how… how can I…,' his words trailed off. How could a mortal defy a god?

'You have already given us your word that you would bear our message. Haven't you, Nala?' Indra asked, reminded, Nala.

'Find someone else. Please,' pleaded Nala.

'No one but you will do, Nala.'

'How will I enter her palace to give her this message? I can't just saunter into her heavily guarded palace, can I?' Nala asked hopefully.

'We will make sure of that. No one will stop you when you do,' Indra replied. 'Off you go.'

Nala found himself outside Damayanti's palace. And then he found himself inside the palace. He walked. Guards didn't stop him, they didn't notice him. Soon enough he saw Damayanti, surrounded by her friends. He gaped at her, blinded by her beauty; he stood there tongue-tied, his words stuck in his throat. Damayanti too was dazzled by Nala. Even her attendants and friends all wondered who this man was. Only the gods could be as handsome as he was. They too stood there, tongue-tied.

In her radiance, she seemed to dim the light of the moon.[17]

Damayanti, however, had more presence of mind than her companions. As events would show, she had more presence of mind than even Nala. But, for now, she approached Nala and asked him all the questions that should have been asked—who he was, how he had entered her well-guarded palace, what did he want.

'I am Nala, the king of Nishadha,' Nala introduced himself.

'You are Nala, are you?' Damayanti's heart skipped a beat.

'I have come to you as a messenger of the gods,' Nala said, each word like a stone around his heart, threatening to pull it apart.

Damayanti looked on.

'Indra, Agni, Varuna, Yama…,' Nala stopped. His words wouldn't come out.

'What do they want, O Nala?' Damayanti asked. Just saying his name out brought her joy.

'Pick one of them as your husband—the gods have asked me to tell you,' Nala replied.

Damayanti stood there, staring at Nala.

'I cannot do that. I won't do that,' she said, her voice choked. 'It is my swaymavara. It is my choice,' she declared.

'If you don't pick one of them, if you refuse their message, then the wrath of those gods will fall on me. Only you can save me,' Nala replied.

'I will, Nala; I will save you. Let those gods come to the swayamvara. If I choose you instead of them, it won't be any fault of yours, will it?' Damayanti said.

Nala nodded and departed.

I love you. If you reject me, for your sake, I will have to find refuge with poison, fire, water or the rope.[18]

Nala returned to the gods. There he briefed the four gods what had transpired. He had conveyed his message to Damayanti. He had asked her to pick one of the gods. Damayanti had refused. She would, she had said, pick Nala at her swayamvara. The gods could come to her swaymavara and witness her make her own choice.

'Damayanti said she will pick Nala?' asked Indra.

'Yes, O Indra,' replied Nala.

'Well, then, there is nothing more to be said, is there? You have done your job, Nala. You may leave,' Indra said, a smile playing on his lips.

Nala departed.

'Damayanti will pick Nala and no one else, will she?' Indra mused out loud.

Agni, Varuna, and Yama looked at him.

'Well, then let her pick Nala,' Indra shrugged. "If she can."

The appointed day and hour of the swayamvara arrived. All the kings assembled, waiting, hoping. Damayanti walked in, stealing the hearts and attention of all the kings assembled. She looked around the gathered assembly as the names of the kings who were there were called out. There was Nala. She smiled. She looked on. Her smile faded. She stared, stupefied.

Yes, there was Nala. And Nala. And Nala. And Nala. And Nala. There were five kings identical in appearance to Nala. Obviously, one of them was the real Nala. Obviously, the other four were the gods—Indra, Agni, Varuna, and Yama. Who was the real Nala? That was not obvious at all.

Damayanti stood, rooted, frozen with indecision. She could not take a chance and garland one of the five kings resembling Nala at random, for this was no game of dice; and no one gambled with such high stakes in a game of dice, at least not those in possession of common sense, and Damayanti was practical. Whatever traits and physical characteristics the gods had, they had all been subsumed within their human forms now. The five Nalas were identical. Damayanti had to choose.

A problem created by the gods would be resolved by the gods themselves. Damayanti prayed to the gods. The gods had decided that Damayanti should garland Nala. The gods, seeing her love and devotion for Nala, acceded to her prayers. She would marry Nala. The characteristics that would distinguish them from Nala were now visible. But Damayanti would have to spot them.

Garland in hand, Damayanti approached the five. With the exception of one, the other four stood there with their feet not touching the ground, their eyes unblinking, not a drop of sweat on them, their garlands untouched by dust. Damayanti smiled, blushed, and then garlanded Nala—her Nala, the king, the mortal. The other kings gathered there lamented. The sages and gods assembled exulted. The gods accepted defeat.

The gods, before departing, gave Nala a total of eight boons, each of the four gods giving two boons. Yama blessed Nala with the ability to taste the essence of food; Varuna promised to come whenever Nala so wished and handed him a fragrant garland. The gods departed.

Nala and Damayanti settled into a blissful state of marital union.

Dark Clouds

Shortly after Nala and Damayanti's marriage, the gods started to make their way back to heaven. On the way they ran into Dwaapara and Kali,[19] the manifestation of two yugas. When asked by the gods, Kali answered he was going to Damayanti's swayamvara. He too wished to marry the princess of Vidarbha. Too late, the gods replied; the swayamvara was over. Damayanti had chosen Nala as her husband over the other kings and the four gods.

How could Damayanti have chosen a mere mortal in the presence of gods, Kali asked. If Damayanti had snubbed the gods for a mere mortal, she deserved to be taught a lesson in humility. But this was with our approval and blessings, said the gods. Besides, Nala was a good person who followed dharma. But this was not good enough for Kali.

> Truth, perseverance, generosity, austerity, purity, self-control and pacification can be found in him.[20]

But I don't care, said Kali. Nala was truthful, generous, was self-controlled. None of it mattered, said Kali. Nala would have to suffer, and by extension, Damayanti too.

Kali asked Dwaapara to help him enter dice. Gambling was the root of much misery. A dice loaded with a vengeful Kali would bode ill for Nala. Dwaapara obliged. Nala and Damayanti, meanwhile, lived in a blissful state of marital union. Unaware.

Kali waited, biding his time. Mortals were imperfect, they were flawed. Nala too would slip. On the scale of a yuga, days and months and years were but a blink of an eye. Twelve years passed—the same number of years that Yudhishthira and the Paandavas would have to spend in the forest.

Finally, time and fate conspired to present Kali with the opportunity he had been waiting for. Before performing his evening rituals, Nala forgot to wash his feet. Like a sentry that forgets to shut a small, unobtrusive door of a fort at night, Nala too had left his defences open. Unclean was unprotected. Kali seized the opportunity and entered Nala. Nala remained unaware.

One half of the stage had been set. Kali then went to Nala's brother, Pushkara, and goaded him to challenge Nala to a game of dice, assuring him that victory would be his; all he had to do was challenge Nala. Pushkara coveted Nala's wealth. And then there was Nala's wife, Damayanti. Pushkara agreed.

Nala and Damayanti lived in a blissful state of marital union. Oblivious.

When his brother Pushkara approached and challenged him to a game of dice, Nala found himself unable to resist. It was Kali's time now. Despite Damayanti's misgivings and his advisors' entreaties, Nala listened to none. News spread. King Nala was gambling. The subjects assembled outside the palace. Nala's charioteer, Varshneya,[21] went to Damayanti, beseeching her to tell Nala that his subjects were worried at the king's sudden addiction to gambling. Damayanti did so. Nala heard but didn't listen. Nala continued to gamble. Weeks and months passed.

A king lost in addiction to gambling, unwilling to listen to his wife, his ministers, advisers, and his people was a king truly lost. Damayanti realized dark days lay ahead. What fate had in store for her, she would face. But her children had to be protected. She summoned Varshneya and told him to take her twins[22]—Indrasenaa and Indrasena—to her father's capital in Kundina. She also gave Varshneya freedom to either stay in Vidarbha or leave. Varshneya took the twins to Vidarbha and left them in the care of their grandfather, King Bheema. He wandered around till one day he found himself in Ayodhya. He went to King Rituparna[23] and took up employment as a charioteer.

Nala kept gambling and he kept on losing. But Kali was not done yet. Even though Nala had by now lost everything—his kingdom, his wealth, Pushkara taunted him to stake Damayanti too if he so wished. After all, he still had something he could stake. No, unlike Yudhishthira, Nala did not stake Damayanti. Instead, he threw down all the ornaments on his body and left the hall, clothed in a single garment. Damayanti too followed, attired in a single garment.

If you think it proper, let Damayanti be your stake now.[24]

Kali was not done yet. Pushkara announced that anyone supporting, feeding, or sheltering the king and queen would be put to death. Fear ensured that no subject sided with Nala. Not a single door opened to give them shelter. Not a single hand extended to support them. Not a single morsel of food was offered to them. For three nights, Nala and Damayanti survived only on water. Hunger gnawed at them.

Kali was not done yet. One final act of retribution, one final humiliation had to be inflicted. Now out of the capital, wandering in the forest, a famished Nala saw some birds with feathers that seemed to be made of gold. If he could catch those birds, they could provide him with both food and wealth, Nala thought. But he needed a net. But he had nothing that could be used as one. All he had was the single garment on his body. That would have to do in these desperate times. Nala took off his single garment and threw it on top of the birds. Nala watched in horror as the birds clasped the garment and flew with it into the skies. Nala was left without a stitch of clothing. Gambling had robbed him of his last possession. As they soared, the birds spoke. They were the dice. They had conspired with Pushkara. They had taken away everything from Nala. And now they had taken away even his clothes.

> O greatly foolish one! We are the dice. We came here to take away your garment. For we would have found no pleasure had you gone away with your garment.[25]

Bereft of possessions and pride, Nala turned to Damayanti. He had nothing left—neither wealth, nor the support of his subjects. Nala pointed out to Damayanti the four directions—there was Avanti, there was Mount Rikshavat, Vindhyas, hermitages of sages, Vidarbha, Koshala; and then there was Dakshniapatha[26] towards the south. The implication was clear, though Nala could not bring himself to utter the words. Damayanti would be better off without Nala.

> It is the view of physicians that for all kinds of misery, there is no medicine that is equal to a wife.[27]

A marriage was not a union of convenience, to be abandoned when times were hard. Damayanti would have none of this. Nala protested that he had no intentions of abandoning her. Well, why had Nala pointed the directions to her, Damayanti asked. Seeing Nala's state of confusion, she suggested that they could go to Vidarbha together, her father's kingdom.

No, that was not something Nala could bring himself to do. With neither hope nor a plan, the two wandered around till they came to an abandoned hall. Tired, hungry as ever, they lay down. Damayanti fell asleep; Nala couldn't. He thought, his mind frantically exploring options.

He could stay, he could leave, he could give up his life. If he left, surely Damayanti would go to her father's kingdom. That's what she had suggested, in any case. That would be infinitely better than staying with him, he thought. Following this line of thinking, Nala decided that the best course would be to abandon her. However, he couldn't leave as he was. He was naked. He needed at least a small garment to cover himself. But if he tore off a piece of Damayanti's clothing, the sound would wake her up. He got up and wandered around.

As luck, or fate, would have it, Nala found a sword lying on the ground. He picked it up and returned. Bending over Damayanti, he used it to slice off a piece of her garment. Covering himself as best as he could, he left. Minutes later, he returned, pulled back by the thought of his wife he had just abandoned. He left again, only to return yet again. Finally, he left. At least she would find some peace, he thought. He was wrong.

> Departing again and again, King Nala returned to the dwelling house again and again. He was drawn away by Kali but was drawn back by his love. It seemed as if the heart of the miserable one was divided into two. Like a swing, it went to the dwelling house and back from it.[28]

Alone, Apart

When Damayanti woke up in the morning, she didn't see Nala. She knew. Nala had done what he had hinted at the previous night—abandoned her. Seeing a piece of her clothing missing only confirmed her suspicions. She was heartbroken. She searched for Nala, she ran here, she ran there, she lamented. Nala had abandoned her. Her troubles were going to get worse, much worse.

> There has been enough of this jest. Let it not go any further. O Invincible One! I am terrified. O Lord! Show yourself to me. O King! I have seen you! I have seen you! O Nishadha! Stay there! I have seen you hidden behind the creepers. Why don't you reply to me?[29]

Exhausted and hungry, oblivious to the world, she didn't spot a huge python[30] slither up to her. It rose and it struck, coiling itself around Damayanti. Much like the grief and circumstances that had her in their coils, so did the python. Damayanti struggled vainly. Death was imminent. In her last moments, she called out to Nala. At least she would die with his name on her lips. Someone heard her cries.

Someone rushed there. It was not Nala, but a hunter who happened to be in the vicinity and had heard her screams. Weapon drawn, he rushed and slashed at the serpent. It lashed out, loosening its grip on Damayanti. The hunter struck again, and again. Finally, the serpent lay dead.

The hunter extricated Damayanti from the coils of the dead serpent and offered her water. A grateful Damayanti accepted the water. As she drank, he inquired who she was and what had brought her to the forest, alone, and in this dishevelled state. An indebted Damayanti told him all that had transpired and how she had ended up in the forest. The hunter listened as Damayanti spoke; he also saw. And then he spoke soft, sweet words, slithering closer to her as he did. The serpent was dead, but now another viper had arisen—of lust. The hunter coveted her. What he saw, he now sought. Physical possession and violation of the companionless, defenceless, scantily clad, young, beautiful Damayanti; Damayanti who even the gods had once coveted. Damayanti at first cringed from the lecherous hunter, and then let out a curse, for the time for words of reason was over.[31] The hunter deserved no less. Her love for Nala had been true, so was her curse. The hunter stopped midtrack, and then collapsed, dead, bereft of both life and lust.

Damayanti left that forest and wandered about, not knowing where she was, not knowing where to go. From one forest to the other, she wandered, searching for Nala, lamenting her fate. She travelled north and entered yet another forest. Unlike the previous forests, this one had hermitages and where sages like Vasishtha, Atri, and Bhrigu lived, performing their penances. Relieved, she walked ahead. The sages saw her and invited her to their hermitage. They asked who she was. She introduced herself and then told them how Nala had been deceived in a game of dice, how they had come about in the forest, and how Nala had left her in the middle of the night. She asked the sages if they had seen Nala. The sages replied that while they had not seen Nala, they however could tell her that she would soon be reunited with Nala and that his affliction would soon be over. The next instant, the sages disappeared, as did the cluster of hermitages.

Damayanti was left alone again in the desolate forest. It had all been a mirage. Perhaps there was a vision of the future that the sages had held forth. Perhaps she was becoming delusional and losing her grip on reality. She continued to walk.

Damayanti entered yet another forest and came upon an Ashoka tree and poured out her grief to the tree, asking it to be true to its name,[32] in much the same way as Sita had beseeched the Ashoka trees in Raavana's grove to remove her sorrow.[33]

She moved on again. Hunger and thirst meshed with a path that clawed at her, shredding her clothes, caking her body, face, and feet with mud. Walking, stumbling, wandering, she chanced upon a caravan. Elephants, horses, and chariots formed the long caravan. With some trepidation, not knowing what to expect, not knowing whether this was yet another illusion, Damayanti approached it. The travellers noticed an unkempt woman, dressed in rags, thin, dirty, and not quite looking in her senses. Some were repulsed. A few took pity and asked her who she was. She answered, not quite sure whether anyone would believe she was the queen of Nishadha and the daughter of the king of Vidarbha. The leader of the caravan[34] noticed the throng and walked over to investigate. He listened as Damayanti talked, ranted, babbled, pouring out her woes.

Taking charge of the situation, he told Damayanti that he had not seen Nala. Their caravan belonged to Subaahu, the king of Chedi. He offered and Damayanti accepted his offer that she ride along with the caravan. Where it would lead her, she didn't know. Where Nala was, no one knew. The days went by, uneventfully. Perhaps the worst was behind her, or perhaps it was just taking some time to catch up with her.

> I am the daughter of a king of men. I am the daughter-in-law of a king and I am the wife of a king.[35]

One day, the caravan came upon a pond filled with clean water and with many fruit-laden trees surrounding it. The leader decided to halt there. Everyone refreshed themselves with the cool waters of the lake, ate the fresh fruit to their heart's content. As night fell, everyone slept peacefully. All was quiet. Till a herd of elephants ambled there towards the pond. Not quite expecting a large caravan there, nor willing to return, the elephants stampeded. In the melee, many travellers were trampled underfoot the elephants, many animals ran away, the travellers' goods stomped underfoot, destroyed. When daybreak came and the surviving travellers took stock, they saw devastation all around. The caravan had been all but destroyed. Damayanti too saw the havoc that had been wreaked and lamented again, even more, sure this time that misfortune was her fate. There was also surely the wrath of the gods she had invited when she had spurned them at her swayamvara. She walked, leaving the caravan, more despondent than ever.

The caravan had been going towards Chedi, which was ruled by King Subaahu, and that's where Damayanti steps found herself going after yet another long trek. Unkempt and dirty, and yet unstained in her regality, she entered its capital. Taunted by curious onlookers, she trudged along till her steps took her near the king's palace. The questions, taunts, and the commotion drew the attention of the king's mother. She had Damayanti brought up to meet her. Despite Damayanti's appearance, the queen mother saw in her a person of noble birth. Prodded, Damayanti unburdened her tale of woe, but leaving out that her husband was a king and that she was a queen. She called herself a sairandhari, a servant, who worked where she could, who stayed wherever she was when night fell—if working as a maid in a queen's chambers was what she had to do to survive, she would, and search for Nala.

> You blaze like lightning in the clouds.[36]

The king's mother was moved by her plight and asked her to stay. Damayanti agreed but put forth certain conditions—she would not eat leftover food, she would not wash anyone's feet, she would not speak with any man, and if any man tried to solicit her, that he be punished. However, since she would not abandon her search for her husband, she would take the help of brahmanas. The king's mother agreed to these conditions and told her daughter, Sunanda, that Damayanti would stay as a sairandhiri.

Where was Nala? Having abandoned his wife, having left her to her fate in a forest at night, Nala walked as far from Damayanti as he could. So far that she would be unable to catch up with him. So far that he would neither hear her voice nor even see her in his heart. Nala walked and walked into a deep part of the forest where a great fire raged.

From within that conflagration, he heard a voice crying out for help. But that voice wasn't just calling out for help—that voice took Nala's name and cried out for Nala to come and save him. Without a moment's hesitation, Nala jumped in and saw, much to his surprise, not a human, but a serpent lying there, unable to move, surrounded by the blaze. Nala was even more surprised when he saw the serpent speak in a human voice.

It was evident to Nala that the serpent had been reduced to this state as the result of a curse. Yes, the serpent affirmed. He was indeed a serpent, and his name was Karkotaka. He had once seized a brahmarshi who had cursed him. Because of that curse, he had been paralyzed. Without Nala's help, he would perish. Karkotaka pleaded with Nala to save him. Nala hesitated. Rescuing a serpent that could bite him would not be wise. Karkotaka, sensing Nala's hesitation, again spoke. If Nala rescued him, Karkotaka would return the favour—a quid pro quo. To make Nala's job easier, Karkotaka reduced himself in size and weight, becoming no bigger than a thumb. Nala made up his mind. He dashed forward, avoided the leaping tongues of the flame, scooped the serpent up, and jumped out of the conflagration to safety.

> 'Be well; go on your way, Karkotaka,' Nala panted, catching his breath.
>
> 'But I want to help you; you must let me,' the serpent hissed as sweetly as it could, slithering around Nala, eager to help.
>
> 'How will a serpent help me?' sighed Nala.
>
> 'Trust me.'
>
> Trust a serpent. The thought was ludicrous. Nala smiled.
>
> 'If you don't believe me, just do this once—walk. As you do, count your steps.'
>
> Nala looked at the serpent, then sighed and started walking, counting the steps as he did. One. Two. Three. Four.... He felt like a fool. Eight... nine... ten. And he felt his body on fire. The serpent had bitten him. He looked at Karkotaka. He had trusted a serpent. He was truly a fool.
>
> 'You bit me! You vile reptile! After what I just did? I saved you from certain death and you repay me by stinging me? What a fool I am,' he cried out. 'Trusting a serpent. Yes, a fool like me deserves this fate.'
>
> Nala looked down. He was no longer the handsome youth he had been. His body had bent over, his face now an ugly, unrecognizable image of its past, his erect frame now stooped.
>
> 'I bit you for your own good,' replied Karkotaka.
>
> 'Are you out of your mind? How can getting bitten by a serpent do me any good? Look at me! I have become a deformed cripple. How is this good?' cried out Nala.
>
> 'You have enemies, Nala. Enemies that will stop at nothing to do you harm. No one will recognize you in this form. Am I right?' said Karkotaka.
>
> 'Yes, I suppose you are right,' Nala responded. Yes, he had enemies.

'The one who did you the most harm is still inside you.'

'Inside me? I lost everything to Pushkara because of those vile dice.'

'He who truly hurt you and is the cause of your tribulations resides inside you. My venom will neither harm you nor cause you pain, but it will torment him every single moment.'

'I see. I had no idea,' Nala said.

'And now you must leave.'

'Where?' Nala asked, hopeful.

'Go to Ayodhya. The noble ruler, King Rituparna,[37] will give you employment. Don't use your real name. Go by the name, Baahuka. Bide your time.'

'Till when?' asked Nala.

'Time and fate will tell you. When you want to regain your old form, wear these garments and think of me,' Karkotaka handed Nala two divine garments.

Nala accepted them and made his way towards Ayodhya.

The choice of King Rituparna had not been random. Rituparna was skilled in dice. Nala was skilled with horses. Nala could now understand why Karkotaka had recommended what he had. After all, if Nala had to win his kingdom back, he could either challenge his brother to war, for which Nala had no allies, no army, and no wealth to raise an army either. Or Nala could pay back Pushkara in the same coin. Surely Rituparna would want, and benefit, from Nala's skill in handling horses.

After ten days of travel, Nala reached Ayodhya. Nala now had a sense of purpose; he went to Rituparna's palace and told the king that his equestrian skills were unmatched, as were his culinary skills. In return he asked to be given employment. Rituparna found that an agreeable bargain. He agreed and asked Nala to come up with ways to make his horses go faster. This was what Karkotaka had suggested; perhaps the tide had begun to turn, in just a tiny, tiny way. Perhaps.

Rituparna fixed a salary for Nala and assigned Varshneya[38] and Jivala, his charioteers, to him. Nala was a deformed and unrecognizable cripple; no one would recognize him, not even his own charioteer, Varshneya. Life started afresh for Nala in Rituparna's palace. Like the Paandava Bheema would as a cook, like Nakula would as a keeper of horses, much later, in King Viraata's kingdom of Matsya, Nala lived in Rituparna's palace, cooking in the kitchens and tending to his horses.

Nala had abandoned his wife but not her thoughts. At night, when the palace was quiet, when he was alone with only her memories, Nala's mind would return to Damayanti.

> O Ascetic! Hungry, thirsty, fatigued and miserable, where are you? Do you keep thinking about that unfortunate one? Whom are you attached to now?[39]

The Search

When news of the tragedy that had befallen his daughter and son-in-law reached Damayanti's father, Bheema, he had sent out brahmanas in search of both. Rewards were offered to anyone who had information about their whereabouts. Thousands of cows would be given to the one bringing good news. Brahmanas could travel far and wide without arousing suspicions. One such brahmana in Bheema's kingdom was Sudeva. His search brought him to Chedi. He made his way to the king's palace. As luck would have it, he spotted Damayanti in the palace with Sunanda, the king's sister. His search was over.

Sudeva got entry into the palace and approached Damayanti. There he introduced himself. He gave news of King Bheema, his sons, and relatives. Damayanti had also recognized Sudeva. Hearing his voice and hearing him talk about her family, she could not restrain herself. Tears flowed freely from her cheeks. Sunanda, the queen's daughter noticed this. She sent word to her mother. The queen mother summoned the brahmana. Sudeva told the king's mother the entire story of Damayanti and how she had come to be in that state. Not a maid servant, she was Queen Damayanti, married to King Nala, the daughter of King Bheema, daughter-in-law to King Veerasena.

Joy came in pairs. A mole on Damayanti's forehead, partly hidden, provided confirmation of Damayanti's identity to Sudeva. This same mole is what the queen mother was now eager to see clearly. Sunanda was puzzled, but she obeyed. She wiped Damayanti's forehead. The mole was now clearly visible. The queen mother saw the mole, a smile appeared on her lips, tears streaming down her eyes. She enveloped Damayanti in a tight embrace. Who was Damayanti?

The queen mother said they were related. She and Damayanti's mother were sisters[40]—she was Damayanti's mausi.[41] Aunt and niece embraced, wept, smiled, and hugged again.

Damayanti had had no complaints during her stay at Chedi. But her heart now longed to return to her father's kingdom Vidarbha. If not Nala, at least she could be with her children again. If her father had succeeded in locating her, perhaps the same brahmanas could find Nala too. Perhaps her days were turning for the better. The matter was discussed, and the king agreed. As befitting a queen, a palanquin was arranged for Damayanti. Escorts of armed soldiers with adequate provisions escorted her to Vidarbha, where there was an outpouring of joy. Sudeva was rewarded by a grateful Bheema. The twins were not orphans. If their mother had been located, perhaps the father too would be found.

The Search for Nala

The next morning Damayanti spoke with her mother. She asked her mother for one and only one thing—that Nala be found. Damayanti's mother talked to Bheema. The king ordered messengers to be sent to search for Nala. Damayanti gave a message to the brahmanas that they were to repeat verbatim wherever they went. If anyone responded to this message, they were to report back. Once more, the brahmanas spread out, carrying Damayanti's message, in search of Nala.

The messengers went to kingdoms; they traversed cities, towns, and villages; they searched cowsheds, they looked in hermitages. One of those countless messengers was a brahmana named Parnaada. One day he found himself in Ayodhya. He spent some days there, looking, observing, and then returned to Vidarbha. He had some information for Damayanti.

Once in Vidarbha, Parnaada told Damayanti that after meeting Rituparna,[42] he had repeated her message for all to hear—not once, but several times. Neither the king nor any of the courtiers responded because it meant nothing to them. Except one. One small, deformed cook named Baahuka, who served in the king's kitchen, met Parnaada alone. Tears flowing, he said that someone like Damayanti should not be angry with her husband, and that her husband too was tormented by grief. Parnaada looked at Nala. He saw a mere cook. Nala was more handsome than the gods themselves; this cook was bent, and ugly, with short arms. But this cook was skilled in driving chariots, just as Nala had been. He was also a good cook, just as Nala had been.

But this could not be Nala. Yet he was the only one who had responded to Parnaada.

The short, deformed man was Nala, no one else—of this, Damayanti was convinced. However, the cook would never admit to being Nala, of that too Damayanti was sure; else he would have revealed himself as Nala to Parnaada then and there. Love for Damayanti had made Nala abandon her; love for her would have to draw him back again.

Damayanti sat, thinking. The contours of a plan slowly formed in her mind, taking shape. A plan most audacious, even outrageous; some would have called it unacceptable. But she saw no other way. It required her mother's cooperation and for her father to be kept in the dark for some time. Between Sudeva and Parnaada, Damayanti chose Sudeva[43] for the task this time.

Damayanti asked Sudeva to depart for Ayodhya, to meet King Rituparna and deliver a message.

> 'What is the message, O Queen Damayanti,' Sudeva asked.
>
> 'Tell King Rituparna that a swaymavara is going to be held in Vidarbha,' Damayanti replied.
>
> 'Whose swayamvara?' a puzzled Sudeva asked.
>
> 'Tell the king that Damayanti has decided to marry again,' a hard look in her eyes.
>
> Sudeva's jaw dropped.
>
> 'Tell the king that no one knows whether Nala is alive or not. Damayanto desires a husband again.'
>
> 'But O Queen,' Sudeva started.
>
> 'Tell the king that the auspicious time calculated for the swayamvara will be the next day, and no other,' Damayanti ignored Sudeva's protestations. 'Tell the king that as the sun rises the next day, Queen Damayanti will choose a second husband.'
>
> 'As you wish,' Sudeva replied.

> Bheema's daughter Damayanti wishes for a husband again
> and will again hold a svayamvara.[44]

As instructed, Sudeva made his way to Ayodhya and sought an audience with Rituparna. The king listened as Sudeva spoke. Damayanti's beauty had beguiled kings and enraptured gods. If she had decided to marry again, Rituparna would try his luck. However, if the swayamvara was being held the next day, time was short. No chariot, no charioteer, no horses could get him to

Vidarbha in time. But he was wrong, he realized. There was one person who could help him. Rituparna summoned Baahuka, the short, deformed, stubby, cook, Baahuka.

Nala listened as Rituparna spoke, curious at first, and then stunned. How could Damayanti have decided to marry again? Perhaps she thought he was dead. Perhaps she had lost her senses because of grief. Nala ruminated but could not make sense of what he had heard. He would have to go to Vidarbha and see matters for himself. He went back to Rituparna and assured him that if the king wished to reach Vidarbha the next morning, he would get the king there—in one day. Nala selected the swiftest horses from the king's stable—the ones from Sindhu were the best. Rituparna had been expecting muscular horses; what he saw were lean but strong horses. Perhaps his faith in Baahuka had been misplaced. A little irked, he made his annoyance known. Baahuka stood his ground. Rituparna yielded to Baahuka. The horses were yoked to the chariot. Nala took the reins and asked Varshneya[45] to climb aboard the chariot. Rituparna set out with Nala to attend Damayanti's swayamvara.

> In this world, feminine nature is fickle. My sin was also terrible. So must it then be.[46]

The chariot threaded its way towards Vidarbha. Soon enough, the horses were flying like the wind, whisking the chariot along. Yes, Baahuka was good, thought Varshneya. So good, in fact, that Varshneya could think of only three charioteers as good as Baahuka—Shaalihotra,[47] Maatali,[48] and his former king, Nala. Varshneya had no proof that this deformed charioteer, Baahuka, was in fact Nala. He therefore kept his thoughts and doubts to himself. Rituparna too marvelled at Baahuka's dexterity with horses. He too observed but kept quiet.

The chariot continued to race ahead. So great was its speed that once Rituparna's upper garment fell off. In the time it took for the king to ask Baahuka to stop and pick up the garment, they had already travelled a yojana. To turn back to retrieve the garment would cost them time which they didn't have. Both were intent on getting to Vidarbha at the earliest. Rituparna hoped to marry Damayanti; Nala hoped to save his marriage to Damayanti.

Their chariot entered a forest and stopped near a Vibhitaka[49] tree. Seeing its fruits, branches, twigs, Rituparna felt the urge to give Nala a demonstration of his counting prowess. Why, we don't know. He told Nala he could count the number of leaves and fruits on the tree, and that they outnumbered those that had fallen by a factor of hundred. Nala was taken aback by this skill. Perhaps Rituparna's was a wild guess, perhaps not. Nala got down to verify for himself. But they didn't have time, Rituparna remonstrated; they had to get to Vidarbha by sunrise. Well, Nala was going to count the fruits, twigs, and leaves on the tree. If Rituparna was in a hurry, he could leave for Vidarbha with Varshneya, also a good charioteer.

Rituparna acceded, though reluctantly. Nala did a count and stood back, astounded. Rituparna had been right. The numbers tallied. But how? Nala wanted to know; he wanted to learn this art from Rituparna—to accurately estimate the count of the total from a sample of a few. But they had to hurry to reach Vidarbha. He also knew the art of playing with dice, Rituparna said. Nala wished to learn that too. But time was running out. Rituparna offered a bargain—he would teach Nala the art of the dice, which he did. He wanted to learn from Nala his equestrian skills, but they didn't have time for that. Nala agreed to teach Rituparna at a later time.

Kali had resided inside Nala all this time. Ever since Karkotaka had bitten Nala, the venom had twisted and tormented Kali every single moment. The agony had now become unbearable even for Kali. Damayanti had been found. Nala was on his way to Vidarbha. Husband and wife would be re-united. Nala had also learned the art of playing dice. All was lost for Kali. No sooner had this knowledge entered Nala than Kali exited his body, vomiting Karkotaka's venom as it did.

Kali was invisible to all but Nala. No sooner had Kali exited Nala that he stood over him, wanting nothing more than to curse Kali. A terrified Kali pleaded for mercy. Nala relented and let Kali go, who fled into the vibhitaka tree. What Rituparna and Varshneya saw was a change in Nala's countenance—a radiance, that had so far been missing, now exuded from him. Nala was still deformed, but that was now only a matter of his own choice and time to correct.

Much time had been lost. All three—Nala, Varshneya, and Rituparna—sped once more towards Vidarbha, the horses galloping even faster. By sunset, earlier than Nala had promised, their chariot was at the gates of the capital, Kundina. The roar and rumble of the horses announced their arrival. King Bheema was informed of King Rituparna's approach. Great was the old king's surprise, for Rituparna, the King of Ayodhya, had arrived on a lone chariot, without a retinue that usually accompanied a king, and without any ostensible reason, either.

The roar and rumble of the horses reached everyone, including Nala's horses in the royal stables. They recognized the cadence, the tempo of their master's equestrian skills. They neighed; they clomped their feet in joy. The thunder and reverberations from the chariot reached Damayanti's ears, too. She rushed out.

Damayanti watched, now confused. Where was Nala? There was Rituparna—had he become the equal of Nala in driving chariots? There was Varshneya—had he learned this skill from Nala? Then there was the third person—crooked, deformed. Who was he?

> If I am not engulfed today in the arms of that brave one, whose touch brings pleasure, there is no doubt that I will perish.[50]

Rituparna got down from the chariot and presented himself before King Bheema, who welcomed him with customary honours and then asked him his reason for arrival.[51] Now it was Rituparna who was surprised. He had seen no signs of a swayamvara, no pomp or gaiety in the capital, no sign of other kings who would surely have come for Damayanti's swayamvara. The wise, calm, and mature Rituparna,[52] therefore, replied that he had come to pay his respects to the king. The aged and wise Bheema inferred that Rituparna was being diplomatic. Merely wishing to pay respects could not have been the reason for his unexpected arrival. Nonetheless, Bheema asked Rituparna no further questions. He asked him to rest; they would talk in the morning.

Damayanti, meanwhile, had surmised that the short, deformed man might be Nala. She asked Keshini, her messenger, to go talk to him and deliver the same message as had Sudeva. Keshini went up and asked Baahuka whether Varshneya knew where Nala was. Nala, disguised as Baahuka, replied that neither did Varshneya know where Nala was, nor did anyone else. Keshini then repeated to Baahuka the same message that Sudeva had delivered. Keshini wanted Baahuka to repeat what he had told Sudeva, for this was Damayanti's wish. Baahuka started to repeat his words but couldn't finish. Overcome with emotion, he broke down. Keshini returned to Damayanti and told her what had transpired.

Damayanti was now almost certain that the deformed person was Nala. She asked Keshini to keep an eye on Baahuka and to report back to her. Keshini did so and came back to Damayanti, filled with wonder at the many deeds she had seen Baahuka perform. Fire didn't singe Baahuka. He was able to light a fire merely by holding up the kindling, and more such happenings that she could not explain. Damayanti asked Keshini to bring some food that Baahuka had cooked. When Damayanti ate a morsel; it tasted identical to how Nala used to cook it. As a last test, she sent her twins, Indrasena and Indrasenaa, with Keshini to Baahuka. When Baahuka saw them, he embraced them and placed them on his lap, weeping. At long last he had set eyes on his children and held them in his arms. But he was Baahuka, not Nala. Realizing this behaviour would seem unusual, he told Keshini those children were just like his own, which is why he had been overcome with emotion. That, and that alone, had been the reason for his sentimentality. He asked Keshini not to misinterpret his show of emotion. She had been seen visiting Baahuka frequently. People were apt to gossip and speculate; he requested her to leave.

Damayanti was now certain that Baahuka was Nala. She sent Keshini to her mother with a message—she wanted to meet and see Baahuka for herself, either at his place or hers, with or without her father's knowledge. Her mother shared this with her husband, Bheema, who approved of it. Baahuka was thus summoned to Damayanti's chambers. The short, deformed man stood in front of Damayanti, not daring to speak.

Nala and Damayanti

Damayanti looked Baahuka in the eye and asked him if he had ever known of a man who knew about dharma and yet who had abandoned his wife in the middle of a forest. A cruel and pointed question, but a question that needed to be asked.

> Have you ever seen any man, who is said to know about dharma, abandon his sleeping wife in a deserted forest?[53]

Baahuka replied that their misfortune had been brought upon by the curse of Kali, and now that both Kali and its curse had been expelled from his body, they could be reunited. But Baahuka could not bring himself to believe that Damayanti would want to marry a second time. Why, he asked. Damayanti replied that this was the only way she could think of getting Baahuka—Nala—to Vidarbha since she knew of no other warrior capable of driving a chariot over more than a hundred yojanas in a single day.

I rejected the gods and chose you.[54]

No, Damayanti had never wanted to marry a second time. One who had rejected the gods themselves to marry Nala could never think of taking anyone else as a husband. Nala was overjoyed. His suspicions had been without reason. It was now time. Nala put on the garment that Karkotaka had given him and remembered him. In an instant, he was transformed to his old form—the handsome, youthful, Nala. The separation and pain of four years was forgotten in an instant as they found each other's arms, after four years.

The next morning, both Nala and Damayanti presented themselves before King Bheema and paid their respects. Bheema embraced Nala like a son. There was great joy throughout the city. Even Rituparna, when he heard the news, was delighted. Seeing the ill-fated couple, Nala and Damayanti, reunited gave him no small measure of happiness. Nala asked for Rituparna's forgiveness, while Rituparna asked Nala to excuse any transgressions on his part.

Before Rituparna departed Kundina, Nala imparted his knowledge of handling horses to him. Rituparna left for Ayodhya with a different charioteer,[55] happy that husband and wife had been reunited, even though there had been no swayamvara.

For a month, Nala spent his time at Kundina, in his father-in-law's kingdom, thinking and planning his next steps. All that had gone wrong had been set right, except for one—he had to get his kingdom back from his brother, Pushkara. After one month, Nala took leave of Bheema and departed for his kingdom.

Nala met his brother, Pushkara, and challenged him to another game of dice. Pushkara smiled, smirked. His fool of a brother had learned nothing. Not an iota of doubt entered his mind, not even when Nala offered to stake everything—his riches, lives, everything. Even his wife. Perhaps Nala was still demented. Pushkara accepted the challenge.

> The aged have laid down the ordinance that an ancestral kingdom must be obtained back, through whatever means.[56]

Nala even offered Pushkara an alternative—if he didn't want to gamble—he could choose a chariot duel. No, Pushkara preferred the game of dice. Contemptuous, laughing derisively, he accepted Nala's challenge to a game of dice. In fact, he looked forward to the game of dice and its stake, for he always had his eye on his brother's wife, Damayanti, he confessed. What had tempted the gods and Kali had not escaped his gaze, either. As apsaraas served Indra, so would Damayanti satisfy Pushkara.

Unsurprisingly, the game began and was soon over. Nala defeated Pushkara. Nala then let Pushkara in on a secret—he knew that Pushkara had won the first time because of Kali, but Pushakara didn't know that Nala had learned the art of controlling dice this time. Pushkara's life was now at Nala's mercy. Nala was merciful. He banished an indebted brother away to another city.

Was there anyone as or more miserable than him, Yudhishthira had asked. By the time Brihadashva finished his account of Nala and Damayanti, the answer was clear. Both Nala and Yudhishthira had fallen prey to gambling, both had lost their kingdoms because of the addiction, but Nala had also suffered separation from his wife. He had lost even the last stitch of clothing on him. Kali had permeated him—temporarily (unlike Duryodhana[57]), and he had become a deformed cripple. Only Arjuna had left for the heavens and would return; Yudhishthira still had the company of three other brothers and Draupadi. Nala had had none.

Yudhishthira had learned something. Over the next dozen years in exile, he would spend time in the company of the wise, absorbing wisdom from them, learning from the accounts of those who had undergone tribulations not very different from his.

> O King! I will destroy the fear that you see, that you may be challenged again by someone skilled with dice.[58]

Brihadashva had one last parting gift for Yudhishthira. He knew that the king had a lingering fear that if he were challenged to a game of dice again, he would lose again, for he was not skilled at the game. Brihadashva offered to teach it to Yudhishthira. The king accepted. Thus did Yudhishthira, who had lost everything in a game of dice that he was not skilled at, finally learn the art from Brihadashva, lest history repeat itself.

Years later, on the battlefield of Kurukshetra, Duryodhana would hatch a plan to have Drona capture Yudhishthira and force the Paandava into another game of dice.[59] Not knowing that Yudhishthira was now adept at dice, one can only speculate what the results of such a game would have been, had it occurred. Would history have repeated itself?

The elders, including Vidura, had warned Dhritaraashtra against that fated game of dice. Dhritaraashtra had given in to his son's badgering. Years later, as the blind king lamented the daily decimation of his army at the hands of the Paandava army, Sanjaya, as blunt as Vidura in his criticism, reminded the king that the blame lay at none other than his own door.

> Your faults have been great. When waters have receded after a flood, the construction of an embankment is useless.[60]

Nevertheless, a game of dice would be played again; but on the battlefield of Kurukshetra; the tools would be different. If a game of dice was what the Kauravas wanted, Arjuna would give it to them.

> O Krishna! Today let Soubala know that my arrows are dice, Gandiva is the box used to throw them and my chariot the spread on which the game is played.[61]

14

AGASTYA

An Epic Appetite

Parva: Aranyaka (3) | Upa parva: Teertha-yaatra (33)
Chapters: 94-108 | Shlokas: 357

The Kaamyaka forest now held one Paandava less—Arjuna. The Paandavas knew the coming battle with the Kauravas was inevitable. It would require them to have more than just courage. They needed celestial weapons. Arjuna was the most qualified to attain them. It still didn't lessen the sadness the Paandavas felt at Arjuna's absence, however. His memories were everywhere the Paandavas went in the forest.

Keeping the Paandavas company in the forest were sages who kept visiting from time to time, sharing words of wisdom and answering questions. On one such occasion, they were joined by Sage Naarada. He uplifted their spirits by telling them the benefits of various teerthas (pilgrimage sites).[1] That helped the Paandavas take their minds off Arjuna. Soon enough, their preceptor, Dhaumya, also stopped by. They were also joined by Sage Lomasha. After some time Naarada departed.

Lomasha had comforted Yudhishthira by reminding him that the prosperity of the wicked was fleeting.

> As a result of not following dharma, they were first filled with insolence. Insolence gave birth to vanity and vanity gave birth to anger. Anger resulted in a lack of shame and shamelessness destroyed their conduct.[2]

The twelve years of exile were a period of learning for the Paandavas. Staying in one place would have meant stagnation. Also, their stay in any one place was not good for the deer in the forest.[3] They set out from the Kaamyaka forest and made their way to the famous Naimisha forest—the same forest where, generations later, Sage Lomaharshana would recite the Mahabharata at Sage Shaunaka's hermitage. The same account that Lomaharshana would have heard at Janamejaya's sarpa satra. The same account that Janamejaya was now hearing from Sage Vaishampaayana.

Vaataapi's End

In the Naimisha forest, at a place called Durjaya,[4] the Paandavas saw Sage Agastya's hermitage. The Paandavas had heard of the famous sage, but Yudhishthira was curious to know how a diminutive sage like Agastya had accomplished the feat of killing the formidable asura, Vaataapi.

In the city of Manimati, began Lomasha, there lived daityas Ilvala and his younger brother, Vaataapi. Ilvala had a particularly nasty boon he had obtained from the gods. Driven by a desire to harm as many brahmanas as he could, Ilvala possessed the ability to call anyone who had died[5] back to life. All Ilvala had to do was to take that person's name. The dead would be restored to life in their original form. Ilvala put that boon to deadly use against brahmanas.

Ilvala had a reason, or so he believed, to harbour ill-will against brahmanas. He had once requested a brahmana to grant him the boon of a son who would be Indra's equal. Granting daityas such boons was usually not a good idea. The brahmana refused. Ilvala did not take kindly to the refusal. All brahmanas would have to pay the price—death—Ilvala vowed.

Ilvala started sending meal invitations to brahmanas. He asked his brother, Vaataapi, to change his form. He ordered his cook to make a dish with Vaataapi as an ingredient, literally. Ilvala then served his brahmana guests that fiendish meal. The unsuspecting brahmana ate. Vaataapi now resided inside the brahmana. Once the brahmana had finished the meal, Ilvala invoked his boon and called out Vaataapi's name. No sooner had Ilvala uttered Vaataapi's name than his brother came back to life in his original form, springing forth gleefully from the brahmana's belly, ripping it to shreds. The two daityas exulted. This most macabre dance gave them so much joy that they decided to do away with as many brahmanas as they could using the same demonical ploy.

Meanwhile, Sage Agastya once came across his ancestors hanging upside down in a cave. Alarmed, perturbed, he inquired why that was the case. The ancestors lamented that they were waiting for Agastya to have offspring so they could be saved from the hell named 'put'.[6] Agastya resolved to remedy the situation.

Paandu too had had a debt to repay; but he had a wife; but he could not mate with her because of a curse.[7] Agastya too had a debt to repay, but his problem was that he was not married. Agastya set about searching for a woman who could be his wife and who would bear him children. Only then would his debt to his ancestors[8] be paid. Agastya had stringent criteria, however, on what he sought in a wife. No one met that criteria; Agastya kept searching in vain. He came to the conclusion that if a woman who was perfect enough to be his wife didn't exist, he would have to create one. He had the powers and he had the need. He thus created a human child. Having done so, he gave the child to the king of Vidarbha. The infant grew up to be a beautiful young woman named Lopamudra.

When Lopamudra was old enough to carry out the duties of a householder, Agastya approached the king and asked for her hand in marriage. The king was in a dilemma, for the idea of marrying his daughter to Agastya, a sage who lived off alms and was neither a prince nor a king, was unpalatable. On the other hand, he dared not refuse the sage for fear of his anger. Wasn't it known that a king's sword would kill one, but a brahmana's curse could kill countless?

> He was incapable of refusing and he was unwilling to give.[9]

Lopamudra resolved her father's dilemma. She went to the king and asked him to marry her to Agastya. The king acquiesced. Agastya and Lopamudra were married. She went with Agastya to his hermitage, clad not in expensive clothes and jewellery but in less than simple clothes and bark. She would live like an ascetic's wife, not a princess. She would do as Saavitri had done.

Time elapsed. After Lopamudra had settled down, Agastya approached her, wishing to mate with her for begetting offspring. His ancestors still hung upside down, waiting to be delivered from the hell they were in. Lopamudra had been a princess. She was now the wife of a sage. She had accepted the hard life of an ascetic's wife, but some desires still lingered. She put forth a condition—that Agastya provide a bed as comfortable and ornate as the one she had been used to in her father's house, and both of them be well-dressed.

But I am an ascetic; I don't have wealth, replied Agastya. Yes, but the sage possessed a wealth of austerities; surely they could be used to summon untold wealth, Lopamudra countered. Fair enough, but this meant his store of austerities would be diminished. This was not what he had performed great penances for. Lopamudra stood firm. She wished for Agastya to mate with her in no other way than how she wished. But neither did she want the sage's store of austerities to be diminished—that would be against dharma. The dilemma was for Agastya to resolve.

Agastya pondered the matter over. Austerities he possessed, but wealth only kings did. Agastya would have to approach a king for wealth.

Agastya made his way to the very wealthy King Shrutarvaana and asked him to share only that portion of his wealth that he could without depriving his subjects. Shrutarvaana opened his books of account, sharing details of his income and expenditure with Agastya. The king and sage sat, poring over the balance sheet. Agastya assessed that the king ran a balanced budget, perhaps a rarity even in those times, and that Shrutarvaana could not give anything without depriving his subjects.

Agastya could not take anything from Shrutarvaana; he would try his luck with some other king. Shrutarvaana was now intrigued—how would the sage resolve this dilemma? Agastya left; Shrutarvaana accompanied the sage. Together, the two proceeded to King Vadhryashva where Agastya repeated his ask. Vadhryashva readily agreed but asked the sage to examine his accounts and take whatever he wished. Agastya repeated the exercise he had done with Shrutarvaana and came to the same conclusion—that Vadhryashva also could not spare anything for Agastya without taking something away from his subjects. Adharma was not an option for the sage.

Agastya left for a third king, Trasadasyu. Shrutarvaana and Vadhryashva tagged along. Trasadasyu was a generous king, but his income and expenditure balanced; he had nothing left to spare. The three kings, sympathetic to Agastya's predicament, wracked their brains. A name finally struck them. The daitya Ilvala. Agastya agreed. The four of them—one sage born from a pot[10] and three kings—trekked their way to Ilvala's kingdom.

Ilvala received Agastya with the respect due a brahmana and a sage as venerable as Agastya. But Ilvala being Ilvala, he scampered off to the kitchen as soon as his guests were comfortable. He gave their meal great attention, personally supervising the preparations. Vaataapi would be Agastya's meal, death his dessert. The meal was served. The three kings knew the great evil that the sibling duo of Ilvala and Vaataapi had perpetrated on brahamanas before. They warned Agastya. The sage listened to the kings and then proceeded to scarf down the meal. Agastya gaily ate, chewed, and ingested morsel after morsel.

The meal over, all that remained now was for Ilvala to call out to Vaataapi, and the world would be rid of one more sage. A brahmana as formidable as Agastya, no less.

'O Sage, did you enjoy your meal?' asked Ilvala, smiling.

'Yes, I did,' replied Agastya, leisurely rolling his hand over his stomach. 'Yes, I did.'

'I thought so,' said Ilvala. *Last meals should be enjoyed.*

Agastya let out a small burp.

'Vaataapi, O Vaataapi,' Ilvala called out softly. Vaataapi would burst forth from the belching sage.

Silence.

'Vaataapi,' Ilvala called out, louder.

Agastya sat, looking contented. Ilvala saw no movement from his stomach. No sign of discomfort.

'Vaataapi!' Ilvala shouted, now in a panic.

There was a loud noise. Ilvala stared at Agastya's stomach. It had contracted. Vaataapi would burst forth any moment now. No. And then a stench pervaded the room. Ilvala brought his hand to cover his nose, as did the other kings. He looked at Agastya, disbelief in his eyes. The venerable sage had just passed wind.[11]

'Vaataapi...,' the words died in Ilvala's throat.

'I must apologize, Ilvala; that's all that's left of Vaataapi,' Agastya said, waving his hand around.

Ilvala looked around. No Vaataapi.

'He's now gone with the wind that I just broke,' Agastya continued.

Ilvala stared at Agastya.

'You see, I have a fondness for food. My digestive system is also fairly robust. It can process food good and bad. I have digested Vaataapi, who you so thoughtfully cooked and served to me.'

Ilvala sat, defeated.

'What can I do for you, O Sage,' he said, defeat and despondency in his voice.

Agastya repeated what he had asked kings Shrutarvaana, Vadhryashva, and Trasadasyu—that Ilvala spare what riches and wealth he could, but without taking from others. Yes, Ilvala had wealth to spare, and he was not going to refuse the sage, but giving so easily was not in his nature. Ilvala put forth a condition that, yes, he would give to the sage, but only if he could guess what Ilvala intended to give away. That was not a big problem for a sage possessed with knowledge and insight that Agastya did. The sage paused a moment and then correctly told Ilvala what the king had been thinking of giving him as well as the three kings—thousands of cows, gold, and much more. To the sage, among other gifts, Ilvala also wished to give a golden chariot drawn by two steeds[12] that could travel at the speed of thought. Had Ilvala thought of giving Agastya and the kings more? No. Would Ilvala admit to having thought of giving them any less? No. A morose Ilvala accepted defeat and gave away those riches to the kings and Agastya.

Agastya returned, having fulfilled Lopamudra's desire. He also gave her a choice—she could either have a thousand sons, or a hundred sons who would each be equal to ten, or ten sons who would each be equal to a hundred, or one son who would be equal to a thousand. Lopamudra chose the last option—one son who would equal a thousand. A son named Dridhasyu[13] was born to Lopamudra.

Agastya repaid his debt to his ancestors, saving them from hell, fulfilled his wife's wishes, and also rid the world of an evil daitya like Vaataapi. Yudhishthira's thirst for knowledge about Agastya was not sated. He asked Lomasha to tell him more about the sage.

The Drinking of the Ocean

This was the time of Krita yuga. Huge numbers of terrible daanavas known as the Kaleyas, led by Vritra, wreaked havoc in the three worlds. The gods fought but couldn't get the better of Vritra. Determined that there had to be a way to kill Vritra, the gods, with Indra at the forefront, approached Brahma[14] for help.

Of course, anyone born had to die, and so would Vritra, assured Brahma. But no ordinary weapon could kill Vritra. Not even the weapons of the gods. Till such a weapon was crafted, Vritra would live and continue to wreak havoc. Only Sage Dadhicha could help the gods.

Brahma's advice to the gods was to seek the sage's blessings for victory over Vritra, and his bones. Brahma was clear—only the sage's bones would do, nothing else. From Dadhicha's bones would be crafted a weapon, the vajra, that would be capable of killing Vritra.

The gods trekked to Sage Dadhicha's hermitage by the banks of River Saraswati and asked him for the boon of his bones. The sage who had attained the highest levels of enlightenment now gave up his breath of life over which he had attained mastery and control. With only his mortal body left behind, the gods collected Dadhicha's bones and took them to Vishwakarma,[15] the celestial architect. Vishwakarma, who had sculpted the perfect apsaraa to distract and bring about Sunda and Upasunda's destruction.[16] His task now was to put his craftmanship and formidable skills to fashion the potent vajra from Dadhicha's bones. Vishwakarma completed the vajra and presented the divine weapon to Indra.

Merely holding the vajra infused Indra with energy and vigour he had never felt before. He led the other gods in a renewed offensive against Vritra and the Kaleyas. The daanavas stood huge, tall as mountains, and fiercer than ever. They launched a vicious counterattack against the devas. Unable to withstand the assault, the devas retreated. Even Indra wilted.

Seeing the devas retreat and Indra's falter, Vishnu imparted a portion of his energy into Indra. Other gods and brahmarshis did the same. Having gained in strength but still lacking in courage, Indra nonetheless unleashed his vajra against Vritra. The weapon crafted from Dadhicha's bones found its mark. Vritra fell, dead.

Indra's fears didn't subside, however. Was Vritra truly dead? Or would he rise again? Wasn't Vritra a brahmana's son? Hadn't Indra committed the sin of killing a brahmana? Doubts, fears, anxiety besieged Indra. He fled the battlefield, taking refuge in a lake.[17]

The gods, meanwhile, confident of their success now that Vritra had been killed, renewed their onslaught against the daanavas. The daanavas and the Kaleyas saw Vritra fall on the battlefield. Lost without their leader, they lost their nerve and fled. Seeking a safe haven, they made way for the ocean to hide themselves, confident that the gods would be unable to follow. Having secured themselves, out of reach of the gods, temporarily at least, the daanavas plotted revenge. Their line of thinking followed a logical course. Peace and prosperity in the worlds rested on the austerities and devotion of the virtuous. When the virtuous and the dharmic were destroyed, so would the world.

> Whatever virtuous ones exist on earth, ascetics, knowledgeable in dharma and wise, their slaughter must swiftly be ensured.[18]

The danavas emerged out of the ocean at night and wreaked havoc. They struck Vasishtha, Chyavana, and Bharadwaaja's hermitages. A dozen killed here, a hundred devoured there, the daanavas massacred the virtuous. Their rampage done for the night, they would retreat to the refuge of the ocean before daybreak. All that could be seen when dawn came were bones strewn around.

Some tried to save themselves by running away, hiding in caves, to no avail. Some even died out of fear. There were some who were brave enough to venture after these daanavas. Armed with bows and arrows, they searched for these killers, to no avail. The daanavas had hidden themselves in the ocean, out of reach.

The gods, at a loss at what to do, approached Vishnu[19] and beseeched him for help, reminding him of the avatars he had taken to rid the earth of evil, time and again, reminding him that it was on the austerities of the devoted that the earth's prosperity rested.

> If the brahmanas decay, the earth will also decay. If the earth decays, heaven will also decay.[20]

Vishnu informed the gods that it was the Kaleyas who were responsible for these macabre deeds and who had now hidden themselves in the ocean. The gods could not enter the ocean. The option? Destroy the ocean itself. That was, however, easier said than done. This was not a lake or a pond that could be drained. Vishnu interjected once more, suggesting a solution to the problem. Emptying the ocean would require someone with an epic appetite. There was only person Narayana could think of. The same person who had digested the daanava Vaataapi—Agastya.[21] Drinking up the ocean would be child's play for him.

The gods trudged to Agastya's hermitage and reminded him how he had saved the worlds from Nahusha[22] and then from an angry Vindhya. Nahusha had been appointed Indra after the king of the gods had disappeared after killing Vritra. The newfound power and prestige maddened Nahusha, who then started desiring Shachi. It was Agastya's curse that turned Nahusha into a serpent, thus facilitating Indra's return to the throne.

But what about Vindhya? What had the mountain done and why had that been a problem and how had Agastya resolved that problem, Yudhishthira wanted to know. He posed his question to Lomasha.

It turned out that one fine day the mighty mountain Vindhya asked Surya, the sun god, to circumambulate him the same way as it did mount Meru. Surya gently reminded Vindhya that he did so not out of his wish or whim but because that was the path the universe had set for him. Vindhya was adamant. Angered by Surya's refusal, Vindhya decided that if not him, then Surya should not revolve around anyone. And Vindhya began to grow, and grow, and grow. Its threat loomed a certainty now. The gods were troubled at first, then they panicked. The order of the universe was at risk of falling into chaos if celestial and terrestrial objects deviated from their prescribed paths. They approached Vindhya and requested the mountain to stop growing. Vindhya was like a rock, impervious to all entreaties. The gods, at their wits' ends, scooted to Agastya for help.

Agastya lent the gods a patient ear. Agastya didn't quite know how to stop a mountain from growing, but not all battles needed to be fought with brawn. He, along with his wife, made his way to Vindhya and requested him to stop growing till he had returned from the south. Vindhya agreed and did as requested. He stopped growing. Agastya crossed the Vindhyas and made his way to the south. Vindhya waited for the sage to return. But Agastya didn't. He settled down in the south. Vindhya's growth was halted. The universe was again in order.

Resuming his account, Lomasha said that the gods approached Agastya for his help yet again. The sage and his appetite would have to rescue the gods from the havoc the Kaleyas were causing. They suggested, requested, Agastya that he drink up the ocean. No water, no refuge for the Kaleyas, and the gods would no longer be fettered. Would Agastya be up to the task, they wondered.

Agastya nodded and made his way to the ocean. The gods, nagas, kinnars, gandharvas followed—none of them were going to miss this spectacle for anything in the world. By the time he reached Varuna's abode,[23] Agastya had built up both an appetite and the temperament needed for the Agastyan task. The gods watched in awe, they sang Agastya's praises, the gandharvas sounded musical instruments, flowers showered from the heavens. And Agastya set about drinking up the ocean. He took a sip, then another; he chugged, gulped, quaffed, swallowed, swigged, and sponged up the ocean.

The ocean's levels dipped; its shore receded. It took time, but slowly, surely, the ocean started to dry up. And then there was no water left in the ocean. The Kaleyas, deprived of the security of their lair, now stood exposed. The gods descended into the ocean bed with their weapons and set upon the daanavas. The imprecations of the sages who the daanavas had hounded and the fury of the gods left these daanavas with no hope of fighting back. Countless daanavas died, while those who could, ran and took refuge again—in the nether world.

Now that the danavas had been defeated, the gods thanked Agastya and requested him to refill the dried-up ocean. Agastya looked at the gods, smiling, shaking his head. The gods wondered. They had forgotten one small thing. When Agastya had eaten Vaataapi, he had not only ingested him, he had also digested the daitya. The same was the case with the ocean. Agastya replied that he had already digested the ocean's water. It wasn't coming back, or out, from him. The gods would have to find some other means to fill up the ocean! Saying so, the sage took the gods' leave, leaving the gods to ponder over their new predicament, having learned a lesson about unintended consequences.

The distraught gods went to Brahma this time with their newest problem. Brahma replied that the ocean would be filled up with water, but only with the passage of time and the efforts of King Bhagiratha. The gods and the world would have to wait.

> A great deal of time must pass before the ocean returns to its natural state.[24]

Ganga's Descent

Yudhishthira was curious, naturally. How did the ocean come to be filled up again because of Bhagiratha, he wanted to know. Lomasha began with the story of King Saagara.

Saagara was a king in the Ikshvaaku lineage. He was a kind, just, and noble king. Wives he had two, but sons he had none. Seeking to obtain a son, he went to mount Kailasa with his wives—Vaidarbhi and Shaibi,[25] to perform austerities in the hopes of getting a son. Shiva[26] was eventually pleased with their devotion and penances. He[27] blessed both his wives with children, but with a caveat. They had prayed to him at a particular moment in time[28] and now, when he was granting them a boon, yes—both his wives would have sons. But one of Saagara's wives would have sixty-thousand sons, while the other would have a single son. But all of them would perish before their time. Saagara's lineage, however, would be continued by a single descendant born to the single son. Sons were sons, thought Saagara as he and his wives returned from Kailasa.

Events were not without further twists and turns. One of Saagara's wives, Vaidarbhi, gave birth not to sixty-thousand sons, but to a gourd. The other wife, Shaibi, gave birth to a lovely son who was named Asamanja. A son had been born. The king was happy. As for the gourd, he decided to throw it away. However, a voice from the skies told him to take the seeds out of the gourd and keep them in a warm pot filled with ghee, not unlike how the Kauravas had been born. From this were born the sixty-thousand sons prophesied. True to the second part of the prophecy, Sagara's sixty-thousand sons were cruel and fought with everyone. They fought with the gods, they quarrelled with the gandharvas, they took issue with the raakshasas, they bickered with humans. They didn't meet anyone they didn't find a reason to pick a fight with. Saagara put up with these sixty-thousand sons as best as he could.

Once Saagara decided to hold a horse sacrifice, not unlike the one that Yudhishthira had conducted. As was the custom, the horse would be left free to roam the earth, and whichever kingdom it entered had the choice of either accepting the king's suzerainty or fighting the king. As protection, Saagara's sixty-thousand sons accompanied the horse. Unknown to the sixty-thousand sons, unknown to Saagara, the wheels of time were turning. They had never stopped, and now they approached a fateful turn.

The sacrificial horse eventually reached the shores of the ocean that was still bereft of water. There, the horse disappeared. Naturally, Saagara's sons thought it had been stolen. They would find the thief and then there would be someone new to quarrel with. They searched everywhere for the horse. Neither could they locate the horse nor the thief. Frustrated, they returned to their father to inform him they had searched far and wide, they had searched the four corners of the earth, but the horse was nowhere to be seen. The sixty-thousand sons had been perpetually querulous, but they were still Saagara's sons. But now they had failed to do the one job the king had entrusted them—keep track of one solitary horse. A frustrated father, an enraged King Saagara ordered his sons to begone and not return till they had found the horse.

Saagara's sons resumed their search. They returned to the ocean-bed where they had last seen the horse. They scoured the area. This time, searching with a keener eye, they spotted a hole in the ocean bed. Their hopes up, they set about making that hole wider, and wider, and wider, unmindful of the havoc and chaos they were creating. The horse, however, was still nowhere to be seen. Undeterred, frustrated, irritated, furious, they continued their excavations. They dug their way through the ocean bed till they reached paataala—the lowest level of the nether regions.

They entered paataala and were rewarded with success. The sacrificial horse was sauntering about, unmindful of the chaos it had caused. If the horse was there, so must its thief, Saagara's sixty-thousand sons reasoned. They looked around and saw someone they assumed was the crook. They approached the man.

The man they approached sat, immersed in penance. It was Sage Kapila. They didn't care. A thief was a thief. Why couldn't a sage be a thief? Or perhaps the sage had facilitated the theft. They would first take the horse and then deal with the sage, they decided. Without acknowledging the sage's presence, without paying him the respect due, they grabbed the horse and started to drag it away. The horse neighed, it whinnied, it created a ruckus. Kapila's penance was disturbed. The sage looked at the insolent sixty-thousand, and the energy created from his gaze burned down the sixty-thousand princes to ashes. Shiva's second prophecy had come true. Sage Naarada conveyed this news to Saagara.

Saagara grieved. He remembered Shiva's words. Shiva's prophecy had to come true, and it had. Saagara took solace in the fact that his lineage survived through Asmanja's son, Anshuman. But what had happened to Asmanja? Saagara had abandoned him. Why?

Bad as Sagara's sixty-thousand sons had been, Asmanja had been worse. For no sane reason, Asmanja's pastime was to grab young children and throw them in the river. Whether they sank or swam, he didn't care. The kingdom's subjects beseeched Saagara with their pleas and petitions. Saagara had tried but couldn't get his son to mend his ways. Saagara ordered that his Asmanja be banished from the city. What happened to Asmanja, no one knew, and no one cared—least of all the subjects. Thus, Asmanjaa's son, Anshuman, was the sole surviving descendant of Saagara, as prophesied by Shiva.

Evil though they had been, the sixty-thousand sons that had perished in paatala had still been his sons. Saagara had another reason to grieve. His yagna had stalled. The horse was still in paataala. He asked his grandson, Anshuman, to retrieve the horse; nothing could be done about the sixty-thousand sons, now dead.

Anshuman went down to paataala and bowed before Kapila and paid his respects. Anshuman had neither the wicked ways nor the wicked nature of his father and uncles. Kapila was mollified and granted Anshuman two boons. Anshuman had the sage's permission to take the horse back with him. Second, his grandson would be the one to bring Ganga down to earth. With Sagara's sixty-thousand sons having perished in paataala, only the holy waters of the Ganga could purify them. Anshuman returned with the horse and the news to his father. Saagara's grief was lessened to some extent. The wait would be long, however.

Anshuman returned with the horse. The yagna was completed. In due course of time, Saagara succumbed to the laws of time and was succeeded by his grandson, Anshuman. Anshuman was succeeded by his son, Dileepa. Dileepa had heard about the fate of his granduncles, and though he tried his entire life, was unsuccessful in finding a way to bring Ganga down to earth. He eventually retired to the forest and was succeeded by his son, Bhageeratha.

Bhageeratha was Anshuman's grandson, the one Sage Kapila had foretold would be the one to enable Ganga's descent to earth. Bhageeratha was equally, if not more, determined to get his ancestors moksha (salvation) through the Ganga. Bhageeratha recognized that such an endeavour could not be accomplished with efforts undertaken on a part-time basis. He could either spend his time governing the kingdom or he could devote that time in penances. Taking a decision, he handed over the reins of the kingdom to his advisors and proceeded to the Himalayas to perform penances and worship Ganga, the celestial river.

The days turned to nights, the nights back to days; the weeks passed, time passed, but Bhageeratha's penances continued undeterred. Finally, Ganga appeared before Bhageeratha in a human form. Bhageeratha requested that she come down to earth so that her waters would send his forefathers, the sixty-thousand sons of Sagara, to heaven.

Ganga agreed. But there was a hitch. Ganga was no ordinary rivulet, stream, or tributary. She was the mightiest of rivers. Her descent from the heavens was not something the earth could bear. Someone was needed to take the river's initial descent on his head and lessen its impact when it landed on earth. One, and only one could do that—Shiva.[29]

Undeterred by this new hurdle, Bhageeratha proceeded to Mount Kailasa and pleased Shiva[30] with his penances, who agreed to bear the river.

Finally, Ganga descended, plunging first on to Shiva's head, where she resembled a garland of pearls, and then plummeted on to the earth. This sight was one to behold, and the gods, gandharvas, sages, nagas, raakshasas, all witnessed this spectacle. Ganga the river, young and tempestuous, followed a straight path here, circuitous path there, curving in one place, looping in another. Where she went, life sprang. Bhageeratha guided Ganga to where his forefathers lay. Ganga followed, and her holy waters purified the bodies of the dead sons of Saagara.

The ocean was filled once more.

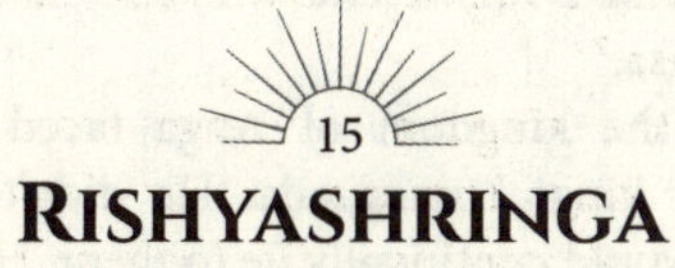

15

RISHYASHRINGA

The Horns of Desire

Parva: Aranyaka (3) Upa parva: Teertha-yaatra (33)
Chapters: 110-113 Shlokas: 101

The Paandavas trekked to Mount Hemakoota, stopping by the Nanda and Apaarnanda rivers on the way. On that mountain they saw many inexplicable phenomena, including showers of stones that prevented people from scaling the mountain. Sage Lomasha told them that this was the place where the son of Sage Kashyapa had been born with the horn of a deer on his head and who had brought rain to the parched kingdom of Anga. A torrent of questions poured forth from Yudhishthira. They had reached the Koushiki river where Sage Kashyapa's and Vishwamitra's hermitages were.

Sage Vibhaandaka[1] was once engaged for a long period in penances. Exhausted, he was washing up in the lake when he spotted the apsaraa Urvashi, known in the three worlds for her beauty. Her beauty caused the sage to lose control over his senses; he spilled his seed into the lake. The water was lapped up by a doe that happened to be there. From that water the doe gave birth to Rishyashringa.[2] The father, Vibhaandaka, and the son, Rishyashringa, lived in the forest.

A long time back, something similar had happened. The apsaraa Adrika lived in river Yamuna as a fish, cursed by Brahma. She ended up ingesting King Uparicaravasu's seed and gave birth to twins. The son became King Matsya, while the daughter was brought up fishermen. The girl was named Satyavati. Satyavati gave birth to Krishna Dvaipaayana, who also came to be known to the world as Vyaasa.[3]

Meanwhile, the kingdom of Anga faced tribulations on account of their king, Lomapaada. He didn't get along with brahmanas and would continually lie to them. He was a friend of the kindly King Dashratha, but that didn't help Lomapaada rectify his wayward ways. Weary of the king's bearing, the brahmanas abandoned him and left his kingdom. Without sagacious advisers, Lomapaada went even further astray. The consequences of the king's actions and the abandonment of the kingdom by brahmanas resulted in a drought. Indra[4] stopped showering on a kingdom where neither the wise lived nor did the king follow dharma. A kingdom could survive without a dharmic king, but life could not go on without rain. A chastened Lomapaada went and sought the advice of wise brahamans for ways to rectify matters, for without rain, the subjects and the kingdom and the king would all perish. Indra[5] had to shower again over his kingdom. But how, was the question.

Each sage had a different opinion that he shared with Lomapaada. Finally, one sage, wiser than the rest, told the king that the only way to get the rains to return was to get Sage Rishyashringa to his kingdom. Getting the sage to the kingdom would also be a conciliatory gesture to the brahmanas whom Lompaada had insulted.

Lomapaada accepted the advice. His first act of reconciliation was to perform penances. This mollified the brahmanas. Their king had had a change of heart. They trekked back to the kingdom. But the rains didn't return, yet. That would happen only when Rishyashringa set foot in his kingdom, of his own accord, not by force or coercion. The king consulted his advisors and the sages on how to get Sage Rishyashringa to leave the forest and make home in his kingdom. Rishyashringa lived with his father, Sage Kashyapa, practicing brahmacharya. Kashyapa's anger was well-known and much feared. What needed to be done would have to be done with some subterfuge. The king's advisers and sages arrived upon a plan they thought would work.

Rishyashringa had spent all his life with his father, in the hermitage, in the forest, away from any female company. So much so that he had not even set eyes on a woman before. The solution to enticing Rishyashringa out of the forest and to the kingdom was, therefore, via a woman. Lomapaada summoned the royal courtesans and told them to make haste for the forest and tempt the sage to follow them to Anga. The courtesans refused.

They knew of and feared Kashyapa's anger. It was common knowledge what fate had befallen apsaraas who found themselves on the wrong side of kaama with these sages. The king sat, dejected, again. Then a lone voice spoke up. The king looked up, hopeful, once more. From among the throng of courtesans, one had stepped up. The king looked at her and his hopes fell again. The courtesan who had stepped up was an old woman; with neither youth nor beauty on her side. Out of options, Lomapaada nonetheless agreed. The old woman had some demands.

No, the old courtesan was not going to attempt to tempt luring Rishyashringa to Anga on her own. Time had dispossessed her of beauty, but not brains. She made her way to the forest with several beautiful women. There she had a beautiful hermitage constructed on a boat in a lake. She then had the boat moored close to Vibhaandaka's ashram, but still out of sight. She then spent the next several days scouting the area and getting to know Vibhaandaka's routine. Once she had firmed up her plans, she sent her daughter, who was young and beautiful, to the ashram at a time when Rishyashringa's father wasn't there. The young temptress stepped foot in the hermitage.

Imagine Rishyashringa's surprise to see another person enter the hermitage. He didn't know she was a woman because he had never seen a woman. She was different. Curious, he inquired what had brought her to his hermitage. Only to visit him, she replied. Only to visit, of course. The two conversed. She gave Rishyashringa fruits that she had brought from her hermitage, along with garlands and clothes and drinks.

Curvaceous, vivacious, enticing, young, beautiful, the old courtesan's young daughter and Rishyashringa played with a ball. During the game, she sometimes touched his body, accidentally, of course; sometimes embraced him, unintentionally, of course, as if under the influence of liquor. And then she left, as if unwillingly, as if she had no choice.

Rishyashringa didn't know what afflicted him, except he felt unhappy, lonely, and longed for her company—whoever she was. He sat, thinking about her, pining for her, wanting her. When Rishyashringa's father, Vibhaandaka, returned to the hermitage, he didn't see the courtesan's daughter, for she had left by then, but he also didn't see many other things either.

Vibhaandaka didn't see wood chopped for the sacrificial kindling; he didn't see the agnihotra as having been performed; nor did he see the ladles cleaned. But he did see his son in a state he had not before—listless, despondent. Had something happened? Had someone come to the hermitage? What ailed his son?

Rishyashringa didn't know what a woman was, nor what one looked like. Perhaps it was just another brahmachari who had stopped by their hermitage. A most unusual brahmachari, however. He described the visitor to his father. He described her anklets, her ornaments around her waist, her waist, earrings, garments, skin, even the parting of her hair. The feminine touch had awakened the poet in Rishyashringa. He likened her voice to a cuckoo's calling, and the fragrance of her body to a redolent forest in spring. Rishyashringa wished to go to this brahmachari, follow the rites he did, to be with him, for he pined for that person now.

> During the spring months, the forest is fragrant when fanned by the wind. O father! Like that, there was a supreme and sacred fragrance when the wind fanned him.[6]

There was no reason for a woman to come by their hermitage. It must have been raakshasa in human form, Vibhaandaka assumed. He warned his son to beware of such creatures, for they were fierce and dangerous and lethal. They had to be, to have succeeded in enticing his pious son. As for the beverage the raakshasa had served his son, it must have been wine, not meant for ascetics like them. Vibhaandaka set out in search of the raakshasa. While he was gone, the courtesan's daughter again entered the hermitage.

This time, Rishyashringa came to the point—he wanted to go her hermitage. The sage's son had expressed a desire to leave his father's hermitage of his own accord. She took the sage's son to her boat, and from there to Anga. King Lomapaada had a grand hermitage in a wood nearby constructed for Rishyashringa and named it Rajashrama.

As Rishyashringa stepped foot in Anga, the rains descended on the kingdom. And it rained gloriously, continuously, till the parched earth was sated with Indra's gift. But now another danger imperilled the kingdom.

Kashyapa Vibhaandaka, Rishyashringa's father, would come in search of his son; his ascetic powers would reveal where his son had gone. Vibhaandaka would come in search of him; and he would rain curses on the king and the kingdom. Lomapaada ordered cattle be placed on the path that Vibhaandaka would take, and the land be tilled. If the sage inquired, he was to be told that all this belonged to his son. Perhaps that would assuage the sage, calm him, Lomapaada hoped.

When Vibhaandaka returned to his hermitage and found his son missing, he used his divine powers to figure out it was not the work of some raakshasa, but of the king. Enraged, he determined to travel to Anga and curse the king in person. On his way, however, as planned by Lomapaada, he was greeted by herdsmen who showed him respect. Everywhere he stopped, he was greeted and paid homage. Slowly, step by step, the sage's anger ebbed. By the time he arrived in the capital, Vibhaandaka's anger had subsided.

Lomapaada, meanwhile, had married his daughter, Shaanta, to Rishyashringa. When Vibhaandaka arrived in the capital and saw his son along with his wife, any lingering anger was replaced by affection. He blessed his son and daughter-in-law and gave them permission to stay in the kingdom, but only till such time as a son had been born to them.

16

KAARTAVIRYA, JAMADAGNI, RAAMA

When Fate Skipped a Generation

Parva: Aranyaka (3) **Upa parva:** Teertha-yaatra (33)
Chapters: 115-117 **Shlokas:** 74

A sage who had destroyed the race of kshatriyas. A sage who had descended from a kshatriya and a brahmana. A sage who had challenged Bheeshma but failed to defeat him. A sage who was more heard about, rarely seen. It was this sage that Yudhishthira wanted to know more about.

The Paandavas had made their way to Kalinga, where Sage Lomasha, still accompanying them, told them this was the spot where the gods had resolved, after a brief spat, that Shiva would also get a share in sacrifices. The Paandavas had continued their travels, eventually reaching Mount Mahendra, where Lomasha introduced Yudhishthira to all the sages there—descendants of Bhrigu, Angiras, Vasishtha, and Kashyapa. Meanwhile, Sage Akritvrana[1] had also joined them, and seeing him, Yudhishthira asked when they would get to see and meet Parashuraama—Raama,[2] the wielder of the axe. He also asked Akritvrana to share more about the valorous son of Jamadagni.[3] Akritvrana agreed. He started to recount the story of Parashuraama. All listened.

Gaadhi was the king of Kanyakubja. He retired to the forest, spending his time in penances. There he had a daughter named Satyavati.[4] When she came of age, a brahmana in Bhrigu's lineage named Richika expressed a wish to marry her. Gaadhi was pleased that a wise and learned person like Richika would be her husband, but he told the sage about a custom in their family—a thousand white horses was the bride price. Furthermore, each of those thousand white horses had to have one black ear. However, for Richika, Gaadhi was willing to forgo this custom. Richika didn't want charity from Gaadhi. He would meet this condition. Where would a hermit get a thousand horses from?

Richika approached the god, Varuna, with his request. Varuna agreed without hesitation. Richika returned to Gaadhi with the thousand horses. Richika and Satyavati married. Time passed. One day, Sage Bhaargava and his wife came to see them. Remember, Bhaargava was Richika's father. Son and daughter-in-law paid their respects. Bhaargava granted his daughter a boon. Satyavati asked for a son for both herself and her mother. Bhaargava acceded. Both Satyavati and her mother would have to observe the proper rites. When the right time came, both were to embrace two different kinds of fig trees. Fate willed something different, however.

At the appointed hour, mother and daughter observed the prescribed rituals, but mixed up the trees.[5] Bhaargava got to know about the mix-up. Well, there was no huge harm done here, for both would still be blessed with sons. However, the mother—the wife of a king, would be blessed with a kshatriya son who would live the life of a brahmana. As for Satyavati—the wife of a brahmana, her son would be a brahmana, but live the life of a kshatriya. For all practical purposes, there was no real harm done. Or so he thought.

This was unacceptable to Satyavati. Was it possible that her son was born a brahmana but also lived the life of a brahmana, and her grandson instead took on the traits of a kshatriya? Could the effects of a boon be made to skip a generation, asked a hopeful Satyavati? Bhaargava agreed.

Jamadagni was born to Satyavati. He, as prophesied, grew up to be a learned sage, knowledgeable about the Vedas and even acquired the knowledge of dhanurveda—weapons, though he himself didn't use weapons. His son, however, would be the one to acquire this knowledge of weapons and would use it to devastating effect. He would pass on this knowledge to Drona,[6] who too would prove to be a formidable warrior on the battlefield.

When Jamadagni was grown up, he went to King Prasenjit and asked for his daughter's hand in marriage. The king accepted and his daughter, Renuka, married Jamadagni. In due course of time, they had five sons—Rumanvat, Sushena, Vasu, Vishvavasu, and Raama. The world would know of three Raamas—Kodanda-Raama, Raama with the bow and son of King Dashratha; Bala Raama, the strong Raama, and brother of Krishna; and Jamadagni's son as Parashu Raama—the axe-wielding Raama.

Renuka once went to the lake for her bath. There she saw that the king of Marttikavata, Chitraratha, was also there, along with his wives. Seeing the handsome king and his wives in the water, Renuka felt a rush of desire sweep through her, overcoming her senses. Abashed at these unchaste feelings, she hurried back to the hermitage, hiding her state of disconcertedness and mental upheaval. This did not remain concealed from Jamadagni, however. This act of unchastity infuriated him. He was a brahmana, not given to violence. Yet his rage was extreme.

Jamadagni wouldn't act against his wife, but he ordered his sons to kill his wife, their mother. Jamadagni had five sons. Who among the five would be the one to act like a kshatriya? Hadn't Bhaargava prophesied it? Jamadagni's first four sons demurred. They were cursed by a frustrated and enraged Jamadagni. Raama—the fifth and the youngest—agreed and sliced off his mother's head with his axe. No sooner had this act been committed than Jamadagni was mollified and perhaps just a little bit contrite about the extreme act he had made his son commit. He granted his son as many boons as were in his heart. Raama asked for five boons.

Raama asked first that his mother be restored to life, that he have no memory of his act, that his brothers be freed from their father's curse, that he remain unrivalled in battle, and that he have a long life. Jamadagni granted these boons without hesitation. His mother was restored to life. It was as if that ghastly act had never been committed. All the other boons would also come true. Except one.[7]

Time passed uneventfully, till one fateful day the king of Haiyaha, Kaartavirya—also known as Arjuna and Kaartaviryarjuna—came to the hermitage, fresh from a battle, still intoxicated by the dance of violence on the battlefield. He was welcomed by Jamadagni's wife, Renuka. The king ignored the welcome and in an act of utter insolence, laid waste to the hermitage. Not content, he also carried off the sacrificial cow's calf, even as it cried and bellowed.

Raama returned to the hermitage. His father updated him on what had transpired in his absence. The brahmana son listened, but the kshatriya in him was awakened. What his father and brothers wouldn't do—pick up arms—he was fated to. He had the temperament, and he also had his father's boon of being unconquerable in battle. Raama set out for the insolent king and soon caught up with Kaartavirya. He challenged the king to a battle. The encounter was short. Raama sliced off Kaartavirya's thousand arms, but let the king go alive.[8] Raama brought back the calf to the hermitage. All was well, for the time being. But a chain of events had been initiated by Kaartavirya whose consequences would stretch for twenty-one generations.

Kaartavirya Arjuna's sons, when they found out what the brahmana had dared to do, were incandescent with rage. They marched on to Jamadagni's hermitage. Raama was not there; he had gone to collect firewood. But in the hermitage was his father, Jamadagni. Never mind that the sage was unarmed and defenceless. They set upon him, hacking him dead. When Rama returned, he saw his father dead and his mother crying her heart out. To have killed in such cowardly a fashion, many against one, armed against an unarmed, defenceless brahmana, hacking away with swords and countless arrows, was no ordinary crime. Retribution was called for. But Raama had to first perform the funeral rites for his father. Which he did, the flames leaping out from the pyre, fanning the inferno igniting inside Raama.

The last rites of his father finished, Raama took an oath as terrible as had ever been taken. Not just Kaartavirya's sons, but the entire race of kshatriyas deserved to be wiped out. If those whose dharma was to protect had forsaken that path, then it had to fall on someone to restore dharma. That someone would be Raama, armed with his parashu (axe).

Raama killed Arjuna's sons and then the kshatriyas who were their followers. He then rid the earth of the kshatriyas twenty-one times. So great was the bloodshed that he dug five lakes to hold this blood. All five lakes brimmed with the blood of the twenty-one generations of kshatriyas.

Having built these five lakes, Raama made offerings to his ancestors there. Richika, Raama's grandfather, arrived there and persuaded him to put a stop to this massacre. It was time, he said, for the bloodshed to stop. Rama accepted his grandfather's injunction. The entire earth at that point, in some ways, belonged to Raama, for there were no kshatriyas left. He performed a huge yagna, constructed a golden altar, and gave the earth to Sage Kashyapa. Raama then retired to Mount Mahendra to live the life of a sage once more.

The Paandavas finished listening to Akritvrana's account of Raama and waited. On the fourteenth lunar day, Raama arrived and the Paandavas offered homage to the sage. After spending a night there, Parashuraama departed.

These five lakes Raama built were in Kurukshetra. The land thus also came to be known as Samantapanchaka. Over time, the blood seeped into the earth, the place again became known a holy pilgrimage site. The land awaited an even bigger massacre of warriors that would take place many, many years later.

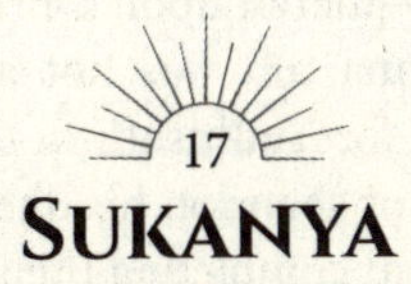

SUKANYA

The Thorns of Desire

Parva: Aranyaka (3) **Upa parva: Teertha-yaatra (33)**

Chapters: 122–125 **Shlokas: 97**

The Paandavas did not linger in one place for long. When they did, it was not without consequences. If nothing else, it was a reminder of the environmental depredations that accompany human habitations.[1] The Paandavas moved on, accompanied by Sage Lomasha, travelling to Prabhaasa, where they met and conversed with Balaraama,[2] Krishna, Samba, Saatyaki, and others. Balaraama, moved by the Paandavas' plight, wondered about the justness of dharma, or even its existence, that would allow a person as devoted to dharma as Yudhishthira to suffer so much at the hands of Dhritaraashtra's sons.

> O Krishna! The pursuit of dharma does not lead to good and the pursuit of that which is not dharma does not lead to defeat.[3] Should one forsake dharma and prosper?[4]

These words were not new to Yudhishthira. Hadn't Draupadi expressed similar sentiments when she had told him that while it had been heard that dharma, when protected, protected, it did not appear to be true in Yudhishthira's case.

> I have heard from aryas that a king protects dharma and dharma in turn protects him. But I think it does not protect you.[5]

Saatyaki[6] interjected here, telling Balaraama that lamentations were futile; their time was past. He urged the Vrishnis to do what could be done instead—march upon Dhritaraashtra and slay the Dhaartarashtras.[7] Krishna too was not averse to the plan, but the time for battle was for Yudhishthira to choose. Yudhishthira replied that he would not abandon his dharma for the sake of the kingdom. Dharma meant completing their period of exile. That is what he had agreed to in the second game of dice with Shakuni. He would not resort to casuistry.

Taking leave of the Vrishnis, the Paandavas departed, along with Draupadi and Lomasha. They made their way to Mount Vaidurya and River Narmada. Lomasha informed Yudhishthira that this was not only the site of Sharyaati's[8] sacrifice, but also where Sage Chyavana, in anger, had paralyzed Indra. Naturally, Yudhishthira had questions for Lomasha, about Sharyaati and Chyavana. Who was Chyavana who had done this to the king of gods?

Sage Bhaargava[9] Chyavana was Maharshi Bhrigu's son. It was near Lake Payoshini that he had chosen to perform penances. There Chyavana sat and meditated, staying rooted to the spot for such a long time that an anthill grew over him. Creepers covered the anthill. Chyavana became unseen to the world. The world ceased to exist for Chyavana, so lost was he in his penances. Nothing could disturb his meditation. Almost nothing.

One day King Sharyaati came to that lake along with his entourage. Also accompanying him was his daughter, Sukanya. The young, brash, and beautiful Sukanya walked around, taking in the sights of the forest, picking up a twig here, snapping off a branch there, its blossoms showering on her head. Chyavana, still ensconced in the anthill, still meditating, heard someone moving around. He opened his eyes and saw the young, brash, and beautiful Sukanya. Through the pits in the anthill, his eyes followed her. If not love, then certainly desire swelled in the sage. He tried to speak to her, but his broken voice didn't permeate through the anthill. But his eyes still followed her, shining brightly, taking in the sights to which he had for so long shut his eyes to. Sukanya finally set eyes on the anthill. She didn't see Chyavana, still entombed inside the anthill, but his eyes, bright, did shine from behind. Sukanya mistook them for fireflies. Out of curiosity, desiring to get them to fly out of the anthill, she poked them with a thorn. The sage screamed out in pain. Sukanya fled from the spot, terrified at what she may have done. A subdued Sukanya kept her act to herself.

Blinded now, and blinded with rage too, Chyavana pronounced a most unusual curse on Sharyaati's soldiers—that their bowel and bladder movements cease. And they did. A person can survive his entire life without an intelligent thought entering his mind; but life without bowel and bladder movements was well-nigh impossible. Sharyaati saw that not one or two or a few or many, but all his soldiers had been afflicted this way. This could only be the result of a curse. There was only one sage with the power of austerities to do so who was known to live in this part of the forest. That sage was Chyavana, who was also feared for his quick temper. Sharyaati surmised someone must have slighted the sage. But who, he wondered?

Sharyaati asked his soldiers if anyone of them had caused him an injury, knowingly or unknowingly. None of the soldiers had wronged the sage; none of them stepped forward. Sukanya had kept quiet, but seeing that the soldiers' distress was only increasing, she stepped up and confided all in her father. She didn't know who it was underneath the anthill. There was only one way to confirm.

Sukanya pointed the way and Sharyaati went to the anthill. His worst fears were confirmed when he saw Chyavana, still seated inside that anthill. He guessed the rest. With folded hands, he begged the sage's forgiveness. Chyavana, his temper having subsided, understood that it had been the king's daughter who had poked his eyes out, and the beautiful princess had done so by accident. So yes, he would revoke his curse and the soldiers would be rid of the affliction. However, said the sage, and the king's heart stopped. However, the sage said, he would do so only if the king married his daughter to him so she could take care of him. Sharyaati agreed.

Sukanya and Chyavana were married. Sukanya, a princess till a short while back, lived with Chyavana in the hermitage, now an ascetic's wife. Over time, she too learned to live the life of an ascetic, observing the same rules of austerities that Chyavana did; over time, she came to love the old sage. Time passed. It kept moving, turning the wheels of fate as it did.

One day, as she came out of the lake after bathing, the Ashvin twins, who chanced to be in the same area, saw her. She had been beautiful with her clothes on when Chyavana had espied her; and she was even more alluring without them, as the Ashvin twins now gazed. They approached her and asked who she was, even as the sage's wife hastily covered herself up. She was Chyavana's wife, she said. A woman to rival the most beautiful of apsaraas was the wife of the old, decrepit, loveless, Chyavana, the twins were astonished. It was inconceivable that her father had married her to such an old person. She deserved better; much, much better, they asserted. She deserved them. Sukanya didn't care.

The Ashvins persisted. They proposed that they could make Chyavana young and handsome. She could then choose from any of the three as her new husband. Sukanya accepted. When she told Chyavana about the twins' offer, the old sage was also agreeable to the idea. He went to the lake, and along with the Ashvin twins, entered the lake.

After a short while, the three emerged. All three were young, all three were handsome.[10] Sukanya had not got a choice the first time. This time she did. Sukanya chose. She chose Chyavana. Chyavana too was happy. He was now a young man again. He had gained Sukanya as a wife again. He blessed the Ashvin twins that they had now the right to drink soma[11] even in the presence of the gods. This was a big deal for the twins.

A long time ago, Indra had proscribed the Ashvin twins from drinking soma. Sulking, upset, they had descended on earth, and eventually found themselves in this forest and then met Sukanya and Chyavana.

Sharyaati had not made the decision to marry his daughter to Chyavana lightly. He had done this under compulsion. But now news reached Sukanya's father, Sharyaati, that his son-in-law, Chyavana, had been transformed into a handsome youth. His joy knew no bounds. He made his way to the forest where father-in-law was received by the son-in-law. Both, along with Sukanya, sat and talked.

Chyavana had, after all, coerced the king into giving his daughter in marriage to him. He now wished to do something in return for Sharyaati. Chyavana decided he would hold a grand sacrifice[12] for him. Sharyaati made his way back to his capital and issued orders for preparations for the sacrifice—a spot was chosen, the ground tilled, ingredients procured, and the yagna commenced with Chyavana presiding.

The auspicious time arrived and Chyavana picked a cup to offer soma to the Ashvin twins. That irked Indra no end. Hadn't he forbidden the twins from partaking any soma? In his opinion, they were unfit to be worshipped. They were not gods. They were merely the physicians of the gods. And he, Indra, was the king of the gods. It was his decision to make. Mortals would have to abide by it. Chyavana had to be stopped. The sage with a formidable store of austerities and a short temper had to be stopped.

Indra descended on earth and forbade Chyavana from proceeding. The sage's anger started to bubble, but he held his temper in check, for now. He was talking to the king of the gods. He reasoned with Indra that the twins were, after all, gods, and they had restored his youth to him. Therefore, they were deserving of the soma, with all due respect to the king of the gods.

Indra was adamant. Irked, Indra now threatened Chyavana. He warned the sage that he would unleash his vajra[13] at the sage. Chyavana looked at Indra as one would look at a foolish child. He then proceeded to offer the soma to the Ashvins.

Indra had warned Chyavana and now Indra acted. He raised his arm to hurl the vajra at Chyavana and destroy the insolent sage. But raise his arm was all he was able to do. With a mere glance, the sage froze Indra's arm. Indra stood there, his arm raised, paralyzed. Chyavana proceeded to complete the yagna. Only after that did he turn his attention to the king of the gods.

Indra didn't deserve to be cursed, Chyavana concluded. However, some form of chastisement was called for. Chyavana created a gigantic asura named Mada, who was not only huge but also terrifying. Its tongue darted as randomly as lightning, and his fangs looked like giant spears. So gigantic was the asura that his lower jaw touched the earth and the upper jaw skirted the heavens. This asura started to advance towards Indra. The king of gods paled in fear.

Indra had learned his lesson. He had no wish to test his might against this asura that had been created by Chyavana. Even if he wanted, he couldn't, for his arm was still paralysed. A fearful and contrite Indra beseeched and pleaded with Chyavana. Yes, the sage was right, of course. The Ashvin twins from that day henceforth would be considered equal to the gods and be deserving of the soma; and of course, he, Indra, the king of the gods, was telling the truth; and yes, all this had only been a ploy to get Chyavana's fame to be known across the three worlds; and not just Chyavana, charmed Indra, even the fames of Sukanya and Sharyaati. Indra was desperate.

The king of gods had apologized and accepted Chyavana's diktat that the twins get a share of the soma. A pacified Chyavana freed Indra.[14] This now left the matter of Mada, the gigantic asura. He could not be wished away. As the sage had created, so did the sage resolve. He divided Mada into four pieces, and one piece each went into liquor, women, gambling, and hunting, making these four seductive and attractive; but also intoxicating and addictive.

18

MAANDHAATAA

Where There is a Way, There is Fate

Parva: Aranyaka (3)	Upa parva: Teertha-yaatra (33)
Chapter: 126	Shlokas: 43

Sage Lomasha's accounts of sages, gods, kings, and teerthas kept Yudhishthira enraptured. Lomasha had barely finished his account of Sukanya, Chyavana, the Ashvin twins, Indra, and Mada than Yudhishthira asked the sage about the famous kings Maandhaataa and Somaka. Lomasha obliged.

In the Ikshvaaku lineage there was a king named Yuvanaashva. He was a great king, but a king without sons. Despondent, he handed over his kingdom to his ministers and headed for the forest to meditate, contemplate. Life continued in the forest for him. Till one day, thirsty, searching for water, he found himself in Sage Bhrigu's hermitage. Knowing who he was and why he had retired to the forest, Bhrigu decided to perform a yagna so the Yuvanaashva would be blessed with a son. The king attended the sacrifice that took place all day long.

When night fell, the exhausted king lay down, but thirst kept him awake. There was no one awake he could call out to for water. Nor did he want to wake anyone up. Yuvanaashva got up and stumbled around in the dark, hoping to find a pot, tumbler, a jar, a pitcher, anything to quench his thirst. In the dark, he spotted what looked and felt like a pot of water. He took hold of it and drank the cool, refreshing water. His thirst quenched; he went back to sleep.

Morning came and everyone woke up. The water pot was seen, but empty. The sages inquired what had happened to that water. Yuvanaashva came forward and owned up that it was he who had drank the water during the night. It was only water, after all. Yes, it was only water, but it was not just any kind of water. Bhrigu looked the king[1] in the eye and explained two things to him.

First, Bhrigu said, the water that Yuvanaashva had drunk the previous night had been consecrated with mantras from the yagna so that the king may get a son. It wouldn't be just any son, but one who would equal Indra in valour. That water had been meant for the king's wife, not him.

Second, the person who had drunk the water would be the one to give birth. If not his wife, then it would be Yuvanaashva himself. The water, sanctified with and infused with the power of Bhrigu's mantras, had acquired a potency that would see Yuvanaashva himself give birth to a son.

As fated, Yuvanaashva gave birth to a son, who emerged from the king's stomach. A son who was resplendent like the sun, truly Indra's equal. So much so that Indra himself came down to earth to see this boy, a boy that Bhrigu had proclaimed would be his equal. The newborn infant cried out for milk. Indra offered his finger to the infant, who suckled it. Indra proclaimed that this infant would be named Maandhaata.[2] The boy grew up, learned in the Vedas through the power of his thoughts, armed with a bow named Ajagava, and was instated on the throne by none other than Indra himself.

This was one of those rare occasions when the birth of a human deemed to be his equal by the sages did not elicit envy from Indra.

19

JANTU

One for a Hundred

Parva: Aranyaka (3)	Upa parva: Teertha-yaatra (33)
Chapters: 127-128	Shlokas: 40

Yudhishthira had asked Sage Lomasha about Maandhaata and Somaka. No sooner had Lomasha finished Maandhaataa's story than Yudhishthira asked the sage about King Somaka.

Dhritaraashtra may have had a hundred sons and one wife,[1] but King Somaka had a hundred wives but no son. His plight was similar to Yuvanaashva's in that respect. The years went on, but no son was born. Then one day, when Somaka had grown old, the stars and the gods took pity on his plight and a son was born. He was named Jantu.

The birth of a child after years of wait brought untold joy to the royal household. Expectedly, everyone doted on this child. What Jantu wanted, Jantu got, and why not—with a doting father and a hundred mothers, he was the apple of everyone's eyes. When Jantu laughed, happiness coursed through the palace. When Jantu cried, the palace was plunged in sadness. One day, an ant bit Jantu on his hip. Jantu cried out in pain. His mothers too cried, pained by their son's agony. Somaka too rushed to his son, consoling, comforting him. Soon enough, all was well. But the king was lost in thought.

> Shame on having a single son. It is better to have none.[2]

Somaka gathered his advisors and shared his thoughts. A hundred wives and only one son. Only one son on whom the hundred mothers doted. Both he and his wives had grown old. He then posed a question that was more than rhetorical.

'We have only one son. He is our life. None of us can bear to see him in any discomfort,' Somaka began.

'Yes, O King, your love for Jantu lights up this palace,' the officiating priest concurred.

'But only one son—just one. Look at how all our lives and happiness are tied to that one son. I am old, and so are my wives. And yet, only one son,' Somaka said.

The priest nodded. He didn't know where the king was going with this conversation.

'You know of many ceremonies and rituals, don't you?'

'Yes, O King,' the priest nodded.

'Can't you suggest something—big, difficult, I don't care—to get a hundred sons?'

The priest was lost in thought. He weighed the pros, he judged the cons, the dharma, the adharma. Finally, he spoke.

'There is, O king. But…,' the priest stopped.

'Whatever it is, I am willing to do it. As long as it gets me a hundred sons,' Somaka perked up.

'Yes, there is a ceremony. It is a sacrifice,' the priest dared not utter the words.

'Yes, yes, there is a ceremony—good! There is a sacrifice—good! Of course, there is an offering at yagna, isn't there. What is the hurdle?' Somaka was agog with anticipation.

'Jantu will be reborn, along with ninety-nine other sons. You will get your hundred sons.'

'Great!' Somaka said, and then paused. 'What do you mean, *reborn*?'

'It means Jantu will be the offering at the sacrifice. From the smoke of that sacrifice your wives will give birth to a hundred sons. Jantu will be one of them.'

Somaka sat, not knowing what to do. One son, the darling of the palace. One son, in exchange for a hundred?

'Is there no other way?' he asked.

'None other that I know of,' the priest answered.

'Then let it be. What has to be, to get what must be obtained, then to do what has to be done, must be done,' Somaka said.

The priest nodded. Yes, Jantu would be reborn. It was not his rebirth he was concerned with, however. Between death and rebirth lay an eternity.

The sacrifice commenced. Jantu was brought to the altar. The hundred mothers tugged at him, grabbed him, wouldn't let him go. But grabbing him by the left arm, the priest pulled him away, and he was offered to the sacrificial fire. Acrid smoke rose from the altar; the hundred mothers gathered there inhaled it and fainted, their grief unbound.

However, time passed. Ten months later, just as the priest had prophesied, a hundred sons were born to the hundred mothers. The eldest of the hundred was Jantu. As the priest had said, the son so born had a golden mark on his left side. All was well that ended well. At least, in this life.

The years passed and the chief priest succumbed to the laws of time. He was followed shortly thereafter by Somaka. In the afterlife, hell awaited them.[3] Somaka saw his chief priest being barbequed in naraka. Whatever for, the king wondered. Because he had, the priest replied, committed the sin of killing a child. As crimes went, this was one of the most heinous ones. Just a shade less reprehensible than the killing of a foetus, that Ashwatthaama had been guilty of. As had been his crime, so would have to be his punishment.

But that crime was not the priest's alone, Somaka argued. If the priest was guilty, so was he, the king. He had consented to and ordered that sacrifice. Somaka turned to Dharmaraja[4] and asked him to set his chief priest free. He would take his place instead, Somaka volunteered. No, that was not possible, Dharma replied. The priest may have committed the act, but it was at his behest, Somaka replied. The deeds were identical, and the punishment, therefore, too must be identical, the king argued. That was acceptable to Yama. King Somaka and his chief priest both suffered for an equal length of time.

No one ever obtains the fruits of someone else's action.[5]

Lomasha concluded by telling Yudhishthira that the hermitage they were all at was Somaka's hermitage. He suggested that they spend the next six nights there. They agreed. They had six nights and many years to pass in the forest.

SHIBI

Dharma and the Self

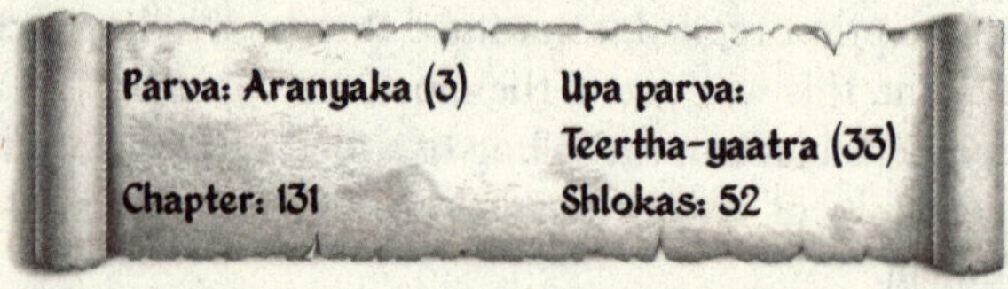

Their travels took the Paandavas to Kurukshetra, a place that had been sacred since time immemorial, and where the Paandavas would fight their biggest and bloodiest of all battles. At Kurukshetra, they were accompanied not by chariots and an army, but by Sage Lomasha, who told Yudhishthira that Daksha[1] had once said that those who die at Kurukshetra would go to heaven. He also pointed out the spot where River Saraswati went underground.[2] To the north, Lomasha pointed, was the region of Kashmir,[3] a region as sacred as any and the abode of many sages.

> The men who die here will have conquered heaven.[4]

King Shibi[5] had been praised by many as equal to a god. Indra, the king of the gods, decided one day to find out for himself, Lomasha began. Shibi at the time was holding a grand yagna. The test of Shibi's greatness would not be one of strength, but of dharma. Indra enlisted Agni's help in this test. Indra took the form of a hawk while Agni became a dove. Together the two descended on earth, the dove flying for dear life, the hawk in hot pursuit. Just when it appeared that the hawk would have the dove in its talons, the dove found refuge. It landed on Shibi's thigh. The hawk hovered overhead and then settled on a perch close by. The dove begged the king for protection from the hawk. The hawk watched.[6]

Seeing that neither would the dove move nor did the king show any inclination to disturb the bird, the hawk spoke. Why was Shibi interfering with the natural order of things—wasn't dove the natural food of hawks? Wasn't it adharma, to deprive it—the hawk—of his natural food? The hawk posed its questions to the king.

But wasn't it dharma to protect those who had taken refuge, Shibi responded. How could the hawk expect the king, the protector of dharma, to give up the dove which had taken refuge with him. Wasn't abandoning one who had taken refuge the biggest sin of all? When Maaya had taken refuge with Arjuna at Khaandava, hadn't even Krishna relented and spared the asura's life?

> Dharma that stands in the way of another dharma is not dharma at all. It is evil dharma.[7]

If it was a question of dharma, wasn't the king aware that it would die if it didn't get food, the hawk asked? If it died, so would its family that depended on it for sustenance. Wouldn't the king be responsible for those deaths? Would that be dharma? Wouldn't that be a greater adharma than handing over the dove to the hawk? What kind of dharma would it be that itself went against dharma? The king was stumped. The hawk asked the king to decide what was dharma in this situation. Presented with a dilemma most dharmic, how Shibi resolved it would be a test of his greatness. Indra, the hawk; and Agni, the dove; waited.

> O King! Not knowing a plantain tree, do not climb it.[8]

No ordinary bird could possess such wisdom; surely this was a god or Garuda in the form of a hawk, Shibi wondered. In any case, the hawk's dilemma was easily solved, Shibi responded. He was a king and had the resources of the entire royal kitchen at his disposal. Whatever the hawk desired would be cooked for it—a buffalo, deer, bull, boar, anything. No, no, no, no, and no—these were not the natural food of the hawk, it replied. Only birds, like the dove that perched on the king's thigh, were. The bird that the king was unwilling to part with. But Shibi was amenable to any other offer. The hawk took the king up on his offer.

The king could part with an amount of flesh equal to the weight of the dove. No adharma would happen then, surely. The king agreed. He placed the dove on one scale of a balance. He cut some flesh from his body and placed it on the other scale. The dove was heavier; the scales didn't balance. He cut some more flesh and placed it on the scale. The dove was heavier; the scales still didn't balance. There was only so much flesh Shibi could cut from his body. The dove sat on one scale, looking at Shibi. To what extent would the king go in upholding dharma? The hawk watched Shibi's flesh on the other scale, still lighter than the dove. Would Shibi give up?

Seeing the situation untenable, pieces of his flesh lying scattered and bloody on the scale, Shibi stepped up and stood on the scale—if his flesh didn't suffice, his entire body would have to. Dharma, when protected, would protect.

Indra was left speechless. The king had passed the test in a way they had neither expected nor imagined. Indra assumed his true form, as did Agni. The two blessed Shibi. His wounded, lacerated body became whole. Indra blessed Shibi with everlasting fame because of his deed. It was only by giving, wholly, unquestioningly—through his deeds—that Shibi demonstrated his greatness.

21

ASHTAVAKRA

An Age of Dharma

Parva: Aranyaka (3)	Upa parva: Teertha-yaatra (33)
Chapters: 132-134	Shlokas: 86

A deformed twelve-year old who had bested the most formidable intellect in the land. That lad was Ashtavakra and that was his and Shwetaketu's hermitage, Sage Lomasha pointed out to Yudhishthira. Who was Ashtavakra,[1] Yudhishthira asked.

Ashtavakra was Sage Kahoda's son. Who was Kahoda? He was Sage Uddalaka's disciple, and pleased with his knowledge and devotion, Uddalaka married his daughter, Sujata, to Kahoda. Uddalaka also had a son named Shwetaketu.

In due course of time, Sujata conceived and the unborn Ashtavakra started to grow in his mother's womb. Though they were poor, life carried on in the hermitage. Kahoda used to spend his time in rituals and studies. One night, he spent the entire night studying some texts, struggling with particularly difficult verses. The unborn Ashtavakra listened all night long. When morning came, a voice emerged from Sujata's stomach. It was that of the unborn Ashtavakra. The young one corrected his father. While his father had spent the entire night studying, he had still not grasped the meaning of the texts; the unborn corrected the twice-born. Kahoda's pride and ego couldn't bear this. He cursed his own son. Ashtavakra would be born crooked in eight ways.

Time passed. Sujata was due to give birth. A new-born would have material needs that the poor brahmana couple couldn't provide in their penurious state. Perhaps some help from the king can be solicited, she suggested. Kahoda pondered the point and agreed with his wife. Perhaps he could get some wealth from King Janaka. With that in mind, Kahoda proceeded to Videha where he was met, not by Janaka, but by the redoubtable Sage Bandi.

Bandi was no ordinary person—he was very, very skilled in debating, and he loved challenging sages to debate. Bandi challenged Kahoda.

'You are a very learned sage, O Bandi,' Kahoda began.

'Yes, I am,' agreed Bandi.

'How can I debate you?'

'Why would you not want to debate a learned person, O Kahoda? Or is your learning limited to rote memorization of texts?' smirked Bandi.

'But all I wanted…,' began Kahoda.

'If you want something, you should be prepared to give something. All I am asking is for some time from you, am I not?' asked Bandi.

Yes, that was true. What harm could a debate do?

'So do you agree to the debate?' asked Bandi.

He wanted money from the king. He needed it for his unborn child.

'I do, O Bandi.'

'Let us start,' Bandi smiled.

The debate was short. Bandi was a skilled debater. Kahoda soon conceded defeat.

'I have lost, O Bandi,' conceded Kahoda.

'That you have,' Bandi sat back.

'Now can I…,' Kahoda started.

'Yes, you may now know the stakes of the debate,' Bandi completed the question that Kahoda had not asked.

'The stakes?'

'Every debate has stakes, does it not?'

'Yes, I suppose it does. What do I give?' What did he have that Bandi could want?

'Your life.'

'What?' Kahoda's blood froze in his veins.

'Anyone who loses to me will also lose his life. There is a lake, the one you saw on your way in, and that's what you will enter to give up your life,' Bandi added helpfully.

'I never agreed to this!'

'Yes, you did, when you agreed to the debate,' reminded Bandi, getting up.

Kahoda sat frozen. But not for long. His fate sealed, he was taken to the lake nearby. Sujata was widowed. The unborn Ashtavakra was orphaned.

Ashtavakra was born, deformed in eight places, just as his father had cursed. He grew up under Uddalaka's care. He had Shwetaketu for company. The two were approximately the same age and Ashtavakra believed Shwetaketu to be his brother. He believed Uddalaka to be his father. Uddalaka had told Sujata not to share the truth with her son, his grandson. Sujata also couldn't bring herself to tell Ashtavakra that his father had died trying to get material comforts for him that she had asked him to go get. Life continued as best as it could under the circumstances. The years passed.

Twelve years had gone by. Memories of loss had faded to a dull ache of emptiness. Then one day Shwetaketu saw Ashtavakra sitting on Uddalaka's lap. Jealous, he pulled him away, saying that Uddalaka was his father, not Ashtavakra's. Children could be very possessive about their parents, after all. Hadn't Dhruva faced the same affront at the hands of his stepmother, Suruchi, and stepbrother, Uttama, when he had sat on the lap of his father, Uttanpaada?

A hurt and surprised Ashtavakra ran crying to his mother and asked who his real father was, where he was, and why wasn't he here, with them. A terrible secret that had remained unsaid in the hermitage for twelve years now spilled open. Ashtavakra listened as Sujata told him how his father had gone to Janaka's court, agreed to a debate with Bandi, lost, and had been ordered to drown as punishment.

Dhruva's journey had taken him on a quest of enlightenment and to seek Narayana himself.[2] What course would Ashtavakra take? Losing a debate was one thing, but to pay such a heavy price was manifestly unfair, Ashtavakra said. If the loss of debate meant death, then perhaps it was time Bandi found himself on the losing end. The son would avenge his father's death at the hands of a person as cruel as Bandi.

The young brahmana, Ashtavakra, would go confront Bandi. But he couldn't tell anyone about it, yet. So he went to his uncle, Shwetaketu, and told him it would be a good idea to go to King Janaka's court, for wise brahmanas aggregated there, and they would get to hear wise men chanting shlokas. And, of course, a king's court would also have delicious food. A young Shwetaketu found the proposition eminently agreeable, and the two children, not quite teenagers, and certainly not adults, set about their journey to Videha.

Along the way they came across a narrow path where the king was also coming, but from the opposite direction. Naturally, the king's guards asked the two children to make way for the king. A similar situation had arisen, hadn't it, when King Kalmaashpaada and Vasishtha's son, Shakti, had come face to face on a narrow path?[3] What would Janaka and Ashtavakra do in this case? As far as the young Ashtavakra was concerned, the rules of precedence were clear. He told the king that while the road belonged to everyone, precedence was to be given to a brahmana. Janaka was a wiser king than Kalmaashpaada; he agreed with Ashtavakra's reasoning, and his chariot made way for Ashtavakra.

> The road belongs to a blind one. The road belongs to a deaf one. The road belongs to a woman. The road belongs to a bearer of loads. The road belongs to a king. But when a brahmana is encountered on the way, the road must belong to the brahmana.[4]

At the palace gates, Ashtavakra and Shwetaketu were stopped by the gatekeeper. Two young children, unaccompanied by an adult, seeking to the enter the palace were surely up to some mischief. Ashtavakra told the gatekeeper that they had come as guests to witness Janaka's sacrifice. They also wished to meet the king. The gatekeeper refused. He was merely following instructions, not the king's, but Bandi's—learned brahamanas were to be admitted, but not brahamana children.

> If touched, a young fire also burns.[5]

If knowledge were the criterion, then they qualified, Ashtavakra reasoned, since they were learned.[6] It was the intellectual age that mattered, not merely the passage of years. Gray hairs were no indication of gray matter. But to have become learned at such a young age was unheard of, the gatekeeper responded. Be that as it may, Ashtavakra replied; the sages had not decreed that wisdom would accrue only to those whose hairs had turned white. The gatekeeper relented, and the two stepped foot in Janaka's court.

> One does not become old because one's hair has turned white.[7]

Once in Janaka's court, Ashtavakra addressed the king and revealed why he had come there—to debate Bandi, and to defeat him, much to Shwetaketu's surprise. Like the sun's brilliance made the stars bleach into the sky, so would his intellect vanquish Bandi. Shwetaketu understood; the son was in the king's court to avenge his father. He stood, silent, observing.

Janaka was taken aback. These were mighty words from a child! Perhaps the child didn't know the true might of Bandi's intellect. If someone chose to debate Bandi, adult or child, the loser's fate would be the same—death by drowning. Janaka didn't want a child to suffer such a fate. He tried to dissuade Ashtavakra.

Bandi may be wise, but he had not debated one like him, Ashtavakra averred. These words had been spoken by a great warrior in earlier times to a great warrior sage, and a frightful war had taken place that lasted twenty-four days—between Bheeshma and Parashuraama.[8] Was another battle about to be witnessed, this time, of intellects? If the child was adamant about debating Bandi, Janaka would not let that happen till he had satisfied himself as to the child's competence.

Janaka asked Ashtavakra what had six parts, twelve axles, twenty-four segments and three hundred and sixty spokes. Ashtavakra replied that it was time that had six parts (seasons), twelve axles (months), twenty-four segments (hours), three hundred and sixty spokes (days).

Janaka asked Ashtavakra more questions, to which Ashtavakra gave correct replies. Pleased and satisfied, Janaka allowed Ashtavakra entry to where Bandi was.

> When he meets me today, he will be destroyed, like a cart on the road with its axle broken.[9]

Ashtavakra entered the assembly and challenged Bandi. Bandi guffawed. He chided the young lad about wanting to take on the redoubtable Bandi.

> The extremely weak man is insolent and strikes a mountain, only to lacerate his hands and nails himself. No wounds can be seen on the mountain.[10]

Ashtavakra asked Bandi to desist from this meaningless palaver and instead start the debate. Each would ask a question; each would respond. His pride challenged, Bandi accepted the challenge. He had done what he could. The child's death would not be on his hands. The debate began.

Bandi started—there was one fire, one sun, one Yama, and one Indra.

Ashtavakra opened with his reply. Indra and Agni were two; there were two Ashvins; and the husband and wife were two.

Bandi took it to the next level. Beings were born thrice; there were three sources of light, and so on.

Ashtavakra talked about four directions, four varnas, and the four ashramas.

This went on. Neither Bandi nor Ashtavakra relenting. Both were learned, wise, and both knew the stakes.

Bandi said there were eleven sacrificial stakes and there were eleven animals used in the Ekadashi rite.

Ashtavakra responded that there were twelve Adityas, twelve months in a year.

Bandi started with the thirteenth shloka and then fell silent midway. He didn't know what completed it. He had never yet debated anyone where the back-and-forth had continued for as long. If Ashtavakra too didn't know, the battle would end in a stalemate. But what if Ashtavakra completed the verse..., Bandi wondered.

Ashtavakra resumed where Bandi had abandoned his shloka. There were thirteen syllables in the atichhanda meter, and Keshi had travelled for thirteen days.

The assembly of brahmanas was silent for a moment. It took some time for the import of what had happened to sink in. They had witnessed the undefeated Bandi just get bested by a child barely twelve years old. They burst into applause. Ashtavakra had won.

Janaka stepped in and declared that as Bandi had lost, he was Ashtavakra's to do as he pleased. Ashtavakra was clear—the dharma that Bandi had imposed on those who had lost was to be his now. Bandi replied that he was Varuna's son, that his father had been conducting a sacrifice that had lasted twelve years, that it was now drawing to a close, and that all the brahmanas who had lost and had been drowned in the lake would in fact be returning shortly.

Ashtavakra was unmoved—if Varuna was Bandi's father, then it was all the more reason for him to be drowned in the same waters that were his father's abode.

> To a weak one may be born a strong son, to a foolish one an intelligent one and to an ignorant one a wise one.[11]

Bandi, Ashtavakra, and others went to the lake. They stood waiting, and then, one by one, Kahoda and the other brahmanas emerged from the lake. Father and son had a tearful reunion. Bandi praised Janaka and returned to his abode, entering the same waters into which he had sent the defeated brahmanas for twelve years. Ashtavakra returned with his father, Kahoda, along with Shwetaketu.

22

YAVAKREETA

The Curse of Shortcuts

Parva: Aranyaka (3) **Upa parva:** Teertha-yaatra (33)
Chapters: 135-139 **Shlokas:** 123

After spending time at Shwetaketu's hermitage, the Paandavas and Sage Lomasha continued their pilgrimage, reaching a river that Lomasha pointed to Yudhishthira as the place where Indra had freed himself of the sin of killing Vritra. Not only was Sage Raibhya's hermitage present here, but it was also known as the spot where Yavakreeta, Bharadwaaja's son, had died.

A place where the venerable Sage Bharadwaaja's son had died must have had an intriguing history behind it. Yudhishthira posed his questions to Lomasha.

Bharadwaaja and Raibhya, Lomasha began, were two sages who were also the best of friends. While Raibhya had two sons, Arvavaasu and Paravaasu, Bharadwaaja had one son named Yavakreeta. The two sages, friends though they were, led very different lives. As he grew up, Yavakreeta noticed that his father was an ascetic and was content to be ignored by all. Raibhya and his sons, on the other hand, were visited by and honoured by brahmanas. The years went by, and Yavakreeta's rancour over this differential treatment grew. He too craved the attention that his father's friend, Raibhya, got. A day came when Yavakreeta could stand this no more.

Yavakareeta resolved he would obtain complete knowledge of the Vedas and become as great a sage as possible. To him too would people flock for learning. He too would become famous. To this end he repeatedly singed his body in a big fire. The gods would have to bestow the wisdom on him that he desired. He would not wait.

Sages performing great austerities were a constant source of worry for the ever-insecure Indra. Yavakreeta's penances, unusual though they were, were no different. Indra decided to investigate.

Employing a simple and direct approach, Indra went down to Yavakreeta and asked him why he was doing what he was doing. Yavakreeta replied he wanted to acquire the entire knowledge of the Vedas; and no, he had neither the patience nor the time to do so the traditional way by becoming a student of a learned preceptor and spending years and years and years under his tutelage. He wanted that knowledge, and he wanted it now. Indra reminded Yavakreeta that there were no shortcuts to acquiring knowledge. Having dispensed this advice, hopeful that it would dissuade Yavakreeta from his misadventures with fire, Indra departed.

Indra's hopes were belied. Repeatedly, Yavakreeta tormented his body, and repeatedly Indra tried to reason with him. One day, tired of this constant charade going on, Yavakreeta gave Indra an ultimatum—either Indra would grant him the knowledge he sought, or he would cut off his limbs and offer them into the fire. His death, a brahmana's death, would be on Indra's hands.

Indra did not want the sin of having caused a brahmana's death on his head. He knew what troubles brahmanas could cause, whether alive or dead. Chyavana, Agastya, Gautama, … the list was endless. Since arguing with Yavakreeta had had no effect, Indra decided to change tack. He took the form of an old and feeble brahmana and went to the banks of the Bhagirathi River. There he started scooping fistfuls of sand from the bank and flinging them into the river.

Soon enough Yavakreeta came by and saw the old brahmana engaged in what looked like a fruitless endeavour. Bemused, he asked the brahmana what and why he was up to. The brahmana replied that he was building a bridge across the river to ease the difficulties of passengers attempting to cross the river. Yavakreeta let loose a burst of raucous laughter, deriding the foolish brahmana, telling him for good measure that his was an impossible and fruitless task. The next instant the brahmana disappeared and Indra appeared in his own form. As Yavakreeta stood gaping, Indra told him that it was no more impossible than what Yavakreeta was attempting. There were no shortcuts.

Realization and a sliver of wisdom finally dawned on Yavakreeta. He posed a question to Indra—if what he was doing was impossible, then Indra, the king of the gods, should tell him what was possible. Indra told Yavakreeta that yes, the knowledge of the Vedas would manifest in not just him, but his father too. Indra went one step further. Not just the Vedas, but all other desires that Yavakreeta had would also be fulfilled. Indra departed, leaving behind a euphoric Yavakreeta. Ecstatic, Yavakreeta rushed to his father and broke the news of Indra's boon. Had Indra granted a boon or a curse in disguise?

They, Yavakreeta told his father, would soon be imbued with the knowledge of the Vedas. They would be better, superior, than the others, he said. His father, Bharadwaaja, far wiser than his young son, knew better. A boon obtained without effort was not a blessing. A boon as one obtained by Yavakreeta would have its consequences. Pride would overcome Yavakreeta, Bharadwaaja feared. With pride would come his downfall. What would come to pass had happened in the past, too. Bharadwaaja spoke about Sage Baaladhi.

Baaladhi was a sage who prayed to the gods to obtain an immortal son. The gods had the same answer for him that they had for everyone who had asked the same question—a mortal person was subject to the laws of time. Asuras had tried asking for such boons of immortality from the gods. Raavana, Hiranyakashyipu, Sunda and Upasunda, Madhu, Kaitabha, and many others. Perhaps Baaladhi thought himself wiser than those who had asked such boons. If he had a son, he would find a way to ensure his immortality, he declared. His son would have the same lifespan as the mountains around him. In due course of time, Baaladhi was blessed with a son named Medhaavi.

Medhaavi grew up and learned that his father had blessed him with a lifespan that was as good as immortality. With this knowledge came pride, for Medhaavi had earned this boon without any effort. With pride came insolence. Armed with a boon of near-immortality, Medhaavi developed a quick temper. Commoners or sages, he didn't hesitate to insult one and all. He was immortal, after all. Wasn't he? Who could harm him?

Almost immortal, completely insolent, one day Medhaavi came across a sage named Dhanushaaksha. True to his nature, Medhaavi insulted the sage. The sage, angered, cursed Medhaavi to be burnt to ashes. But Medhaavi stood unharmed, laughing. Medhaavi was protected by his father's boon, wasn't he? As long as the mountains stood, so would Medhaavi. For every curse, there was a cure; every boon of protection carried with it its own fatal flaw. Dhanushaksha goaded a herd of buffaloes to charge at those very mountains. People witnessed, but they could not believe the spectacle that unfolded before their eyes. The buffaloes charged, slammed against, and then crushed and trampled those mountains underfoot. Where there had been mountains, now stood a pile of rubble. As the mountains crumbled, so was Medhaavi's lifespan. The mountains came crashing down, and so did Medhaavi.

The sages who witnessed this were moved by Balaadhi's grief. They uttered a verse.

> Under no circumstances, can one who is mortal change his destiny.[1]

Concluding this cautionary tale, Bharadwaaja counselled his son Yavakreeta to never cross Raibhya's path or antagonize him, since the sage was not only very learned but also easily angered. Yavakreeta assured his father he would do no such thing. Promises were easier to make than to keep. Yayaati had learned this. So would Yavakreeta.

The wisest of counsel from the most sagacious of sages sometimes comes to naught in the face of pride. As fate would have it, Yavakreeta found himself at Raibhya's hermitage one day. The sage was not there, but his daughter-in-law was. Arrogance and desire generated the basest of emotions inside Yavakreeta. Approaching her, he told her to submit to him. Alone, defenceless, fearful of Yavakreeta and his power, she yielded to Yavakreeta, who violated her. His vile deed done, the impenitent Yavakreeta departed.

When Raibhya returned and saw his daughter-in-law weeping, he asked her what had happened. She told him what had transpired and of Yavakreeta's shameful act. To a sage or a commoner, to someone short tempered or not, Yavakreeta's was an unpardonable act. Enraged, Raibhya plucked a hair out of his locks and offered it to the sacrificial fire. Out of the fire arose a Krityaa[2] identical to Raibhya's daughter-in-law. Raibhya threw another lock into the fire and from it arose a fierce looking raakshasa. They asked Raibhya for instructions. He gave them only one directive—to kill Yavakreeta.

Hadn't something similar happened after Daksha's[3] sacrifice where Shiva had been insulted, and unable to tolerate her husband's humiliation, Sati had immolated herself?[4] From an enraged Shiva's locks had emerged two beings—Veerabhadra and Bhadrakaali, who Shiva had ordered to go kill Daksha.

Hadn't something similar happened in the Mahabharata itself? Hadn't Drupada, looking to seek revenge against Drona, got the sages Yaaja and Upayaaja to perform a yagna,[5] from which had emerged a son, Dhristadyumna, and a daughter, Draupadi? Hadn't Dhristadyumna killed Drona on the battlefield of Kurukshetra several years later, and hadn't Draupadi's insult at the Kauravas' hands resulted in the destruction of their entire clan on that same battlefield?

Tasked by Raibhya, the krityaa followed Yavakreeta, waiting for an opportunity. She succeeded in distracting Yavakreeta and took away his Kamandalu (water pot). Without his water pot, Yavakreeta was now unclean and vulnerable. The raakshasa took this opportunity and charged at Yavakreeta. Yavakreeta fled towards a pond, but that pond had dried up. There was no water for Yavakreeta to clean himself. He then ran to his father's hermitage, hoping to find refuge there. However, fate and time had willed otherwise.

A blind gatekeeper stood guard outside Bharadwaaja's hermitage. He stopped Yavakreeta.[6] The raakshasa meanwhile caught up with Yavakreeta and plunged its spear into Yavakreeta's heart, killing him instantly. Having accomplished their task, the raakshasa and the krityaa departed.

When Bharadwaaja returned and entered his hermitage, he saw something miss. He turned to the blind guard. The guard responded that the sage's dim-witted[7] son, Yavakreeta, had gone to Raibhya's hermitage and had been killed by a raakshasa.

Happy are men to whom sons have not been born.[8]

A heartbroken Bharadwaaja wept over his son's corpse. He lamented that despite warning him to not go to Raibhya's hermitage, Yavakreeta had, and he now lay dead. Raibhya had killed him, leaving the old sage without any support in his old age. He too would embrace death soon enough. But just as Raibhya had become the cause of Yavakreeta's death, so would Raibhya's own son soon kill him, he cursed.

Having cursed his friend, Bharadwaaja realized what he had done. Not only was his son dead, but in his anger, he had cursed his dear friend. Bharadwaaja couldn't take his burden of woes any longer. He cremated his son and thereafter, entered a fire, immolating himself.

Raibhya knew nothing of the events that had unfolded after Yavakreeta's death. He had been appointed the sacrificial priest for King Brihaddyumna's yagna. The king also appointed Raibhya's sons, Arvavaasu and Paravaasu, as assistants. One day, Raibhya stayed back at his hermitage. As night fell, Paravaasu too returned to the hermitage, tired and sleepy. His father had stepped out into the forest, covering himself in a black antelope skin. Mistaking his father for an animal, fearful for his own life, mistaking it to be a predator, driven by fate and propelled by Raibhya's curse, Paravaasu killed what he believed was a predator. Bharadwaaja's curse had come true. Paravaasu had killed his father.

When he realized his mistake, Paravaasu grieved over his dead father. What had been done could not be undone. He performed the last rites for Raibhya. As he sat grieving, he remembered that Brihaddyumna's sacrifice was still going on. Paravaasu hurried back. There he broke the news to his brother Arvavaasu that he had killed their father, by mistake. Events were about to take a very curious turn.

Paravaasu told his brother, Arvavaasu, that there were rituals left to be performed for their dead father and it was appropriate that Arvavaasu perform them. The brother agreed and added that he would also perform the rituals needed to atone for the sin of killing a brahmana on his brother's behalf. Arvavaasu departed and Paravaasu took over the rituals for Brihaddyumna's sacrifice.

After finishing the vows and rituals and rites, Arvavaasu returned to the site of the sacrifice. Paravaasu, however, told the king not to let his brother enter the site. His brother, Paravaasu averred, was a killer. He had killed his own father. Such a person had no business being anywhere near a sacrifice. The king's guards didn't let Arvavaasu enter, deriding him as the killer of a sage, ignoring his cries that he had observed the vow on his brother's behalf. The killer had successfully led the world to believe his brother was the culprit, not him.

No human could corroborate Arvavaasu's innocence. But the gods had witnessed the goings on. They manifested themselves.

Paravaasu was expelled from the sacrificial site, Arvavaasu was reinstated, and Agni himself granted him a boon.

What did Arvavaasu ask for? That first, his father, Raibhya, be brought back to life. Then, that his brother, Paravaasu, be absolved of the sin of killing a brahmana. And lastly, that both Bharadwaaja and Yavakreeta also be brought back to life. This tragic sequence of events had gone on far enough.

One last question remained. When Yavakreeta was brought back to life, he asked Agni and the other gods how had Raibhya managed to kill him. Weren't the Vedas manifest in him. Hadn't Indra himself blessed Yavakreeta with the boon of the Vedas?

Yavakreeta may have known the Vedas, the gods said, but that knowledge had been acquired the wrong way, without the guidance of a preceptor, and with too little effort. Raibhya, on the other hand, had learned the Vedas over after intense a long course of time, and under the tutelage of a guru. Nothing good came easy. Knowledge acquired the right way was superior to shortcuts.

23

VAINYA

An Indra among Kings

Parva:	Upa parva:
Aranyaka (3)	Maarkandeya-samasya (37)
Chapter: 183	Shlokas: 32

Arjuna was still gone on his quest to acquire the knowledge of celestial weapons in heaven. The Paandavas waited for their beloved sibling's return. They did not stop their travels, however. Draupadi once asked Bheema to get her some fragrant flowers the breeze had blown her way. That search took Bheema on a journey to Gandhamadana, where he came across his divine half-brother, Hanuman.[1]

> Amidst enemies, my body becomes gigantic through its own energy.[2]

Later, Bheema encountered and killed the raakshasa Jatasura[3] and had a duel with yakshas.[4] Bheema also killed a raakshasa named Manimana, a friend of Kubera.[5] Distressed and pleased in equal measure, Kubera met with the Paandavas. They learned from Kubera that Manimana had been cursed by Sage Agastya, and the redemption of the curse had been his death at a human's hands. Even Kubera had been cursed by Agastya, and to free himself from the curse required Kubera to meet the human who would kill Manimana. Five years passed.

After five long years, Arjuna returned from the heavens, escorted by none other than his celestial father, Indra.[6] Arjuna gave an account of his time in heaven, including his encounter with the nivatakavacha daanavas, whom he defeated as his guru dakshina to Indra.

> "O Yudhishthira! Perseverance, steadfastness, place, time and valour—these are the five principles that determine results in this world.[7]

Arjuna had returned after several years with much sought celestial weapons. Unable to contain his inquisitiveness at these weapons Arjuna had just described, Yudhishthira expressed a desire to see those weapons in action. Arjuna got ready to oblige. But before he could, the mountains shook, the wind stopped blowing, the sun no longer shined, and rivers and oceans quivered. Something was amiss. Even before the weapons had been discharged, their mere presence threatened to wreak havoc on earth. No less a god than Brahma appeared, accompanied by Shiva, Naarada, and other gods, intervening on behalf of all those who inhabited the world. Arjuna had to stop.

These were not toys to be brandished for whimsical reasons, or to satisfy someone's juvenile inquisitiveness, Naarada admonished Arjuna. These were divine weapons, not to be treated trivially. He then turned to Yudhishthira and told him to have patience and wait till Arjuna deployed those weapons in battle. There was a time and place for everything.

> Do not discharge these divine weapons. They should never be used when there is no target.[8]

After that, the Paandavas continued their travel, all five brothers and Draupadi, visiting King Subaahu. From there they proceeded to the banks of the River Saraswati. Bheema got encoiled by Nahusha. Nahusha was not only Paandavas' ancestor, but also a king with such great powers that he had been elevated by the gods themselves to become an Indra. However, pride became his undoing, and cursed by Agastya, he had been reduced to the state of a boa.[9] To save his brother, Yudhishthira engaged Nahusha in a debate. Yudhishthira would do the same again, that time to save all his four brothers.[10] At the end of the debate, Nahusha thanked Yudhishthira, for it had been foretold that it would be his descendant, Yudhishthira, who would free him from this curse. Reverting to his celestial form, Nahusha returned to heaven.

> Truthfulness and knowledge of the brahman can be found in all the four varnas.[11]
>
> If these traits, not even found in a brahmana, are seen in a shudra, he is not a shudra. A brahmana in whom a brahmana's traits are not found, is a shudra.[12]

The Paandavas returned to the Kaamyaka forest, just in time for the rainy season, which brought respite from the summer heat to all.[13] There they were visited by Krishna and his wife, Satyabhaama. While the Paandavas and Krishna engaged in a conversation, Sage Maarkandeya arrived there. Upon the Paandavas' request, and Naarada's approval, Maarkandeya agreed to share words of wisdom with them.

Maarkandeya was a worshipper of Shiva, and whose blessings had saved him from the clutches of Yama. His wisdom and knowledge were unparalleled. The unjustness of the Kauravas' deeds still rankled Yudhishthira. That the Kauravas had suffered no consequences for their evil deeds troubled Yudhishthira. He shared his thoughts with Maarkandeya.

> How can the good and evil fruits of an embodied being follow him in this body and how are they united with him after death? Do we reap the fruits in this world or in another world after death?[14]

Not just humans, but what happened to the deeds committed by animals is what Yudhishthira wanted to know from the sage. Deeds followed a person, even animals, like a shadow follows the body, Maarkandeya replied. Some of what happened to beings was because of fate, some by accident, and some because of one's own karma. The ones who stayed devoted to dharma enjoyed both the current life and the next. Those addicted to desires enjoyed neither.

In response to Yudhishthira's next question, Maarkandeya elaborated on the greatness of brahmanas.[15]

Once there was a king and there was a sage. Vainya[16] was the king. Wise, knowledgeable, and regarded as a rajarshi, he once conducted a horse sacrifice.[17] On the completion of such rituals, it was a practice for kings to donate wealth, in the form of cows, gold, and other valuables, to brahmanas present there.

Atri[18] was the sage. His wife suggested that her husband go to the sacrifice and obtain the wealth that Vainya would donate. It so happened that Atri, at one point, had also wanted to go to this sacrifice for the same reason—to obtain wealth. However, upon reflection, he had concluded that in his stage of life, his dharma didn't require him to have this wealth. Therefore, he had retired to the forest. But circumstances had changed.

The demands of dharma had changed, his wife told him. They needed some wealth to distribute among their sons and servants. Atri rethought his decision. This was wealth not for himself, but for reasons that were entirely consonant with dharma. There was, however, one catch.

Vainya himself was a noble king, well-versed in dharma. The problem was the company he kept, Atri said. He was surrounded by brahmanas who hated him—so Sage Gautama had told him. Atri wanted nothing to do with those sages. He would go and bless the king with wise words on artha, dharma, and kaama. But things were not so simple. The brahmanas present there, out of spite, would either argue with him or contradict him. That bickering would render the entire exercise futile, he said. However, Atri maintained, there was wisdom in what his wife had said; hence, he would go to Vainya's yagna. What had to happen would happen.

Atri left for the sacrificial site. Once there, he praised Vainya as the first among all kings. As expected, he was contradicted. The surprise was that it was Gautama who spoke out against Atri. Gautama's retort was that Indra was the greater of the kings. Atri responded that Vainya sustained the earth as much as Indra did the heavens. Gautama responded, but not to Atri's argument, but with an ad hominem attack on Atri. Gautama held Atri to be immature and lacking wisdom. Atri opined that it was Gautama who was ignorant and deluded. Gautama countered that Atri had grown old but still remained a fool; the implication being that intellectually, Atri was a juvenile. A veritable shouting match ensued between the two, in full sight of all the other brahmanas. The cacophony of the fracas reached Vainya's ears.

At that moment Sage Kashyapa intervened. Gautama told Kashyapa and the assembled sages that he and Atri were arguing over whether Vainya was as great a sustainer of dharma as Indra. To resolve this, they all decided and agreed to go to Sage Sanatkumara,[19] who they all considered to be learned, and who they agreed could adjudicate between the two sages.

Sanatkumara replied that the king, as the ruler, was like Shakra (Indra), Shukra (preceptor of the raakshasas), and Brihasapati (preceptor of the gods). How could the king, adorned and addressed with appellations such 'the conqueror in battle', 'the fortunate one', 'the one who propagates dharma and truth', not be great, he asked? Therefore, Sanatkumara said that he favoured the sage who had spoken for the king; viz., Atri.

Vainya was much pleased with this resolution, and with Atri's forthrightness in the assembly of brahmanas. He showered wealth and gifts upon Atri, who returned and distributed them among his children, and having completed this last pending act of dharma, retired to the forest.

24

MATSYA

The Law of the Jungle

Parva: Aranyaka (3) **Upa parva: Maarkandeya-samasya (37)**
Chapter: 185 **Shlokas: 54**

After finishing Vainya's account, Sage Maarkandeya told Yudhishthira about goddess Saraswati's reply to Sage Tarkshya on the prescribed behaviour for a person on earth, lest he stray from the path of dharma.[1] When Maarkandeya had finished, Yudhishthira requested the sage to talk about Vaivasvata Manu.

Vaivasvata Manu was so named because he was the son of Vivasvat.[2] Manu was a great sage (literally, a maharshi). Like sages, he too meditated deep and hard. He practiced his austerities in Badari under a vishaala[3] tree, standing on one foot, head facing down, clad in a wet bark.

It was when Manu was immersed in these austerities that a small, tiny fish swam up to him on the banks of the River Virini and asked him to protect her. Why? Because there were bigger fish in the river that would, otherwise, eat it up. Why? Because that was the rule of the fishes—the bigger fish ate the smaller fish. Not just the rule of fishes, but this was also the practice in societies where dharma had decayed and where the king had abdicated his duties.

> It is the rule among fish that large fish prey on smaller ones.[4]

The fish asked Manu to protect; it would return the favour. How could a fish as tiny as the one that had swum over to Manu help and protect him was a baffling question.

Vaivasvata Manu was a compassionate sage. He took pity on the fish and placed it in a small water pot. Manu took care of the fish, and over time, the fish grew, to the point where the pot was not big enough to hold it. Manu took the fish out of the pot and placed it in a large pond where it would be safe. The fish lived in that pond, feeding, but still growing. The years passed. The fish didn't stop growing. It now had become too large for even that large pond. The fish again spoke to Manu, asking that he place it in the Ganga. Manu took the fish to the Ganga. The fish lived there, still growing. Eventually, it was too big for it to move around comfortably in the Ganga. Eventually, it was time for it to find a bigger pond, a larger river. There were none—neither a larger pond nor a bigger river. Manu took it to the ocean. By now Manu had realized this was no ordinary fish; certainly, no fish he had seen, heard of, or known.

Once in the ocean, the fish looked at Manu with kindness and gratitude and said what it had been waiting to say all these years. The time and moment were now ripe. The end of the world was nigh; everything was going to be destroyed. What needed to be saved, what needed to survive to the next cycle of creation, Manu would have to save. The fish asked Manu to build a sturdy boat and tether it with a rope. In the boat, the fish continued, Manu was to first place the saptarishis,[5] followed by all the seeds that the fish mentioned. Manu collected all that the fish had instructed him to and set sail on the ocean. At the right time, the fish reappeared, large as a mountain, and now sporting a huge horn on its head. To this horn, Manu attached the rope. The boat was now tethered to the fish's horn.

A great storm raged in the ocean and in the swirl of the waters; nothing except the fish, Manu, and the sages could be seen. The world was immersed in water—the earth, the heavens. Time and space ceased to exist. For years that no one counted, the fish pulled the boat. Till one day when the fish pulled the boat to the highest peak of the Himalayas. In that great swirling ocean of possibilities, only the peak of the Himalayas was visible above the water. The fish asked Manu to tie the boat to the peak. Since then, the highest peak of the Himalayas has also been known as nau-bandhana.

It was then that the fish revealed itself to be none other than Prajapati Brahma.[6] He tasked Manu with creating all beings. To enable him to do that, Brahma infused Manu with the powers of creation. The cycle of creation began afresh. The asuras, devas, humans, the worlds, and everything mobile and immobile, sprang into existence. This was the account of Vaivasvata Manu, Maarkandeya concluded.

25

MANDUKA

As was the Seed, So was the Fruit

Parva: Aranyaka (3) Upa parva: Maarkandeya-samasya (37)
Chapter: 190 Shlokas: 82

Yudhishthira's next question was as expansive as one could imagine, for he asked Sage Maarkandeya to talk *about the reasons behind everything.*[1] Or the question was as precise as could be, for the answer to that one question would answer any other.

Maarkandeya, however, did not get into the details of 'everything'. He nonetheless talked about the yugas, which encompassed everything. He talked about the age of yugas—krita yuga, spanning four thousand years, and which was both preceded and followed by a twilight[2] period lasting four hundred years each, and where dharma stood on four legs[3], like a bull; treta yuga, spanning three thousand years, preceded and followed by a twilight lasting three hundred years each, and where dharma stood on three legs; Dwaapara yuga, spanning two thousand years, preceded and followed by a twilight lasting two hundred years each and where dharma stood on two legs; and finally Kali yuga, spanning one thousand years, preceded and succeeded by a twilight lasting one hundred years each, and where adharma had taken away three legs, leaving dharma to stand on only one leg.[4] This added to a total of twelve thousand years.

> People who are devoted to dharma, decay. The evil ones prosper. Dharma loses its strength and that which is not dharma becomes powerful.[5] Overcome by the burden of taxation, brahmanas will flee in the ten directions.[6]

After Maarkandeya had finished, Yudhishthira asked him a question on the greatness of brahmanas, again. Maarkandeya had expounded on the same subject in the Vainya upakhyaana,[7] but he nevertheless began his answer afresh by talking about a king of Ayodhya named Pareekshit,[8] from the Ikshvaaku lineage. One day, on a hunt and in pursuit of a deer, he became tired and thirsty and found himself in a forest with many trees and a large pond. There he quenched his thirst and rested. As he lay there, resting, he heard a beautiful and melodious song wafting through the air.

Looking around, he saw a beautiful woman singing. Immediately and completely lovestruck, Pareekshit spoke to her and expressed a desire to marry her. The maiden agreed but put forth a condition that the king take an oath to never show her water. The king agreed, not pausing for a second to consider the outlandish nature of the request.

In short course, his soldiers caught up with Pareekshit. As per the king's instructions, they arranged a palanquin for the maiden, and together all returned to the capital. The king spent his time with the maiden, in private, away from prying eyes, and away from water. Soon enough, the king's prime minister became worried enough with the king's absence from matters concerning the kingdom to come over and inquire from the women who attended on the king.

The women apprised him. The prime minister, learning from the women attendants that no water was to be brought there, had a grove built with beautiful trees and flowers, but with no water, and invited the king and queen to spend time there. At least the king would spend time outside the palace, even if it was in a private grove, without water.

Events, however, have a way of taking their own twists and turns. One day, as the king and queen strolled around in the large grove, they came across a cluster of creepers. Entering it, they came across a pond. A pond with water. The king saw it; the queen saw it. The king had forgotten about the oath he had taken—the one where he had promised to never show the queen any water. The king suggested to his queen that they enter the pond. The queen agreed and entered the pond. The king waited. The queen didn't emerge from the pond. The king waited some more. No queen.

A frantic king summoned his soldiers and had them empty the pond. The soldiers got to work. Soon enough the pond was empty; only dank, soggy, slippery mud remained. And a hole. And a frog at the mouth of the hole. But no queen. The king, earlier frantic with worry, then eager with anticipation as the pond was emptied, and now driven to beyond the edge of frustration at not finding his beloved queen, assumed, somewhat irrationally, that the frog had killed or eaten the queen. Pareekshit flew into a most frightful rage and ordered that for the alleged, unproven crime of one frog, all frogs be killed. He even decreed that anyone coming to meet him had to bring a dead frog as a tribute.

With this began a slaughter of frogs. In desperation, the frogs approached their king, who decided to appeal to Pareekshit. There was one hitch in this plan. If the king of the frogs stepped into the king's court in the form of a frog, he was liable to be killed much before he could get a chance to open his mouth, and it would be his corpse that would parlay with the king. He, therefore, decided to take on the form of an ascetic and went to meet Pareekshit.[9]

Aasteeka had approached Janamejaya's sarpa-satra, requested him to stop this sacrifice of snakes, and succeeded. As Takshaka lay suspended mid-air, Vaishampaayana had narrated the history of Janamejaya's ancestors. Would the king of the frogs succeed in stopping another slaughter?

In Pareekshit's court stood the king of the frogs, disguised as a hermit, beseeching the king to put an end to this senseless slaughter. Pareekshit refused, and there the matter stood. The ascetic, bereft of all options, chose to reveal what he had been hoping to keep hidden from the king. He disclosed to Pareekshit that he—the ascetic—was the king of the frogs, that his name was Ayu, and that the queen who had married Pareekshit and then disappeared in that fated pond was none other than his daughter, Sushobhana. She, Ayu told the king with a heavy heart, was in the habit of deceiving kings, and Pareekshit had only been the latest in a long line of people she had taken for a ride. Perhaps, Ayu hinted, the king would be better off without the queen.

No, never; it didn't matter, responded Pareekshit, for he loved her and desired her. Seeing the king's persistence, Ayu brought his daughter to the palace and told her to be with the king and serve him, and to desist from any misadventures. Pareekshit was overcome with joy, emotion, and gratitude. The royal edict on the matter of the slaughter of frogs was rescinded. He then prostrated himself before Ayu, his father-in-law. Ayu blessed him and departed, but not before prophesizing that since Sushobhana had deceived many and uttered many lies, her sons would be hateful towards brahmanas. With those fateful words hanging, Ayu left.

Time passed and the king and queen had three sons—Shala, Dala, and Bala. The years rolled on and it was time for Pareekshit to hand over the reins of his kingdom to his eldest son. He instated Shala, the eldest one, as the king, and then retired for the forest.

Once, on a hunt, Shala spotted a deer. He shot an arrow at it, but the deer sprinted away. Shala urged his charioteer to pursue the deer. The charioteer obeyed, but the deer was faster. Shala ordered his charioteer to go faster. The charioteer demurred, for those horses that Shala's chariot was yoked to couldn't go any faster. Only Vaaamya horses could go fast enough to catch the deer, the charioteer replied. Time's arrow, once fired; and words, once uttered, cannot be taken back. The charioteer had a sense of foreboding that he had started a most fateful chain of events with his words. Neither his words nor time could be turned back, however.

What were Vaamya horses, Shala wondered out aloud. It was not a rhetorical question. But the charioteer kept quiet. Shala suspected his charioteer knew more than he was letting on. Not for Shala were the ways of persuasion. He threatened his charioteer with the death penalty because, of course, he could—he was the king. The charioteer was now caught between the devil and the deep sea. On the one hand, if he kept quiet, Shala would kill him; on the other hand, if he did open his mouth, who knew what the consequences would be. Choosing to save his life, he told the king what he knew—that the Vaamya horses belonged to Sage Vaamadeva.[10]

Shala ordered his charioteer to steer his slow horses towards Vaamedeva's hermitage. Had Ayu not prophesied that Pareekshit and Sushobhana's sons would be deceitful towards brahamanas? Was Shala not the eldest son? Was Vaamadeva not a brahmana? Was there any reason Ayu's words would not come true? Was Shala now not headed towards Vaamadeva's hermitage?

Once they reached Vaamadeva's hermitage, Shala asked the sage to lend him two of his famed Vaamya horses so he could catch the deer he had been hunting. The sage agreed but asked the king to return the horses as soon as he was done with them. Talk was cheap. Shala agreed. The sage handed the king his horses. The king took the horses and went in pursuit of the deer.

The horses' gait and speed were as his charioteer had described. These horses were just what would befit a king. Doubts and dishonesty entered Shala's mind. After all, didn't everything in the kingdom belong to the king? After all, what use could a brahmana have for such speedy steed? Having convinced himself thus, Shala pursued and caught the deer, and then returned to his capital, with the Vaamya horses.

Vaamadeva waited for the king to return the horses he had borrowed. And he waited. When a month had passed and the king had still not returned the horses, Vaamadeva asked his disciple Atreya to go Shala and ask him to return the horses. The king sent Atreya back with the message that brahmanas had no use for horses and that he, the king, was keeping what in any case belonged to the king. True to Ayu's prophesy was Shala's behaviour.

Atreya returned and conveyed Shala's message to Vaamadeva. This breach of promise, by none other than the king—the protector of dharma—did not go down well with Vaamadeva. The annoyed sage made his way to Shala's court and demanded that the king, a descendant of the famed Ikshvaaku lineage, keep his word.

The sage had a point, Shala reasoned. After all, he had taken something that had belonged to Vaamadeva. No, the horses would stay with him, but he offered Vaamadeva bulls, donkeys, ordinary horses—anything but the Vaamya horses.

> 'O Sage, what do you need horses for?' asked Shala.
>
> 'What do you mean, O King?' Vaamadeva asked, seeing the smirk on the king's face.
>
> 'Why do you need horses to carry you? Don't the words of the Vedas bear brahmanas like you?' Shala said, letting out a chuckle.
>
> 'Are you mocking me?' asked Vaamadeva.
>
> 'Why would I mock you, O Sage?'
>
> 'The Vedas bear me, O King, but only in the next world. Return the horses, as you had promised, and honour the kshatriya code and your lineage's steadfastness to truth.'
>
> 'I will give other horses, I will give you bulls, whatever you want. I am not returning those horses to you.'

> The chants indeed bear someone like me, but that is in the next world.[11]

Vaamadeva lost his patience and temper. He cursed Shala that he would be killed by giants made of iron and wielding spears who would slice his body into four pieces. Even as the two were arguing, raakshasas[12] emerged and wielding spears, hacked the king to death, whose last words were that come what may, he would never give the horses up as long as he lived. True to his word, as long as Shala lived, he did not part with the horses.

With Shala dead, Dala was instated as the king. The Vaamya horses were still with the king. Vaamadeva now went to Dala and repeated his request for his horses to be returned. If Shala had been something of a reprobate, Dala was even worse.

> 'Ha! Return those horses to you, O Sage?' spat Dala.
>
> 'Yes, those were my horses. Your brother, Shala, had promised to return them. He didn't. He is dead because of my curse. Now I am asking you, the king, to return those horses,' Vaamadeva replied.
>
> 'Guards!' Dala shouted. 'Bring me the sharpest of arrows dipped in the most virulent of poison. I will stab this wicked sage with my own hands and then sit back to watch you die a miserable death.'
>
> Vaamadeva looked in disbelief at the king.
>
> 'And then,' Dala was not done yet, 'I will feed your body to dogs. Yes, that is what I will give you. No Vaamya horses for you!'

Vaamadeva pronounced a second curse now—that the king's ten-year old son would soon be killed by the king himself. Refusing to pay heed to the brahmana's words or learn a lesson from his elder brother's fate, Dala shot an arrow at Vaamadeva. Driven by destiny and Vaamadeva's curse, the arrow instead killed the king's ten-year old prince.

But Dala was not done yet. Despite having lost his elder brother and now his son, he asked for even more poisoned arrows. Vaamadeva replied that the king would not even be able to release those arrows, let alone shoot them.

Soldiers brought more arrows to Dala. Dala took them and that was all he could do. He found himself paralyzed. He could not move, much less release those arrows. Finally, Dala admitted defeat.

Vaamadeva asked the king to touch his queen with the poisoned arrow to free himself from his sin. The queen then asked Vaamadeva for his blessings. The sage blessed the queen and returned with his Vaamya horses.

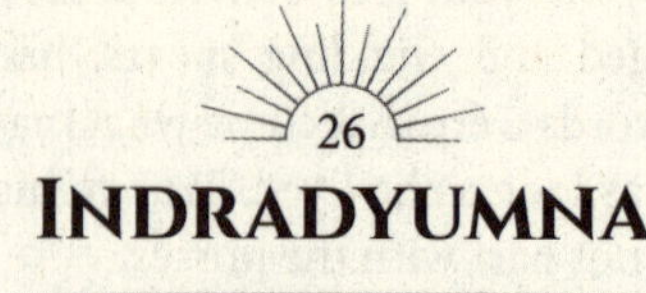

26

INDRADYUMNA

The Life of Deeds

Parva: Aranyaka (3) **Upa parva:** Maarkandeya-samasya (37)
Chapter: 191 **Shlokas:** 28

As Sage Maarkandeya finished his account, the sages and Paandavas assembled there asked him a question—was there anyone who had a longer life than him?

Maarkandeya pondered over the question and after some thought, replied that yes, there was one such person—a rajarshi named Indradyumna. After death he had gone to heaven. But, as was the course of heaven, when Indradyumna's store of merits was exhausted, so was his stay in heaven, and he fell back to earth. He wandered around, trying to remember who he was, searching for someone who would recognize him.

His search brought Indradyumna to none other than Maarkandeya. The sage looked at Indradyumna and thought long and hard but could not recall who the king was. No, he had not heard of Indradyumna. Perhaps a wise owl named Praakaarakarna, who lived far away in the Himalayas, did.

Indradyumna took the form of a horse and carried Maarkandeya there. They reached the Himalayas and Indradyumna posed the same question to the owl. Praakaarakarna thought long and hard and then shook his head. No, he too didn't know who Indradyumna was.

If Maarkandeya didn't know who Indradyumna was, and if the owl Praakaarakarna didn't know who Indradyumna was, then perhaps someone older than even the owl may. The owl again reflected on the king's question and then came up with a name—a crane named Naadijhangha[1] who lived in a lake. The name of the lake? Indradyumna, coincidentally, or not.

With renewed hope, Indradyumna took both Maarkandeya and the owl to the lake, for the owl too was curious to know. In any case, Indradyumna, Maarkandeya, and Praakaarakarna reached the lake named Indradyumna. They posed the same question to the crane. The crane, Naadijhangha, however, also had no memory of Indradyumna. But, like both Maarkandeya the sage and Praakaarakarna the owl, Naadijhangha too had a suggestion. There was a tortoise named Akupura who lived in the same lake. Perhaps the tortoise who lived in the lake named Indradyumna would know something about the king named Indradyumna. The three agreed. The crane called out the tortoise's name.

Akupura the tortoise heard its name being called out. It craned its neck out and emerged from the lake. It ambled toward the four. Maarkandeya, Indradyumna, Praakaarakarna, and Naadijhangha all asked it the same question—had he heard of Indradyumna the king? They looked expectantly at the tortoise, who was now lost in thought. After a long time, the long, lost memory of the name surfaced, and the tortoise became emotional. Of course, yes, he had heard of the king. Wasn't Indradyumna the same king who had conducted a thousand sacrifices, and who had given away so many cattle at these sacrifices that this very lake had been formed from the hooves of the cattle he had given away? Ever since he, the tortoise, had dwelt in this lake so formed from the king's generosity.

So, yes, someone did remember the king. For long beyond a person's life on earth, his generosity and its memory are what lived on.

As Akupura's, the tortoise, words rang out, a celestial chariot descended from the heavens, ready to escort Indradyumna back to heaven.

Thus, Markandeya did his bit to restore Indradyumna back to heaven. Even though he had led a long life, he had not heard of Indradyumna's deeds till then. So yes, there was someone older than even him.

The words about sacred deeds touch the heaven and the earth. As long as there is their sound, so long does man live.[2]

27

DHUNDHUMAARA

Smoke and Fire, and an Asura

Parva: Aranyaka (3) Upa parva: Maarkandeya-samasya (37)
Chapters: 192–195 Shlokas: 125

The questions for Sage Maarkandeya kept coming at a furious clip. First about Vainya, then about Matsya, followed by Manduka, and then Indradyumna—the sage had recounted four upakhyaanas in rapid succession. No sooner had Maarkandeya finished telling those assembled about Indradryumna than Yudhishthira asked him why Kuvalaashva had been renamed as Dhundhumaara.

Who was Kuvalaashva? He was a king in the Ikshvaaku lineage, just as Pareekshit in the Manduka upakhyaana had been, and was a ruler of Ayodhya. How had Kuvalaashva descended from Ikshvaaku? The lineage could be traced as follows: Ikshvaaku's son was Shashaada; his son Kakutstha; Kakutstha's son, Aanena; his son, Prithu; his son, Vishvagashva; his son, Aardra; his son, Yuvanaashva;[1] his son, Shraavasta; his son, Brihadashva; and finally, Brihadashva's son was Kuvalaashva.

Who was Dhundhu? He was an asura, and the son of Madhu and Kaitabha.[2]

How did Kuvalaashva get the name of Dhundhumaara—which meant, literally, the slayer of the formidable asura, Dhundhu? The implication was that Kuvalaashva had killed Dhundhu; but how?

For that, Maarkandeya said, one had to go to a time and place when Sage Uttanka[3] sat immersed in penances in his hermitage, in the middle of a desert, to appease Vishnu. Pleased with Uttanka's austerities, Vishnu appeared before him. Delighted at beholding the Lord, Uttanka recited many shlokas in Vishnu's praise,[4] at the end of which the lord granted Uttanka a boon. The sage considered Vishnu's vision as boon enough, but Vishnu insisted. Uttanka then asked Vishnu that his mind be always centred on the lord, on dharma, truth, and self-control.

Vishnu not only granted this boon but also told Uttanka that because of the powers of yoga that would manifest themselves in the sage, he would also become the vehicle for the destruction of a powerful asura named Dhundhu at the hands of Kuvalaashva.

Eventually, in the lineage of Ikshvaaku was born Kuvalaashva as the son of Brihadashva. Eventually, Brihadashva instated his son as the king and retired for the forest. When Uttanka heard the news, he went to meet Brihadashva at his hermitage and tried to dissuade him from this act of renunciation. He told the king that protecting his subjects was the dharma of kings and he would be ill-advised to discard such a course of action.

> There is no dharma that can be seen, which is like protecting the subjects.[5]

Who was Dhundhu? Near Uttanka's hermitage was a huge desert called Ujjaanaka and in which lived a daanava named Dhundhu. Dhundhu lived underground and was the son of Madhu and Kaitabha, two asuras who had been disposed of by Vishnu. It was their son who was creating havoc. If the king wanted to retire to the forest, Uttanka argued, he should do so only after killing Dhundhu. Not the gods, not the daityas, nor the raakshasas or nagas or yakshas or gandharvas could kill him. Which meant that the task of killing Dhundhu had to fall on a human.

Dhundhu was no ordinary demon. So great was his power that he could hold his breath for long periods of time. When he did breathe out, once a year, the exhalation caused the earth to shake for seven days. If the king was not strong enough to take on Dhundhu, Uttanka continued persuading Brihadashva, he would give his own energy to the king. It was what he had obtained as a boon from Vishnu. Brihadashva could meld it with his own. Perhaps that would be enough.

Brihadashva listened patiently to all that Uttanka said. He told the sage that it would be his son who would be the one to kill Dhundhu since he himself had laid down weapons and wouldn't pick them up again. Disappointed though Uttanka was, he left with the knowledge that his visit had not been in vain. The path to Dhundhu's destruction now looked clearer.

Yudhishthira by this time was very curious to know how Dhundhu had become so powerful as to be out of the reach of the gods themselves. It had so happened, Maarkandeya explained, that at the time of the dissolution of the world, when nothing existed, Vishnu once slept, on Shesha, alone in the ocean. From his navel emerged a lotus, from which emerged Brahma. While Vishnu slept, two daanavas, Madhu and Kaitabha, saw Brahma emerge from the lotus and stalked him. This commotion woke Vishnu up.

Upon seeing Madhu and Kaitabha, Vishnu[6] granted them a boon. Drunk with power and deluded with arrogance, they scoffed at Vishnu's offer and instead told Vishnu to ask them for a boon. Well, if that's what the asuras wanted, that was acceptable to Vishnu. The lord responded that his wish was to kill the two of them for the welfare of the world. Would Madhu and Kaitabha grant Vishnu this boon?

The two asuras were cornered. They hadn't expected Narayana himself to take up their offer, but a boon was a boon. The two daanavas granted Vishnu the boon but added a rider that he should do so only at a spot that was uncovered by water. This posed a problem, for the entire universe was submerged in water; there was not a dry spot to be found. After looking around everywhere, Vishnu looked down on his thighs, which were dry. He dragged the two daanavas to his thigh and sliced their heads off with his chakra.

Madhu and Kaitabha had had a son named Dhundhu. He prayed to Brahma and got a boon, much like Raavana, that he couldn't be killed by the gods, daityas, raakshasas, nagas, yakshas, or the gandharvas.

Armed with the invincibility of this boon, Dhundhu defeated the gods and the gandharvas. He then went to the expanse of sand named Ujjaanaka and hid himself there to acquire more powers through austerities.

Time passed. One day, Kuvalaashva, Brihadashva's son, came to Uttanka's hermitage there along with his sons. Taking advantage of the opportunity and Vishnu's boon, Uttanka requested Vishnu to infuse Kuvalaashva with his energy. Even the gods, maharshis, and gandharvas assembled to watch the looming battle between Kuvalaashva and Dhundhu.

Kuvalaashva had the place dug up and after seven days, Dhundhu was unearthed. Dhundhu awoke from his austerities and launched an assault on Kuvalaashva's soldiers. Kuvalaashva repulsed Dhundhu with arrows and spears and other weapons, all of which Dhundhu swallowed. Flames emitted from his mouth which burnt up all of Kuvalaashva's twenty-one thousand sons. Such was the spectacle that it was reminiscent of Kapila's[7] wrath or of Kumbhakarna being awakened from his slumber.

Kuvalaashva doused Dhundhu's flames with jets of water that spouted from his body. Finally, after a long and fierce encounter, Kuvalaashva unleashed the brahmaastra. Dhundhu fell.

From that day on, Maarkandeya concluded, Kuvalaashva came to be known as Dhundhumaara.

28

VYAADH GITA

What is Dharma

Parva: Aranyaka (3) **Upa parva: Maarkandeya-samasya (37)**
Chapters: 196-206 **Shlokas: 433**

Yudhishthira now turned to the topic of women and their greatness. Much later, he would pose a very different question about women to Bheeshma.[1] But for now, Yudhishthira was fascinated by the question of women's greatness. Hadn't one, his wife Draupadi, rescued them from the calamity they had found themselves in? Yudhishthira's opinion was that staying devoted to husbands seemed a difficult task. Damayanti had managed it despite Nala's passion for gambling. Draupadi had stayed faithful, despite Yudhishthira gambling her away. Perhaps other women were not as strong. Women also bore children, underwent great difficulties, pain, and brought their children up with a lot of love. He wanted to know from Sage Maarkandeya the greatness of devotion to husbands.[2] Maarkandeya began speaking.

> Some hold the mother to be superior, others the father. However, the mother performs the most difficult task, she propagates the species.[3]

It was a devoted wife's rebuke that sent a learned sage named Kaushika on a journey to the city of Mithila where a hunter educated him on the infinite subtleties of dharma. Where did this hunter come from, who was he, who was Kaushika, who was the wife who rebuked him and why? Expounding, Maarkandeya told Yudhishthira that there was once a learned brahmana named

Kaushika. Once when he sat under a tree, a female crane perched on a branch of the same tree dropped some faeces on top of him. Angered, Kaushika dropped the bird dead with his angry stare. However, the next instant he was overcome with remorse at his rashness. But what was done was done.

> After undergoing such great difficulties, one obtains a son, difficult to obtain, and one wonders about what this son will end up doing.[4]

Pensive, regretful, and still lost in thought at his actions, Kaushika walked about in the village, begging for alms. He came to a dwelling where the lady of the house asked him to wait while she cleaned the vessel used for giving alms. While she was doing this, her husband returned and the wife tended to her husband first, following her dharma. She gave him water, seat, and food. She waited on him as he ate. The brahmana was neglected as a result. When her gaze finally fell upon the brahmana, still waiting at the door, she was mortified at this unintentional lapse.

> The gods know him to be a brahmana, who is in control of his senses, is devoted to dharma, is always engaged in studying, is pure and is in control of desire and anger.[5]

She went out to give alms to Kaushika. The sage's temper, meanwhile, had started to rise once more. Straightening himself up with self-righteous indignation, he berated the woman. It was not proper, he said, for her to have asked him to wait and then kept him waiting for as long as she had. The wife replied that she had got busy serving her husband—her greatest god. Kaushika was not impressed and reminded her that a brahmana's anger, like a fire, could burn down the entire world. And he was angry. And she was the cause of his anger. The wife accepted the potency of the anger of brahmanas, citing the example of the fate of Dandaka and Vaataapi. But the true brahmana was one who had controlled his anger and was not provoked.

> It is evident that dharma can be seen in many ways and that it is subtle.[6]

But there was more, the wife continued. The brahmana didn't seem to be well-versed with the true nature of dharma, she declared.

Oh yes, he was learned and well-read, but literacy and wisdom were two separate things, weren't they? Yes, he possessed the anger to bring down a crane, but he didn't have the traits of a true brahmana.[7] To learn about dharma, she advised the brahmana to go to Mithila and meet a hunter there who could educate Kaushika about the true nature of dharma.

Kaushika was stunned by the woman's injunctions. She not only knew about his act of rashness against the bird, but she had not been daunted by the brahmana's anger or his implied threat. Anger had dissipated and had now been replaced by inquisitiveness. Who was this hunter in Mithila who seemed to be so knowledgeable about dharma? Kaushika thanked the lady and announced he was leaving for Mithila to improve himself.

After a long journey, Kaushika finally entered Mithila, then ruled by King Janaka. He walked in that beautiful city, with large roads teeming with horses, chariots, carts, and elephants; buildings and dharmic institutions that lined the roads, and masses of people milling about who looked cheerful and happy. Kaushika walked around, asking people about the hunter. Yes, the brahmanas knew who the hunter was, and pointed him the way. Kaushika made his way to the hunter's shop, this great ascetic who knew dharma. He saw the hunter and paused. There was the hunter, seated in a slaughterhouse, surrounded by the carcasses of deer and buffaloes, with blood, skin, and gore strewn all around, with a line of buyers queued up. This was the person who would instruct Kaushika on dharma. Kaushika waited, bemused.

Soon enough someone informed the hunter that a brahmana had come to see him. The hunter got up, stepped out, and greeted Kaushika. Yes, he knew who had sent Kaushika, and why. Kaushika was taken aback, again. The hunter suggested that they talk at his house and not in the slaughterhouse. Kaushika thought that to be a most amenable suggestion. Once at the hunter's house, they sat down and started to talk.

Kaushika was disappointed that a person supposed to be as learned as the hunter had to make a living through such a profession as the selling of meat, spending his time in the middle of a slaughterhouse, surrounded by meat, skin, and worse. No, he didn't feel any sorrow, much less shame, in this profession, the hunter replied. It was his ancestral profession and he practiced it as per his dharma.

> The deeds performed earlier, always follow the actor.[8]

Wasn't what he was doing wrong? No, said the hunter. He lived in Janaka's kingdom, he reminded Kaushika. A king as true to dharma as Janaka would have stopped him from pursuing a line of profession if it went against dharma. He hadn't, had he? The king, the hunter said, was such that he would punish even his own sons, were they to stray from the path of righteousness. The hunter said that neither did he kill the animals whose meat he sold, nor did he himself eat meat.

As Kaushika listened, the hunter expounded on dharma. Compassion, donations, devotion and adherence to dharma were paramount. A liar and evil person were like a bag full of air. A dharmic person, on the other hand, was given neither to boasting nor repeated a sin if he committed one.

> Just as wells are covered by grass, evil ones cloak themselves under dharma.[9]

The brahmana asked the hunter how to recognize righteous conduct. The hunter said that the righteous served their elders, gave up greed, arrogance, and anger. Steadfast in their dharma, they sought out those who were equally devoted to dharma.

> Sacrifices, donations, austerities, study of the Vedas and truthfulness—these are the five sacred things that always characterize good conduct.[10]

Theists were humble, had righteous conduct, honoured brahmanas, and entered heaven. Atheists, on the other hand, were cruel and crossed limits of righteous behaviour.

> Dharma is the conduct of the righteous and the righteous are characterized by their conduct.[11]

Yes, though he neither ate meat nor killed animals, his was still a terrible profession. The hunter was paying for his past karma. But how could this profession be as per dharma, the brahmana wondered. So much violence was unacceptable, Kaushika averred. Was it, asked the hunter?

As to the deed of killing animals, the hunter said that in King Rantideva's[12] kitchen, two thousand animals were sacrificed every day. Yet the king's fame was unmatched. Hadn't King Saudasa[13] turned a man-eater on account of a curse? The hunter said that a person who ate meat according to rituals was considered a vegetarian.

> It is considered to be adharma to give up one's own dharma.
> It is certainly dharma to adhere to one's own dharma.[14]

> Men who are righteous do not praise other righteous ones. Relatives do not praise relatives, even if they are prosperous. Foolish ones, thinking themselves to be learned, criticize preceptors.[15]

What act did not involve violence and killing? Cultivating did, eating did, walking did, even breathing involved violence. Even the virtuous occupation of agriculture, the hunter started, involved the killing of many insects as the ground was ploughed. Even when trees were cut and herbs plucked, it involved the killing of organisms that grew on trees and fruits. Even the mere act of walking on the ground meant trampling underfoot insects on the ground. Knowingly and unknowingly, acts of violence were committed by people. Where would one draw the line?

> Many things can be said about the dharma or adharma of our deeds. But he who adheres to his own dharma attains great fame.[16]

Was this dharma or adharma? What was the brahmana's view on all this, asked the hunter. In the view of the hunter, the course of dharma was subtle. A person obtained the fruits of one's deeds, but that was only if those deeds didn't depend on anything else. Past deeds determined and explained facts that were contrary. If everything could be determined by a person's actions and past deeds played no role, then no one would be unhappy in this world. Those with tasty food in front of them would not suffer the irony of indigestion. A person was never every truly the complete master of his own fate.

> There are those who endeavour a lot and obtain nothing. Wretched ones worship the gods and perform austerities to obtain a son. They remain in the womb for ten months and are born, but turn out to be a stain on the lineage. Others enjoy the riches, grain and objects of pleasure accumulated

> in immense quantities by their fathers and obtained through auspicious means.[17]

The body was perishable, but the soul was eternal. Determined by past deeds, the soul took birth again. Past deeds determined the new birth,[18] in which new karma was accumulated, and the chains of bondage continued. It was by following one's own dharma that one obtained happiness and fulfilment.

> The course of dharma is subtle. It has many branches and is infinite.[19]

Engrossed, Kaushika now asked what the senses were and how they could be controlled. The hunter said that the properties of the five elements—sky, wind, fire, water, and earth—were sound, touch, shape, taste, and smell, respectively. The hunter said that it was the mind that generated perception. From perception were generated desire and anger. From desire and anger came attachment, avarice, and delusion. With all this, only a pretence of following dharma is practiced. Sin in thought, speech, and deed are committed, and companionship with similar, evil-minded people is all one gets.

> There is no end to dissatisfaction.[20]

The hunter then moved on to talking about the properties of the five elements. Sound, touch, form, taste, and smell were the properties of the earth. Water had all these properties except smell. Fire had sound, touch, and form. Air had the properties of sound and touch, whereas the sky had only sound. These five elements were universal. What these five senses created was the manifest;[21] what the senses could not grasp formed the unmanifest.[22] If a person could rise above the senses, he could be united with the brahman. The senses, when controlled, led to heaven, if not, to hell. Bringing these senses under control was the key to yoga.

The hunter then drew an image for the brahmana. The body was like a chariot, the senses like the horses, the soul controlling them. If the senses ran wild, like horses on a road, one lost one's intelligence and became like a boat being tossed by the wind.

> It has been seen that a man's body is like a chariot. The senses are like horses and the soul controls them.[23]

Having listened to all this, the brahmana now asked the hunter to talk about the qualities of sattva, rajas, and tamas. The hunter replied that defining characteristic of tamas was ignorance, while action was the characteristic of rajas. Sattva had the characteristic of illumination. A person under the influence of tamas was ignorant, lazy, foolish, prone to anger and dreaming. A person under the influence of rajas was prompt in action and speech, without enemies, hardworking, and proud. A sattvic person persevered, wasn't attached to anything, and was wise and self-controlled.

The brahmana's next question to the hunter was what happened to the fire in the body when it was combined with the elements of the earth. The hunter gave a lengthy response to the brahmana's question, detailing the different fires in the body and how they functioned. Tamas, rajas, and sattva were the attributes of life, he said.

> One must always protect austerities from anger. One must protect one's riches from envy, one's learning from vanity and insults and one's soul from distraction.[24]

The brahmana marvelled at the hunter's knowledge of dharma and complimented him. At the hunter's invitation, the brahmana now entered his house where he saw the hunter's parents. He paid them respects and the parents inquired of the brahmana's welfare. The hunter said that whatever he did was to serve his parents.

> It has been said that a man prospers through five gurus—the father, the mother, the fire, he himself and the preceptor.[25]

The hunter told the brahmana that it was through his dharma of devotion and austerities that he had gained the knowledge he had and that is why the devoted wife had asked Kaushika to go to Mithila and meet him. He then told the brahmana that he had left his house without his blind parents' permission, even if it was to go study the Vedas. He asked the brahmana to go back to his parents and to serve them, for there was no greater dharma than that.

> Grief is a terrible poison.[26]

The brahmana was grateful to the hunter for having saved him from a hell into which he had been unknowingly descending.

But one question still nagged—the hunter was knowledgeable, adhered to dharma, and yet he lived the life as a shudra. Surely this must have been the result of past karma, the brahmana speculated.

The hunter replied that he had been a brahmana in his earlier life, well-versed in the Vedas and Vedangas.[27] He had also been friends with a king and had learned archery as a result. Once on a hunt with the king, the brahmana shot an arrow to kill a deer, but ended up piercing a rishi. Paandu had committed the same sin and had been cursed. In this case, the rishi cursed the brahmana to be born as a hunter in the next life, just as Animaandavya had cursed Dharma himself to be born as the son of a maid. Wise, but fated to serve those less knowledgeable than him.

The brahmana begged forgiveness from the dying rishi, that it was an act of ignorance. The rishi relented. He said that even though the brahmana would be born as a hunter, he would still remember his previous life. The brahmana then took the arrow out of the rishi's body and took him to his hermitage, where he recovered.

> I think him to be a brahmana who becomes a brahmana because of his conduct.[28]

The brahmana took leave of the hunter and returned to his village, back to his parents. He now knew what dharma was and followed it assiduously. A path that had been forged from an angry stare, on which he had been set upon by the devoted wife of a householder, and which had led him to a discourse on dharma finally ended at his parents' house.

29

MUDGALA

The Man Who Spurned Heaven

Parva: Aranyaka (3)	Upa parva: Vreehi-Drounika (41)
Chapters: 246-247	Shlokas: 83

After Sage Maarkandeya had finished talking about the Vyaadh Gita, which had started with Yudhishthira's question to the sage about the greatness of women and their devotion to husbands, he talked about the origins of fire and the different kinds of fires that existed.[1] He also told Yudhishthira and the assembled Paandavas about the origins of the birth of Kartikeya.[2]

There was a short discussion between Draupadi and Satyabhaama.[3] While the Paandavas lived in Dvaitavana, the Kauravas decided to initiate a journey to the forest.[4] Ostensibly, it was to see the cowherds assembled in the forest, but the real intent was to gloat over the plight of the exiled Paandavas.

The principal instigator here was Karna, again. Just as he had goaded Duryodhana in the game of dice, so did he provoke Duryodhana here also.

> Go there with your supreme prosperity and torment the sons of Pandu with your energy, like the sun. You are established in your kingdom and they have been dislodged from their kingdom. You have wealth and they are deprived of wealth. They are without prosperity and you are full of prosperity.[5]

It wasn't enough for Karna that Duryodhana now ruled over the Paandavas' kingdom also, and that the treasury was under his control; he had to see for himself the destitution of Yudhishthira, Arjuna, Draupadi, and others.

> The birth of a son or the obtaining of a kingdom does not bring as much bliss as seeing one's enemies in misery.[6]

Karna even provided Duryodhana with an excuse to go to the forest—the assembly of cowherds in Dvaitavana. Dhritaraashtra, the blind king, turned a blind eye, as usual, and gave Duryodhana permission. The 'dushta chatushtaya'—the gang of the evil four: Duryodhana, Duhshaasana, Karna, and Shakuni—proceeded to the forest. There, they ran afoul of the Gandharvas who were encamped there. There was an altercation, which escalated into a skirmish, and which culminated with Duryodhana and Duhshaasana being taken prisoner by the Gandharvas.[7] Against the assault of the Gandharvas, the Kaurava army, along with Shakuni and Duhshaasana, fled. While Karna fought the Gandharvas for some time, he too couldn't withstand their onslaught and use of magic; he also fled,[8] leaping onto Vikarna's chariot and whipping the horses into flight.

The Kaurava army's soldiers ran for help—to the Paandavas. Yudhishthira was in the middle of a sacrifice, so he couldn't go to the Kaurava's help, but he asked Bheema and Arjuna to do so. The two brothers got the better of the Gandharvas, who confessed they had had no intention of killing Duryodhana. They had merely captured him to hand over to the Paandavas. Upon Arjuna's request, they freed Duryodhana and the others, who returned shamefaced.

Even after this humiliation, Duryodhana remained implacable. He still wanted to best the Paandavas, go one up on Yudhishthira. He got the idea of equalling Yudhishthira by performing the Rajasuya yagya. He was, however, told by brahmanas that as long as Dhritaraashtra and Yudhishthira were alive, he couldn't perform that same sacrifice. He could, instead, perform another sacrifice—the Vaishnava—which was almost equal in fame to the Rajasuya. When a messenger sent by Duhshaasana went to the Paandavas to invite them for the sacrifice, Bheema gave him a piece of his mind. The Vaishnava sacrifice was completed without the Paandavas.

> Dharmaraja Yudhishthira will go when that king has been hurled into a flaming fire lit with weapons and missiles.[9]

Eventually, the Paandavas decided to leave Dvaitavana. Partially this was because of all the events that had taken place there, but the trigger for the decision was a dream[10] that Yudhishthira had where deer appeared and told him that their numbers had greatly dwindled on account of the hunting of deer. Yudhishthira decided to leave. They proceeded to the Kaamyaka forest.

Eleven years had passed since the Paandavas had been living in the forests and travelling. One more year and they would have to spend the thirteenth year incognito, in a public place, and yet remain undiscovered. The consequences of being discovered would be calamitous.

One day Vyaasa came to visit the Paandavas. When Yudhishthira asked him about the relative difficulty of the dharma of giving and austerities, Vyaasa invoked the name of the ascetic Mudgala[11] who gave up even the one pot of rice on which he subsisted.[12]

> It is said that nothing is more difficult in this world than giving.[13]

Mudgala, started Vyaasa, was an ascetic who lived in Kurukshetra. He would subsist on grains of rice he would go around collecting and with that he would feed himself, his wife and son, as well as the gods and any guests that came. The wondrous fact about this way of life was that whenever Mudgala gave without envy, the store of grains left over would only increase further.

One day Sage Durvaasa, known for his short temper and propensity to deliver fearsome curses when angered, went to Mudgala and told him he had come there for food. Mudgala gave him water to wash his feet and mouth, as was the custom, and then gave him the food he had collected. Durvaasa ate all the food there was and smeared the leftover food on his body and left. There was nothing left for Mudgala and his family. He returned the next day and ate all the food there was, again. Mudgala was left without any food, again. For six days did Durvaasa come and eat the food there was. Yet the sage could detect no anger, resentment, or disrespect in Mudgala's mind.

> Hunger drives away all sense of dharma and removes self-possession.[14]

Durvaasa told Mudgala that even though it was very difficult to part without rancour that which had been acquired with great difficulty, the ascetic had nonetheless done just that. Pleased, Durvaasa told Mudgala that he would ascend heaven in his own body, something even Trishanku[15] had failed to achieve.

> It is difficult to give up with a pure mind that which has been earned through labour and misery.[16]

A celestial chariot appeared, and the messenger of the gods told Mudgala to ascend the chariot to go to heaven. Before he ascended the chariot, Mudgala asked the messenger to describe for him heaven, the qualities of the people who resided there, the happiness one experienced in heaven. Mudgala also wanted to know the drawbacks of residing in heaven, if any.

The messenger was taken aback at Mudgala's question. After all, who would hesitate to accept an invitation from the gods to go to heaven, and that too in their own body? The messenger wondered out aloud why Mudgala was hesitating in accepting such a great honour. He said that those who had practiced the best of dharma went to heaven and that gods, maharshis, gandharvas, apsaraas, and others lived there. In heaven, there was no disease, hunger, thirst, cold, heat. Fragrances pervaded heaven as did pleasant sights and sounds. The drawbacks, Mudgala asked again.

There was heaven, the messenger said, and beyond that was Indra's world, and beyond that lay Brahma's world, where the gods of the gods lived. These gods of the gods did not have a physical form, and neither happiness nor unhappiness tormented them. But what about the drawbacks?

Well, yes, there was a drawback, the messenger confessed. Once the fruits of a person's deeds had been completely consumed, there was a fall. To enjoy the fruits of heaven, one had to pay in the form of fruits earned from good deeds performed on earth. Eventually, the store of good deeds would run out. When that happened, those in heaven would fall. Having experienced the pleasures of heaven, this would cause fear and uncertainty among the residents. Thus dislodged, these people would undergo rebirth.

> It has been said that this is a world of deeds. The next is one of fruits.[17]

Mudgala heard all this and pondered the matter over and concluded that if this was how heaven worked, he did not want to ascend to heaven. With the inevitable fall that loomed, there would be unhappiness. The thought would keep gnawing at the back of his mind. He did not desire such a heaven. If there was a heaven he aspired to, it was one where there would be no unhappiness, misery, or a dislodging once a person had reached it.

> Happiness follows unhappiness and unhappiness follows happiness in circles around a man, like the rim of a wheel.[18]

Mudgala gave permission to the messenger of the gods to depart. He returned to his life of collecting grains for subsistence. Such a person was Mudgala.

30

RAAMA

A Precedent of Misfortune

Parva: Aranyaka (3) Upa parva: Draupadi-harana (42)

Chapters: 257-276 Shlokas: 727

While the Paandavas lived in the Kaamyaka forest, there was yet one more indignity Draupadi had to suffer. Jayadratha, king of Sindhu and husband to the lone Kaurava sister, Duhshala, spotted Draupadi in the Kaamyaka forest.

> Now that I have seen this lady, all other women seem like monkeys to me.[1]

The king of Sindhu took a fancy to Draupadi and tried to persuade her to abandon the Paandavas and go off with him.

> One should be united with a husband when he is united with prosperity, but no longer reside with him when the fortune is destroyed.[2]

When she refused, he forcibly carried her off in his chariot. When the Paandavas returned from their hunt, they saw the hermitage abandoned and in a state of disarray. Upon learning from her maid that Jayadratha had kidnapped Draupadi, they set out after him. Bheema and Arjuna caught up and decimated Jayadratha's retinue. Bheema shaved Jayadratha's head, leaving only five tufts of hair. They carried him back to Yudhishthira and Draupadi, where he was finally set free.[3] Jayadratha would learn no lesson; he would instead pray to Shiva to take his revenge on the Paandavas.

After the Paandavas had foiled Jayadratha's attempt to kidnap Draupadi, Yudhishthira was again saddened by the turn of events. He lamented to Sage Maarkandeya that Draupadi had to suffer all this even though she had been righteous in her conduct and steadfast in her dharma. He wondered if there had ever been any man more unfortunate than him. It was not as if Yudhishthira was bemoaning his fate for the first time. He had expressed a similar sentiment years ago when their exile had commenced.[4] The years had passed, but there seemed to be no end to the woes afflicting Yudhishthira.

> Is there any other man who is more unfortunate than I? Have you seen, or heard of, any such one earlier?[5]

The Lord of Lanka

Sage Maarkandeya, who had assembled there along with other sages, responded with an account of Raama, the scion of Ikshvaaku.

Raama's wife, Jaanaki, was abducted by Raavana, king of Lanka. He carried her off to Lanka after killing Jataayu. It was only through Sugreeva's help that Raama was able to kill Raavana, destroy Lanka, and bring her back. There had been Nala, who too had suffered on account of his addiction to gambling; and now there was Raama, who too had to go through trials and tribulations. Sage Brihadashva had told Yudhishthira who Nala was. Now Yudhishthira wanted to know from Maarkandeya about Raama. Who were Raama, Seeta, Raavana, Sugreeva, Hanuman?

Maarkandeya gave a quick rundown of the principal characters in this saga. There was Raama—the son of King Dashratha. Dashratha was the son of Aja, of the Ikshvaaku lineage. He had four sons through three wives—Raama, the eldest, through Kaushalya; Bharata through Kaikeyi; and the twins Lakshmana and Shatrughna through Sumitra. Seeta was the daughter of Janaka, king of Videha, and had been created by none other than Vishwakarma, the celestial architect.

As for Raavana,[6] he was the great grandson of Brahma himself. Brahma had a son named Pulastya, who had a son named Vaishraavana.[7] For some reason, Vaishraavana chose to stay with his grandfather, Brahma, abandoning his father, Pulastya. In anger, Pulastya created another son named Vishrava from half of his body, from the emotion of anger. Brahma meanwhile granted the boon of immortality to Vaishraavana. Vaishraavana had a son named Nalakubara and ruled over Lanka.

Kubera, in an effort to keep his father in good spirits, sent three raakshasis to serve him. These were Pushpotkata, Raaka, and Malini. Pushpotkata gave birth to Kumbhakarna and Raavana,[8] Malini to Vibheeshana, while Raaka gave birth to Khara and Shoorpanakha.

Raavana was the eldest; Kumbhakarna was the strongest and adept at using maaya; Khara was very good with the bow, hated brahmanas and ate raw flesh; Vibheeshana was the most handsome; Shoorpanakha loved creating obstacles in religious rites. Nonetheless, all of them were learned and knew the Vedas. Yet, all, except Vibheeshana, were of an evil bent of mind.

Once these sons of Vishrava saw Kubera at Mount Gandhamadana and became envious of his prosperity. They were not strong enough to usurp that wealth, yet. They resolved to pray to Brahma and gain boons from him. After all, boons gained from gods were the surest path to prosperity and power. While Raavana, Kumbhakarana, and Vibheeshana prayed, Shoorpnakha and Khara served the three.

A long period of penance passed, but Brahma did not manifest himself before the three. Raavana became frustrated. He cut off one of his ten heads and offered it to Brahma. He then cut off a second head and offered it to Brahma. He then cut off a third head. And then a fourth.[9] He was following the same path as Yavakreeta. Yavakreeta wanted the supreme knowledge of the Vedas, and he wanted it without the time and effort that was required, and if the gods wouldn't oblige, he would coerce them, badger them. Raavana wanted power, and he would compel Brahma into acceding. Brahma relented. Brahma manifested before the brothers. The time for praying had passed; now was the time for asking for boons.

What would these sons of raakshasis ask for? Even before they could ask, Brahma granted two boons to Raavana—that he would regain the heads he had offered as oblations to the fire and that he would be able to assume any form he wanted. The first boon made Raavana whole again. The second boon would enable him to spirit off Seeta many years later, setting off a chain of events in motion that would culminate in his death. In Brahma's boon lay Raavana's destruction.

Even before they could ask, Brahma put forth one condition—they could ask for anything except immortality, for raakshasas and asuras had a habit of asking for immortality, and gods had had to refuse. Sunda and Upasunda[10] had done so, Hiranyakashyipu too had had the same ask of Brahma, and even Sage Baaladhi[11] had thought he had outwitted the gods. Brahma thought it best to nip any such designs in the bud. The asuras, however, decided to be clever; too clever by half.

If not immortality, then the next best would have to do. Raavana asked for and was given invincibility against gandharvas, gods, asuras, yakshas, raakshasas, serpents, kinnaras and demons—all except humans. Raavana didn't ask to be invulnerable against humans; for humans were too puny to be considered a threat to the invincible raakshasa. Furthermore, Raavana was a man-eater—he considered it infra dig to ask for protection from his prey. Would a lion ever ask for protection from deer? Raavana's ego wouldn't allow him. His ego would also be his downfall.

Next came Kumbhakarna. He asked to be able to sleep for long periods of time. Brahma granted that boon—it was perhaps one of the easiest, and most confounding, of boons the grandfather had granted. But if sleep was what the most powerful of the raakshasa brothers wanted, then that is what he would get.[12]

Vibheeshana didn't ask for immortality; he didn't ask for invincibility; he didn't even ask for a boon to sleep as much as he wanted to. But he did ask for two boons. First, that his mind never strays from dharma; and second, that the Brahmaastra weapon be manifest inside him. Brahma granted him both boons, and then added a third one. Brahma granted Vibheeshana immortality. What he had told the three brothers to not ask for, he granted it to the third. Vibheeshana had not asked for it, and perhaps that was the reason why the most dharmic of the siblings got blessed with the boon that his siblings and other raakshasas had craved for, but never obtained.

Armed with Brahma's boons, Raavana set on his campaign to become the lord of all there was. The brothers first turned on their own relatives. They defeated Vaishraavana and snatched his Pushpaka vimaana from him. Then they drove him out of out of Lanka. Yes, Raavana had become the new owner of the famed Pushpaka vimaana, but at a terrible price, for a furious Vaishraavana cursed Raavana.

> This will not bear you. It will carry the one who will kill you in battle.[13]

The raakshasas and pishaachas instated Dashaanan[14] as their king. Intoxicated with power and the ability to assume any form, Dashagreeva plundered the wealth of the gods. Great was the terror he wreaked upon the worlds. Raavana's deeds were true to his name—he caused the worlds to scream out in terror.

From Ayodhya to the Forest

What Brahma's boon had wrought; the gods decided Brahma would only have to end. Agni led a group of sages to Brahma. Agni lamented before Brahma that it was on account of his boon that Raavana could not be killed by the gods. Yes, that was true, Brahma concurred. But if the gods could not kill Raavana, Brahma told Agni,[15] then a human it would have to be. That human would be none other than an avatara of Vishnu. Vishnu had, in fact, already descended on earth to complete this task. The gods could still help, however. Brahma asked the gods to also take birth on earth as sons of monkeys and bears to aid Vishnu in his task. The gods, gandharvas, serpents all readily complied.

All that was needed to kill Raavana was being done. But nothing could be left to fate. There had to be a reason for Raama to confront Raavana in battle. Brahma asked a gandharvi (gandharva woman) named Dundubhi to take birth as a hunchbacked named Mantharaa.

Maarkandeya said that Raama grew to be a dark-complexioned, strong, and broad-chested handsome youth. With the passage of time, his father, King Dashratha, decided that he had become old and that it was time to instate Raama as the heir apparent. He called his priest and asked him to make the preparations for Raama's coronation. Bharata was away at the time.

Mantharaa—the gandharvi that Brahma had asked to take birth as Mantharaa—overheard this and rushed to Kaikeyi's chambers. There she instigated the queen. Relentlessly, she pushed all the buttons that she knew were sure to work on Kaikeyi—Dashratha's young, beautiful, envious, and ambitious queen, who was also Bharata's mother. If Raama became the heir apparent, that would be the end of the good life that Kaikeyi had enjoyed thus far, wouldn't it? Her status would be relegated to a secondary, inferior, queen. Kaushalya, Raama's mother, would be the dominant queen then, wouldn't she? The heir apparent's mother would enjoy an exalted status compared to other queens, wouldn't she? What about Kaikeyi's cherished son, Bharata? With Raama as the heir apparent, he would no longer be one among equals, wouldn't he? Her dream of seeing Bharata become king would remain just a dream. On and on went Mantharaa. Her incendiary words lit a fire of insecurity in Kaikeyi, just as fate demanded, just as Brahma had willed, just as the gods had hoped for.

Kaikeyi put on her best jewellery and went to Dashratha. There she reminded the king of the boon he had once granted her. Of course, he was a man of his word, Dashratha assured Kaikeyi. He belonged to Raghu vamsha, who were known to keep their word, even if it was at the cost of their lives. Kaikeyi demanded that Bharata be crowned heir apparent, and that Raama be exiled to the forest for 14 years. Fourteen years would be sufficient time for Bharata to consolidate his hold on the throne and for the people of Ayodhya to forget Raama. A grief-stricken Dashratha watched as Raama went to the forest, accompanied by Seeta and Lakshmana. The wheels of fate had turned once more, as the gods and fate had willed and waited for.

A heartbroken Dashratha died grieving for his beloved Raama. When Bharata returned to Ayodhya and Kaikeyi asked him to become the king, now that all obstacles to the throne had been removed, an appalled Bharata berated his mother for being responsible for not only her husband's death but for also destroying the entire family line. To become king by depriving his beloved brother Raama of his right was farthest from Bharata's mind. Distraught, Bharata left for Chitrakoota to bring Raama back, taking Kaushalya, Sumitra, Kaikeyi, Shatrughna, Vashishtha, and others with him. Raama, however, would have none of it. A word given to his father was inviolable for one born in Raghu's lineage. The period of fourteen years would be passed in exile.

Bharata did end up becoming ruler. He, however, did not ascend the throne. Bharata ruled the kingdom from Nandigrama, not Ayodhya, and only as Raama's regent, with his sandals on the throne instead. Raama's fourteen years in exile, to be spent in the forests, began. The stage was set for the next set of events, just as the gods hoped for.

While living in the region of Dandakaranya, by the river Godavari, the three—Raama, Lakshmana, and Seeta—were accosted by Shoorpanakha, Raavana's sister. An altercation resulted in Lakshmana slicing off Shoorpanakha's nose and ears. As a result, Khara and Dooshana, two raakshasas, became Raama and Lakshmana's enemies. Raama killed them, along with fourteen thousand other raakshasas in that forest. Raama was acting out his destiny, unaware of his divine origins.

A distraught Shoorpanakha went to her brother Raavana and poured out her woes. His sister's disfigurement enraged Raavana. Shoorpanakha told him what had happened. Raama would have to pay, Raavana pledged. Raama too would have to be humiliated, Raavana plotted. He left Lanka, crossed the ocean, and went to Gokarna to meet Mareecha, his former advisor, but who now lived a life of an ascetic.[16]

If Mareecha had a sense of foreboding on seeing his nephew, Raavana, he didn't show it. He welcomed Raavana and then asked why the king of Lanka was in an agitated state. He listened patiently as Raavana fulminated against Raama. Having experienced the might of Raama, Mareecha advised Raavana to not provoke Raama, lest he also meet the same end as Subaahu. Raavana, bent on revenge, would brook no dissent. Raavana threatened to kill Mareecha if he didn't do his bidding. Come what may, Mareecha saw his death as inevitable.

If he disobeyed Raavana, Mareecha knew he would die at his hands. If he didn't, he would die at Raama's hands. He concluded that it was better to meet his end at the hands of Raama than Raavana. Raavana asked Mareecha to take the form of a golden deer and go tempt Seeta. The sight of a golden deer would make Seeta goad Raama[17] into chasing it. Once he left, Raavana the brave and lord of the three worlds would be free to abduct the defenceless Seeta. That would cause Raama to die of grief, or so Raavana thought, for who would dare taking on the King of Lanka? After all, wasn't Raavana armed with the boon of invincibility? Gandharvas, gods, asuras, yakshas, raakshasas, serpents, kinnaras and demons—none could kill him. None, except humans. And humans were puny, his prey. The predator had no reason to fear his prey. Raavana would hide while Raama hunted Mareecha.

Since death is certain, it is better to die at the hands of a superior being.[18]

Having heard Raavana's designs, Mareecha was even more certain of one thing—not of the success of Raavana's scheme, but of his own death at the hands of Raama. With death certain, Mareecha did what was done for the dead. He performed his own funeral rites.

Mareecha then departed Gokarna and reached the forest where Raama, Seeta, and Lakshmana were. He assumed the form of a deer and danced and pranced in front of Seeta. Raavana, meanwhile, took the form of a sage with a shaven head and a staff[19] in his hand. Seeing the golden deer, Seeta asked Raama to get it for her. As fate willed, as time demanded, as the gods awaited, Raama chased the deer, but not before entrusting Seeta in Lakshmana's protection.

Raama pursued the deer deep into the forest. Realization finally dawned on him that he was chasing not a deer but a raakshaa. Taking aim at the deer, he shot an arrow. The arrow found its mark. The deer fell, fatally wounded.

Before dying, Mareecha, the deer, committed one last act of villainy. It cried out, imitating Raama's voice, calling out to Seeta and Lakshmana for help. These sounds carried back through the forest and to the hermitage where Seeta heard these words and started to run in the direction of the words, but Lakshmana restrained her. He reasoned with her that Raama was a brave warrior and needed no help, and certainly not to hunt down a mere deer. Seeta had no cause to worry on his account. Seeta remained adamant.

No, that wasn't why Lakshmana was not setting out to help his brother, Seeta alleged. She accused Lakshmana of coveting her. His refusal to help Raama was nothing but a pretext to get him out of the way. A mortified Lakshmana covered his ears at her words. He nonetheless left in search of Raama. Fate and time moved in lockstep.

> 'O stupid one! This is not the time for satisfying the desire in your heart.'[20]

No sooner had Lakshmana left than Raavana, now disguised as an ascetic, came to the hermitage. If Seeta should have been surprised at the sight of a sage, we don't know, but she certainly followed her dharma and greeted and invited him. No sooner had he entered that Raavana assumed his true form and revealed his real intentions.

> 'Become my wife and abandon the ascetic Raghava.'[21]

Killing Seeta would have been too easy. If he kidnapped Seeta, or if she left of her own accord, yes, that would be the ultimate act of revenge against Raama. Raavana sought to lure Seeta to go with him, only to be spurned. An aghast Seeta covered her ears at Raavana's words, much as Lakshmana had at her words a few moments ago.

Unwilling to spend any more time persuading her, Raavana grabbed Seeta by the hair and ascended his chariot—the same Pushpaka vimana that Raavana had snatched from Kubera, the same Pushpaka vimana that Kubera had cursed would carry the one that would be responsible for Raavana's end.

Jataayu—Dashratha's friend, king of the vultures, Sampaati's brother, and Aruna's[22] son—saw Seeeta lamenting, 'Raama, Raama!'

> Can a she-elephant, after serving a giant elephant that is in musth and ranges the forest, touch a hog? How can a lady who has drunk choice liquor and drunk nectar made out of honey, be attracted by the juice of the jujube tree?'[23]

A furious Jataayu attacked Ravana, tearing at him with his talons, causing the rakshaasa to bleed profusely. Raavana slashed with his sword, slicing off Jataayu's wings. Jatayaayu fell to the ground, not yet dead. Raavana flew off with Seeta. Despite being abducted by the fearsome raakshasa, Seeta kept her wits about her. Whenever Seeta[24] spotted a hermitage or a water body, she took off an ornament and dropped it. On the slopes of a mountain, she spotted a group of monkeys. As she passed over it, she dropped a yellow garment off. Someone would notice these and somehow, somewhere, help would arrive, she hoped. The Pushpaka chariot was flying over a region known as Pampa.[25] Millennia later, the world would know it as Hampi.

The Search for Seeta

Raama, in the meantime, had killed the deer. He started back for the hermitage. When he saw Lakshmana on his way back, he was mildly annoyed since he had given him explicit instructions to stay back and guard Seeta. Knowing that he had just killed a raakshasa disguised as a deer, an anxious Raama and Lakshmana hastened to the hermitage. There they saw Jataayu lying on the ground, wings clipped, bleeding, at death's door. Jataayu told Raama who he was and what he had witnessed. With a nod of his head, he pointed to Raama[26] that Raavana had taken off in a southern direction with Seeta. His task completed, Jataayu died. Raama and Lakshmana[27] performed Jataayu's last rites. They headed south, towards the Dandakaranya forest, in search of Seeta. The Pushpaka vimaana had carried off the one who would become the cause of Raavana's death. Now the one who would kill Raavana followed.

Shortly thereafter they came across a huge, one-eyed raakshasa named Kabandha, who lifted Lakshmana up in his arms and started to bring him to its mouth. On Raama's advice, Lakshmana cut off the raakshasa's right arm while Raama hacked off its left arm. As Kabandha fell, a divine being arose from its body. It said it was the gandharva Vishvavasu who had been cursed by Brahma to be born to a raakshasa womb. Before disappearing, he revealed what he knew about Seeta—that she had been abducted by Raavana. That much they knew, but he also said that Raama go seek the help of Sugreeva, Vaali's brother, who lived by Lake Pampa near Mount Rishyamukha. The gods who had taken births as monkeys, waited for the one who would kill Raavana to find his way to Pampa.

Raama proceeded to Lake Pampa, where the sights and sounds of lotuses, cool breeze, and smell of amrita only reminded him more of Seeta. Lakshmana advised Raama to stay composed and to think of ways of finding Sugreeva, for that was their immediate mission. After bathing in Lake Pampa, the two brothers climbed Mount Rishyamukha, where they saw the same five monkeys[28] that Seeta had spotted.

Sugreeva sent his advisor, Hanuman, to meet them. Raama and Sugreeva entered into a pact of friendship and agreed to help each other. Sugreeva promised to help bring Seeta back while Raama vowed to kill Sugreeva's brother, Vaali,[29] and instate Sugreeva as the king of the monkeys. Sugreeva as king would be able to marshal the entire army of monkeys to search for Seeta.

Raama and Sugreeva then went to Kishkindha where Sugreeva challenged Vaali. Taara warned her husband, Vaali, that it seemed as if Sugreeva had found a powerful protector. There was no reason otherwise for Sugreeva to emerge now and challenge Vaali to a duel. On Vaali's urging, Taara listened to the voices and surmised that it was Raama who had entered into a pact with Sugreeva. With his four advisors and Raama, Sugreeva was now a formidable foe. However, Vaali not only dismissed Taara's advice, but also suspected her of still being attached to Sugreeva. Vaali went to Mount Maalyavan and challenged Sugreeva.

Sugreeva and Vaali started duelling. Both were equally matched and struck at each other with tree limbs, rocks, fists, claws, teeth. Both bled profusely. The fight continued. Raama watched the fight from afar, hidden, unable to intervene. Why? He could not distinguish one from the other. Hanuman then came up with an idea and placed a garland around Sugreeva's neck. Now identifiable, Raama shot an arrow at Vaali. Struck, Vaali fell down, blood spouting from his mouth. A dying Vaali castigated Raama.

Sugreeva regained the kingdom of Kishkindha as well as Taara. Raama lived on the slopes of Maalyavan, waiting for Sugreeva to assemble an army of monkeys to locate Seeta. Four months passed.

While all this was happening in and outside Kishkindha, Raavana had brought Seeta to Lanka and had her put near a grove of Ashoka trees, guarded by fierce raakshasis who spent their time berating and threatening Seeta in turn. Seeta, fearful and grieving, stuck to her resolve that either she would be reunited with Raama or she had no desire to live. One raakshasi, Trijata, however, was of a better nature and comforted Seeta when she could, telling her what another raakshasa, Avindhya,[30] had shared with her—that Raama was well and had made friends with Sugreeva. She also told Seeta that Seeta was protected from Raavana's desire and lust by Nalakubera's curse.[31]

Nalakubera had cursed Raavana that he could not forcibly possess, or violate, any woman. Trijata said she had seen the portents of the raakshasa's destruction and of Raavana's, Kumbhakarna's, and the other raakshasa's deaths. Only Vibheeshana would remain alive, she told Seeta.

Soon enough, Raavana came again to meet Seeta, as she sat on a slab of stone, sad, sorrowful, hopeful. Raavana, dressed in the best of garments, jewels, and a magnificent crown, crowed about his power, strength, riches, and fame. Hoping to have impressed Seeta, he again asked her to become his wife, like Mandodri was. Seeta, teary-eyed but iron-willed in her resolve, censured Raavana for harbouring unchaste thoughts about another man's wife. If he was, as he claimed, the son of a brahmana, Seeta wondered, how could he not know about dharma.

> The one who was slender in form covered her head and her face with her garment. Her hair was long and was braided well. Hanging from her head, it looked like a delicate and dark serpent.[32]

Raavana in turn wondered why Seeta would not leave Raama, a man who was but food for the raakshasas, and accept Raavana. It was utter foolishness. Nonetheless, he would not have Seeta by force. He couldn't. Raavana departed, frustrated by Seeta's refusal, fearful of Nalakubera's curse. He would try again.

Four months had passed. Raama had waited out the monsoon months patiently. Yet there had been no help forthcoming from Sugreeva. Unable to contain his longing for Seeta, unwilling to wait any longer, annoyed with Sugreeva's attitude and his ingratitude, Raama one day asked Lakshmana to go to Kishkindha and remind Sugreeva of his obligations. Raama gave Lakhmana[33] two choices—to kill Sugreeva, just as he had killed Vaali, if he didn't agree, or to bring him here, if he did. Raama was still serving his fourteen-year exile; he would not enter a habitation, even of monkeys.

An equally incensed Lakshmana entered the gates of Kishkindha where he was met by an anxious Sugreeva. When Lakshmana delivered Raama's message, Sugreeva folded his hands and pleaded that he was neither indolent nor an ingrate. He had, in fact, already dispatched messengers to all four corners, giving them a period of one month to report back with news of Seeta's location. In another five nights, it would be one month since he had sent his monkeys. A mollified Lakshmana returned to Raama. Both counted the days.

The month over, monkeys by the thousands started returning to Kishkindha. They all had the same disheartening message—there was no sign of either Seeta or Raavana. Only one team remained; the one that had travelled south. This was the group that had Hanuman in it.

Though dejected, Raama kept hope that news from the southern direction would be better. Time passed, and two more months went by. Raama hung on to hope by a most slender thread. Then one day some monkeys came rushing to Sugreeva and told him that the monkeys who had gone south had returned and were eating fruits and enjoying themselves in the garden Madhuvana. Sugreeva exulted. The group had traced Seeta. Else they would not have been celebrating. Raama concurred. Hanuman, Angad,[34] and the other monkeys came to Raama. Raama had only one question for Hanuman.

'Will you give me my life?'[35]

Hanuman said that yes, he had indeed seen Seeta. They had travelled a long way in search of Seeta. In their search they had entered a long cave that stretched for many yojanas. Emerging through its other end, they had seen a palace and an old lady named Prabhaavati performing penance there. She told them to continue south. The monkeys proceeded and at the end, saw the ocean, which spread endlessly in all directions. There was water everywhere, but no sign of Seeta or Raavana.

Dejected, the monkeys had all sat down, talking about Jataayu and his message. Hearing this, a huge vulture came towards them. He was Sampaati, Jataayu's younger brother. He said that once both had risen high up in the skies, towards the sun. Sampaati's wings had been burnt as a result, while Jataayu's hadn't. Sampaati had fallen on this mountain, and he hadn't seen his brother since. And now he had heard someone taking his brother's name. Did they know anything about Jataayu, his brother? How was Jataayu, asked Sampaati.

Jataayu was dead, the monkeys informed Sampaati. They had come to the shore in search of Seeta. Sampaati was grief-stricken at news of his brother's death. Composing himself, he told the monkeys that he knew who Raavana was. He lived on the island of Lanka, on top of Mount Trikoota. Across the ocean the monkeys would have to go.

Crossing the ocean was a hurdle in every sense of the word. They could neither swim nor leap across to Lanka. None could, except Hanuman, who agreed and leapt over the ocean. Once in Lanka, he searched and succeeded in locating Seeta. There, he gave her Raama's message, assured her that they would soon be coming to Lanka, along with Sugreeva and his army, to rescue her. Seeta heard Hanuman's message and remembered what Trijata had told her; that Avindhya had told her that Raama had befriended Sugreeva and that an army of monkeys was searching for Seeta. And now here was Hanuman, a monkey, giving her the good news that Raama would soon be making his way to Lanka. For the first time in months, a smile and hope washed over Seeta.

Before Hanuman departed, Seeta gave him a jewel as proof of her existence and proof that Hanuman had indeed seen and met Seeta. As further corroboration, she also told him about an incident that had taken place in Chitrakoot, where Raama had thrown a straw at a crow. That would be proof to Raama that Hanuman had indeed met Seeta. Hearing Hanuman recount all this, hearing him talk about Seeta, Raama was elated. The monkeys assembled to march to Lanka.

Raama, Lanka, and Raavana

The monkeys marched to the ocean. From all corners, they arrived, led by Sushena, Gaja, Gavaya, Gavaaksha, Gandhamaadana,[36] Panasa, Dadhimukha, Jaambavaan, and others, each of whom brought a substantial army of monkeys with them. Thus, they collected, and at the auspicious hour, Raama and Sugreeva marched towards the ocean with this huge army of monkeys, who were armed with rocks and trees as weapons.

Soon enough, this ocean of monkeys reached the ocean, where the insurmountable obstacle presented itself. One monkey, Hanuman, was capable of leaping across the ocean, but what about the countless other monkeys? Raama asked Sugreeva what the best way of crossing the ocean was. The monkeys talked, discussed, debated this question among themselves. Raama reminded everyone that neither could all the monkeys jump over the ocean, nor were there enough boats to ferry all the monkeys across. Varuna, the God of the ocean, himself would have to show the way, Raama said. If Varuna did not comply, Raama promised to dry up the ocean with his arrows and weapons. Come what may, the monkey army would cross the ocean.

Raama's ultimatum presented Varuna with a dilemma. While he did not want to obstruct Raama's passage, if he gave free passage to Raama, others were also liable to use the threat of force to command the ocean. That would set a bad precedent. Varuna, therefore, suggested that Raama take the help of the monkey Nala, son of Vishvakarma Tvashtra, to construct a bridge over the ocean. Varuna, on his part, would bear and float whatever the monkey army decided to use to construct the bridge with—whether it was wood or stone.

On Raama's instructions, Nala constructed a bridge over the ocean. Meanwhile, Vibheeshana, along with his advisors, left Raavana and Lanka and met Raama by the shore. They were accepted by Raama, despite Sugreeva's misgivings, and Vibheeshana was appointed Lakshmana's advisor and king of Lanka in exile.

Once the monkey army crossed over to Lanka, it wrought havoc on the many gardens there. Raavana, to ascertain the strength and size of Raama's army, sent two raakshasas—Shuka and Saarana—as spies disguised as monkeys. Vibheeshana spotted them and they were taken before Raama, who let them go. Raama made one last attempt to avoid a terrible war. He dispatched the wise Angada as his emissary to Raavana.

Raavana, in anticipation of a war with Raama and his army of monkeys, had fortified his city of Lanka. Walls, turrets, moats, watchtowers, stakes, weapons were replenished and fortified. Ignoring all this, unafraid though surrounded by countless raakshasas, Angada entered through the gates of Lanka and strode up to Raavana. There he delivered Raama's message. Even though it was Raavana alone who was responsible for the dastardly act of kidnapping Seeta, it would be the residents of Lanka who would suffer on account of their king, Angada warned Raavana. The raakshasa king had two options—free Seeta or be killed by Raama on the battlefield.

Raavana was enraged upon hearing Raama's message. If not Raama, at least he could teach this mere messenger of the mere human a lesson, or so Raavana thought. Four raakshasas pinned Angada down, each raakshasa holding on to one limb. Seeing that Raavana was beyond reasoning, Angada leapt up onto a terrace, all four raakshasas still clinging to him. As he leapt up, they lost their grip and fell to their deaths. Angada returned to Raama and the war started. A human was fighting Raavana.

Raama's monkey army succeeded in breaching the walls of Lanka, and Lakshmana, Vibheeshana, and Jambavan destroyed the south gate of the city. Once the gate was down, the monkeys swarmed into the city, raining down their chakras, rocks, and other weapons upon the raakshasas on the turrets, who fled. In retaliation, Raavana's raakshasas poured out and fell upon the monkeys. Raama rained a shower of arrows on the raakshasas. As the first day of the war ended, it was clear that Raama and his army had carried the day.

Raavana decided to resort to maaya. He sent some of his raakshasas[37] to attack the monkey army as it rested. The raakshasas made themselves invisible and advanced upon the army. However, Vibheeshana was able to spot them and removed their cloak of invisibility. The monkeys set upon these raakshasas and killed them all.

His army ineffective, his powers of illusion having failed, Raavana decide to lead the charge himself against Raama. Raama faced him in battle, while Lakshmana took on Indrajit,[38] Sugriva battled Virupaksha, Nikharvata with Tara, Nala with Tunda, Vibheeshana against Prahasta, and Patusha faced Panasa. Vibheeshana sliced off Prahasta's head with a spear. Dhumraaksha, another raakshasa, rushed at the monkeys, who fled in terror. It was Hanuman who rallied the monkeys, and after a fierce battle, killed Dhumraaksha. The raakshasas retreated from the battlefield and returned to Lanka, fearful, and recounted their woes to Raavana.

Raavana decided that Kumbhakarna needed to enter the battlefield. However, this posed one problem, and no small one at that. Fortified with Brahma's boon, Kumbhakarna slept. It was with great difficulty that he was awakened. The raakshasa king brought him up to speed on what had happened thus far. Kumbhakarna ordered Dooshana's brothers, Pramathi and Vajravega, to march along with him to the battlefield.

Once on the battlefield, the monkeys attacked Kumbhakarna with all their might, striking him with trees, nails and teeth. However, Kumbhakarna was huge. He shrugged all of them off as mere pinpricks and started to devour the monkeys. Sugreeva sprang to action and hurled a huge shala tree at Kumbhakarna. That had no effect on the raakshasa. Retaliating, Kumbhakarna caught hold of Sugreeva and started to march off with the monkey king. With the monkey king prisoner, the battle would come to a swift end.

Lakshmana sprang to Sugreeva's rescue and shot off an arrow at Kumbhakarna that pierced his armour and body. A wounded Kumbhakarna let go of Sugreeva. He then advanced against Lakshmana, arms raised, a huge rock in his arms. Lakshmana retaliated with more arrows that severed Kumbhakarana's arms. Lo and behold, in their place sprouted four arms, which Lakshmana again sliced off with his arrows. As those four arms were severed, several more seemed to sprout from Kumbhakarna's body. Not just arms, but even legs and heads appeared on the raakshasa's body. Lakshmana sliced off all of them with his arrows. Desperate, bleeding, in a last-ditch attempt, Kumbhakarna assumed a gigantic form and rushed at Lakshmana. Lakhsmana summoned the Brahmaastra and with it, killed Kumbhakarna.

Seeing Kumbhakarna fall in battle, the other raakshasas fled in fear. Where Kumbhakarna had failed, what hope did they have. Only Vajravega and Pramathi attacked the monkey army and Lakshmana. They didn't stay in the battlefield for long. Hanuman killed Vajravega and Neela killed Pramathi.

With losses mounting on the raakshasa army's side, Raavana ordered his son, Indrajit, the one who had defeated Indra and earned the appellation, to enter the battlefield. There would be no half measures any longer. Raavana's orders were clear. Indrajit was to kill Raama, Lakshmana, and Sugreeva. With divine weapons at his disposal, with the strength and cunning that had defeated Indra, Indrajit would surely succeed, Raavana exhorted. Indrajit strode atop a chariot into the battlefield. He challenged Lakshmana to a duel and the two engaged in the fierce battle in the war.

Soon enough, Angada also entered the fray and attacked Indrajit with a huge tree, which Raavana's son destroyed. Angada hurled another tree trunk at Indrajit which destroyed his chariot, charioteer, and horses. Indrajit, on foot now, made himself invisible, and rained an incessant shower of arrows on Raama and Lakshmana. Despite the best efforts of the monkeys, they could not counter Indrajit, and the two brothers fell, wounded, unconscious. Indrajit bound them with arrows. Defeat loomed.

While the monkeys stood around, watching, helpless, Vibheeshana arrived and revived Raama and Lakshmana using the prajna weapon. Now there was the matter of the arrows that had pierced their bodies. Vibheeshana used the vishalya herb to remove these arrows. Once the two had recovered, Vibheeshana introduced them to a guhyaka[39] who had brought holy water that would allow them to see invisible things. Raama, Lakshmana, Sugreeva, Jaambavan, Hanuman, Angada, and many other chief monkeys applied the water to their eyes. Indrajit's potent weapon of invisibility had been rendered useless.

Indrajit meanwhile informed his father of his exploits and then returned to the battlefield. In his exultation, Indrajust had however forgotten to perform his daily rites. He was now vulnerable, just as Yavakreeta[40] had been. Lakshmana, now more determined than ever to bring down Indrajit, battled him, and after a fierce battle, killed him with three arrows. One arrow sliced off the arm that held the bow, the second the arm that held the arrows, and the third arrow his head. His charioteer also dead, Indrajit's horses pulled the chariot back into Lanka.

Enraged, fearful, mourning, Raavana rushed to the Ashoka grove where Seeta was. If he could not win against Raama in the battlefield, he would defeat him another way. If he killed Seeta, Raama would die of grief. The outcome of the battle would not matter. However, he was stopped by Avindhya. Surely the lord of the worlds, the undisputed king of the raakshasas could do better than kill a defenceless woman, he argued. Avindhya reasoned that Raavana would be better off killing Raama instead, since that would kill Seeta also, and no sin would accrue to Raavana. Heeding his advice, Raavana sheathed his sword and resolved to go out into the battlefield.

> 'You are established as a great king. You should not kill a woman. This woman is captive in your house and is already dead. In my view, she will not be killed through the destruction of her body. Kill her husband. When he is dead, she will be dead.'[41]

Raavana advanced with his mighty army of raakshasas, only to be met by the monkey leaders who took on many of his warriors. After a brief battle, Raavana resorted to maaya and countless raakshasas emerged from his body. All of them were killed just as soon by Raama's divine weapons. Raavana used more of his maaya and two beings that looked like Raama and Lakshmana emerged and charged at Raama and Lakshmana. The two brothers however slayed these two apparitions.

It was then that Maatali, Indra's charioteer appeared in a celestial chariot before the two brothers. This, he said, was Indra's chariot named Jaitra. He invited Raama to ascend the chariot and fight Raavana from it. Was this one more of Raavana's illusions? Raama was wary. Vibheeshana assured him that this was not one of Raavana's illusions.

Seeing Raama advance on that celestial chariot, Raavana attacked him with all manners of weapons, which Raama repulsed. The time for Raavana's end had come. Raama took out an arrow, armed it with the Brahmaastra, and released it at Raavana. The raakshasa king was enveloped by the weapon and was killed, engulfed in a huge blaze. Such was the intensity of the Brahmaastra that let alone skin and bones, not even Raavana's ashes could be seen.

> The ingredients of his body, together with his flesh and blood, were burnt so much by the Brahmastra that even the ashes could not be seen.[42]

With Raavana dead, Raama handed over Lanka to Vibheeshana. Avindhya, accompanied by Vibheeshana, escorted Seeta out of the Ashoka grove and out of Lanka. Seeta, for whom Raama had pined for so long, for whom he had crossed an ocean and taken on the invincible king of raakshasas, was finally free, and ready to be reunited with him. However, the Raama who spoke to Seeta was not the Raama that she had known. Instead of delighting at seeing Seeta, he told her that she was free to leave; leave him, leave for anywhere she wished. Cold, uncaring. He said he had done his duty so that Seeta would not have to live in the house of the raakshasa who had kidnapped her. Seeta stood, speechless, stunned, devastated.

> Her face had been flush with delight. But that disappeared in an instant, like breath on a mirror.[43]

As everyone stood, stunned, stupefied at this turn of events, Brahma, along with other gods like Indra, Agni, Vaayu, Yama, and Varuna manifested themselves. Soon thereafter the saptarishis also arrived, as did Dashratha in a divine form. It was in front of all of them that Seeta addressed Raama that if she had committed any wrong act, the breath of life leave her.

Vaayu spoke up, his voice pervading the skies, vouching for Seeta's innocence. Brahma also echoed Vaayu's words. He further told Raama that he had protected Seeta through Nalakubera's curse—were Raavana were to try and force himself on any woman without her consent, his head would explode into pieces.

> O Prince! I do not blame you, because I know the ways of women and of men.[44]

Dashratha gave permission to Raama to rule over Ayodhya. Raama listened to all of them, and acquiesced, accepting Seeta. Indra, before leaving, granted a boon to Avindhya and wealth to Trijata. It was now Brahma's turn to grant Raama a boon. Raama asked for everlasting devotion to dharma, victory over enemies, and for the monkeys killed in the war to be revived. Seeta granted Hanuman the boon of a long life, to live as long as Raama's fame lasted. Hanuman was blessed with immortality.

His mission to Lanka successful, Raama and others left Lanka, and after crossing the ocean, spent some time on the shores of the ocean. He then left on board the Pushpaka chariot for Kishkindha along with Sugreeva and Vibheeshana. There, Raama instated Angada as the heir apparent. After finally reaching Ayodhya, Raama sent Hanuman as a messenger to Bharata, and then himself proceeded to Nandigrama to meet Bharata and Shatrughna.

On the auspicious time, sages Vashishtha and Vaamadeva instated Raama as the king of Ayodhya.

Raama then granted leave to the visitors to leave—Sugreeva for Kishkindha, Vibheeshana for Lanka. He also returned the Pushpaka vimaana to Kubera.

Finishing the upakhyaana, Maarkandeya told Yudhishthira that such had been the misfortunes and hardships that Raama had to face.

> Everything in this world stays with those who have aides.[45]

Maarkandeya told Yudhishthira that with such aides by his side as his brothers, he had nothing to fear from his enemies. Just as Raama had rescued Seeta from Raavana's clutches, so had Yudhishthira's brothers brought back Draupadi from Jayadratha.

Yudhishthira was consoled by these words and regained his composure. Yes, he was not the most unfortunate of men. Nala had experienced more hardships than he had. Raama had seen a greater share of misfortunes than him, even though he had been born as an avatara of Vishnu himself. Fortitude and companions had seen him through the toughest of times and the darkest of days. Yudhishthira, however, had one further doubt, a question.

31

SAAVITRI

A Walk with Death

Parva: Aranyaka (3) | Upa parva: Draupadi-harana (42)
Chapters: 277-283 | Shlokas: 297

Draupadi had suffered much humiliation in the Kuru assembly and yet retrieved Yudhishthira's lost kingdom for him, only to see him lose it again in a second game of dice. Her husband had lost everything and then staked her in the game of dice to Shakuni. Her brother-in-law, Duhshaasana, had dragged her by the hair to the Kuru assembly. Karna had then called her a courtesan[1] who deserved to be dragged in naked.[2] Her five husbands had watched helplessly, and the Kuru elders had been mute spectators as Duhshaasana had attempted to disrobe her. No, most people would not call Draupadi as blessed with good fortune.[3] But that's what Yudhishthira thought of her.

But yes, Draupadi had possessed the courage to ask the question that neither Yudhishthira nor Bheeshma could answer.

> Go back to the assembly hall and ask that gambler from the Bharata lineage whether he first lost himself or me.[4]

She had had the presence of mind to retrieve for the Paandavas the kingdom that Yudhishthira had gambled away in the first game of dice, leaving Karna to wonder in amazement.[5]

Was there anyone who was as devoted and endowed with good luck as Draupadi, Yudhishthira wondered.

> Have you ever seen, or heard of, a woman as immensely fortunate and as devoted to her husbands as Drupada's daughter?[6]

Yes, there had been a wife who had walked seven steps, and then some, with no less than the god of death and returned with her husband's life, Maarkandeya told Yudhishthira.

Who was this woman? She was Saavitri, Maarkandeya began. To learn about Saavitri, we have to go back to a time when a kingdom named Madra was ruled by a kind, just, and generous king named Ashvapati. Time passed, as it does, and the king grew old, as everyone does, but he remained childless. What he could not obtain through human endeavours, he decided to seek divine blessings to attain. He became an ascetic and performed penances to Goddess Saavitri.[7] Pleased, Saavitri granted Ashvapati a boon. The old king asked for sons. 'No, not quite yet,' the goddess replied.

What Ashvapati wanted, Saavitri already knew. She had already consulted with Brahma about this before appearing before the king. Not a son, but a daughter would be born to him. Anticipating, perhaps, questions from the king, the goddess asked the king not to ask why.

> Ask for whatever boon you desire. But do not make the mistake of disregarding dharma.[8]

Ashvapati accepted the boon and returned home. Despite not getting exactly what he had asked for, he was happy. The goddess had granted him a boon, which is what mattered, and that too after consulting none other than Brahma. Ashvapati was content. In due course of time, his eldest queen gave birth to a daughter. Because she had been born from Saavitri's boon, who had been pleased with the offerings of the Saavitri mantra that Ashvapati had chanted in her honour, the infant was named Saavitri.

Saavitri grew up to be a beautiful maiden. Such was her beauty and dazzling radiance that no prince could muster up the confidence to approach her father to ask her hand in marriage. This was a source of distress for her father. Who would step up?

One day after Saavitri had prayed to the gods and offered oblations to the fire she went to her father. Ashvapati opened up. A worry had been gnawing away at his heart. Such was her persona and beauty that no prince in the land had gathered the courage to ask her hand in marriage. He, therefore, preferred that she go and select her own husband. Whoever she selected, he would marry her to him, for it was a father's dharma to give away his daughter in marriage. Saavitri took leave of her father, and accompanied by the king's ministers, left for hermitages and pilgrimage sites. Where she went, she paid her respects to the sages and gave away donations. Eventually, she finished her travels and returned home. She had made up her mind. She had seen the man she would marry.

When Saavitri returned, she saw Sage Naarada seated along with her father. Naarada asked Ashvapati why Saavitri had not been married yet. Of course, the sage would have known more than he let on, but he nonetheless asked the question. Ashvapti replied that he had tasked her daughter with finding a groom for herself, because, well… Saavitri spoke and recounted her travels. She talked about Dyumatsena in particular, a brave king of Shaalva, but who had gone blind and had been driven out of his kingdom by a neighbouring king. His son, born when Dyumatsena was still king, grew up in the forest, and was named Satyavaan. Saavitri paused a beat. It was Satyavaan, she resumed, that she wanted to marry. In her mind, she had already accepted him as her husband.

Naarada listened. Of all the kings, all the princes, that Saavitri should select Satyavaan was nothing but fate. But it was his duty to share with Ashvapati and Saavitri what he knew.

> In her ignorance, Savitri has committed a grave error, by choosing the virtuous Satyavan.[9]

'Hmm,' Naarada sighed.

'What, O Sage?' Ashvapati asked, concerned.

'Of all the kings, all the princes in the land…,' Naarada stopped mid-sentence.

'Why? Is Satyavaan not truthful?' asked Ashvapati.

'He is truthful like Shibi.'[10]

'Is he not intelligent enough?'

'He is intelligent like Brihaspati.'[11]

'Does he have the vice of being lazy?'

'No, he is energetic like Surya.'

'Is he a coward?'

'He is brave like Indra.'

'Is he easily angered? Is that his vice, then?'

'He is forgiving like the earth.'

'Is he a miser? That must be his vice, then,' Ashvapati asked with mounting consternation.

'He is generous like Rantideva.'[12]

'Is he not handsome? Is he deformed or hideous?'

'He is handsome like the Ashvin twins.'

'Then what is his vice, O Sage, please. Please enlighten me. You didn't look pleased when Saavitri revealed her choice,' Ashvapati pleaded with Naarada.

'He has no vices save one, O King. But your daughter has still erred in choosing Satyavaan as her husband.'

'Why do you not approve of this union?'

'He has one vice. Just one.'

'What is it?'

'He is destined to die one year from now.'

Ashvapati stood up. Saavitri stood, rooted. He looked at his daughter.

'O Child, not him. Anyone but him. You cannot marry Satyavaan. You must not marry someone who will leave you a widow in just a year,' Ashvapati pleaded with his daughter.

'Once, O Father, just once,' Satyavati said. Ashvapati looked on, nonplussed. Naarada looked at Satyavati and knew. She had made up her mind. Not even the gods could change her mind now.

'Just once, father. Just as a die is cast only once, just as the daughter is given away in marriage only once, just as the father gives away the daughter only once, so will I choose a husband only once. I have made my choice,' Satyavati said.

> The die is cast only once. The daughter is given away only once. 'I give her away,' is pronounced only once. All these three occur only once.[13]

Indeed, the die had been cast. Naarada realized Saavitri would not budge. Naarada acquiesced. The daughter had made up her mind. So did Ashvapati. He would support her in the choice.

After making all necessary arrangements, Ashvapati set out for the forest along with brahmanas and priests to meet Dyumatsena. Ashvapati offered his obeisance and introduced himself, while Dyumatsena offered the king arghya[14] and a seat. When Ashvapati told him why he had come to meet the blind king, Dyumatsena replied that Saavitri did not deserve to live a hard life in the forest. A king living in the forest in exile would have little to offer a princess like Saavitri. Happiness and sadness were impermanent, Ashvapati responded. He again requested Dyumatsena to accept his proposal. The blind king agreed, and arrangements were made for the wedding.

The wedding took place. Saavitri and Satyavaan both were happy at having found each other as husband and wife. Ashvapati returned home. Once her father had departed, Saavitri shed all her ornaments and donned bark and red garments, for she was now a wife of one who lived the life of an ascetic in the forest. She was no longer a princess. She was Satyavaan's wife. For one year.

Time passed, for the die had been cast by both Yama and Saavitri. If Satyavaan was destined to die as Naarada had told her, then Saavitri needed to know when exactly that day would arrive. She calculated and then counted down each day as it passed.

Time passed. The year drew to a close. Four days, Saavitri calculated. She spent the next three days and three nights fasting and remaining standing. She needed to accumulate whatever extra austerities she could to face what was coming. She felt she could hear, sense, almost see Yama. But death would have to walk past her to get to Satyavaan.

The fated day dawned. Saavitri performed the morning rites and bowed before all the brahmanas and her in-laws, who all blessed her that she may never become a widow. Little did they know. Whether Naarada's prophesy would come true or the blessings of the wise men—would be clear before the end of the day. The die had been cast.

When her mother-in-law asked her to eat, now that her fast was over, Saavitri replied that she would do so only at sunset. Satyavaan, in the meantime, had also got ready to leave for the forest, axe in hand, to chop wood for the sacrificial fire. Saavitri asked to accompany him. She had not once left the hermitage where she had lived since her marriage. Though surprised, since she had never asked to go with him to the forest, and because she was weak from the three days of fasting, he nonetheless agreed. Her company would be a welcome change from his routine in the forest. She took her in-laws' permission, and the two departed for the forest. Of the two, one had an appointment with death; only one knew about it.

The two proceeded to the forest. In the forest, Satyavaan first set about collecting fruits. His basket full, he then began chopping wood. The appointed hour ticked down, and death was now within touching distance of Satyavaan. He started to sweat from his exertions, and then developed a splitting headache. Without the strength to even stand, he lay down. Saavitri placed his head on her lap. She started counting the moments to his death, remembering Naarada's words. She counted the muhurta[15] and the kshana[16] to when death would arrive. In what form, she didn't know.

At the appointed hour, moment, and time, Saavitri saw someone approaching. He was a fierce looking person, dressed in yellow garments, holding a noose in his hand. He stood there, observing. His eyes finally came to rest on Satyavaan, his head in Saavitri's lap. Saavitri placed Satyavaan's head on the ground and got up. Of course, she knew who he was, her heightened sense of misery and the tremors of her heart had already informed her. But she nonetheless addressed him and asked him who he was. Let Death introduce itself first.

The man replied that he was Yama, the god of death. Satyavaan's lifespan had run out, and because he had been a person devoted to dharma, Yama said, he had come himself, instead of sending one of his messengers. Then, taking Satyavaan's life out from his body and binding it with his noose, Yama departed in a southern direction. Satyavaan's body had become cold to the touch, lifeless. As Yama departed, Saavitri followed him; to what end, she didn't know. Yama asked her to desist.

> O Savitri! Go back. Perform the last rites for your husband. Your debt to your husband has been discharged. You have come as far as you possibly can.[17]

How far she would go with her husband was for her to decide. Saavitri replied that it was her dharma to follow her husband. She talked about the words of the wise who had spoken about the importance of dharma. Death had rolled its dice; now it was her turn.

> The learned ones, enlightened about the truth, have said that friendship is established by walking seven steps with another.[18]

Seven steps constituted a friendship. Not death, but certainly the god of death could be her friend. Pleased with her words and devotion, Yama granted her a boon. Smiling, he told her that she could ask for anything, except Satyavaan's life.

> Ask for a boon, other than his life.[19]

Saavitri asked for her father-in-law's sight and strength to be restored. Yama granted her the boon and once again urged Saavitri to turn back. Long was the walk with death; severe would be the exhaustion.

> How can there be exhaustion when I am with my husband?[20]

She spoke more words of wisdom to Yama.

> It is said that a meeting with the virtuous is desirable. It is said that friendship with them is even better.[21]

Pleased again with her words, Yama told Saavitri to ask for a second boon.

> Other than Satyavan becoming alive, ask for a second boon.[22]

So be it. The second throw of the dice also had not been in her favour. But she would again do some good with it. Saavitri asked that her father-in-law regain his kingdom and that he never stray from the path of dharma. Yama granted her this boon and again asked her to turn back lest she tired.

Saavitri demurred. She continued to speak, sharing her knowledge of the etymology of the word Yama. She spoke on the dharma of the righteous, on their capacity to be kind even to those who wished them ill. Pleased, Yama granted her a third boon. She could ask for anything except her husband's life. Saavitri asked that her father Ashvapati have a hundred sons. After all, he had desired sons when he had prayed to Goddess Saavitri. Yama granted her this boon. He again asked Saavitri to turn back. She had travelled a long distance. Saavitri replied that no distance seemed long when she was with her husband.

> My mind travels a greater distance.[23]

Saavitri spoke to Yama, telling him that people trusted the virtuous even more than they trusted themselves, and that friendship also created trust. Pleased, Yama asked Saavitri to ask for a boon. She could ask for anything except her husband's life.

> Other than his life, ask for a fourth boon.[24]

Saavitri asked for a hundred sons through Satyavaan. Sons without a husband? How that would happen was not something for Saavitri to think about. A boon was a boon. Yama granted her this boon and again asked Saavitri to turn back. Saavitri spoke more about the qualities of the virtuous. Pleased, Yama admired her wisdom and his growing respect for her.

> Ask for an unmatched boon.[25]

A fifth boon. She had another boon from Yama. Without conditions or exceptions. She could ask for anything. She wanted only one thing. She seized the moment and asked Yama what she had been waiting for—Satyavaan's life.

> You have not made an exception to your favours, as you did with the other boons. Therefore, I ask for the boon that Satyavan should live.[26]

She said that without her husband, she desired neither heaven, nor happiness, nor even life. As Yama had granted, Yama would have to give.

Yama had two options in front of him—go back on his word or give back Satyavaan his life. Of course, Yama granted Saavitri her boon. Satyavaan would live again. Freeing the noose that held Satyavaan's life, he told her that all his boons would come true. Satyavaan and Saavitri would live long and healthy lives.

The sun had set. The night had advanced. Saavitri didn't care. She walked, she ran, she raced to where she had left Satyavaan. He soon regained consciousness. Had he come back from the dead? Had he just slept a long time? Who had been the person who had been dragging him? Saavitri told him who that man had been—Yama himself. Saavitri had come back from the God of Death, while Satyavaan had come back from the dead. She said she would tell him all that had happened, but the next day, since the sun had set and it was now dark.

Satyavaan wanted to return and not wait till morning since his parents would be worried on his account. The two started back for the hermitage.

Dyumatsena, meanwhile, had regained his eyesight. Together with his wife, they searched for his son, taking in every sound they heard for his arrival. Sage Gautama comforted them and said that he knew Satyavaan and Saavitri to be alive. Other sages, like Bharadwaja, Dalbhya, Dhaumya, and Maandavya[27] reiterated the same.

Soon enough, Satyavaan and Saavitri returned to the hermitage. All gathered around the couple. All wanted to know what had kept them in the forest. His parents didn't need to know everything; least of all the fact that Satyavaan had had a brush with death closer than anyone could imagine. Not yet. What had been prophesied had come to naught, thanks to Saavitri's determination, piety, and presence of mind. He told them he had developed a headache and lain down and slept for a long time.

But what had happened, was the question. Why had Dyumatsena's vision returned? Surely that had to be the result of a divine intervention. For these answers, Satyavaan turned to Saavitri. She explained what had happened, how she had come to know from Naarada of Satyavaan's remaining lifespan of one year, of Yama's arrival, of her walking with him, his boons, and her getting Satyavaan's life back.

The next morning the sages could not stop gushing to Dyumatsena about Saavitri's wisdom. Then came news from Shaalva that the king who had usurped Dyumatsena's throne had been killed by one of his own advisors and the subjects had decided to reinstate Dyumatsena as the king. The king left for the city along with his wife, son, and Saavitri, and was instated as the king. In due course of time, Saavitri had a hundred sons, as did her father.

Just as Saavitri had saved her family from misfortune, Maarkandeya told Yudhishthira, so would Draupadi deliver all the Paandavas. Their grief lessened, the Paandavas continued living in the Kaamyaka forest.

32

Yaksha Prashna

An Interview with Death

Twelve years of the Paandavas' exile were coming to an end. The thirteenth year was upon them, that they would have to spend among people, but without getting recognized. Duryodhana would send his spies to ferret out the Paandavas. There was one more fear that gnawed at Yudhishthira's heart. A fear that he dared not utter out aloud to anyone. Yet, it was a fear that the king of the gods knew about, and he sent a message, via Sage Lomasha, to Yudhishthira.

As long as Karna wore his earrings and armour, he could not be killed in battle. Defeated, perhaps, for he had had to face defeat at the hands of Arjuna in the past[1] and would do so again in the future.[2] But a defeated warrior could rise again, and again.

Bheeshma's advice, as he lay on the bed of arrows, to Yudhishthira would be much the same but several years later.

> A debt that is not repaid, a fire that has not gone out and an enemy who is not eliminated, repeatedly keep on growing.[3]

Arjuna's celestial father, Indra, went to Karna in the guise of a brahmana and asked for his earrings and armour. He got them, but only in an exchange.[4] He had to give his Shakti weapon to Karna. The weapon that could kill whoever it was aimed at, without fail. Karna had lost the protection that rendered him invulnerable, but he had gained a weapon against which no one was.

Yudhishthira's unease and distress at Draupadi's abduction by Jayadratha continued to prey on his mind. Soon thereafter, the Paandavas left the Kaamyaka forest for Dvaitavana[5] and started living there. In that forest, they faced yet more tribulations, though this was one episode that ended on a positive note.

Once when the Paandavas were seated in the forest, a brahmana came rushing to them, lamenting that his kindling and the rod he used to light the fire, which he had hung on a tree's branch, had got stuck on the antlers of a deer. The deer had scampered off, leaving the brahmana without both. He requested that the Paandavas retrieve them.

The Paandavas set off after the deer, following its footprints. They spotted it and shot many arrows at it, to no avail. Every single arrow missed its mark. Even Arjuna's arrows could not even graze the deer, much less bring it down. The deer bolted away, leaving the Paandavas dejected, frustrated, tired, and thirsty. A morose Nakula pondered why such failures had become their fate, even though they had neither forsaken dharma nor were they guilty of sloth. Bheema, Arjuna, and Sahadeva too shared in with their dejections. Yudhishthira consoled them, or perhaps added his own lament to theirs.

> There are no limits to misfortune. Nor effects or causes.
> Dharma distributes it, depending on merits and demerits.[6]

The chase had been futile; they were a long way from their hermitage, and all were thirsty. They could not spot water anywhere. Yudhishthira asked Nakula to climb up a tree and look for water. Nakula did so and spotted several trees and the sounds of cranes. Convinced there was water there, he climbed down and walked over to that spot.

Nakula reached a lake with clear and clean water. As he was about to drink from the lake, a voice arose from the heavens warning him to desist from drinking the water before he had answered a question. Nakula was tired, he was thirsty, his brothers were waiting for him to bring water. He had neither the time nor the inclination to listen to some disembodied voice. He ignored it, scooped up water in his palms, brought it to his mouth, and drank the cool water. The next moment, he fell down. Was he dead? He looked so.

When Nakula didn't return, Yudhishthira sent Sahadeva in search of Nakula. He reached the lake and saw Nakula lying down.

Both distraught and thirsty, he too went to the lake to drink water. He too was stopped by the voice which had the same message and admonition for Sahadeva. Sahadeva too ignored the voice; he too drank the water, and he too fell down. Arjuna and Bheema also followed suit, meeting the same fate as their younger brothers.

Finally, Yudhishthira went in search of both water and his brothers. He saw his four brothers lying on the ground, lifeless. There was no sign of battle, no marks of injuries on their bodies, and no other footprints to suggest they had been ambushed. Four warriors as redoubtable as Bheema, Arjuna, Nakula, and Sahadeva had been felled as if by magic. Yudhishthira was baffled. Perhaps Duryodhana and Shakuni were behind this. Perhaps the water itself had been poisoned. But that did not seem to be the case either, for their complexion looked healthy. There was no discolouration to suggest poisoning. As Yudhishthira entered the water, the same voice spoke out, warning him against drinking the water without answering his questions.

Yudhishthira paused and asked the voice who it was. It was not every day that a voice from the skies spoke to them. The voice said it was a crane that lived in this lake and was its owner. No, not possible, Yudhishthira professed both his curiosity and fear, for none other than Yama could have brought down these four warriors. The voice again asked Yudhishthira to answer his question before attempting to drink the water. He then said that he was a yaksha and made himself visible to Yudhishthira. If that was what the yaksha, or the crane, or whatever it was, wanted then that's how it would be. Yudhishthira told the yaksha to ask his questions.

Yudhishthira said he would reply to the best of his knowledge. Thus began a series of questions and answers between the wise Paandava and the inscrutable yaksha.

> 'What is heavier than the earth? What is higher than the sky? What is swifter than the wind? What is more numerous than men?'[7]
>
> Yudhishthira replied, 'The mother is heavier than the earth. The father is higher than the sky. The mind is swifter than the wind. Worries are more numerous than men.'[8]
>
> The yaksha asked, 'Who is a friend to one who is travelling? Who is a friend at home? Who is a friend to one who is sick? Who is a friend to one who is about to die?'[9]

> Yudhishthira replied, 'A caravan is a friend to a traveller. A wife is a friend at home. A physician is a friend to one who is sick. Charity is a friend to one who is about to die.'[10]

The yaksha then asked a question about dharma to Dharma's son. The delicious irony in that question would be revealed only later.

> The yaksha asked, 'In a single word, what is dharma? In a single word, what is fame? In a single word, what is heaven? In a single word, what is happiness?'[11]
>
> 'In a single word, dexterity is dharma. In a single word, generosity is fame. In a single word, truth is heaven. In a single word, conduct is happiness.'[12]

The yaksha then asked a question that Yudhishthira answered with brevity and clarity, but one which humans have ignored for millennia, philosophers have spent lifetimes trying to come up with better answers, and which management gurus have made fortunes trying to answer.

> The yaksha asked, 'If abandoned, what makes one pleasant? If abandoned, what does not lead to sorrow? If abandoned, what ensures prosperity? If abandoned, what makes one happy?'[13]
>
> Yudhishthira replied, 'The abandoning of pride makes one pleasant. The abandoning of anger does not lead to sorrow. The abandoning of desire ensures prosperity. The abandoning of desire makes one happy.'[14]
>
> The yaksha asked, 'When is a man dead? When is a kingdom dead? When is a funeral ceremony dead? When is a sacrifice dead?'[15]
>
> Yudhishthira replied, 'A poor man is dead. A kingdom without a king is dead. A funeral ceremony performed without a learned brahmana is dead. A sacrifice without dakshina is dead.'[16]

The same Yudhishtira who had answered the yaksha that poverty was death, would, after the war, insist on renouncing the throne and all wealth to head off into the forest to live the life of penury.

> 'What is the right direction? What is spoken of as water? O Partha! What is food and what is poison? What is the right time for a funeral ceremony?'[17]

> Yudhishthira replied, 'The virtuous are the right direction. The sky is water. The cow is food. A request is poison. A brahmana is the best time for a funeral sacrifice. O Yaksha! What do you think?'[18]

Back and forth the yaksha and Yudhishthira had gone. The Paandava had answered all the questions the yaksha had for him. Pleased with Yudhishthira's answers, the yaksha granted him the life of one of his brothers. Yudhishthira chose Nakula. Why not Bheema or Arjuna, the yaksha asked. Because one son of Kunti—Yudhishthira—already lived, said Yudhishthira. He wanted one son of Maadri also to live, hence, Nakula. Pleased with his reply, the yaksha restored all four brothers to life. Who was the yaksha who had this power over life and death at his fingertips?

Seeing his brothers awake, neither hungry nor thirsty, Yudhishthira again asked the yaksha who he was, for no ordinary bird or yaksha could have subdued his brothers so effortlessly. The yaksha replied that he was Dharma[19] and had come down to see his son.

> It is fortunate that you have conquered the six states.[20] Two occur early, two in the middle and two at the end, leading to the hereafter.[21]

Dharma then granted Dharmaputra Yudhishthira a boon. He asked that the brahmana's kindling be returned. Dharma then granted him a second boon. Yudhishthira asked that since their thirteenth year of exile was approaching, they should not be recognized when they lived among people that year. Dharma granted that boon, assuring him that they would spend the thirteenth year in Viraata, undetected. Dharma then granted Yudhishthira a third boon. Yudhishthira asked only that he stay true to the path of dharma. Dharma granted the boon to Dharmaraja that he would stay true to the path of dharma. The coming war would test Yudhishthira's resolve and boon repeatedly.

33

VICTORY OF INDRA

A Renewed Indra

Parva: Udyoga (5) Upa parva: Udyoga (49)
Chapters: 9-18 Shlokas: 304

Much time had passed. The Paandavas had entered the kingdom of Matsya Viraata[1] to spend their thirteenth year of exile, to live amongst people and yet remain undetected. The penalty for being discovered by Duryodhana's spies would be to spend another twelve years in exile and one in disguise.

The Paandavas had Dharma's boon that they would remain unrecognized in their thirteenth of exile.[2] The question that they had before them was to pick a kingdom where they could spend that one year.

Having settled on Viraata, Yudhishthira had decided he would pose as a brahmana named Kanka, skilled in dice.[3] Bheema said he would pose as Ballava, a cook and supervisor of the royal kitchens. When called upon, he would also tame wild elephants and wrestle warriors. As for the handsome and radiant Arjuna, he decided he would live the year as a eunuch named Brihannalla.[4] The handsome Nakula would become Granthika, keeper of horses. Sahadeva would tend to the cows, going by the name Tantipala. Draupadi would become a sairandhari, a maidservant skilled at hairdressing. She would adopt the name Sairandhari and tell Queen Sudeshna she had served both Satyabhaama and Draupadi in the past. They would resort to deception to live incognito for a year, just as Nala[5] had.

The Paandavas, proud princes of the Kuru lineage, would live like commoners for a year. It was important that they knew how to live like commoners. Dhaumya, their priest and counsellor, guided them. Those who had lived as kings needed to now learn how to live under a king.

> Live in the king's abode without assuming that, as a favourite, one can ascend his vehicle, palanquin, seat, elephant or chariot.[6]

> One can live in the king's abode as long as one does not serve those who wish him ill, as long as one does not consort with those who seek to harm him and as long as one does not stray from one's station.[7]

> Do not reveal to men the lies the king utters. Do not converse with men the king does not like.[8]

Thus did the thirteenth year pass, almost without incident. Bheema was once called upon by the king to wrestle a famed wrestler named Jeemoota.[9] Unable to refuse the king, Bheema wrestled him. Unable to restrain himself, he ended up killing the wrestler.

> I think that if I grant you residence, I will bring about my own destruction.[10]

Sudeshna had expressed reservations at employing Draupadi as a sairandhari, seeing her beauty. Draupadi had assuaged her fears by telling her that she was married to five gandharvas who protected her. The implication was that Draupadi was a chaste woman who would not let another man near her. The thirteenth year would have passed off uneventfully had it not been for Queen Sudeshna's brother, Keechaka, who was also the general of Viraata's army. One day, his roving eye fell on Draupadi.

> This beautiful one's form intoxicates me, like scent generated from liquor.[11]

When she wouldn't succumb to his sweet words, he chased her around the palace. She ran to the court where Keechaka kicked her in the presence of the king and Yudhishthira, who stayed silent, again, as his wife was ill-treated, again. A distraught Draupadi decided to end matters and Keechaka's life, and to that end she approached Bheema at night.

> How can a woman, who has Yudhishthira as a husband, not be sorrowful?[12]

Goaded and riled up by Draupadi, Bheema agreed to put an end to Draupadi's miseries and Keechaka's life. She lured Keechaka to a dancing hall where Bheema did the rest. Such was his repressed rage at the indignities Draupadi had had to bear and at Yudhishthira's reluctance to act, that Bheema didn't stop at killing Keechaka. He pummelled his head, hands, and legs into his trunk,[13] leaving people the next morning to gape in horror at the lifeless lump of mass that had once been the mighty general, Keechaka. When Keechaka's 105 brothers tried to take revenge by carrying off Draupadi to the cremation ground to burn her alive along with Keechaka, Bheema dispatched all 105 to Yamaloka.[14]

> I do not think that you have ever been caressed the way you are going to be caressed now.[15]

Just as this crisis was brewing over, another erupted. Keechaka's death prompted Susharma, the king of Trigarta and a long-time rival who had been bested by Viraata under an army led by Keechaka, to decide to invade Viraata. The Kauravas joined Susharma in this misdeed, and separated by a day, their armies attacked Viraata. A lone Arjuna, with the king's son, Uttara, as his charioteer, repulsed the Kaurava army.[16]

When the Paandavas's identity was finally revealed, Viraata married his daughter Uttaraa to Arjuna's son, Abhimanyu.[17] This union would lead to the birth of Pareekshit, but not before Abhimanyu had been martyred on the battlefield of Kurukshetra on the thirteenth day of battle, and not before Pareekshit himself would be killed by Ashwatthaama's brahmaastra while still in his mother's womb. It would fall upon Vaasudeva Krishna to revive the young prince.

With the thirteenth year of exile over, negotiations commenced between the Paandavas and Kauravas for the return of Indraprastha and the Paandava's kingdom to them, as per the condition of the second round of dice that had taken place. Half the kingdom should be returned to the Paandavas—this was Krishna, Balaraama, and others' view. But it was also certain that Duryodhana had no intention of returning the kingdom to the Paandavas. Krishna and Balaraama wanted an emissary to be sent to Dhritaraashtra. Saatyaki didn't think that would yield any results. Drupada also concurred. He wanted to start approaching friendly kingdoms for support in a war he saw as inevitable.[18]

> Duryodhana will not hand back the kingdom sweetly.[19]

Even as Drupada sent an old and learned priest as his emissary to Hastinapura with the dual purpose of asking for half the kingdom back for the Paandavas and to sow dissension among the Kaurava elders and their army,[20] he also dispatched messengers to other kingdoms to rally support for the war that everyone saw as a distinct possibility. Krishna meanwhile departed for Dwaarka, followed closely by Arjuna.

News of these activities reached Duryodhana through his network of spies. He too had the same idea as Drupada and others, for he too knew the Kauravas would need allies in the coming war. Drupada and Saatyaki had assessed Duryodhana correctly—he had no intention of giving back the Paandavas their kingdom. In case anyone harboured any doubt, Duryodhana would utter those infamous words to Krishna in the assembly of the Kurus.

> O Keshava! As long as I am alive, I will not give to the Paandavas even that much of land that can be held on the point of a sharp needle.[21]

Krishna had reached Dwaarka. Duryodhana also arrived there, getting there ahead of Arjuna. Once at Dwaarka, Duryodhana entered Krishna's chamber, followed shortly by Arjuna. Both Kauravas[22] stood there, waiting for the sleeping Krishna to awake. When Krishna awoke, he saw both. Since both had asked for his help, Krishna offered his Narayana army to one and himself to the other. Since Arjuna was the younger of the two, Krishna asked him to choose first. Arjuna chose Krishna; Duryodhana exulted at having obtained a large army.[23] Both departed happy.

Among the kings that had received information about the preparations for the inevitable war, Shalya, Maadri's brother, and uncle of Nakula and Sahadeva, was one. He had started out to the Paandavas to offer his help and army. This was a large army and would be an asset to the Paandavas. Duryodhana too got to know of this army's movement through his spies. Shalya's large army was on the move. It would end up siding with the Paandavas against the Kauravas. Duryodhana thought up a stratagem and deployed it to full effect.

Duryodhana had grand pavilions constructed on the route that Shalya's army took. As that army marched, as Shalya halted, they were as greeted by resplendent pavilions and multitudes of servants. Vanity vanquished Shalya; he thought of himself as above Indra himself, for perhaps not even the king of the gods would have received such lavish hospitality.

Wanting to reward the builders of such grand pavilions, when Shalya asked for them to be shown to him, he got a surprise when Duryodhana presented himself, instead. Shalya asked Duryodhana to ask for anything he wished. Duryodhana seized the opportunity and asked that Shalya become the general of his army; where Shalya went, so would his army. An indebted Shalya acquiesced. He had partaken of Duryodhana's hospitality, even if in ignorance. Duryodhana had scored two hits with one strike.

Shalya proceeded to Upaplavya, where the Paandavas and Drupada were camping, and recounted what had transpired to Yudhishthira. What had happened could not be undone, but Yudhishthira saw a silver lining in this dark cloud. Knowing Karna and his nature, he was certain that when events came to pass, and if Karna became commander of the Kaurava army, he would want a redoubtable warrior like Shalya to become his charioteer. Yudhishthira asked Shalya to agree when Karna asked him to become his charioteer. Having done so, Shalya's task, Yudhishthira said, would be to sap Karna's pride and energy. Thus enervated, emasculated, Karna would be easier to vanquish and kill in battle.

> When he wishes to fight in the field of battle, it is certain that I will speak words that do him harm. O Paandava! They will make him lose his pride and lose his energy. He will then be easy to kill.[24]

If one maternal uncle, Shakuni, could spend his entire life in plotting the downfall and demise of the Paandavas, then the Paandavas could return the favour through Shalya, maternal uncle of Nakula and Sahadeva.

Shalya now turned his attention to Yudhishthira and the fact that they had suffered the last thirteen years on account of that cursed gambling match. But from such unhappiness would arise happiness, Shalya said, just as Indra and Shachi had to undergo sufferings, but eventually emerged victorious. Yudhishthira asked him to elaborate.

Shalya started his account with Prajapati Tvashta.[25] Harbouring a longstanding hatred of Indra, the Prajapati created a three-headed son named Trishiras. Fierce in form, Trishiras studied and chanted the Vedas with one mouth, drank liquor with another head, and cast an eye around the entire world with his third head. He was equally steadfast in his austerities. With such severe penances and dedication, Indra began to experience unease at a potential rival to his throne. Indra was quick to imagine threats to his throne, but this time the peril was real.

Indra employed all the strategems at his disposal. He dispatched apsaraas to distract Trishiras. That had worked with Vishwaamitra, but the seduction failed with Trishiras. The beautiful, perfection personified, flawless apsaraas failed.

> One who is stronger must not ignore a weak enemy who is strengthening.[26]

What could not be accomplished by the wiles of beauty would be completed with weapons. Indra launched his vajra at Trishiras. The vajra found its mark and Trishiras lay dead. Yet Indra felt no peace. The energy from Trishiras' corpse continued to blaze in all the directions. Indra fretted over the matter and concluded that Trishiras' three heads needed to be severed from his body. But who would, could, perform such a task?

Indra spotted a woodcutter and asked him to cut off Trishiras' three heads. The woodcutter replied that not only was his axe not sharp enough to cut through Trishiras' broad shoulders, but he was not going to become a sinner by committing such an act. Indra assured the woodcutter that he would ensure that his axe was sharp enough to do the job.

The sharpness of the axe aside, the woodcutter wanted to know who Indra was and why he had killed this giant. Indra answered the woodcutter's questions. He was Indra and the asura who lay dead was Trishiras. That he was the king of the gods didn't matter to the woodcutter. He chided Indra for having committed the sin of killing a brahmana. The deed was done, and he would atone for the sin, Indra replied.

All matters settled, the woodcutter finally obliged Indra and sliced off Trishiras' three heads with the axe that now was sharp enough for the job. From those three severed heads emerged three types of birds. The woodcutter returned to his home and Indra returned to heaven.

The matter didn't rest there. When Trishiras' father, Tvashta, heard of his son's death at the hands of Indra, he was enraged. His son had caused no harm to Indra, and yet he had been murdered by Indra. There would be retribution. He resolved to create Vritra, who would destroy Indra, and through his austerities, he did. When Vritra thus appeared, Tvashta asked him to grow in power through the strength of his austerities. And so did Vritra grow. When he was as tall as the skies, Vritra asked his father what to do next. Accepting his father's command to destroy Indra, Vritra went to heaven and there commenced a terrible battle between him and Indra.

Vritra was not only huge, but he was also growing in strength because of his father's austerities. As the battle progressed, things worsened for the gods. At one point, Vritra opened his mouth up and swallowed Indra. The gods scrambled to save their king. They created a yawn, and when Vritra yawned, Indra slipped out of his mouth. That was, however, a momentary respite, for Vritra's powers continued to grow. Unable to withstand his onslaught, the gods fled. Fearful and defeated, the gods went to Vishnu on Mount Mandaara for help and advice.

Approaching Vishnu, the gods and rishis addressed him, praising him for his past deeds in saving the gods and in defeating Bali through his three strides[27] and instating Indra as the king of the gods. Vishnu pondered over the matter and decided that before Vritra could be killed, he had to be lulled into a sense of complacency. He asked the gods to broker a truce between Indra and Vritra. He would enter Indra's vajra to give it more power.

Their confidence bolstered, the gods and sages went to Vritra and asked him to forge a friendship with Indra. Vritra bowed his head and asked the sages how could the two become friends, since both were powerful. Friendship or enmity could be decided, the gods said, only after a meeting of minds.

> Righteous ones should meet, at least once. After that, what is destined will happen.[28]

The sages asked Vritra to meet Indra at least once, as both were righteous and virtuous. Vritra acquiesced. He would listen to the words of the wise, and he had anyway nothing to fear from Indra, who lacked the strength to kill him. Vritra said that neither Indra nor the gods, nothing that was wet or dry, not during the day nor during the night, nor any weapon made of stone or wood could kill him. Such overconfidence was not a good trait. Vritra should have learned from itihaasa—what had happened, as it had happened, to Hiranyakashyipu, Sunda and Upasunda, Raavana, and others.

Friendship was a means to an end—Vritra's. Though an uneasy friendship had formed between Indra and Vritra, the king of the gods was always on the lookout for an opportunity. One day, as dusk approached, Indra saw Vritra by the ocean. Hadn't Vritra said that he could be killed by nothing that was dry, nor by anything that was wet? Indra looked at the foam the ocean's waves had brewed up. They were neither wet, nor dry. The foam could become an instrument of Vritra's death, Indra reasoned. It was neither day nor night. The foam was a weapon, but neither of stone nor of wood. The agreement that the two had was not on Indra's mind; only the destruction of his enemy mattered. He aimed and hurled his vajra at the foam, aiming it at Vritra. Vishnu's energy infused itself into the foam. Vritra fell, dead.

Everyone rejoiced at Vritra's demise. But Indra now carried the burden of having killed not one, but two, brahmanas. He had broken an agreement with Vritra. Less the guilt and more the sin weighed immeasurably on him. With that sin and falsehood came a loss of the powers and wisdom that once had been his. Distraught, bereft of his powers, dislodged from his position, Indra was no longer the king of the gods. He fled to some far, remote corner of the world. With no Indra, there were no rains, and the earth suffered. None of the gods wanted to be Indra, either.

The situation had to be remedied. The gods and sages consulted and concluded that Nahusha was the worthiest among mortals to be the king of the Gods. When they approached Nahusha, however, he was diffident. After all, being a great king was one thing, but to be the king of the gods quite another. Indra's powers far exceeded anything he possessed. The sages assured him that that would not be the case for long. Indra had been the king of the gods. If Nahusha became the new king, then Nahusha would get the same powers that Indra had. Nahusha would be the new Indra, even though the designated span of the reign of the current Indra had not yet passed. Unprecedented situations called for unprecedented solutions. Unintended consequences would come along for the ride.

> You will absorb the energy of gods, danavas, yakshas, rishis, rakshasas, gandharvas and all beings as soon as you behold them. You will then be powerful. Always placing dharma at

> the forefront, be the lord of all the worlds and the herdsman of the brahmarshis and gods in heaven.[29]

Nahusha was now Indra. The divine Nandana Garden was his to roam as he pleased. The apsaraas were at his beck and call, to dance for him when he so wished. The gods waited upon him, as did the gandharvas, Naarada, and the six seasons.[30] Where he sat, where he went, a pleasant breeze blew, cooling him. Nahusha enjoyed the power and pelf that accrued to him. He immersed himself in everything that heaven had to offer. The heaven so far had one thing that Nahusha didn't have or know he could have. Matters might have rested that way, had it not been for the inevitable twist of fate.

> He had always had dharma in his soul. But he now became addicted to desire.[31]

One fateful day Nahusha laid eyes on Shachi, Indra's consort. Was he not the new Indra, Nahusha reasoned? Wasn't everything that had once been Indra's now his, Nahusha argued. Wasn't Shachi also to be his, by that right, Nahusha asked. Shachi had to come to him and become his, Nahusha demanded.

Thus did Nahusha decree. An appalled Shachi rushed to Brihaspati for help and advice. Her Indra's absence was temporary, she said. Brihaspati consoled Shachi and then assured her that her Indra would soon return. When? How? In the meantime, Nahusha was furious when he heard that Shachi had taken refuge with Brihaspati.[32]

The gods went to Nahusha and tried to assuage his anger, reminding him that not only was such wrath unbecoming of the king of the gods, but also that Shachi was the wife of Indra. If that were the case, Nahusha reminded the gods, this was the same Indra who had violated Ahalya and committed many other questionable acts. Surely the gods could have restrained Indra when he had coveted Ahalya, Sage Gautam's wife. They hadn't.

Nahusha concluded by reminding the gods in a not-so subtle threat that it would be good for Shachi and it would be good for the gods if she came to him willingly. He would wait, but not indefinitely.

> Let the goddess serve me. That will be the best for her. And that will always ensure welfare for the gods too.[33]

At their wits' ends, the gods went to Brihaspati and asked Shachi to accept Nahusha as her new husband. Without Indra around, and with Nahusha as their king who they themselves had elevated to the throne, the gods had few options. A distraught Shachi beseeched Brihaspati to help her. Brihaspati turned to the gods and told them that he would not give Shachi up to Nahusha and perform an act of adharma. He reminded the gods of what Brahma had once said.

> He who hands over to the enemy someone who has sought refuge, his seed will not grow at the time of sowing.[34]

If Brihaspati was not going to hand over Shachi to Nahusha, the gods certainly were not going to forcibly evict her from the hermitage. However, the situation could not continue indefinitely in this state of limbo, either. Nahusha's insolence and arrogance would lead to his downfall, of that Brihaspati was certain; all they needed was some time, that they didn't have.

> Time brings many impediments. It is time which leads to another time.[35]

Perhaps, what if Nahusha could be persuaded to give some more time? But who would ask Nahusha? Not the gods, fearful of his wrath as they were. But if Shachi herself were to ask for some time, Nahusha's ego would make him accede to her request. Brihaspati asked the gods to go to Shachi and have her ask Nahusha for some time. The gods put their request to Shachi, who agreed.

Seeing Shachi walk down his court gave Nahusha's heart a leap. Even more when she told him that while she was ready to become his consort, she needed some time. She needed time to ascertain where Indra had disappeared, and if she failed to locate him, she would then willingly come and serve him as a wife. What more could the new Indra want. Nahusha granted her permission, reminding her that he would hold her to her promise.

Having bought a little time, the gods then went to Vishnu and asked him for advice. Indra's killing of Vritra had set off a chain of events in motion. They reminded him that it had been his energy that had helped Indra kill Vritra. Killing Vritra had been an imperative. But the killing of Vritra, a brahmana, had enervated Indra. The gods implied that it was Vishnu who was now also on the hook for finding a way out of the predicament they faced. Vishnu assured the gods that Nahusha's downfall was nigh and he would become the cause his own downfall. But Indra would have to expiate the sin of killing a brahmana first. Without that he would not be able to ascend the throne again. Vishnu advised the gods to tell Indra to perform a sacrifice in his honour.

Indra did as advised and performed a horse sacrifice.[36] He felt unburdened of the sin. He felt ready to battle Nahusha. He marched against Nahusha. However, Nahusha was still king of the gods; he had been infused with the energies of the gods. Indra could not muster up the courage to take him on. He slunk away. He would wait, remain invisible till an opportune moment, whenever that arrived.

Indra was nowhere to be found. His disappearance plunged Shachi in grief. He had been her only hope. With the darkness of hopelessness engulfing her, she prayed to goddess Raatri,[37] asking for her help. Upashruti[38] also appeared before both. The Goddess Raatri asked Upashruti to reveal to them where Indra was.

Upashruti and Shachi travelled. They crossed forests, mountains, and went past even the Himalayas. They went past its northern slopes to a great body of water, in the middle of which was a large island. In the middle of that island was a large lake. In that lake were many lotuses. In one of those lotuses was Indra, the former king of the gods. Assuming a tiny form, Shachi and Upashruti entered the stalk of one such lotus. There they saw Indra, in a tiny form, hiding inside that lotus. Shachi told Indra why she had come there, what Nahusha's intentions were, and asked Indra to assume his true form and defeat Nahusha.

Indra had tried that once before. Just the very sight of Nahusha had driven Indra to the farthest corner of the world, to take refuge in that tiny lotus. How could he take on the new god of the kings? But perhaps there was a way, Indra mused. For someone whose ego and arrogance had been driven beyond all measure, perhaps there was a way to bring about his downfall. Hadn't his own ego led to his downfall, because of Sage Durvaasa's curse?[39] Indra suggested a course of action to Shachi. He advised her to follow that with the utmost of secrecy. The plan? Shachi was to go Nahusha again and tell him to come to her in a celestial palanquin. Yes, that was the plan—for Shachi to invite Nahusha to come and become her new lord.

Shachi walked into Nahusha's court a second time. Nahusha watched her walk.

'Yes, O divine beauty, what brings you to my court a second time?' Nahusha said, admiring Shachi and her gait.

> 'I am ready, O Nahusha,' Shachi said. She would not address him as Indra.
>
> 'I knew you would see the wisdom in my words,' Nahusha said with an air of nonchalance. His heart and loins, on the other hand, were already giddy with excitement and anticipation.
>
> 'But…,' Shachi said.
>
> 'Do not hesitate, O goddess. Your walk captivates me, the sound of your words intoxicates me. I am already yours. Be mine, now, and forever.'
>
> 'I have a request, a condition, if you will,' ignoring Nahusha's libidinous litany.
>
> 'A condition?' Nahusha frowned. 'You are not going to talk of locating your coward of a husband, Indra, again, are you? One look at me and the coward slunk away. This time I will not be as generous.'
>
> 'No, it is not about Indra, but you,' Shachi ignored Nahusha's jibe.
>
> 'You shall have me—all of me, soon enough, O Fair Goddess. What more do you want of me?'
>
> 'When you come to my place, it should be in a manner befitting my stature and your status,' Shachi said.
>
> 'What is it that you crave from me?' Nahusha indulged Shachi.
>
> 'A palanquin like none ever, none before, none after. Not even Brahma and Vishnu possess one.'
>
> 'Done. I am the lord of all that is past, what is present, and what will be the future, am I not? A palanquin made of the finest gold, adorned with the brightest and biggest jewels shall be. Just for you.'
>
> 'No.'
>
> 'Then?' Nahusha asked.
>
> 'I said a palanquin like no other, O Nahusha,' Indraani[40] said.
>
> 'Command me, then, O Shachi,' Nahusha said, ego, desire, and destruction goading him.
>
> 'Borne by the seven sages (saptarishi[41]),' Shachi said.
>
> Nahusha was quiet for a moment. Yes, such a palanquin had never been before, where the seven sages, the wisest, would bear the strongest and greatest of gods, the king of the gods, the new Indra. Yes, he liked the suggestion.

Nahusha accepted her request. He got a celestial chariot prepared and which was yoked by the seven sages.

> One who makes the sages carry his vehicle cannot be weak in strength. I am a powerful ascetic. I am the lord of the past, the present and the future. When I am angry, the universe ceases to exist.[42]

The moment of Nahusha's arrival neared ever so fast. Time was running out like sand from a clenched fist. Shachi's anxiety knew no bounds. Brihaspati, meanwhile, offered oblations into the fire. From the fire appeared Agni himself, the god of fire. Brihaspati asked him to search out Indra. Agni searched far and wide and came back, having failed in his search. He had searched everywhere but failed to locate Indra. He had searched everywhere, except the waters, since entering the waters would mean his own destruction.

Brihaspati told Agni that he[43] had emerged from water, so entering water would not destroy him. Additionally, his mantras would ensure Agni's safety. Thus assured, for Agni trusted the preceptor of the gods, he entered the waters and renewed afresh his search for Indra. Eventually, he came across the same lake and the same lotus that Shachi and Upashruti had found Indra in. Agni propitiated Indra and asked him to come resume his rightful place as the king of the gods.

Indra had a question for Agni. How had Nahusha, a mere king at one time, had come to be so powerful and become the new king of the gods? Agni told Indra how Nahusha had been approached and requested by the gods to become their king and that Nahusha had absorbed the energy of whoever he looked at.

Word had spread discreetly that the Agni himself had taken up the search for Indra. Where there was life, there was fire. And wherever Indra was, Agni would soon find him. Other gods like Yama, Kubera, Varuna, and Soma also arrived there. In that tiny stem of the lotus did the gods confer. They all joined in bolstering Indra's confidence. Indra, in turn, made Varuna the lord of the waters, Yama of ancestors, and Kubera the lord of wealth and yakshas.

The gods were so busy bolstering Indra's confidence that they didn't notice Sage Agastya join them. When they turned around in surprise, Agastya gave them the news that Indra's problem had been solved. Nahusha had been ejected from heaven. The gods asked Agastya to share with them how that had happened.

As planned and agreed upon, the seven sages had started out for Shachi's abode, carrying a palanquin with Nahusha, king of the gods, atop. When the sages were carrying Nahusha in the palanquin, they asked him a question. Nahusha and the sages started arguing, and in that argument, Nahusha's foot touched Agastya's head.[44] Agastya cursed him for having done this act of adharma. Nahusha would have to spend ten-thousand years as a snake, only after which he would return to the heavens. The curse was instantaneous. Nahusha lost his form, his status as king of the gods, and his place in heaven. Down he fell. There he would remain for a long, long time, till he met his descendants, the Paandavas.[45]

Reinstated as the god of the kings, Indra ascended Airaavata.[46] Surrounded by the sages, gods, gandharvas, and apsaraas, he was reunited with Shachi.

Ending his account, Shalya told Yudhishthira to not be distressed by their travails and to take heart from Indra's struggles. If the king of the gods could turn around his fate, so could and so would Yudhishthira. This account of Indra, Agastya had said, was equal in importance to the Vedas.[47]

Yudhishthira listened to this remarkable account. Before they departed, Yudhishthira reminded his maternal uncle Shalya that in battle his task would be to sap Karna's energy on the battlefield.

Shalya took leave and went back with his army to Duryodhana. Shalya would remain true to his word. He became Karna's charioteer on the seventeenth day of battle. He engaged Karna in a war of words, belittling him and eulogizing Arjuna. Such was their exchange that by the time Karna entered the battlefield, he had been mentally drained and driven to distraction by Shalya's jibes.[48] After Karna's death, Shalya was instated as the commander of the Kaurava army. As commander of the Kaurava army, Shalya led the remnants of the Kaurava army into battle and met his end at the hands of none other than Yudhishthira.

> The one with dharma in his soul had fought in accordance with dharma and was killed by Dharma's son.[49]

Karma, dharma, and bhaagya (fate) were relentless, subtle, and ruthless, indeed.

> The bull among men fell down affectionately on the ground, like a beloved wife who falls down on the chest of her dear husband.[50]

34

DAMBHODBHAVA

Dumb is as Dumb Does

Parva: Udyoga (5) **Upa parva: Bhaagavat-yaana (54)**

Chapter: 94 **Shlokas: 45**

Even as Duryodhana plotted to entice Shalya and his army into serving him instead of the Paandavas, Drupada's aged and wise priest from Upaplavya[1] arrived at Hastinapura with a message for Dhritaraashtra. In that assembly of the Kurus, the messenger delivered his missive.[2] The Kurus all listened as the aged messenger reminded the assembly of what the right of the Paandavas was but had been denied them, of the game of dice where they were cheated of their kingdom even as the Kuru king had looked on, and of the attempts made on their lives by Duryodhana over the years. The Paandavas' seven akshauhinis were less compared to the Kaurava's eleven, but on the Paandavas' side was Arjuna. The thirteen years had passed. It was now time for returning to the Paandvas what was rightfully theirs.

Bheeshma didn't disagree with the brahmana messenger's words,[3] though he did feel his words were sharper than they should have been. Karna, ever eager to weigh in and wade in, retorted that the brahmana was repeating what was known to all, and therefore wasting everyone's time. What was relevant, in his opinion, was that the Paandavas had not completed the thirteen years of exile, and as per the terms of the gambling match to which the Paandavas themselves had agreed, they should return for another period of thirteen years of exile.

As great and brave a warrior as Karna was, Bheeshma had to remind him that he had been bested by Arjuna not too long back in Viraata.

> O Radheya! How can you speak? You should remember your own deeds, when Partha alone vanquished the six charioteers in battle.[4]

Their internal squabbles aside, Dhritaraashtra sent the messenger back with a promise to send his response soon enough. The messenger selected was Sanjaya. Dhritaraashtra summoned him and asked him to proceed to Upaplavya. The king was clear—Sanjaya was to use words of peace, words of reconciliation, words of praise. He was to offer the Paandavas everything except their kingdom. He was not to, under any circumstance, incite the Paandavas to war. The message had to be delivered with finesse.

> O Sanjaya! At the right time, whatever you think should be said for the welfare of the Bharatas, say that in the midst of the kings, but do not say anything that incites them to the war.[5]

In the assembly of kings at Upaplavya, Yudhishthira heard Sanjaya's words, understood their import, and returned Sanjaya with the message that he too desired peace, which could be had if the Kauravas returned Paandavas their half of the kingdom. Krishna added that he also wanted peace, but it could not be without restitution. To ensure peace, to prevent war, to avoid bloodshed that was otherwise inevitable, Krishna decided that he would go to the Kauravas as a peace emissary.

> I am as ready for peace, as I am for war. For the sake of dharma and artha, I can be mild. But I can also be terrible.[6]

By the time Sanjaya reached Hastinapura, it was late at night. An anxious Dhritaraashtra could not wait till morning. He granted Sanjaya an audience and listened as he spoke, his words casting a darker pall of gloom than the night itself. Such was Dhritaraashtra's despondency that he called for Vidura, who came forthwith. Vidura's words calmed the king down somewhat.[7]

Vidura finished his discourse. Dhritaraashtra asked a question that Vidura did not wish to answer. He instead pointed the king to Sage Sanatsujata, who had just arrived, and who proceeded to talk to the king about death, immortality, and more.[8]

> I am telling you that confusion is death.[9]

The next morning, to the entire assembly of the Kurus, Sanjaya delivered Yudhishthira's message. Listening to those words were Bheeshma, Drona, Kripa, Shalya, Kritavarma, Jayadratha, Ashvatthaama, Vikarna, Somadatta, Bahlika, Vidura, Yuyutsu, Duhshaasana, Chitrasena, Shakuni, Durmukha, Duhsaha, Karna, Ulooka, Vivimshati, and Duryodhana. Dhritaraashtra was convinced that if there were a war between the Paandavas and Kauravas, then defeat for the Kauravas was inevitable. Duryodhana thought differently. He was confident in the skills his guru, Balaraama,[10] had imparted him. Sanjaya described the preparations for war the Paandavas were making, the armies that were gathering to support them. To no avail. Duryodhana remained as adamant as ever. When he would finally change his mind, it would be too late.

As Krishna had prepared to depart, Yudhishthira had addressed him, confiding and putting forth his point of view and why it was important that there be peace between the Paandavas and Kauravas, but not at the cost of what was rightfully theirs. It was the principle that mattered. Even five villages would have done, but that offer had been rejected by Duryodhana.

> A man who has naturally been poor, does not suffer as much as one who has possessed fortune and prosperity and enjoyed happiness, having subsequently descended to an inferior state.[11]
>
> Lack of prosperity is like death to a man.[12] Everything is established in prosperity.[13] When one faces great hardships because of one's own crimes, one blames Indra and the other gods, but never one's own self.[14]

Here was Yudhishthira telling Krishna as well as reminding himself that without artha there could be no dharma. Yet, after the war, the same Yudhishthira would need to be reminded by Arjuna, who would quote Nahusha, that dharma's existence required artha.

> Without riches, cruel deeds are perpetrated. Shame on poverty.[15] Dharma, kaama, and heaven result from artha. Without artha, the world will not be able to sustain its life.[16] One who possesses riches possesses friends. One who possesses riches possesses relatives. One who possesses riches is a man in this world. One who possesses riches is learned.[17]

There was much that Yudhishthira unburdened to Krishna, but the outcome of a war was always uncertain, for many could unite to kill one, a coward could get lucky and kill a bravehearted warrier. As for one who died on the battlefield, it didn't matter whether his side won or lost, for both were the same to one who perished.

This, Krishna replied, was precisely the reason why he intended to go to Hastinapura and make the case for peace, once again, even though he knew Dhritaraashtra was under his son's control and would turn a deaf ear to overtures of peace. Yes, Krishna also knew about Duryodhana's nature and his proclivity to using means unfair and foul, but that didn't perturb him. It was not the dharma of the kshatriya to live by begging or displaying weakness. In any case, even if his mission failed, he would still return with the consolation that no one could blame them for not having tried for peace one last time.

As a parting message, Bheema reminded Krishna that there had been eighteen kings[18] whose evil actions had resulted in the annihilation of their entire lineages. Duryodhana was now on course to be the nineteenth. And then, much to everyone's surprise, even shock, Bheema asked Krishna to not incite Duryodhana to war. Krishna wondered aloud if the same Bheema who had sworn to avenge Draupadi's insult and break Duryodhana's thighs was now speaking like coward. No, Bheema responded, he was neither weak nor afraid! He just didn't want to be held responsible for the inevitable annihilation of the race of the Bharatas on their account. Even Bheema was capable of restraint.

Arjuna, Nakula, and Sahadeva also spoke their minds. Saatyaki echoed everyone's thoughts that war was inevitable, war was imminent, and that war would take place. It had to. Lastly, Draupadi spoke.

Draupadi's words cut like a knife—just as it was a sin to kill, it was equally a sin to not kill someone who deserved to be killed. And there was no one who deserved death more than Duryodhana. Krishnaa[19] gathered her hair in her left hand and showed them to Krishna—the tresses that Duhshaasana had grasped and dragged her by to the assembly of the deaf and mute Kurus.

Krishna consoled Krishnaa—the time for those Kuru women to weep the tears of the widowed was nigh. His words wouldn't come to naught.

Krishna left for Hastinapura the next morning, and stopping at Vrikasthala for the night, he arrived at Hastinapura. Vidura advised Dhritaraashtra against trying to bribe Krishna with lavish gifts the king proposed, reminding him that if he wasn't inclined to give the Paandavas even the five villages they had asked for, then all these gifts were of no use.

Krishna arrived, was greeted along the way by all, met by the Kurus and escorted to Dhritaraashtra and the elders. After paying his respects to the king, Krishna went to Vidura's house, and then to his aunt, Kunti's.[20] Kunti's message to Krishna was frank—this was the time for which kshatriya mothers gave birth to sons. The time for talking and waiting was over. Her kshatriya warrior sons would have to show their valour and take back what was and had been rightfully theirs, else they were as good as dead to her.[21] Her sons would not fail her, Krishna assured Kunti. Krishna departed Kunti's house, assured that she was ready to see her sons do battle.

Krishna then proceeded to Duryodhana's residence, where Karna, Shakuni, and Duhshaasana had also gathered. He tried to make Duryodhana see reason. The Kaurava's only response was that he had no quarrel with Krishna and therefore Krishna had been unwise to speak the words that he did. Krishna refused their food and instead went to Vidura's house where he had his meal.

> Food should be accepted because of love, or because of necessity.[22]

Vidura lamented that Krishna's words of peace would fall on deaf ears. Worse, in that assembly of elders would also be kings who had one or the other reason to be antagonistic towards Krishna. Among the kings in the assembly were some who had once allied with Jaraasandha. On Krishna's counsel, Bheema had duelled with and killed Jaraasandha. Those kings had come to ally with Duryodhana against the Paandavas. Vidura feared for Krishna.

The night passed. A new day dawned. Krishna woke, bathed, meditated, offered oblations in the fire, and prayed to the sun. Duryodhana and Shakuni arrived to invite Krishna to the assembly, for Dhritaraashtra had arrived. It was time for the blind king to see Krishna.

Like the sun that parts the clouds with its radiance, Krishna entered the assembly with Vidura and Saatyaki by his side. Once seated, Krishna spoke. He addressed Dhritaraashtra, beseeching him to weigh upon his son to accept peace, to act as a just king, to bring the feuding cousins together, for none in the world would dare stand against an army that had the combined might of the Paandavas and Kauravas. The alternative, Krishna warned, was a fratricidal war that would bring happiness to none and sorrow to all. He concluded by requesting the king to control his son who had forgotten the path of both dharma and artha. The Paandavas, Krishna said, stood as ready to fight as they were ready to serve the king. The choice was the king's. Krishna sat, silent. All welcomed Krishna's words. None spoke.

Silence was not an answer. Worse, it could be construed as a rejection of Krishna's peace overture. Parashurama broke the silence.[23] He addressed the assembly of Kurus and told them the story of a king named Dambhodbhava. He was as great a warrior as he was a vain egotist. Every day he would ask whether there existed anyone as brave as him. His brahmana advisors cautioned him against such pride. The advice fell on deaf ears. Each day the king would ask the same question.

One day, the brahmanas, fed to the teeth with Dambhodbhava's constant crowing and strutting, told the king about two that he could never equal in valour. Not warriors, but these were two ascetics, Nara and Narayana.

Where were they, asked Dambhodbhava. The brahmanas replied the two ascetics, Nara and Narayana, were performing penance somewhere in Gandhamaadana. A new challenge had finally presented itself. Dambhodbhava was ecstatic. Gathering his army of six divisions, he marched. He located the two ascetics. He saw Nara and Narayana, emaciated, cold, hungry, all skin and bones. Yes, great would be the fame that would accrue to him when he defeated them. He bowed before them and asked that they fight him.

Nara and Narayana responded that this was a hermitage that knew neither war nor weapons. But Dambhodbhava would not hear 'no' for an answer. Relenting, Nara then picked up a blade of grass. Dambhodhava sniggered. This was weapon enough, Nara said. Dambhodhava could bring whatever weapons he wished.

A delighted Dambhodbhava attacked with his army. Arrows rained like rains in the monsoons. With his blade of grass, Nara repulsed all. It was now time for Nara to retaliate. A single blade of grass is what he released at the six divisions of Dambhodbhava's army. A single blade turned into infinite. Each blade of grass scythed through Dambhodbhava's army, decimating it—slicing off the soldiers' eyes, noses, and ears. Such was the power of Nara's maaya. His army defeated, his pride crushed, Dambhodbhava fell at Nara's feet, begging for mercy.

Nara counselled the king. Pride and haughtiness were not desirable traits. Vanity was a person's undoing. Nara asked Dambhodbhava to return and lead a life of dharma. With his pride pricked, the king led the rest of his life following dharma.

This was the doing of Nara, Parashurama concluded. Narayana, on the other hand, was even greater. Why had he told the assembly this historical account? Arjuna was none other than Nara, reborn. Not merely a blade of grass, Arjuna had eight weapons.[24] Before he affixed even one to his Gandiva, the Kurus were well-advised to go seek peace with the Paandavas, Parashuraama counselled the assembly. Such was Arjuna's prowess, who was Nara reborn. And Krishna was Narayana reborn.

Whether they embraced peace or invited destruction was up to the Kauravas now, Parashurama concluded.

35

AMBAA

The Celibate Warrior and the Fiery Princess

Parva: Udyoga (5)	Upa parva: Amba-upakhyaana (60)
Chapters: 170–193	Shlokas: 673

Krishna's words to the Kuru assembly fell on deaf ears. His peace mission to Hastinapura failed. He tried to win over Karna over to the Paandava side but couldn't.[1] War, that had loomed on the horizon for thirteen years, now began its descent like a dark cloud over the plains of Kurukshetra. The Paandava and Kaurava armies marched to Kurukshetra.[2] Bheeshma was appointed and consecrated as the commander-in-chief of the Kaurava army.[3]

Not willing to let go of one last opportunity of playing mind games against the Paandavas, Duryodhana sent Ulooka, Shakuni's son, as a messenger to the Paandavas.[4] Ulooka's mission was to taunt the Paandavas, in Krishna's presence, to challenge them to fulfil the boastful words Krishna had uttered, Duryodhana told him. Ulooka was to remind the Paandavas to be 'men', to remember how Draupadi had been insulted and molested in the assembly of the Kurus.

> Wrath is manliness.[5] If you are capable, drink Duhshasana's blood.[6]

On the eve of the war, Duryodhana asked Bheeshma to share his assessment of the warriors on both sides of the armies lined up to face-off the next day on the battlefield of Kurukshetra. Bheeshma assessed all the major warriors on both sides. Kritavarma was an atirathi; so was Shalya; Jayadratha equal to two rathas; Shakuni equal to a single ratha. Bheeshma refused to assess Ashwatthaama as equal to even one ratha because of one fault—he loved his life too dearly. He concluded by saying that he would not kill the sons of Kunti,[7] nor would he fight or kill Shikhandi.

> But I will not kill the mighty-armed Shikhandi from Panchala, when I see him with weapons raised, marching against me in battle.[8]

Duryodhana may have been disappointed, but not surprised, upon hearing that Bheeshma would not kill the Paandavas. But Shikhandi? What was so special about him? Perhaps Shikhandi was not great enough a warrior for Bheeshma to consider worth fighting. But why single out Shikhandi in that case, for there were countless warriors who wouldn't measure up to Bheeshma? Furthermore, Bheeshma had assessed Shikhandi as a foremost among rathis.[9] There was more to it than met the eye. Duryodhana asked for more. Thus began a tale about a princess in a previous life.

Shikhandi, Bheeshma said, had been a woman[10] in a previous life, had been born a woman in this life, but had later turned into a man. That was why he had declared he would not fight or kill Shikhandi. That act would fall upon Drona's son, Ashwatthaama, after the war had ended, in the middle of the night.[11]

Bheeshma talked about a time many years past, before Duryodhana's birth, before Dhritaraashtra's birth, when Dhritaraashtra's father had been a minor; to a time when Bheeshma had only recently made the transition from Devavrata, the crown prince of Hastinapura, to Bheeshma, its lifelong celibate regent.

Bheeshma's father, Shaantanu, had died. Since Bheeshma had renounced the throne, he instated Shaantanu and Satyavati's eldest son, Chitraangada,[12] not quite an adult, on the throne. Before long, Chitraangada died in a battle with a gandharva also named Chitraangada on the plains of Kurukshetra,[13] the same plains where entire generations of Kuru warriors would perish much later. With his death, Chitraangada's younger brother, Vichitraveerya, became the king.

Till such time as Vichitraveerya became an adult, Bheeshma ruled as a proxy for his stepbrother. When Vichitraveerya reached adulthood, Bheeshma discussed matters with Satyavati and concluded that the three princesses of Kaashi—Ambaa, Ambika, and Ambaalika—would make ideal brides for his stepbrother. Arming himself, he proceeded to Kaashi where a swayamvara[14] was to be held for the three princesses.

Ambaa is a Princess

Bheeshma arrived in Kashi. He declared his intention of taking the three princesses as brides for Vichitraveerya. The assembled kings were free, he said, to challenge him; to stop him; to perform an act of bravery, if they could. The kings took up the challenge and all launched an assault against Bheeshma. They were, one and all, no match for Bheeshma—Ganga's son and Parashuraama's disciple.

Bheeshma took the three princesses to Hastinapura and handed them over to his stepmother, Satyavati, to marry off to Vichitraveerya. Two princesses said nothing. One did. The eldest one. Ambaa. She told Bheeshma that she had already accepted the king of Shaalva as her husband. Bheeshma decided marrying her to Vichitraveerya would be improper.

Bheeshma informed the elders, including Satyavati, and gave permission for Ambaa to leave for Shaalva, accompanied by brahmanas and her nurse. A happy, beaming Ambaa reached Shaalva's capital. She would be united with the one she had desired. Destiny, however, had chosen a decidedly devious detour.

Shaalva looked at Ambaa and declared that he now no longer wished to have her as his wife. After all, he reasoned, she had been won by Bheeshma. After all, hadn't she looked pleased as punch when he had abducted her? In any case, he concluded, as a king he could no longer accept her as a wife.

A stunned Ambaa protested that not only had Bheeshma placed her on his chariot against her will, but that she had been weeping all the time. Could the king not differentiate between tears and a smile? She requested, pleaded with Shaalva to accept her, that she loved him, and had never thought of anyone else as her husband.

> Love me. A maiden has come to you of her own accord.[15]

But try as she might, Shaalva had already abandoned her. He was unmoved by either her pleas or her tears, nor by her anger. He also admitted, inadvertently perhaps, that he feared Bheeshma's anger and considered her to be Bheeshma's property.

> It has been rightly said that where there is virtue, there is truth.[16]

A heartbroken Ambaa departed. The humiliation heaped on her by Shaalva now lit a fire of rage in her. She sought revenge now. Love, marriage, happiness were all alien to her now. Only revenge would bring her peace.

Ambaa blamed herself for not having jumped from Bheeshma's chariot in Kaashi when she had the chance. Undoubtedly, Shaalva was a coward. But what about her father, she told herself, who had treated her like chattel and organized a veeryashulka, to auction her off to the one who displayed the most prowess? Even the gods weren't without blame, who had given her such a father, lover, and fate. But none of this would have come to pass had it not been for one person. That one person alone was responsible for all the wrongs she had been subject to. Bheeshma.

Take revenge against Bheeshma? That was easier said than done. Ambaa, a mere woman, had no chance of success against a warrior like Bheeshma. Perhaps she could persuade other kings to pick up arms on her behalf. She would have to enlist the support of the sages for that. Ambaa made her way to a hermitage.

One of the residents of the hermitage was a learned and aged ascetic named Shaikhaavatya. He asked Ambaa why she had come, what she wanted, and how they could help her. Ambaa wanted the counsel of the sages and she wanted to spend some time in the hermitage. Shaikhaavatya agreed. Ambaa opened up, talking about her travails.

The ascetics discussed the matter among themselves. Opinion was divided. Some thought it best that Ambaa return to her father; some were of the opinion she would be better off with Shaalva. The sages were also unable to arrive at a consensus whether Bheeshma deserved to be censured or not. After much cogitation the sages decided it was best for Ambaa to go back to her father.

> For any arya lady, the husband or the father is the refuge. A husband is the refuge when things are smooth. A father is the refuge when things are rough.[17]

This was unacceptable to Ambaa. Her father shared blame for her predicament. Even if she returned to her father, there would be the barbs, the taunts, the snide remarks from her relatives. She didn't want to hear those gibes. Yes, she had grown up in that palace as a child. Time had changed, so had circumstances. She again expressed a wish to stay at the hermitage.

The sages returned to their deliberations. Ambaa was in for a pleasant surprise. Rajarshi Hotravaahana came by the hermitage. He was not only a learned sage in his own right, but also Ambaa's maternal grandfather. He comforted Ambaa as she poured her heart out to him. Hotravaahana too, like the sages, pondered over the matter. Unlike the sages, he didn't believe that returning to her father in Kashi was the best course of action. But what could Ambaa do? Hotravaahana didn't know, he confessed. But he knew someone who could. Someone who was not only wise but also whose words even Bheeshma would be unable to defy; a person who had taught Bheeshma. A sage who was feared the world over.

Parashuraama, more commonly known as Raama.[18] If Raama could be convinced of Ambaa's cause, and if Raama instructed Bheeshma, Hotravaahana was confident that Bheeshma would dare not defy the sage. Raama was not known to brook disobedience. A ray of hope lit afresh in Ambaa's heart.

Raama was on Mount Mahendra. Hotravaahana advised Ambaa to proceed to the mountain, pay her respects to the sage, and taking his—Hotravaahana's—name, tell him everything. While grandfather and granddaughter conversed, Ambaa got support from another unexpected quarter. Raama's follower, Akritavrana, arrived there. Hotravaahana brought Akritavrana up to speed on who Ambaa was and why she was there.

Akritavrana listened. If he were to intercede on Ambaa's behalf with Raama, it was important that he understood the issue. He put forth to Ambaa the choices she had. She could have Raama tell Shaalva what to do, or he could instruct Bheeshma to set things right. What did Ambaa prefer? Ambaa thought the matter over and requested that Akritavrana himself suggest a course of action. Akritavrana opined that the source of her troubles was Bheeshma since his actions had initiated this chain of events. What Bheeshma had done he would have to undo.

> That has always been the great desire in my heart, if only I could kill Bhishma in battle.[19]

Ambaa agreed with Akritavrana's view. Her hate for Bheeshma had been rising, and by now she wished for nothing more than his death. Could she kill him in battle? That was unlikely. Forget women, even the mightiest of warriors of the land hesitated to take up arms against Bheeshma. And Bheeshma would not fight a woman. What choices did she have? Thus, in conversation, the day passed. They did not have to wait till the next day to go to Mount Mahendra and meet Raama. As night fell, Raama[20] arrived with his followers, with a bow in one hand and an axe in the other.

After the customary welcome had been accorded to Raama, Hotravaahana and he started to talk. The conversation shortly turned to Ambaa. Taking the cue, Ambaa approached the sage and told Raama everything, tears of grief, rage, frustration escaping her eyes.

As Akritvrana had said earlier, there were two options open to Ambaa. Raama too gave Ambaa the option of either making Shaalva or Bheeshma heed his instructions. Ambaa requested Raama to defeat and kill the haughty Bheeshma in battle, in much the same way that Indra had killed Vritra.

> 'I will order Bheeshma to do as I say, but I will not pick up arms,' Raama said.
>
> 'All I ask is for you to kill Bheeshma, O Sage,' Ambaa said.
>
> 'I will pick up arms only for the sake of the learned. Not for revenge.'
>
> Ambaa kept quiet.
>
> 'Just say the word, dear child, and I will order Bheeshma,' Raama said.
>
> 'I want nothing more in this world, or this life, than for you to kill Bheeshma,' Amba said.
>
> 'I won't pick up arms unless the learned, the brahmanas ask me to. Bheeshma will surely listen to me,' Raama said.
>
> 'Only Bheeshma's death will bring me happiness.'

Akritvrana spoke up at this moment, urging Raama to take up weapons and kill Bheeshma, just as Ambaa was requesting him. Bheeshma was no less than an asura, Akritvrana goaded Raama. Hadn't Ambaa sought refuge with Raama and hadn't Raama resolved to help those who sought his help, even at the cost of his own life, Akritvrana provoked Raama.

Raama made up his mind. He would first ask Bheeshma to do as instructed; failing which he would kill him, for he had not forgotten how to fight. Raama was confident of his prowess. Even proud. Perhaps arrogant.

> The arrows that I unleash do not remain in bodies.[21]

Raama proceeded to Kurukshetra. Ambaa and the other brahmanas followed. They all set up camp by the Saraswati River. On the third day after setting camp, Raama sent word to Bheeshma that the sage wanted to meet him.

Bheeshma went to Kurukshetra. He met the sage and paid his respects. Raama told Bheeshma why he had come here and asked him to take Ambaa back, presumably to marry Vichitraveerya. His words were sharp, but his tone conciliatory, for now.

> Bheeshma weighed his words, for this was Raama he was speaking to.
>
> 'O Sage,' Bheeshma began. 'I am blessed that you have come to see me.'
>
> Raama looked at Bheeshma, silent, seeing.
>
> 'The princess of Kashi, Ambaa, had already taken Shaalva as her husband,' Bheeshma continued. 'She agreed when I suggested that she go to Shaalva.'
>
> Raama's brows furrowed.
>
> 'I cannot now take her back and give her to my brother, Vichitraveerya, a second time,' Bheeshma continued. 'So, O Sage, I cannot take Ambaa back, even if the one issuing the request, instruction, command, is as venerable a sage as you.'

> Because of fear, compassion, avarice or gain, I cannot abandon the dharma of kshatriyas.[22]

In everyone's presence, Bheeshma had refused to carry out Raama's instructions. Raama's temper started to rise. Bheeshma tried to placate him, reminding him that he had learned the knowledge of weapons from Raama himself; he could not bring himself to raise weapons against his preceptor. Raama would have none of this. Bheeshma could not call Raama his preceptor on the one hand and refuse his instructions on the other. Bheeshma could choose to take Ambaa back or he could choose to see himself and his lineage destroyed, Raama warned.

Bheeshma saw Raama was not going to budge from his position; nor was he going to take Ambaa back. Bheeshma's stance hardened.

> Since this cannot be done, what is the point of striving towards it?[23]

'O Sage, what you have asked me to do, I cannot,' Bheeshma said.

'Cannot, or will not?' Raama asked, his eyes reddening with rage.

'*Will not, cannot*—what difference does it make? What you have asked for is not going to happen, O Sage. What is the point of this back-and-forth bickering?' Bheeshma said, his words harder than his voice.

'Have you forgotten how to behave with your preceptor, O Bheeshma?' Raama growled.

'A preceptor, a brahmana who picks up arms is no longer either a brahmana or a preceptor, O Sage,' Bheeshma responded.

Raama stood up.

'But if you want to fight; if the great Raama wants to fight, then I, Bheeshma, assures you that I will fight you. I also promise you that you will lose, O Sage. But I cannot kill my guru, and so I won't,' Bheeshma said, his voice mild, his words biting even more

> If a preceptor does not know what should be done and what should not be done, if he deviates from the right path and if he is arrogant, it is one's duty to abandon him.[24]

The escalation between the two had now spiralled beyond anyone's control. Raama had talked of how he had destroyed entire generations of insolent kshatriyas. Bheeshma didn't let that taunt go unchallenged. Perhaps Raama had not yet met a kshatriya like Bheeshma.

> O Rama! You have often boasted in assemblies that you have exterminated kshatriyas from the world. But listen to my words. At that time, Bhishma had not been born and there were no kshatriyas like me, who could dispel your insolence about war and your love for fighting.[25]

Raama challenged Bheeshma to proceed to Kurukshetra and fight him there, confident that his arrows would kill Bheeshma soon enough, a spectacle that his mother, Ganga, could also watch. Bheeshma returned to Hastinapura, brought Satyavati up to date, took her blessings, and then proceeded to Kurukshetra on a silver chariot drawn by white horses, and equipped with all weapons imaginable.

Once at Kurukshetra, Bheeshma blew his conch and soon enough, brahmanas, ascetics, gods, and sages collected there to witness this battle.

Even Ganga, Bheeshma's mother, appeared. She knew and had heard of Raama's valour and ferocity. Fearful for her son, she approached Raama and implored him to not fight Bheeshma. Raama was unmoved. Frantically, she returned to Bheeshma, but to no avail.

Before the battle could begin, there was one point of order that Bheeshma brought up. He was on a chariot while Raama was on the ground. It would be a battle of unequals. No, it wouldn't be, Raama responded. He was on a chariot—the earth itself was his chariot, the Vedas his horses, and the wind his charioteer.

> The earth is my chariot. O Bhishma! The Vedas bear me, like well-trained horses. The wind is my charioteer. The mother of the Vedas is my armour.[26]

Even before Raama had finished speaking, the truth of his words became apparent to Bheeshma. He saw Raama atop a celestial chariot, one that the warrior sage had created from the powers of his mind. Akritavrana was his charioteer. Both warriors would be on chariots.

Getting down from his chariot, Bheeshma approached Raama and asked for his blessings. Raama appreciated the gesture and blessed Bheeshma, but not for his victory, for Raama himself was his foe and who wished to defeat him. Many years later, many generations later, Yudhishthira would get down from his chariot and approach Bheeshma for his permission and blessings.[27] Bheeshma would bless Yudhishthira, but also lament his plight, reduced to fighting on the side of adharma because of the Kauravas' pelf.[28]

The battle commenced. Raama was the first to attack with 969 arrows. Bheeshma retaliated with 900 arrows of his own, wounding Raama. Raama shot more arrows at Bheeshma. Bheeshma's counterattack left Raama unconscious. Thus ended the day's battle.

> I will not strike the Vedas that are there in your body, your great brahmana characteristics, or the extremely great austerities that you have collected. O Rama! I will strike the dharma of kshatriyas that you have resorted to.[29]

The second day dawned. The two warriors prepared to do battle again. Bheeshma paid homage to Raama before starting battle. This day, celestial weapons were used.[30] One of Raama's arrows struck Bheeshma in the chest, causing him to faint. Bheeshma's charioteer steered the chariot away. Once he had recovered, he brought Bheeshma back to the battlefield. Bheeshma retaliated with a flaming arrow that struck Raama, causing him to faint. The scales were even so far. Once Raama recovered, he shot arrows at Bheeshma which not only wounded him but also killed his horses. Throughout the day, countless arrows were shot by both warriors, covering the skies. Even the sun was hidden from view. The second day's battle ended.

The third day's battle was no different. A divine weapon fired by Raama enveloped Bheeshma, his chariot, charioteer, and steeds. Its arrows destroyed his chariot's wheels, yoke, and axle.

On the fourth day, Raama's assault killed Bheeshma's charioteer. A sliver of fear entered Bheeshma's heart, perhaps for the first time in his life. Even as he struggled to recover, Raama pierced Bheeshma with an arrow that caused him to fall in a faint. He recovered and resumed battle. He discharged an arrow that caused Raama to faint. When night arrived, the battle was paused, and both warriors, alive but injured, retired.

Thus did the battle rage for twenty-three days.[31]

Raama had been unable to defeat Bheeshma, much less kill him. Bheeshma too had arrived at the conclusion that he could not defeat Raama. The battle could continue for another twenty-three days, or another two thousand, but it would still end in a stalemate. Bheeshma turned to the gods for help. That night he prayed to the gods, brahmanas, and to night[32] itself. If he was capable of defeating Raama, then the gods had to show a way, for it was beyond his mortal means. With these thoughts, Bheeshma fell asleep.

As dawn neared, eight brahmanas appeared before Bheeshma in his dream. These were the same eight brahmanas who had held up Bheeshma when he had lost consciousness in the battlefield against Raama. They told him that not only would Raama be unable to defeat him, they, the brahmanas, were going to reveal to Bheeshma how he could vanquish Raama in battle. A weapon that Raama had no knowledge of, or defence against.

In an earlier life Bheeshma had learned how to wield a weapon called 'prasvaapan' that had been created by Vishwakarma. No one, not even Raama, knew about the existence of this weapon. Yes, and not even the warrior sage who had taught Bheeshma knew how to counter this weapon. The brahmanas advised Bheeshma to go ahead and use it in the battle against Raama the next day. Better still, this weapon would not kill Raama, and thus no sin of killing a brahmana would accrue to Bheeshma. Why? Because the weapon didn't kill; it put its target to sleep.[33]

> Whether one is asleep, or whether one is dead, we regard the two as equal.[34]

The twenty-fourth morning dawned. The two warriors faced each other; the battle resumed. The two warriors fired increasingly devastating weapons at each other. When Raama unleashed the brahma weapon, Bheeshma retaliated with a similar brahma weapon of his own. The two weapons collided mid-air. All that could be seen was a mass of energy and light. Havoc ensued. Bheeshma decided that the battle had to come to an end. He invoked the prasvaapan weapon. It manifested itself before him. Bheeshma got ready to release it at Raama.

Bheeshma did not fire the prasvaapan weapon. Sage Naarada appeared before Bheeshma and requested him to not release the weapon. Why? Because Raama was an ascetic, a brahmana, and it did not behoove Bheeshma to use it against him. Even the eight brahmanas who had appeared in his dream the night before and told him about the weapon now concurred with Naarada. Bheeshma withdrew the prasvaapan weapon and took out another weapon to fire at Raama.

Raama was crushed. He had been defeated by Bheeshma. Bheeshma had drawn and then withdrawn a weapon against him—Raama considered it his defeat. He stood, defeated, angry. His forefathers[35] appeared before him and counselled him. Yes, it was for a purpose that Raama had picked up weapons. However, it was unwise to continue to fight Bheeshma. He was a kshatriya, the eldest of the Vasus, Ganga and Shaantanu's son. Raama was fortunate to be alive, they said, notwithstanding his prowess. They told Raama that he had been defeated by Bheeshma and it was time for him to give up his weapons and return to austerities.

> I will not refrain from this battle. That is the vow that I observe.
> I have never withdrawn from the forefront of battle earlier.[36]

Raama accepted his forefathers' advice. But he would not withdraw from the battle. He had never done so, and he would never do so. He would not be the first to withdraw. He wanted Bheeshma to be the first to withdraw; only then would he do so. Naarada approached Bheeshma with Raama's condition. Bheeshma would not relent, either. He would not be the one to withdraw from a battle. The sages and Narada went back to Raama and requested him again to withdraw. While this seesaw continued, the eight brahamanas spoke to Bheeshma and asked him to do what was right. Bheeshma decided to not stand on ego. He bowed before the brahmanas and went up to Raama and paid his respects. Raama blessed him and thus the battle came to an end.

> I will never withdraw from a fight. I will not withdraw and retreat. I will not be pierced by arrows on my back.[37]

Raama went back to Ambaa. He had failed, he told her. He had failed to make Bheeshma heed his words; he had failed to defeat Bheeshma; he had failed to kill him. There was nothing left to say. Ambaa understood that Raama had done all he could, and that Bheeshma was a greater warrior than all, even Raama. Perhaps Ambaa would be wise to reconsider and go back to Bheeshma. Never. That was one thing that would never happen. Not in this life, not in any.

Where Raama had failed, she—Ambaa—would have to find a way to succeed.

Ambaa is an Ascetic

Ambaa departed for the forest. Ramaa returned to Mount Mahendra from where he had come down to fight Bheeshma. Bheeshma returned to Hastinapura where he gave Satyavati an account of the events. He was a worried man.

Bheeshma had glimpsed Ambaa's strength of resolve and sensed her depths of hate. Ambaa was not going to let matters rest. He had spies deputed to keep an eye on her. He feared for what the future would bring. He confided these fears in Naarada and Vyaasa. They told him to stop worrying about destiny, for what had to happen would happen. Neither humans nor gods could alter destiny.

Ambaa began a series of fierce penances by the banks of the Yamuna. Standing, unmoving, resolute, she even gave up food. She entered the river, stood on one toe, and prayed. This continued for twelve years. From there she went to several holy places, bathing at those teerthas and continuing her penances.

Gangaa rose from her waters and asked Ambaa why she was performing such penances. Ambaa replied, truthfully, that she wanted to kill Bheeshma, and if that meant taking birth in another body, she was prepared for that. Bheeshma's destruction is what she wanted in her life—this or the next. Gangaa, Bheeshma's mother, counselled her to not follow that path, warning her that if she persisted in this path, she would become a river that flowed only during the monsoon, remaining dry for the other eight months, infested with crocodiles. Ambaa remained undeterred. Gangaa's prophecy came true. Ambaa merged with and became a seasonal river. Yet she persisted in her austerities.

Ambaa's penances finally brought fruit. Shiva appeared before Ambaa and granted her a boon. Ambaa didn't ask for the means; she asked for the end. She didn't want to become immortal, or the most powerful person in the three worlds. No, all of those were only means to an end—Bheeshma's end. Bheeshma's end at her hands. Shiva acquiesced.

Ambaa stood stupefied for a moment. How could she, a woman, defeat and kill Bheeshma when even the great Raama had failed, she asked. Shiva told her that it would happen when she donned another body—a man's body. She would be born in Drupada's line, her memory of this previous life preserved. Saying so, Shiva disappeared.[38]

If the next birth was what it would take to kill Bheeshma, then Ambaa would speed matters along. She lit a pyre and entered it. The fire of revenge that had been burning inside all those years finally consumed her, in every sense of the word.

> When the fire was blazing, with rage igniting her senses, she said, 'This is for Bhishma's destruction.'[39]

That was how Ambaa's life had ended. Her story had not ended, however. How had Ambaa, the princess of Kaashi, become Shikhandi, Drupada's son, Duryodhana asked Bheeshma.

Ambaa is Shikhandi

Drupada had been bested by Drona's pupils, the Paandavas, and had to cede half his kingdom to Drona. Humiliated, seeking revenge, Drupada obtained from a sacrifice a son, Dhrishtadyumna; and a daughter, Draupadi. But even before that, he had desired a son who could bring about Bheeshma's destruction. Presumably, this was because he held Bheeshma also responsible for having appointed Drona as the teacher of the Kurus.

Drupada had prayed to and obtained a boon from Shankara that a daughter would be born for the destruction of Bheeshma. The same Shiva had also granted a boon to Ambaa that she would be born in Drupada's line and become the cause of Bheeshma's death. But Drupada had wanted a son! Shiva had replied that the daughter would become a son, and that was the way it would be.

When the daughter was born to Drupada's wife, the king proclaimed that a son had been born instead. Confident that Shiva's prophecy would come true, Drupada hid this fact from everyone. Only Bheeshma knew the truth.[40]

The daughter, destined to kill Bheeshma, born to the father who wanted to kill Drona, learned archery from the same Drona. When she came of age, Drupada and his wife debated and decided that she be married to a princess, still confident were they of Shiva's words coming true. Thus, the daughter of Hiranyavarma,[41] the king of Dasharna, was chosen as her bride. The marriage took place. But was not consummated.

Hiranyavarma's daughter, the princess, found out the truth about Shikhandi being a woman. Ashamed, she confided in her nurse, who sent a message to the king. That Drupada had deceived him infuriated Hiranyavarma. An insult as severe as this could be avenged only by wreaking destruction on Drupada. He sent a message to Drupada to the effect.

> Drupada was like a thief who had been caught in the act and could not utter a word.[42]

Drupada tried his best but could not pacify Hiranyavarma, who decided to invade Paanchala. Seeing the efforts being made to protect the city and the frantic discussions between Drupada and his ministers, Shikhandi the princess was filled with shame. It was on account of her, her gender, that all these troubles had arisen. She ran away into the forest.

The forest was ruled by a yaksha named Sthunakarna. In his abode, Shikhandi fasted for days. Sthuna appeared before her and asked what she craved and he, the follower of Kubera, would make it possible. At this moment in time, Shikhandi wanted nothing more than for the calamity that was about to befall her father to be averted. She told Sthuna everything. If only Sthuna could turn her into a man. That would convince Hiranyavarma that rumours of Shikhandi being a woman had just been that—rumours.

Sthuna pondered over the matter. If Shikhandi thought that disaster could be staved off by her becoming a man, then he, Sthuna, would loan her his male organ, and bear her female organ for her. But this exchange would be temporary, for only as long as Shikhandi needed to avert the looming war. Shikhandi agreed, promising to come back for the exchange once Hiranyavarma had returned to Dasharna. Shikhandi returned to Kaampilya, a prince, a man. One part of Shiva's boons had come true.

A delighted Drupada welcomed Shikhandi. He sent a messenger to Hiranyavarma. A skeptical Hiranyavarma sent women to ascertain the truth of Shikhandi's gender. They came back with the news that Shikhandi was indeed a man. The crisis passed.

Meanwhile, in the forest, Kubera[43] happened to arrive at Sthuna's abode. Kubera was welcomed and well-received, but Sthuna was nowhere to be seen. Peeved, Kubera inquired of Sthuna's whereabouts. The yakshas told Kubera about Shikhandi's visit and why Sthuna was not appearing before Kubera. A furious and outraged Kubera ordered Sthuna to be produced before him. One simply did not go about exchanging gender organs. What Sthuna had done was unprecedented. Kubera decreed that this exchange of organs would be permanent, and Sthuna would forever remain a woman.

The yakshas tried their best to pacify Kubera and asked for the curse to be limited in duration. Kubera, after many entreaties, yielded. Sthuna would again become a man, but for that he would have to wait till Shikhandi was killed in battle. Only when that happened would Sthuna receive his male organ back. Sthuna counted the days, weeks, months, and years to Shikhandi's death.

Shikhandi, meanwhile, true to his word, returned to the forest to hand back the genders and again become a woman. Sthuna told him what had transpired, about Kubera's curse, and told Shikhandi to return. Shikhandi would remain a man for the duration of his life. As a man, he would get to fight Bheeshma, whenever that opportunity presented itself. Mahaadeva's boons would come true, as they had to.

> Thus, Drupada's offspring is both a woman and a man.[44]

Bheeshma ended his account of the past and present of Shikhandi and why he would not fight him.

> I will not shoot arrows at a woman, one who has earlier been a woman, one who has the name of a woman and one who has the form of a woman.[45]

Shikhandi qualified on not one, not two, but all four counts. He had been a woman in this life; he had been a woman in a previous life as well; and still retained the form of a woman.

The war would begin. Bheeshma would fall to Shikhandi on the tenth day. Drona would fall to Drupada's son, Dhrishtadyumna on the fifteenth day. Drona's son, Ashwatthaama, would avenge his father's death by killing Dhrishtadyumna and Shikhandi after the war had ended. This last act would also happen with Shiva's blessings. Narayana would protect that which needed protecting; Shiva would destroy what had to be destroyed. The cycle of creation was impossible without the act of destruction.

36

VISHWA

Fighting the Infinite

Parva: Bheeshma (6)	Upa parva: Bheeshma-vadha (64)
Chapters: 61-64	Shlokas: 149

Much water had flown under the bridge since Bheeshma had shared Ambaa's past and present with Duryodhana and the other Kaurava warriors on the eve of the war. For one, the war had finally commenced, the war no one had wanted to fight, but no one had found a way to avoid. Even Narayana himself—Krishna—had tried and failed. The plains of Kurukshetra would be reddened once more with the blood of kshatriyas. For adharma to fall, dharma would have to pay a heavier price than had ever been paid.

It was Nara—Arjuna—who would suffer pangs of doubt over the morality of fighting a war that pitted brothers against brothers. It took Narayana—Krishna—as his unarmed charioteer to settle his doubts in a discourse that would come to be known as Bhagavada Geeta.[1]

With doubts removed over the justness for the war that would uphold dharma, the battle began in which no quarter would be given or asked for.

> In that battle, the father killed the son and the son killed the father. The sister's son killed the maternal uncle and the maternal uncle killed the sister's son. O King! A friend killed a friend and a relative killed a relative. Thus was the battle between the Kurus and the Paandavas.[2]

The first day of the war saw King Viraata's son, Uttara, falling to Shalya.[3] On the third day, seeing Arjuna's intensity flagging and his persisting reluctance to take the battle in earnest to his grandfather, Bheeshma,[4] Krishna lost his temper and patience. He rushed at Bheeshma to slay him, only to relent when Arjuna promised to change his apathetic attitude towards Bheeshma.[5]

Bheema, meanwhile continued his decimation of Duryodhana's brothers. He killed fourteen on the fourth day,[6] eight on the eighth day.

On the fourth day, Duryodhana and Bheema engaged in a fierce duel. After Bheema had severed Duryodhana's arrow, the Kaurava grasped a stronger one and discharged an arrow that struck Bheema's chest, causing the great Paandava to fall down in his chariot, unconscious. The other warriors, including Abhimanyu, rushed to Bheema's aid, taking on Duryodhana. Once Bheema regained consciousness, he took up arms again, and soon thereafter, killed fourteen of Duryodhana's brothers. This slaughter sent waves of fear through the remaining Kaurava siblings. Bheeshma ordered a fresh assault against Bheema. Bhagadatta, the redoubtable warrior, from atop his elephant shot arrows that again caused Bheema to lose consciousness. Ghatotakacha, Bheema's son through Hidimbaa, became furious at seeing this, and using his powers of illusion, attacked Bhagadatta and his elephant. Other Kaurava warriors, including Drona and Duryodhana, raced to Bhagadatta's help.

The day was drawing to a close. Dusk and then night would fall. Raakshasas like Ghatotakacha would become powerful; much more powerful. This is something Duryodhana would realize, at great cost, on the fourteenth night, after Jayadratha had fallen. Bheeshma recognized the portents; they would only be fighting an increasingly losing battle. He announced the cessation of hostilities for the day. The Paandavas roared at this victory and returned to their camp.

> I do not wish to fight with Hidimba's evil-souled son. He is full of strength and valour now and has support. The wielder of the vajra himself is incapable of vanquishing him in battle now.[7]

Hearing this account from Sanjaya of the Kaurava army's woes, Dhritaraashtra was distressed. He asked what boons the Paandavas possessed to cause such a slaughter of the Kaurava army.

> Nothing was accomplished because of mantras and nothing was caused by maya.[8]

Sanjaya bluntly told Dhritaraashtra that this was because of the Kaurava's own doing. Where there was dharma, there was victory, and since dharma was with the Paandavas, they could not be killed in battle. The king, Sanjaya reminded, had been advised by such elders as Bheeshma, Drona, and Vidura, but chose to disregard those words.

> Where there is dharma, victory exists there.[9]

Continuing his narration of the events on the battlefield of Kurukshetra during the day and in its camps at night, Sanjaya told Dhritaraashtra that it was Duryodhana who raised the question how the Kaunteyas could be victorious on the battlefield time after time, despite the Kaurava side fielding such warriors as Bheeshma, Drona, Shalya, Kripa, Ashwatthama, Kritavarma, Sudakshina, Bhurishrava, Vikarna, and Bhagadatta.

Bheeshma replied that the Paandavas were protected by Krishna, the wielder of the Shaarnga bow. For Duryodhana's benefit, Bheeshma told him an ancient account to emphasize his point.

Once on Mount Gandhamaadana, the sages and gods worshipped Brahma. Even as all were present there, a great vimaana appeared in the skies. Brahma knew what it was. He stood up. Seeing Brahma stand up, all the gods and sages too stood up in salutation. Then followed a stuti, several verses in praise of Narayana. He was addressed by several of his thousand names.

> You are the end of the universe. You are the creator of the universe. You are supreme. You are supreme dharma. You are the glory of the universe. You are the manifestation of the universe. You are the refuge of the universe. You are the action of the universe. You are the controller. You are the lord of the universe. You are Vasudeva. You are the soul of yoga. You are divinity and I seek refuge in you.[10]

The god who was Vishnu, who was Naraayana, who was Krishna, told Brahma that things would be just as he had asked for; and then disappeared.

All the assembled gods were amazed at what they had just witnessed. They requested Brahma to explain the phenomena that they had witnessed. Brahma replied that what they had seen was the supreme brahman. What was it that Brahma had wanted and which the great god knew and acquiesced to? Brahma said that he had requested Narayana to be born in the world of men, as Vasudeva, to annihilate all the daityas, daanavas, and raakshasas who had been born on earth in human form. Brahma said it would be a great folly to mistake Vasudeva as a mere human, for He was the unmanifest, the eternal one, without decay.

This was neither a new incident nor a secret one. Bheeshma told Duryodhana he had heard this account from wise sages, read about it in texts, and heard it from Raama,[11] Maarkandeya, Vyaasa, and Naarada. This was the reason, Bheeshma said, he had constantly counselled Duryodhana to not wage war against the Paandavas. Of course, Duryodhana had chosen to disregard all good advice, and therefore this is where matters stood.

> Where there is Krishna, dharma exists there. Where there is dharma, victory exists there.[12]

Duryodhana, despite everything, was curious. He asked Bheeshma about Vasudeva's origin and his glory. Bheshma expounded about Vasudeva, who had been created by the gods, to whom no one was superior, and who had created the three elements of water, air, and energy, and who was the god who had created the earth.[13]

> He created fire from his mouth. He created wind from his breath of life. Through his mind, the undecaying one created Sarasvati and the Vedas.[14]

Bheshma ended with a stuti[15] that had been sung by Brahma himself in Vasudeva's praise. After hearing this account Duryodhana's opinion of Krishna changed, but he still rebuffed Bheeshma's appeal to make peace with the Paandavas. The path to destruction was decked with petals of wisdom that Duryodhana had chosen to trample underfoot.

37

TRIPURAA VADH

When He Became Mahaadeva

Parva: Karna (8) Upa parva: Karna-vadh (73)
Chapter: 24 Shlokas: 161

Fate and Shiva had dictated that it would be Ambaa who would become the cause of his death, Bheeshma knew. But the arrows that would take his life had to be Arjuna's, Bheeshma wished.

He had a boon from his father to decide his moment of death. Thus, as the tenth day of battle drew to a close, Bheeshma fell.

Karna came to Bheeshma at night.

'Don't hate me; at least now,' Karna whispered.

'I can't hate you. I never have,' Bheeshma mustered the strength to say. 'I could never hate a son of Kunti.'

Karna looked at Bheeshma, unasked questions filling his eyes.

'Yes, I have known. Naarada, Vyaasa, and Krishna all know, and they told me.'

'Then why?' Karna asked. Why the harsh words all these years? Why the constant belittling? Why the public putdowns?

'To stop you from fighting your brothers, the Paandavas. You are the Sun god's son, you are invincible in battle, there is no one like you. Don't fight the Paandavas, don't fight your brothers. Stop.'

'There are some things in life that are beyond our control, beyond our ability to change them with our endeavours. They are…,' Karna stopped.

'Destiny,' Bheeshma completed Karna's sentence. The eldest Vasu, cursed by Vasishtha to be born on earth and live the longest life among all the Vasus, borne by Ganga and blessed by her to live

> the longest, granted a boon by Shaantanu to choose his moment of death, at the receiving end of a boon that Shiva granted Ambaa who would become the cause of his death. Yes, he knew the dictates of destiny better than anyone else.
> Karna departed.
> Duryodhana came next.
> 'Make peace before Arjuna destroys your army; make peace while you still have some of your brothers alive; make peace before Bheema finishes off your army. Make peace while I am still alive. Make peace with my death if you can,' Bheeshma beseeched Duryodhana.

Duryodhana paid no heed to Bheeshma's advice. The war continued. Soldiers, charioteers, horses, elephants, all fell one by one. The biggest of them, Bheeshma, had fallen to Shikhandi and Arjuna's arrows on the tenth day.[1] He would lie on the bed of arrows and wait, for the war to end, for Uttarayaana[2] to begin, for Krishna's permission, before he would finally leave this world, ending a curse and a cursed life that had begun in another time, another world.[3]

Karna, who had taken a vow to not fight alongside Bheeshma, finally joined the Kaurava army after seeking Bheeshma's permission and forgiveness for past acrimony.[4] Duryodhana's sorrow at Bheeshma's fall was lessened when he saw Karna astride a chariot, armed. The two conferred, and Karna recommended Drona as the next commander of the Kaurava army.[5]

> However, all of them cannot be the leader at the same time.
> There must be only one, who possesses special qualities.[6]
> Drona, supreme among those who wield all weapons, should
> be made the commander.[7]

On the thirteenth day,[8] with Arjuna drawn far away from the main battle by the Samshaptakas warriors, it fell upon the young Abhimanyu to break through the chakra vyuha that Drona had formed. Abhimanyu broke through the formation, but could not exit it, for he did not know how to break out. None from the Paandava army, not even the four Paandavas, could break in, for neither did they know how to, nor could they follow Abhimanyu's lead, for they had to contend with Jayadratha's boon.[9]

One warrior would not fight another; six would gang up on one. Drona, once the teacher of the Paandavas, now advised the Kauravas how to defeat and kill Abhimanyu, his favourite pupil's son.[10] A lone

Abhimanyu was surrounded and felled by six Kaurava warriors—Drona, Kripa, Karna, Ashwatthama, Brihadbala, and Kritavarma.

A grief-stricken Arjuna vowed to kill Jayadratha before the end of the next day's battle.[11] If he failed, he would immolate himself, he vowed. Jayadratha fell to Arjuna moments before sunset the next day.[12]

Duryodhana had pinned his hopes for a swift end to the war on Arjuna's failure; if Arjuna failed, he would immolate himself. If he did, the Paandava morale would crumble. Without Arjuna, there was no Paandava army. An enraged and frustrated Duryodhana goaded Drona into ordering the fight to continue into the night.

> The angry Kurus and Srinjayas will fight, even during the night.[13]

Night advanced. The tired warriors fought through the night, not knowing whether they were awake or asleep, alive or dead. Jackals howled through the night, waiting for the living to join the assembly of the dead and the dying.

As the night advanced, the raakshasa warriors, led by Ghatotakacha, grew stronger by the minute, wreaking havoc on the Kaurava army. A hapless Duryodhana watched his army get decimated. Much against his wishes, relenting to Duryodhana's entreaties, Karna deployed his fearsome Shakti weapon against Ghatotakacha.[14] With Karna's one sure weapon against Arjuna expended, Krishna danced with joy.[15]

Drona, the eighty-five-year-old commander of the Kaurava army, continued to fight with the vigour of a sixteen-year-old. The Paandavas watched in dismay as the warrior guru gutted their army. Krishna approached Yudhishthira with a plan.

> 'There is only way to stop Drona,' Krishna told Yudhishthira. 'There is no other.'
>
> 'No, we will try harder. Can't we?' Yudhishthira said, asked.
>
> 'If you wait any longer, even half a day, there won't be any army left to fight with,' Krishna replied.
>
> 'But it will be a lie!' Yudhishthira stated.
>
> 'A lie uttered for the sake of saving lives is not a lie.'
>
> 'And it is not a lie, in any case, dear brother,' Bheema interjected.
>
> 'It is not?' Yudhishthira asked.
>
> 'Of course, it isn't. There was an elephant named Ashwatthaama in Indravarma's army,' Bheema said.

'An elephant with the same name?' asked Yudhishthira.

'Yes, amazing coincidence, isn't it?" remarked Bheema. 'And I killed it. I killed Ashwatthaama. Ashwatthaama is dead. Now, tell me—is that a truth or a lie?' Bheema asked.

Krishna smiled at Yudhishthira. Bheema could be relied upon to find practical solutions to the toughest of problems. Yudhishthira looked helpless.

'But it is not the complete truth,' Yudhishthira muttered.

'You will have neither a complete army nor a partial one left by the end of the day, Yudhishthira, if you start quibbling over complete and partial truths. Now, we can debate the subtleties of dharma or act on the imperative of winning this war. The choice is yours,' Krishna said.

The desire for victory won over the fear of a lie. Yudhishthira spoke. The king who would not utter a lie, decide to lie. If it was any consolation, it wasn't a complete lie. He ordered his chariot to be taken to Drona's.

'Yes, it is true that Ashwatthaama has been killed,' Yudhishthira confirmed to Drona. 'The elephant,' he whispered.[16]

One should also utter a lie when one's life is in danger, or at the time of a marriage. Those are the times when falsehood becomes truth and truth becomes falsehood. A person who is always based on truth is but a child.[17]

A hopeful Drona heard Yudhishthira speak that Ashwatthaama was dead. A heartbroken father couldn't hear the second part that it was Ashwatthaama the elephant that had been killed by Bheema. The commander-in-chief dropped his weapons. A vengeful Dhrishtadyumna, seeking payback for his father's death at Drona's hands, beheaded the eighty-five-year-old Drona, flinging away the severed head in triumph.[18]

Senseless with rage at his father's killing through means most unjust, Ashwatthama launched the lethal weapon—Narayana-astra—at the entire Paandava army.[19] In a single strike, an entire akshauhini of the Paandava army was decimated.[20]

With Drona dead, Karna was appointed the commander of the Kaurava army. Who would be charioteer to the new commander-in-chief? Yudhishthira and Shalya had plotted this before the war. They sought to turn Duryodhana's masterstroke on its head. They knew Karna's ego would make him take Shalya as his charioteer. As a charioteer, Shalya would play mind-games on Karna, sapping his morale, confidence, and focus.[21] Because even with his armour and earrings gone,[22] even with his shakti weapon used against Ghatotakacha, Karna still possessed one lethal weapon he could, and would, unleash at Arjuna. Not to mention that this would be a duel to the death between Karna and Arjuna. Hadn't Karna made a promise to his mother, Kunti?[23]

> 'O Mother, the world knows you as the mother of five sons,' Karna had spoken to Kunti.
> 'But you are also my son,' Kunti had replied.
> 'The one you abandoned. The one you never acknowledged publicly. O Mother, five is a nice number. Let it stay that way.'
> Kunti had looked on, hopeful, helpless.
> 'Four of your sons I will spare.'
> Kunti knew who those four would be—Yudhishthira, Bheema, Nakula, and Sahadeva. She held her breath.
> 'Let the battlefield of Kurukshetra decide who the fifth will be to survive. Let the one who is protected by Narayana save himself from the one who has the shakti, given by the king of the gods himself. That is my promise to you, mother. The world will remember you, always, as the mother of five sons; not four, not six.'

Who better to be Karna's charioteer than the maternal uncle of the Paandavas, Shalya. A formidable warrior in his own right, seeing their mother's brother would sap the Paandavas's morale. So Duryodhana thought. So he approached Shalya and requested him to become Karna's charioteer.

> 'You must be joking, O King,' Shalya said.
> 'No, O King, I am most certainly not,' Duryodhana responded.
> 'Karna is not my equal. Nor have I any interest in obeying him. It will make a bizarre spectacle on the battlefield, to watch a warrior give instructions the charioteer doesn't heed. Is that what you want, Duryodhana, to have this war descend into a charade, a joke?'
> 'Certainly not, O King,' Duryodhana began. 'A charioteer must be one the warrior is proud and honoured to give the reins of his chariot to. It is not a matter of debate that Karna is a better warrior than Arjuna; the world knows this. Similarly, the world knows you to be a better charioteer than Krishna.'

> Just as the world thinks that Karna is superior to Dhananjaya in qualities, the world thinks that Shalya is superior to Vasudeva.[24]

Yes, that would make it a battle of equals. Whatever the outcome, it would be a battle for the ages. Shalya agreed, but not before placing one more condition—he would be free to use disrespectful words against Karna if he so decided. Duryodhana and Karna both agreed. A bad decision, as Karna would later find out.

Just as Brahma had become Shiva's charioteer, so would Shalya be Karna's charioteer. Duryodhana asked Shalya to listen to this account that Sage Maarkandeya had told his father, Dhritaraashtra.

This was a time when the gods and asuras had been engaged in fierce battles for longer than anyone could remember. One such battle had been against Taarakmaya.[25] The gods succeeded in defeating him. But that was not the end of the war. For, after his defeat, his three sons, Taaraaksha, Kamalaaksha, and Vidyunmaali prayed to Brahma. After severe penances, Brahma appeared before them and granted them a boon. They asked for—immortality. Raakshasa and asuras had a habit of asking for the impossible. Brahma reminded them that the boon of immortality was not for them.

The three pondered over the matter and came up with an ingenious ask—that they live in three floating cities. As long as they lived in those cities, they would be almost invulnerable. But those cities could not last forever, either. If that was the condition, then the three said that only once in a thousand years would those three cities come in alignment, and only then would they be vulnerable to destruction. Their destruction, however, would be possibly only through the hands of a god. But the destruction of the three cities would have to be done with a single arrow. Only then would, should, death come to them, they asked. It was not for Brahma to question the boon they desired. He granted them the boon.

Armed with the boon, the three set out constructing three such cities, for there were three of them. For this, they summoned Maaya, the architect of the asuras, and asked him to construct three such cities for them. Maaya constructed three magnificent cities—one made of gold, one of silver, and one of iron.

Once the three cities were constructed, daanavas from all over began to pour into these three magnificent citadels. Not only were these three cities impregnable, but they also had all amenities one could think of, thanks to Maaya's powers. As long as Maaya resided in the city, the millions of daanavas residing there had everything they wanted.

Taaraaksha had a son named Hari. Hari too obtained a boon from Brahma—a lake that would revive any asura killed in battle.

Without batting an eyelid, Brahma granted even that boon. It was not a boon of immortality, after all. Lakes could dry up, couldn't they?

Living peacefully was now not on these asuras' minds. Bolstered by the protection these three celestial fortresses afforded, safe in the promise of being revived by the waters of the lake, the three brothers, living in three cities, attacked the three worlds without fear. The residents of Tripuraa made life miserable for all the worlds.

Eventually the gods had had enough. They trudged up to Brahma.

> 'O Grandfather,' the gods bowed before Brahma.
>
> 'Yes, I know,' sighed Brahma.
>
> 'Not to question you, O God, but why give such a boon in the first place to someone as evil as these three brothers? And having given a boon, why give yet another boon to Taaraaksha's son? Why?' the gods pleaded.
>
> 'I cannot take sides; I cannot be partial to one over the other. Anyone who worships me will get a boon from me. That is the way of this creation,' Brahma reminded them.
>
> The gods looked at each other. Nothing? Was there no way out of this predicament?
>
> 'However, these fellows have gone against dharma. I have no issues if these evil ones are killed,' Brahma gave them a ray of hope. 'However, killing them is not my…, how should I put this…, forte.'
>
> 'Then who?' the gods asked. Having created the problem, who would destroy it?
>
> 'Sthaanu. Ishaan. Jishnu, that's who. I create, Vishnu sustains, Shiva destroys. That is the way the cycle of creation has been, and must be,' Brahma answered them.[26]

It would fall on Shiva to undo what Brahma's boon had done.

The gods, with Indra and Brahma leading them, approached Shiva. All they saw was a mass of energy that was Shiva. They bowed before him. Shiva asked them why they had come to him. The gods praised Shiva[27] as the god of the gods, Rudra, Neelkantha, brahman, brahmachari, Ishaan, Kumara's father, Tryambaka, and so on.

Pleased, Shiva asked the gods how he could help them. Brahma spoke of the boon he had granted the three brothers and which was now causing so much trouble.

'Those three brothers are very powerful,' Shiva said.

'Yes, O Tryambakeshwara,' the gods replied. 'That is why we have come to you.'

'I alone cannot kill them. Why don't you take the energy of my weapons and fight unitedly?' Shiva said.

'O Maheshwara! That may not be enough.'

'Then take half my energy too,' Shiva offered.

'All our energies won't be sufficient to defeat those three asuras. However, half of your energy will be too much for us, O Shankara. But why don't you take half our energies instead? You alone can bear these combined energies.'

Shiva agreed. The gods agreed. They gave half their strengths to Shiva. Shankara thus came to be known as Mahaadeva.

To take down the cities constructed by Maaya, the architect of the asuras, Shiva asked the architect of the gods, Vishwakarma, to fashion an immense chariot. It could not be an ordinary chariot. Every god and goddess came forward with their energy.

The goddess earth became the seat for the charioteer.
Mount Mandara became the axle.
The Mahanadi River became the flank.
Dharma, artha, and kaama became the joints.
Herbs, trees, flowers, fruits became the covering for the charioteer's seat.
Indra, Varuna, Yama, and Kubera became the horses.
Sinivali, Anumati, Kuhu, and Raka were the yokes and harness.
Action, truth, austerities, and prosperity became the reins.
Day and night walked as the front and rear flanks.
Saraswati became the chariot's track.

Next came Mahaadeva's armour and weapons. Shiva used the year with its six seasons as his bow, night as his bowstring, Vishnu, Agni, and Soma as the arrows.

Shiva was now ready for battle. He had the charioteer's seat, the reins of the horses to be handed to the charioteer. But he did not have a charioteer.

The gods went to Brahma and prayed to him to agree and become Shiva's charioteer. Brahma listened to the gods and acceded,[28] became Shiva's charioteer, and took charge of the reins.

Shiva advanced towards the three cities of Tripuraa. No sooner had he finished affixing the pashupata weapon on his bow, than the three cities came in alignment. Shiva released the weapon at Tripuraa. The flames and energy of the arrow destroyed Tripuraa and the asuras. Before it could destroy anything more, Shiva restrained the flames.

Thus was Tripuraa destroyed exactly as the three brothers, Taaraaksha, Kamalaaksha, and Vidyunmaali, had wished for from Brahma. Where there was a need for adharma to be destroyed, there would be a way. As for the lake that revived the asuras who had fallen in battle, Nandi, the bull, drank up its water.

Maaya would later also construct the palace at Indraprastha for the Paandavas. Neither had the three cities of Tripuraa survived; nor had the palace at Indraprastha provided the security the Paandavas had desired. Nor, for that matter, the city of Dwaarka that Vishwakarma had extended at the request of Krishna.

Duryodhana finished his account. Shalya would be no ordinary charioteer. He would be to Karna what Brahma had been to Shiva; he was better than Krishna just as Karna was better than Arjuna. Flattery worked its charm. Fate would move as it had to. Karma awaited all; Karna on the seventeenth day, Shalya on the eighteenth; Duryodhana after that.

38

HANSA-KAAK

The Fool's Flight

Parva: Karna (8) **Upa parva: Karna-vadh (73)**
Chapter: 28 **Shlokas: 66**

'Where is Krishna? Where is Krishna hiding?' Karna shouted, astride his chariot.

'I will give carts of gold, women, white horses, hundreds of elephants, all my riches, everything to the person who points out Arjuna to me,' Karna proclaimed.

'I will do so after I kill the two Krishnas in battle,' Karna boasted.

'You will see Arjuna today, Karna, you can be sure of that,' Shalya, his charioteer, responded.

'A jackal cannot bring down a lion. I have never heard of two lions being brought down by a jackal. Never has that happened before, and it's not going to happen today either,' Shalya laughed. 'Everyone's time comes; and it's evident yours has come. Time to leave this earth. Why else would one act in as foolish manner as you. Kill Arjuna in battle, you say? You may as well try to cross the ocean with a stone tied to your neck,' Shalya tore into Karna.

'What would you know of valour, Shalya, for you are without any,' Karna responded.

'I will put it in a manner simple enough for even you to understand, Karna. You are to Arjuna like a rat is to a cat, like a dog is to a tiger, like a fox is to a lion, like a rabbit is to an elephant. Do you get the picture?' Shalya provoked Karna.

On and on and on the two went, arguing, bickering, trading insults. Shalya was, of course, doing what he had promised Yudhishthira—sapping Karna's morale on the eve of his most critical battle, with Arjuna.

> 'If you have still not understood, perhaps this story will help you understand what your stature is compared to Arjuna,' Shalya said.

Karna had no choice but to listen as Shalya spoke.

By the shores of the ocean, there once lived a crow who subsisted on leftovers fed to it by the sons of a prosperous vaishya. Over time the crow became haughty. One day it saw a flock of swan. The vaishya's sons saw the swans and yet praised the crow to be the best among birds. The crow heard their words and drunk with pride, challenged the swans to a test of flight. The swans asked the crow whatever made it think it could compete with them, who could travel vast distances. The crow crowed, describing all the different ways in which it could fly, dive, soar, loop.

> There is no doubt that I will fly in one hundred and one different kinds of ways.[1]

One of the swans replied that the crow could choose to fly in any one of the hundreds of the ways it knew, or even all hundred different ways, but the swans would fly in one and the only way they knew. By this time other crows had also assembled there and they cheered the crow on.

The race began and the crow and a swan started to fly. For a brief period, it appeared to the crow that it was winning. As the shore receded, the swan rose up higher and higher in the sky and increased its speed. The crow tried, it flapped its wings harder, it made all effort it could, but soon lost both, its nerve and energy. It looked down but could see no place in the ocean for it to stop and rest. Soon enough it lost height, sinking closer and closer to the ocean, till it was tottering over the ocean, its body skirting the waters.

The swan took pity on the crow and came to its rescue. It raised the crow on its back and turned back towards the shore. The crow realized it had become vain and haughty for no reason.

> Having fed on leftovers, I became insolent.[2]

Shalya finished the story and looked back at Karna.

> 'Karna, you are like the crow in the story. You have subsisted on Duryodhana's leftovers, and yet you now want to take on Arjuna. You are a delusional fool,' Shalya.

> 'I should kill you first, you insolent man!' Karna shouted.
>
> 'So says the man who ran away when the gandharvas took Duryodhana captive. So boasts the man who could not defeat a lone Arjuna at Viraata, even with the help of Bheeshma, Drona, Kripa, and others. Such is the bravado of the man who retreated against Arjuna at Drauapadi's swayamvara. Go ahead, continue with your bravado boasting,' Shalya sneered.

A frustrated, mentally exhausted, distracted Karna finally entered the battlefield as commander-in-chief of the Kaurava army.

39 INDRA-NAMUCHI

A King's Rise

Parva: Shalya (9) Upa parva: Teertha-yaatra (76)

Chapter: 42 Shlokas: 161

Karna kept his word to Kunti.[1] He spared the lives of all the four Paandavas he had promised his mother.

Karna got the better of Yudhishthira in a duel on the seventeenth day.[2] The Paandava retreated with Karna chasing him. Karna caught up with Yudhishthira and grabbed him by the shoulder. To slay or spare?

> I don't think you know the dharma of kshatriyas well. O Kounteya! Do not fight again and do not advance against brave ones. Do not speak unpleasant words towards them. Do not advance towards a great battle.' Having said this, the immensely strong one released Partha.[3]

Bheema, on the fourteenth day, had to suffer a defeat at the hands of Karna. Karna used the choicest of insults against Bheema, choosing to slay his younger brother with words.[4]

> However, remembering Kunti's words, he did not kill him.[5] ... Eunuch! Idiot! Glutton! You have no skill in weapons, but wish to fight with me. You are only a child and become distressed in battle. O Paandava! You should be where there are many kinds of food and things to eat and drink.[6]

Karna spared Nakula's life on the seventeenth day.[7] Holding Nakula's neck with the string of his bow, Karna reminded his stepbrother that theirs was not a fight between equals.

> Do not fight again with those who are your superior in strength. ... O Son of Maadri! Go home, or go where Krishna and Phalguna are.' ... Though he could have been killed, the son of the suta did not kill him. O King! He remembered Kunti's words and abandoned him.[8]

Sahadeva challenged Karna to a duel[9] on the fourteenth night.

> O Son of Maadri! Fight with those who are your equals.[10] ... The maharatha was devoted to the truth and remembered the words that he had given to Kunti. Though the destroyer of enemies could have killed Maadri's son in the battle, he did not slay him.[11]

With four of Kunti's sons spared by Karna, who would be the fifth to survive was determined as the seventeenth day drew to a close. Karna fell to Arjuna.

Shalya was appointed the commander of the now decimated Kaurava army. He too fell the next day to Yudhishthira.[12] The war was now close to its end. Only a few warriors remained standing on the Kaurava side, and they too fell. Shakuni was killed by Sahadeva, as he had vowed to.[13] Bheema killed Duryodhana's remaining brothers, as he had promised.[14]

> The one with dharma in his soul had fought in accordance with dharma and was killed by Dharma's son.[15]

Duryodhana, tired, wounded, and perhaps even scared now, saw Sanjaya leaving for Hastinapura, and told him to convey the message to his father that his son had entered a lake to recover and hide.[16] Only three other warriors remained alive from the Kaurava army—Ashwatthaama, Kripa, and Kritavarma.

The Paandavas discovered Duryodhana in the lake and goaded him to come out for one last fight to the finish. His peace overture, coming too late, was rebuffed by Yudhishthira. The same Yudhishthira would have agreed to five villages instead of half the kingdom. The same Yudhishthira now insisted on a fight to the finish. For one to be declared the victor, the other would have to die. Duryodhana, who had relied on a gambling match to deprive the Paandavas of their kingdom for thirteen years, now would lose his life to Bheema.[17]

> If, between the two of us, both of us remain alive, all beings will be uncertain about who has emerged victorious.[18]

Rukmi was one of two notable warriors who had not taken part in the war.[19] Balaraama was the second; he had chosen to not fight on either side and had left instead on a long pilgrimage.[20] Just as Duryodhana and Bheema were ready to face off against each other, Balaraama returned after having been away for forty-two days, just in time to witness the duel between his two most capable students.

At this point in Vaishampaayana's narration, Janamejaya asked the sage to expound on the greatness of the teerthas that Balarama had visited and why those teerthas had come to acquire their sanctity.

Vaishampaayana talked about how Soma, who had been inflicted with the curse of tuberculosis, had been freed of the curse at Prabhaasa.[21] Balaraama had proceeded to a teertha called Udapana, where at one point in time the Saraswati River had flowed. This teertha was also associated with Sage Gautama's son, Trita.[22] The next teertha was Vinashana, a place where the Saraswati flowed, invisible.[23] Sage Mankanaka had performed austerities at Sapta-saaraswata, a teertha believed to be situated within Kurukshetra, and where Saraswati had manifested herself in seven different forms—Suprabhaa, Kanchanaakshi, Vishaala, Manasrhadaa, Sarasvati, Oghavati, Suvenu and Vimalodaka.[24] Next was a teertha called Aushanas, also known as Kapaalamochana, so named for a raakshasa's head, severed by Raama,[25] that had got stuck to Sage Mahodara's leg. It was at this teertha that the head was finally freed from Mahodara's leg.[26] Balaraama next went to a teertha Lokaloka, famous for Rajarshi Sindhudveepa who became a brahmana there.[27]

Balaraama had then proceeded to a teertha called Vasishthapavaaha, so named for the strong current that had carried away Sage Vasishtha. As for the origins of the name, one had to go back, once more, to the period of hostility between the sages Vishwaamitra and Vasishtha. Their hermitages were on the western and eastern banks of the river Saraswati, respectively. Shiva had performed great penances at this place, and it came to be known as Sthaanu-teertha.[28]

Wishing to do away with his rival and foe, Vasishtha, once and for all, Vishwaamitra summoned Saraswati.

> 'O Saraswati,' Vishwaamitra began.
> 'Yes, O Sage, what is it you wish me to do?' Saraswati saw his red eyes, his demeanour, his barely concealed rage. She trembled. No good could come out of this, she thought.

'With your strong currents, bring Vasishtha over here.'

'Can't you invite the sage yourself?' she bit her tongue the moment the words left her mouth. Vishwaamitra inviting Vasishtha over? What was she thinking?

'You will do as I say, O Saraswati, and you will do so today and forthwith,' Vishwaamitra dismissed her.

The alternatives were none. To disobey the sage was to invite a curse. Vishwaamitra's curses were never gentle.

A terrified Saraswati went to Vasishtha. The wise sage knew what she had been asked to do. He told her to carry him to Sthaanuteertha and save her herself from Vishwaamitra's curse and anger. He would figure out how to tackle Vishwaamitra himself; there was no point in letting Saraswati suffer the brunt of Vishwaamitra's anger.

Saraswati did as advised by Vasishtha. When Vishwaamitra saw that Vasishtha had been brought there to his side of the river, he looked around for a weapon to kill the brahmana with.

Saraswati may have brought Vasishtha there, but she could not bear to see the sage killed thus. She again bore Vasishtha away to the eastern bank. A grateful sage praised her in a stuti.

Deprived of a chance to do away with his foe, Vishwaamitra's rage turned on Saraswati., cursing that her water would turn to blood, fit only for raakshasas. That spot came to be known as Vasishthapavaaha.

The raakshasas couldn't have asked for a better gift than Vishwaamitra's. They bathed, drank, and revelled in the flows of blood of the Saraswati. The sages and gods were distressed. A river as holy as the Saraswati had been turned into a feast for the raakshasas. The situation had to be remedied. They summoned the river who told them what had occurred. The sages set about cleaning the river. Soon enough, Saraswati had returned to her initial, pristine state.

The raakshasas, however, were now hungry, deprived of their food. The river had sustained and nourished them. They were without food. They beseeched the sages to help them. The raakshasas said they performed evil deeds not of their own accord but because of past deeds. As they had acted, so had they become.

> Those beings who disrespect preceptors, officiating priests, elders and the aged, also become rakshasas.[29]

The brahmanas thought about this. They concluded that just as offerings from sacrifices became the food for the gods, so would there be offerings that could become the share for raakshasas.

> Food in which there are insects and worms, food that has been mixed with leftovers, food that is mixed with hair, food that is mixed with grain that has not been broken and food that has been touched by dogs—these will constitute the share of rakshasas. Knowing this, the learned will always avoid such kinds of food. Those who partake of such food will eat food that is meant for rakshasas.[30]

To help the raakshasas, Saraswati thought up a new form for herself, named Aruna. Bathing in it, the raakshasas gave up their bodies and went to heaven. This was also the teertha where Indra freed himself of the sin of killing a brahmana named Namuchi.[31]

Janamejaya asked Vaishampaayana to tell him about this episode. The sage replied that Indra had broken a peace accord reached with Namuchi. Fearful, Namuchi hid himself inside the sun's rays. Indra made a pledge to Namuchi, promising not to kill him.

> O Best of Asuras! O Friend! I will not kill you with anything that is wet, or with anything that is dry, nor during the day or during the night. I swear this to you truthfully.[32]

Indra however broke the pledge. He lured Namuchi to the ocean, created a mist there, and used the foam of the ocean to slice off Namuchi's head.[33]

Namuchi's head, however, followed Indra everywhere. Panic-stricken, Indra ran to Brahma for help, who told him that Indra had committed the sin of killing a brahmana. He told Indra to perform a sacrifice and then bathe in Aruna teertha. Indra did as was told and was freed from the sin of killing a brahmana. Namuchi's head was immersed in the Saraswati and he also attained the eternal worlds.

40

VRIDDHA KUMARI

Dharma and Desire

Parva: Shalya (9)	Upa parva: Teertha-yaatra (76)
Chapter: 51	Shlokas: 26

So engrossed had Janamejaya become in Sage Vaishampaayana's account of Balaraama's pilgrimages that he put the hearing of the duel between Duryodhana and Bheema on hold. One such teertha that Balaraama visited, Vaishampaayana told Janamejaya, was where an aged maiden had lived. Thus far he had heard about sages, rajarshis, and gods. This was the first time he was hearing about an aged woman and a teertha. His curiosity piqued, the king asked about the maiden and her austerities.

There was once a sage named Kuni-Gargya who created a daughter through the powers of his mind. After the sage's death, his daughter pursued her father's path of austerities and penances. While Kuni-Gargya had been alive, he had desired that his daughter gets married. However, try as she might, she could find no suitor worthy of her. Thus, her penances continued. Eventually, she became old and weak. She resolved to depart this world.

Before she could do so, Sage Naarada came and told her that she should not depart before marrying. But who would marry her? She was now old, weak, and well… old. She was, however, willing to give half of her austerities to whoever accepted her hand in marriage. Sage Gaalava's son, Shringavaan, came forward, but with a condition. He would marry her, but he would leave after one night. The maiden gave her assent.

The marriage took place and as night fell, the old maiden had turned young, with beauty to rival a goddess. The night passed.

When morning came, she told Shringavaan that her pledge was fulfilled, and she would leave. She departed for the heavens, leaving behind a desolate Shringavaan who could not stop thinking of her, the now young and beautiful maiden. Yes, he accepted half the store of her austerities, as that was what she had promised, but he could not get her out of his mind. Soon enough, unable to bear the separation, he also followed her to heaven.

The maiden decreed that anyone who spent a night at this teertha, after performing the necessary rituals, would obtain the fruits equivalent to performing sixty-four years of brahmacharya.

Balaraama was at this teertha when he heard about Shalya's death. Balaraama walked through the gates of Saamantapanchaka and asked the rishis what had happened on the battlefield while he had been gone. Before he entered though, the sages assembled told him why the land was known as Kurukshetra.[1]

41

SRINJAYA

Sorrowing over Death

Parva: Shanti (12)	Upa parva: Raja-dharma (84)
Chapter: 29	Shlokas: 141

Vaishampaayana resumed his narration. Janamejaya listened. The duel between Duryodhana and Bheema ended with Duryodhana losing. His thighs shattered, he lay on the ground, awaiting death.

Kripa, Kritavarma, and Ashwatthaama—the three warriors from the Kaurava army who had survived the war—came by where Duryodhana lay. Once a king, he was now one of the countless warriors who had fallen in this war; alone, dying, vanquished. As night fell, Ashwatthaama, restless and intent on revenge, got an idea when he saw an owl attack a murder of crows sleeping on a tree. Inspired, he entered the Paandava camp at night, killing all he could lay his hands on—Dhristadyumna, Shikhandi, Draupadi's five sons, Uttamauja, Yudhaamanyu, and many others.[1]

The Paandavas, appalled at this cruel and cowardly attack, went after Ashwatthaama. Ashwatthaama invoked the deadly Brahmasheera weapon; so did Arjuna. At Vyaasa's intervention, Arjuna withdrew his weapon. He knew how to fire as well as withdraw the weapon; Ashwatthaama did not, nor did he want to. He directed the weapon towards Uttaraa's womb.

> 'You really love your own life, don't you? Isn't that why you attacked the Paandava camp through deceit?' Krishna asked Ashwatthaama.
> 'Had I fought through fair means, I would have lost. And yes, I would have lost my life too,' Ashwatthaama shrugged.

'Yet you have no compunctions about what you just did, do you?' Krishna asked.

'No, I don't. The Paandavas have committed every evil deed there is, and yet you talk of dharma!' Ashwatthaama retorted. 'It is but fitting that the line of these vile Paandavas end, and even more so that I end it with my weapon. Yours will be a hollow victory. Rejoice, O Keshava, over the dead foetus!' Ashwatthaama shouted.

'You are not only evil but also a coward,' Krishna said, nailing Ashwathaama with his icy stare.

'Don't preach to me, O Krishna.'

'Do you know that when Uttaraa had gone to Upaplavya, a brahmana had told her a son would be born to her, and he would be named Pareekshit. When all had been killed, he would be born.'

'Born? You are deluding yourself, O Krishna. My weapon cannot fail; it will kill Uttaraa's foetus, the foetus that you wish to protect, that you think you can save, that you dream you can save,' Ashwatthaama smirked.

'Karna also believed that the vajra would kill Arjuna, who I protected,' Krishna smiled.

Ashwatthaama's smile waned.

'But your words will come true. Your weapon will find its mark. Yes, the foetus will be stillborn,' Krishna continued, a hint of a smile on his lips now.

Ashwatthaama looked puzzled. What games was Krishna playing now?

'I, Vasudeva, will revive him. The child will live. The boy will one day become a prince, and then a king who will succeed Yudhishthira. He will learn the Vedas from Kripa. He will rule for sixty years.'

A look of dismay clouded Ashwatthaama's face. Realization dawned. It was Narayana who was speaking to him, not a cowherd from Vrindavan. A shiver went through him. It was not fear as much as a growing realization of what he had done and what he would have to undergo as a consequence.

'As for you…,' Krishna paused.

Yes. A pall of gloom consumed Ashwatthaama. What he had done was unforgivable. Would Krishna kill him, a brahmana, for that sin? No. Then what?

'You are not only evil but also a coward, O Ashwatthaama. One who has no compunctions about killing an unborn is worse than the vilest of persons,' Krishna said. 'Yes, I will not kill you, for I will not incur the sin of killing a brahmana; even one as vile as you. But I will curse you, O Ashwatthaama. I curse you to roam this earth for three-thousand years. Alone, unseen, unheard, forever on the move, forever bleeding, forever enveloped in the stench of your deeds.'

Ashwatthaama had loved his life all his life. Now he would have to live for longer than anyone ever had. A life he did not want.

> Sometimes there were fates worse than death. Sometimes there were crimes that deserved a fate worse than death.[2]

News of the death of the last of their sons reached Dhritaraashtra and Gandhaari. The Paandavas went to Hastinapura to meet the bereaved parents. A raging and grieving Dhritaraashtra wanted to crush Bheema to death. Unbeknownst to Dhritaraashtra, Krishna had an iron image placed in front of the king instead. The blind king enveloped it in his arms and crushed it.[3] Bheema survived.

Gandhaari had been dissuaded by Vyaasa from cursing the Paandavas.[4] Vyaasa reminded Gandhaari that she had known who was in the right. She had not showered blessings of victory on Duryodhana. Rather, she had uttered, 'Where there is dharma, there is victory.'[5]

The Pandavas were spared of a grieving mother's curse. Her gaze, suffused with her grief and anger, which fell on Yudhishthira's toe, still ended up disfiguring those toes.[6] Her anger, however, dissipated at Yudhishthira's fear. It was time to move to the battlefield. Gandhaari and other women of the Kuru household made their way to the battlefield to identify and grieve over the fallen warriors.

Gandhaari walked the battlefield, strewn with corpses, the widowed wives trying to locate their dead warrior husbands. Gandhaari walked to her dead sons, weeping, sorrowing over each. Her grief overwhelmed her again. Rage at the slaughter that had taken place looked for an outlet. At one person who could have stopped all this. Krishna. He who controlled the worlds, the past, present, and future, could have, should have prevented this war. He had not. He was responsible. With the store of a lifetime of austerities, she cursed Krishna. He too would die. So would his kin. So would the entire Yaadava race. So would their womenfolk be widowed. So too would they weep.[7]

> When thirty-six years have elapsed, your relatives will be killed, your advisers will be killed and your sons will be killed. You will wander around in the forest. You will confront a horrible death. With the sons slain, with the kin and relatives killed, your wives will be tormented, as the women of the Bharata lineage are now.[8]

Yes, what Gandhaari had cursed would come to pass—Krishna said, accepted, knew, and would allow to happen. What would happen would happen as it had to, as Krishna had determined it would. Krishna, of all, knew this only too well. He smiled.

The funeral rites for the dead were conducted. The funeral pyres were the last act of destruction in a cycle that had begun generations ago. The Bharata race was reduced to one survivor who would carry on the lineage—Pareekshit.[9]

Water was offered to River Ganga for the departed. The river that had descended from the heavens to ferry Saagara's sixty-thousand sons to heaven[10] would now carry the souls of the countless fallen warriors to the other world, accepting their sins and the last remnants of what was once their mortal shell. The bravest of warriors, the most cowardly and craven, all had been reduced to ashes. The Ganga would accept one and all. She would also accept the forgotten, the abandoned, carrying them to another life.

The Paandavas grieved over the dead, their loved ones. Their cup of woe was not full, however. Fate had left some room for more sorrow. Kunti revealed that Karna had been their brother. Brother had truly killed brother.[11] The cup of sorrow was infinite, it seemed. Yudhishthira sank into despondency.

When the time came for the Paandavas to enter Hastinapura as victors, to rule over the entire kingdom, Yudhishthira would not. His heart was tormented by the deaths of relatives and near and dear ones. The war that he had tried to avoid, the war he had then fought to the end, now seemed pointless, futile.

To bring a sense of perspective to Yudhishthira, Sage Vyaasa had recounted what the wise brahman Ashma had told Janaka, the king of Videha. Yudhishthira listened, but stayed quiet, his mind still in turmoil. Arjuna turned to Krishna[12] to rescue Yudhishthira from the ocean of sorrow in which he was immersed. Krishna clasped Yudhishthira's sandalwood-smeared arms and spoke to him.

> Do not indulge in this sorrow that dries up the body. Those who have been slain in the field of battle will not come back. They are like objects one sees in a dream. Once one awakes, they disappear.[13]

Death was inevitable. It spared none. Neither the rich, nor the poor. Krishna then recounted a story to Yudhishthira about King Srinjaya and his conversation with Sage Naarada about sorrow, death, its inevitability, and the futility of sorrow over the dead. Many kings, sages, and illustrious people had had to face the death of the near and dear, Naarada said.

Srinjaya was a king in the Ikshvaaku lineage who had been grief-stricken on account of his son's death. Naarada, his friend, consoled him that happiness and unhappiness were something everyone had to face. He was neither the first father to see his son die, nor would he be the last.

Naarada told Srinjaya about Maruta, son of Avikshit. When Maruta died, the king had a great sacrifice where he invited all the gods and sages, wishing to equal Indra. Who would officiate at that sacrifice? Brihasapati, not wanting to anger Indra, refused. However, Brihaspati's younger brother, Samvarta,[14] who did not get along with his elder brother, agreed to officiate. Naarada told Srinjaya said that when Avikshit ruled, the earth yielded a bountiful harvest and he was four times as meritorious as Srinjaya's son. When he could die, then why was Sinjaya grieving over his son's death, Naarada asked.

What about Suhotra, the son of Vitithi? During his reign, Indra showered gold for an entire year. Suhotra collected that gold, organized a grand sacrifice at Kurukshetra, and gave the gold away to brahmanas. He too was four times as meritorious as Srinjaya's son. He too died.

What about Vrihadratha, son of Anga? He gave away a million white horses, a million bulls, and thousands of cows as donations. No king had ever given as much away in donations as he did. He too was four times as meritorious as Srinjaya's son. He too died.

Wasn't Shibi,[15] son of Ushinaara, famous in the three worlds as a valorous king who was famed for his donations and who was even more valorous than Indra. He too had died.

King Bharata, son of Dushyanta and Shakuntala, was famous for his donations. When he, four times as meritorious as Srinjaya's son, died, what reason did Srinjaya have to grieve, Naarada asked.

Didn't the world know about Raama, Dasharatha's son, Naarada asked Srinjaya. During his reign, not only did the rains shower at the right time, but his subjects also followed dharma. He too was four times as meritorious as Srinjaya's son. He too died.

Bhagiratha, the king, the sage, who brought Ganga down to the earth, was equally valorous, and who defeated thousands of asuras and gave away untold wealth away as donations.

Each maiden was on a chariot and each chariot was drawn by four horses. With each chariot, there were one hundred excellent elephants with golden harnesses. A thousand horses followed each elephant from the rear. A thousand

> cows followed each horse and there were one thousand goats and sheep behind each cow.[16]

The numbers were more than one could imagine, running into millions, billions, trillions, and quadrillions, and they conveyed a sense of the magnitude of donations. When this scion of the Ikshavaaku lineage died, what reason did Srinjaya have to grieve over his son's death, Naarda asked?

Such was also the case with Dileep,[17] son of Ilvala, known for his charity, and at whose abode three sounds—the chants of studying, the twang of bowstring, and that of 'I give'—were always heard. Yet, he too died.

Maandhaataa was Yuvanaashva's[18] son, born from Yuvanaashva himself, and who was sustained from a stream of milk that originated from Indra's hand. He performed many sacrifices and gave brahmanas a huge fish made of gold. When he too, four times as meritorious as Srinjaya's son, died, what reason did Srinjaya have to grieve, Naarada asked.

Then there were similar cases of Yayaati, son of Nahusha; of Ambareesha, Naabhaaga's[19] son; of Shashabindu, Chitrasena's son; of Gaya, Amurtaraya's son—who gave away as many cows in donations as there are grains of sands in the Ganga; of Rantideva, Sankriti's son; of Sagara; Prithu, and Vena's son.

> Shashabindu had a million sons who were excellent archers. All of them were clad in golden armour. Each of those princes married one hundred maidens, who followed him. One hundred elephants followed each maiden and one hundred chariots followed each elephant. One hundred horses, born in the country and adorned with golden harnesses, followed each chariot. One hundred cows followed each horse and one hundred sheep and goats followed each cow.[20]

Srinjaya felt his sorrow reduce, but he could not stop thinking of his son. Despite Naarada's words, he wanted his son back. He requested Naarada to bring him back to life. Naarada said that though Srinjaya's son, Swarnashtheevi,[21] had been given to him by Sage Parvata, he would nonetheless give him his son back.

Perhaps there was a way for those who had died in the war to be brought back to life. If, as Naarada had just said, Swarnashtheevi could be brought back to life, and by none other than the sage himself, perhaps there was hope.

42

NAARADA-PARVATA

Monkeying Around

Parva: Shanti (12)	Upa parva: Raja-dharma (84)
Chapters: 30-31	Shlokas: 89

It was known that in the past men lived long lives. Yet Srinjaya's son, Swarnashtheevi, had died when only a child. Yudhishthira was puzzled by this. He asked Krishna how that had come to be. If Swarnashtheevi had been brought to life, could those killed in the war too be revived? This thought may have been on Yudhishthira's mind.

Krishna said that Parvata's mother was Naarada's sister, and hence the two were nephew and maternal uncle, respectively, and also good friends. Once they came down from the world of the gods. They roamed the world of humans, eating their food, travelling on foot like men did. Not wanting anything to come between their friendship, they made a pact that whatever the other was thinking, good or bad, he would share with the other; if he didn't, he would be cursed.

Travelling the earth, Naarada and Parvata eventually came to King Srinjaya's kingdom. There, the king welcomed them and asked his daughter, Sukumaari, to tend to the two sages as if they were like her father.

Sukumaari was young and beautiful. Naarada could not but fall in love with her. But neither did he tell Sukumaari about his feelings nor did he tell his nephew. Not sharing this with Parvata was a breach of their pact. Parvata was also a sage with great powers. He divined the turmoil inside Naarada's heart. He was enraged at this deception. A curse was called for. That had been their pact, after all.

Parvata cursed Naarada. If Sukumaari was who Naarada desired, then Sukumaari was who Naarada would marry. However, Sukumaari would see Naarada not as who he was, but as an ape.

Naarada too cursed Parvata in retaliation. Sure, Naarada had broken their pact and as per the pact, Naarada deserved to be cursed, but after all, wasn't Parvata an ascetic with tremendous self-control? Could he not have exercised that restraint and not cursed Naarada? But he had pronounced the curse. And thus, Naarada counter-cursed Parvata. He, Naarada pronounced, would not dwell in heaven.

As fated, Sukumaari married Naarada. As cursed by Parvata, the moment the marriage was solemnized, Sukumaari saw Naarada as an ape. She nonetheless served him faithfully.

Time passed. The two sages came across each other in a forest. It was time for bygones to be bygones. Curses too had an age. Parvata, with folded hands, requested Naarada to free him of the curse so he could go to heaven. Naarada had been equally distressed because of Parvata's curse. Both withdrew their curses. Naarada acquired the shape of a human again.

When Sukumaari saw Naarada approach her, she saw not an ape but a sage. That could not be her husband. She ran. Parvata called out and told her that it was none other than Naarada. She returned. All was well.

This is how Naarada had been married to Sukumaari, and how Naarada and Parvata had cursed each other, and eventually freed themselves of those curses. But what about Swarnashtheevi? How had he been born, Yudhishthira asked.

Naarada said that he and Parvata spent a long time in Srinjaya's abode. When it was time for them to leave, they decided to confer a boon on the king. Srinjaya, however, demurred. The presence of the two sages had been a blessing in itself. Parvata persisted. The king relented. He had desired a son, too. Parvata granted him the boon, but there was a condition. Srinjaya had desired a son who would exceed Indra in prosperity and power. That would come to pass, but the son would have a short life. After all, Indra, the king of the gods, was not one to allow rivals and claimants to his throne to prosper. Parvata warned the king to beware of Indra.

Srinjaya was unhappy and requested Parvata to grant his son a long life. Parvata, because of his favourable disposition towards Indra, didn't reply, but instead told Srinjaya to think of him when his son was dead, and he would appear and restore him back to life.

In due course, a son was born to Srinjaya and was named Swarnashtheevi.[1] The boy was brave and radiant. His name and fame spread through the worlds. Indra became apprehensive. A new claimant to his throne had arisen and would need to be put down. He summoned his vajra and told it to assume the form of a tiger and be on the lookout for a weak moment to kill the prince.

Meanwhile, Srinjaya, the queen, and the women had moved to a forest by the Bhagirathi. One day, the prince was running around near the river with only his nurse by him. Seizing the opportunity, the tiger killed the child. Holding his son's mangled body in his arms, Srinjaya grieved. He then remembered Parvata's words. As promised, Parvata restored Swarnashtheevi to life, who grew up to be king and lived a long life.

But no such assurance had been given to those killed in the Kurukshetra war.

43

PARASHURAAMA

Rage, Reignited

Parva: Shanti (12)	Upa parva: Raja-dharma (84)
Chapters: 48–49	Shlokas: 95

Bheeshma lay on the battlefield, waiting for Uttarayaana to start. He thought of Krishna and invoked his name. Krishna heard Bheeshma and went to Kurukshetra, along with Saatyaki, the Paandavas, Kripa, Yuyutsu, Sanjaya, and others.

The battlefield of Kurukshetra had seen more warriors fall than ever had, or ever would. A billion fatalities, that's how many had died. Tens of thousands were missing.

> Yudhishthira replied, 'One billion, twenty thousand and sixty-six crore—that is the number slain in this battle of kings. O Indra among Kings! In addition, twenty-four thousand, one hundred and sixty-five brave ones are missing.'[1]

The battlefield was still a fearsome sight. Corpses still littered the earth, funeral pyres still burnt, the earth still looked red and felt soaked with blood.

> The bodies and bones of elephants and horses were piled up in heaps, like mountains. The heads and skulls of men were strewn around like conch shells. Thousands of funeral pyres had been lit, with armour and weapons piled on. It looked like a drinking ground that had been used by Death and had just been abandoned. Large numbers of demons wandered around and large numbers of rakshasas frequented it.[2]

The Paandavas, Krishna, and others proceeding to where Bheeshma lay. Along the way Krishna pointed out the five lakes created by Parashuraama[3] who had wiped out the kshatriyas twenty-one times and offered their blood as offerings that filled up those five lakes. The blood had long since disappeared; the place had become a teertha. Hearing this, Yudhishthira asked how Parashuraaama had wiped out the kshatriyas and how, once they had been wiped out, they come to be again.

King Jahnu's son was Ajahnu, and his son, Ballava. King Kushika[4] was Ballava's son. Kushika desired a son who would be Indra's equal and performed severe penances to obtain one. Indra, ever fearful of a contender to his throne, decided to be born as Kushika's son. That was one ingenious way of thwarting any contender to his throne. This son was named Gaadhi. Gaadhi had a daughter named Satyavati.[5] She married Sage Richika.[6]

Richika once cooked rice balls mixed with milk. He gave one half of the mix to his wife, Satyavati, and told her to give the other half to her mother. Her mother, King Gaadhi's wife, would have a son equally fierce and brave. Satyavati, on the other hand, now the wife of Sage Richika, would have a son who would stand tall among brahmanas.

As fate would have it, there was a mix-up.[7] When Richika told Satyavati what was going to be the result of this mix-up, she requested him to endow her with a son who would be peaceful and wise. Richika said that what was done was done. However, at her request, he agreed to delay the effects by a generation. Satyavati's son would be a great sage, but the grandson would be one with a great temper. What had happened could not be undone; at best, the consequences could be pushed out by one generation.

Satyavati thus gave birth to Bhaargava Jamadagni who grew up to be a wise sage. Jamadagni's son, however, was the fierce warrior Parashuraama. Gaadhi's wife, meanwhile, gave birth to Vishwaamitra.

The cycle of fate was moving in its own, inexorable way. Around the same time, there was a brave king named Kaartaveerya Arjuna of the Haihaya lineage. Agni[8] once approached Kaartaveerya for alms. Protected by Kaartaveerya, Agni blazed, consuming forests, forts, and hamlets. One such place was Vasishtha's hermitage. Enraged, the sage cursed Kaartaveerya that the same thousand arms with which he had protected Agni would one day be severed by Parashuraama.

As fate willed, one day Kaartaveerya's sons, without his knowledge, went to Jamadagni's hermitage and forcefully dragged away his calf. Parashuraama attacked and retrieved the calf, got into a duel with Kaartaveerya, and severed his arms, as prophesied by Vasishtha.

Kaartaveerya's sons, driven to madness by hubris, anger, and fate, returned to Jamadagni's hermitage. There they didn't find Parashuraama, but his father, Jamadagni, instead. If not the son, then the father would do. They hacked the sage to death, beheading him. When Parashuraama returned and saw the carnage wrought, he went on a destructive spree, killing all the Haihayas and kshatriyas. Eventually, his anger subsided and Parashuraama retired to the forest.

Time passed. Paravaasu, a great sage in his own right and Vishwaamitra's grandson, once taunted Parashuraama in full view of others. Hadn't Parashuraama taken a vow to rid the earth of kshatriyas? Who was Yayaati, if not a kshatriya? Who was Pratardana if not a kshatriya?

> 'Your vow was an empty one, O Raama,' Paravaasu taunted. 'It is as hollow as your axe is blunt.'
>
> The assembled men looked at Parashuraama's face.
>
> 'The truth,' Paravaasu continued, 'is that you are a coward. You are scared of the kshatriyas, and that is why you have chosen to hide. You are so terrified of the kshatriyas that you chose to flee to the mountains.'

Parashuraama's rage was reignited. He stood up, picked up his axe. The cycle of killing started again. This time the carnage was even more severe. Those kshatriyas that had managed to remain alive were killed. Neither were children spared, nor women. Twenty-one times was this cycle of destruction repeated. Twenty-one times did Parashuraama kill the race of kshatriyas.

Finally, the killings stopped, for there were no more kshatriyas left. Parashuraama gave the earth as a donation to Sage Kashyapa. He asked Raama to go to the shores of the southern ocean. Parashuraama obliged.

> When there is no king in the world of the living, the strong oppress the weak. There are no restraints and no one is the lord of his own possessions.[9]

Actions have consequences—foreseen and unforeseen. With no kshatriyas left, order decayed in society. The strong preyed on the weak. People did as they pleased. Neither was property safe nor women. The earth became a veritable hell, descending into rasaatala.[10] At such a time, Kashyapa held her up on his thigh; thus the earth also came to be known as Urvi.[11]

This could be a temporary measure, at best. Goddess Earth requested Kashyapa that she be protected by kshatriyas, for that was the role of kshatriyas in society. Despite Parashuraama's best efforts, some kshatriyas had indeed survived. There were some from the Haihayas lineage that still lived; a descendant of the Paurava lineage; Sarvakarma, born in the Sudasa lineage; Shibi's son, Gopati; Pratardana's son, Vatsa; Dadhivahana's grandson, Anga; and three kshatriyas in the Marutta lineage.

If that were the case, then all was not lost. Kashyapa went looking for all these survivors and brought together all these kshatriyas. He consecrated them afresh as protectors of the earth.

Those five lakes that Krishna, the Paandavas, and others had just passed had a gory past. Pride, arrogance, and the wanton abuse of power would be put down, sometimes with equally gory means. Krishna, Yudhishthira, and the others proceeded to where Bheeshma lay.

44 MUCHKUNDA

A Question of Roles

Parva: Shanti (12)	Upa parva: Raja-dharma (84)
Chapter: 75	Shlokas: 22

Bheeshma, the store of wisdom and governance, awaited Krishna. Lying on a bed of arrows, the grand patriarch of the Kurus counted the days to when his mortal existence would come to an end. The day was coming to an end, and the sun cast long shadows, sinking into the horizon.

> He was like the evening sun or the fire, surrounded by a net of his own rays.[1]

Krishna told Bheeshma that Uttarayaana was still some days away—when the sun would resume its northward journey. Till then, he wished that Bheeshma instructs Yudhishthira on dharma and artha.

> Fifty-six days still remain in your life.[2]

But Bheeshma, who had the boon of choosing his moment of death, who was still alive, was barely conscious. His mind clouded by pain, his body riddled with arrows, speech was the last thing on his mind. In any case, with Krishna there, how could he speak on dharma and artha?

Krishna smiled. He granted Bheeshma the boon that he would suffer from neither thirst nor hunger, not from pain, not from fever. All knowledge would become manifest in him, Krishna decreed.

Thus did Bheeshma receive the boon from Krishna. The day had come to an end. The Paandavas departed; they would return the next day. Yudhishthira finally entered Hastinapura.

The next day, as they prepared to leave to meet Bheeshma, Yudhishthira ordered that they proceed alone, without soldiers, without an entourage. What Bheeshma had to say was best said without a horde listening in. The five Paandavas, like the five elements, proceeded, accompanied by Krishna and Saatyaki.

Among the duties of a brahmana, Bheeshma began, was to bring peace to people from worries unmanifest. This was done through knowledge. As for manifest worries, like safety from thieves, the duty fell upon a king.

Once there was a king named Muchkunda. Valorous, he had conquered all that lay within his sight. Eventually he set eyes on Kubera, the lord of Alaka. Kubera, also known as Vaishraavana, counter-attacked with his army of raakshasas. They slowly gained the upper hand over Muchkunda's army. Vasishtha, Muchkunda's purohit (priest), performed great penances to aid Muchkunda. Those prayers bore fruit. Kubera's army had to retreat. Kubera approached Muchkunda.

> 'O Muchkunda,' Kubera began, 'why are you taking the help of a brahmana in this fight? If you value yourself as a kshatriya, then fight without the help of brahmanas.'
>
> An angry retort came to Muchkunda's lips, but he refrained. He calmed himself and responded. 'O Vaishraavana, how are brahmanas and kshatriyas different? Weren't both created by Brahma? It's just that both have different powers. The strength of a brahmana comes from his penances and mantras; that of a kshatriya from his weapons and his strength to use them. Is it or is it not the case?'
>
> 'I am not in the habit of taking or giving away kingdoms, O Muchkunda,' Kubera replied. 'But in this case, I give you my kingdom. Go, rule it.'
>
> 'O Kubera, I do not rule a kingdom that has been given to me as alms. What I rule is what I have won through the power of my arms,' Muchkunda said.

Kubera was impressed by Muchkunda's kshatriya dharma and paid him his respects.

Bheeshma concluded this account by reminding Yudhishthira that the king who recognized and respected the brahmana gained fame and victory.

45

USHTRAGREEVA

Sloth

Parva: Shanti (12) **Upa parva:** Raja-dharma (84)
Chapter: 113 **Shlokas:** 21

What a king ought to do had been laid out in detail. But sometimes it helped to acquaint oneself with a cautionary tale. For in that tale would be a lesson most eloquent on what not to do and how not to act.

Bheeshma shared an account of a camel with Yudhishthira.

Camels have padded feet to allow them to walk on soft sands without sinking. They have immense stores of water in their stomachs. Their necks are long to allow them to reach leaves and fruits that may otherwise be out of reach. There was once such a camel. He was at the time aware of dharma and performed great penances. So great were the austerities that Brahma was pleased with him and granted him a boon. Food was scarce and an even longer neck would help him reach food with ease, the camel reasoned. Therefore, the camel asked for an even longer neck. A really, really, long neck would mean he didn't have to crane it to reach leaves and fruit high up on trees. As the camel asked for, so did the camel get from Brahma.

A long neck meant food was now within reach of the camel. He didn't have to starve. He had plentiful food. With a little effort he was able to get a lot of food. Soon enough, the inevitable happened—the camel became lazy.

Life went on in this comfortable manner, till one day there was a terrible storm. To take shelter from the storm, the camel placed his head and neck inside a cave. The cave was narrow. The camel's head and neck got stuck there. That wasn't a calamity since the camel was well-fed. A few days or weeks without food or water wouldn't kill him.

Eventually, a hungry jackal and its wife came by, also seeking refuge from the storm and entered the same cave where the camel's neck remained stuck. The camel's soft neck beckoned. The jackal and his wife took a nibble, then a bite. The camel thrashed around in desperation but could not extricate its neck out from the cave. The inevitable happened—the jackal and his wife made a meal of the camel.

> Behold the great sin that progressively comes about because of laziness.[1]

Bheeshma narrated this tale to serve as a warning against indolence. He quoted Manu who had said that intelligence is the foundation of victory (*buddhimūlaṁ hi vijayaṁ*). The best tasks were those that were performed with intelligence, the worst those performed with the thighs since they were meant for bearing loads.

DANDA UTPATTI

The Rod and the Right

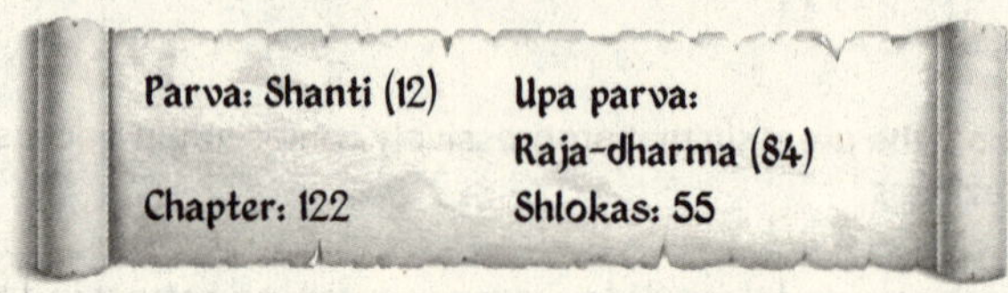

Five hundred years ago there lived the poet and saint, Tulasidaas. He wrote in his epic poem, Ramcharitmanas, that without fear there could not be love.[1] A few thousand years before that, Bheeshma, when talking about crime and punishment, had made the same point to Yudhishthira, elaborated over several chapters. He quoted Brahma, as repeated by Vasishtha, that the three objectives of life—dharma, artha, and kaama—flowed from the rod of chastisement.[2] Bheeshma even recounted twenty-five names of the rod to Yudhishthira.[3]

> It is out of fear of the rod that they do not kill each other.[4]

The rod of punishment was one of the limbs of the kingdom and was united with judgment.[5]

> Where the Vedas are, dharma exists there. Where dharma exists, the path of virtue is there.[6]

Yudhishthira had asked Bheeshma about the origins of this rod of punishment. For that answer, Bheeshma recounted an ancient example of Vasuhoma, the king of Anga. Once when he was in the Himalayas with his wife, he was visited by King Maandhaataa.[7] Maandhaataa had had the same question for Vasuhoma that Yudhishthira had of Bheeshma.

Once Brahma wished to perform a sacrifice but couldn't find an officiating priest equal to himself. He therefore created a foetus from which was born Kshupa, a Prajapati, and thus the sacrifice began. However, since Brahma, as the officiating priest, had to be calm and collected, the rod of punishment vanished. If he had chosen to adopt a fierce demeanour, the sacrifice itself would go in vain. Therein existed a dilemma.

The consequences were not merely philosophical. With the disappearance of the rod of punishment, there was no longer any restraint on the conduct of people. A dog-eat-dog world loomed.

> One's own property and that of others became the same. They snatched from each other, like dogs after meat. The weak were killed by the strong and no one exhibited any respect.[8]

Seeking a way out, Brahma prayed to Vishnu, who manifested himself. This was no small problem that the great Brahma had presented before Vishnu. Vishnu thought about the problem, pondered over solutions, weighed their pros and cons, and finally came to a resolution.

Vishnu created the rod of punishment from his own self. From the rod was created Saraswati, also known as dandaneeti—that would be the policy of dharma. But Vishnu was not done. He meditated some more and appointed Indra as the king of the gods; Vaivasvata Yama as the god of the ancestors; Kubera as the god of riches and raakshasas; Meru as the god of the mountains; the ocean as the god of the rivers; Varuna as the god of the waters; Mrityu[9] as the god of the living; Shiva[10] as the lord of all the Rudras; and so on.[11]

At Brahma's sacrifice, Shiva gave the rod to Vishnu, and Vishnu gave it to Angiras, and from Angiras it passed to Indra, then to Maarichi, to Bhrigu, to the sages, to Kshupa, and to Manu, who gave it to his sons.

This, then, was the history of how the rod of chastisement came to be.

47

RISHABHA GITA

The Fine Thread of Hope

Parva: Shanti (12) **Upa parva: Raja-dharma (84)**
Chapters: 125-126 **Shlokas: 86**

Hunger does not atrophy the body as much as hope does. Hope could drive a person insane with anticipation. Hope, on the other hand, was what had sustained the Paandavas in their exile; it had kept Nala and Damayanti going after Nala had lost everything to his brother; hope is what had driven Ambaa to desperate measures in her quest for vengeance against Bheeshma. Where was hope generated from, what was its nature, asked Yudhishthira. Hope was difficult to obtain, and when hope was dashed, it led to great misery, Yudhishthira said. He had experienced that pain when the great hope generated in his heart at the thought that Duryodhana would do the right thing had been dashed.

Bheeshma told Yudhishthira what had transpired between Sumitra and Rishabha. Sumitra was a king and a rajarshi. He once went out on a hunt. In the forest he struck a deer with his arrow. The arrow, however, had not killed the deer; for it scampered away. Sumitra gave chase. This was no ordinary deer, for Sumitra chased it over rivers, lakes, and woods; he shot arrow after arrow at the deer, to no avail. The chase went on for a long time. Eventually, Sumitra came across a hermitage. The sages there greeted the king as per the rites and then asked him his reason for coming to the hermitage.

Sumitra introduced himself as a king in the Haihaya lineage, the son of King Mitra. It was a deer that had led him on this chase and to this hermitage, Sumitra confessed. His hopes on making a kill had risen when his arrow had struck the deer, but now that the deer was nowhere in sight, they had been dashed. The disappointment felt like a crushing burden. Sumitra felt a despondency greater than if he had lost his entire kingdom. There was no comparison between a kingdom and a mere deer, and yet the disappointment he had felt on losing out on the hunt was greater than if he had lost his entire kingdom. He didn't understand this.

Since he was amidst wise sages, perhaps they could shed light on this question that he had. Of course, he did not want to distract the sages from their austerities, nor would he press for an answer if it were a secret. Was it?

> **Which seems to be greater in this world, the hope of a man, or the sky?[1]**

Among the sages was a brahmana named Rishabha. He told Sumitra about his travels to various teerthas and one which had led him to the hermitage of Nara and Narayana, where Vishnu himself had recited the Vedas. Wishing to spend some time there, Rishabha found a spot a short distance from the hermitage. There he saw a very emaciated sage named Tanu there. Rishabha bowed and touched Tanu's feet, introduced himself, and the two got talking.

Did Rishabha want to talk about hope? Tanu smiled wanly. He had decided, a long time back, to not take anything from anyone. Expecting someone to give him something only led to hope, and the dashing of that hope was a crueller blow than he cared for. Experience had led to this insight.

As Rishabha and Tanu conversed, a king named Viradyumna arrived there along with his retinue and queens. Many years ago, the king's son, Bhuridyumna, had wandered off and had got lost in this jungle. The king had spent years in search of his son. The years had passed but hope had not dimmed in the king's heart.

Tanu saw King Viradyumna approach. Fate indeed had its ways. Wasn't Viradyumna the same king Tanu had once approached with hope. He had asked the king for some wealth—a golden pot and bark to use as clothing. Viradyumna had turned Tanu down, insulting him in the bargain. A humiliated Tanu had vowed then to never take anything from anyone.

For what it was worth, Tanu had reacted less virulently to Viradyumna's insult than Drona had to Drupada's. When Drona had approached his childhood friend and now king of Paanchala, Drupada,[2] he had been insulted by the king and reminded that friendship could only be between equals. A humiliated Drona had left Drupada's court. Nursing that insult, he had bided his time and avenged his insult years later. An insulted Drupada did not forget that humiliation and had his revenge years later when his son, Dhrishtadyumna, killed Drona on the battlefield of Kurukshetra. Drona's son, Ashwatthaama, avenged his father's death by killing Dhrishtadyumna with his bare hands. A small hope, dashed, had led to a fatal chain of events.

Fate had brought now brought Viradyumna and Tanu face to face again. The king had forgotten their past meeting; Tanu had not. Viradyumna too posed the same question that Sumitra had posed to Rishabha—was there anything as difficult as hope.

> There is nothing that is as emaciated as hope.[3]

Much water had flowed under the bridge since; Tanu had acquired much wisdom since; the king had mellowed since; time had taught much to both.

> It is rarer to find a petitioner who is satisfied with what he has got. It is rarer to find a person who does not disrespect a petitioner.[4]

Tanu replied that there were those who could help but did not; yet hope remained in petitioners so rejected. That hope was thinner and more emaciated than he was. There were aged women and rich people alike who wished for a child; hope remained thinner in them than he was.

But not all hope needed to be dashed. A wiser, calmer Tanu used the power of his austerities and knowledge to locate Viradyumna's son, Bhuridyumna. Only after father and son had reunited did Tanu remind Viradyumna of their past encounter. Viradyumna was mortified.

But who really was Tanu? How had his austerities been powerful enough to locate Viradyumna's son after so many years? The sage was none other than Dharma,[5] Rishabha said.

Sumitra heard this account from Rishabha. He sat ruminating on the import of the sage's words. Worry, desire, hope against hope over a deer? Sumitra now knew better. He realized that some things were not meant to be. He discarded the hope he had been clinging to. He felt unburdened, freed from distress.

Bheeshma thus counselled Yudhishthira.

48

KAPOTA

Unwanted, Unwelcome, but Still a Guest

Parva: Shanti (12)	Upa parva: Apad-dharma (85)
Chapters: 141-145	Shlokas: 111

Bheeshma had talked at length about the dharma of kings. He had now moved to a related aspect of governance—of the dharma of kings in difficult times. Dharma was subtle, and never unchanging, never ossified. As times changed, so did the dharma to be followed.

Arjuna had given sanctuary to Maaya, saving him from certain death at the hands of Krishna. A grateful Maaya had built a palace for the Paandavas more wondrous than anything before, or since.[1] Yudhishthira had spared Jayadratha's life, saving him from certain death at the hands of Bheema. Kidnapping Draupadi was not an offence that deserved pardon, but Yudhishthira had let Jayadratha go.[2] An ingrate Jayadratha repaid that debt by playing a pivotal role in Abhimanyu's death years later.

Yudhishthira now wanted to know from Bheeshma what the dharma was of protecting a person who had taken refuge.

What Parashuraama had once told King Muchkunda, Bheeshma now repeated to Yudhishthira. There was once a hunter named Lubhdaka who would catch birds, kill them, and sell them. Hunting was a profession, but Lubhdaka pursued it in a cruel and wicked manner. He lived with his wife, without family or friends.

One day Lubhdaka went to the forest to hunt animals. Deep in the forest, it started to rain. He took shelter under a tree, waiting for the rain to subside. It didn't. It poured and poured. Trickles turned to rivulets, rivulets turned to streams, water gushed everywhere. Anxiety loomed large in the hunter. Night advanced. Drenched, the hunter started to shiver with cold. Hunger pangs stabbed at him. But he could not head back home in this downpour. He had no choice but to spend the night under the tree.

Up in the branches of that tree lived a pigeon (also called a kapota) and his wife. The bird had his own reason for distress. His wife had not yet returned to the tree. Darkness had enveloped the forest, but he could neither see nor hear her. He fretted out aloud.

> It has been read that a wife is a man's supreme protector and that in this world, a man who does not have her as a companion along the journey, is helpless.[3]

He could not know that his wife, that the male pigeon was so anxious about, was close by. How close? Under that very tree. She had been captured by the fowler who now slept under that same tree. She heard her husband's lament and felt equally distressed. However, she had a bigger concern—the fowler.

As the female pigeon spoke, her husband listened. The fowler, the same fowler who had caught her, the same fowler who had now taken refuge under the tree that was their house, was now their guest. What was the dharma towards a guest? That the guest be taken care of. The husband agreed. But how?

He asked Lubdhaka, the fowler, what he needed. The fowler, surprised at first, confessed to being cold. The bird, in the pouring rain, got about collecting twigs and branches. He managed to kindle a fire by bringing a piece of burning coal. The fire warmed Lubhdaka. Soon enough he confessed to being hungry. The bird did not have any store of food, but it did have its own body. It lit another fire, circumambulated the fire thrice and entered it. The bird gave its life up for the sake of dharma. The fowler could not believe what he had just witnessed. When the full realization of what the pigeon had done sank in, the hunter felt ashamed, wracked by guilt at having driven the bird to kill itself.

What had happened had happened. But the fowler repented; he resolved that his adharmic, wayward, evil ways had to come to an end. He got up and threw away the stick, the net, the cage—all the implements he used to catch birds. He freed the birds he had trapped and left.

The pigeon's wife, now freed, looked at the fire that still burned, into which her husband had thrown himself. She saw no point in remaining alive without her husband. She stepped up, one tiny step at a time, and plunged into the fire. The light blinded her momentarily; she clenched her eyes shut, waiting for the flames to singe her, waiting for death. She opened her eyes after a few moments. To her utter amazement and delight, she saw her husband on a celestial chariot.

Where was he? Where was she? Both had gone to heaven. Their deeds had been such.

Lubdhaka, meanwhile, having abandoned his tools, was walking away, lost in his thoughts about the two pigeons who had followed dharma more assiduously than he ever had. He turned around to look at the fire one last time. He saw the fire, but he also saw the celestial vehicle carting the two pigeons away. Overcome by guilt, he too decided to give up his mortal body. He gave up all attachments and desires and subsisted only on air. He made his way to a forest in which once a great fire was ignited. Like the pigeons before him, he entered the fire and was consumed by it.

Thus did Lubdhaka and the pigeons go to heaven. Bheeshma told Yudhishthira that there was atonement for the greatest of sins, but for those who neglected one who had taken refuge, allowing them to perish, no refuge existed anywhere.

49 KRITAGHNA

He Who Even the Raakshasas Wouldn't Have

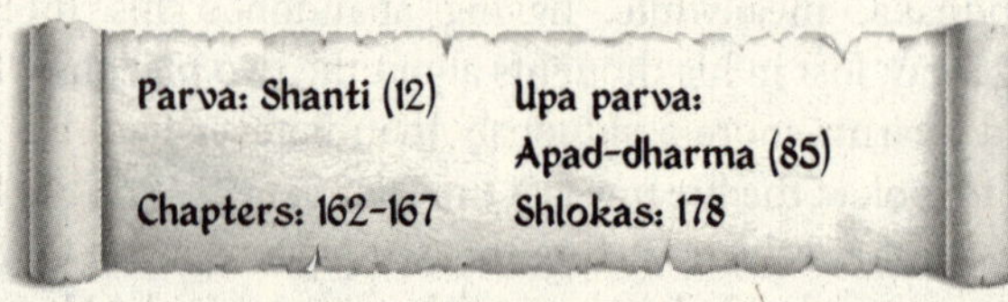

A friend was not necessarily a well-wisher. Nor could be relatives be well-wishers. Wealth too was fickle, though its possession did grant an illusion of knowledge to the one who possessed it. Yudhishthira wanted to know from Bheeshma who were the kinds of people who were well-wishers.

Bheeshma listed the kinds of men to avoid. People who were lazy,[1] procrastinators,[2] suspicious of everyone, shameless, paranoid, who broke agreements,[3] slanderers, gamblers, who lost interest for no reason—dilletantes, who were confused as to what was for their own good. Among all the undesirable traits listed, Bheeshma said the worst was ungratefulness.[4]

> [A]n evil-minded person who is not satisfied even if someone gives him a lot and to the best of giver's capacity...one who is wicked and swiftly abandons his well-wishers for a benefit... one whose friendship is for an ulterior motive...
>
> You should never have an alliance with someone who is looking for your weakness.[5]

Conversely, Bheeshma said, the kinds of people one should consort with were those who were devoted to friends, grateful, knowledgeable, were not given to boasting, and so on.

Yes, it was a truism, but Yudhishthira still wanted to hear from Bheeshma why alliances with the ungrateful were ill-advised.

Bheeshma elucidated with a story about a brahmana named Gautama. Gautama, however, was a brahmana only in name, for he had long abandoned all the traits of a brahmana. He once went to a village in the hopes of begging for alms. In that village lived a rich bandit who was nevertheless noble enough to follow the dharma of daana (donations). Going from house to house, Gautama reached the bandit's house and begged for alms. Seeing the bandit's willingness to give, Gautama not just begged for alms sufficient for one day, he asked for enough alms to last him a year. On top of that he also asked for a house. The bandit gave to the brahmana—enough alms to last a year, then gave him a grand place to live, new clothes, and also married him to a widow.

The brahmana was delighted. He had got all that he had asked for, and more. He helped in the bandit's household. In the bandit's company, Gautama learned archery. With this newfound skill, he started to practice it. In the company of bandits, he too became one; hunting birds and cranes where and when he found them.

Time passed; the months went by. One day another brahmana, from Gautama's country, happened to pass by the village, also in search of alms. He too went from house to house, begging for alms. His path brought him to Gautama's house. The brahmana waited for someone to come out of the house. No one came out of the house but the brahmana saw someone walking towards the house. It was none other than Gautama. But what a sight he presented to his fellow brahmana—dead cranes dangling from his hand, clothes smeared with blood. This was no longer a brahmana; in the company of a bandit, Gautama had become a bandit.

Aghast, the brahmana derided Gautama, chiding him, castigating him, reminding him of his dharma that he had abandoned and forgotten. A penitent Gautama begged his friend's forgiveness. He was poor, Gautama pleaded; he had no means of subsistence; he had been reduced to this wretched state solely so he could subsist on whatever he could find. He had seen the wickedness of his ways, Gautama confessed. He requested his brahmana friend to stay the night. In the morning they would both leave this wretched village, Gautama said.

The brahmana relented and agreed to spend the night in Gautama's house. When morning came, the brahmana left, and so did Gautama. Along the way, Gautama came across a caravan of traders going towards the ocean. He decided to accompany them. As fate would have it, a crazed elephant descended on the caravan and killed most of the traders there. Gautama escaped with his life. Alone again, he wandered around till he came to a beautiful forest inhabited by birds, animals, yakshas, and kinnars. He saw two-headed birds[6] too, so magical was the place.

Walking, exploring, gazing, wondering at the place, Gautama came to a spot near the ocean with golden sand all around. Amidst all the dazzling sand, he saw a huge banyan tree. He walked over and stood under the tree's shade. A pleasant breeze blew, providing respite. Gautama sat under the tree, and tired from his travels and travails, fell asleep.

The sound of the flapping of wings woke Gautama up. He opened his eyes but couldn't see anything. It took a few moments for him to realize it was night. He had slept long. The sound? It was of a bird's wings. Above in the tree lived a celestial crane named Naadijangha,[7] also known as Raajadharma. It had returned to its nest and the flapping of its wings as it settled had caused the disturbance. Gautama, awake now, was also hungry. The hunter of birds looked up, saw the bird. Hunger pains stabbed at him.

Having lived off the largesse of a bandit, living the life of a hunter, having forgotten his vows as a brahmana, Gautama didn't see anything immoral, reprehensible, or wrong in making a meal of the bird. Raajadharma, the king of the cranes, on the other hand, saw in Gautama a guest who had taken refuge under his tree. He asked Gautama to spend the night under the tree and leave in the morning. Raajadharma swooped down to join Gautama.

Raajadharma and Gautama got talking. It told Gautama that it was a descendant of Kashyapa and Dakshayaani;[8] and was a friend of Brahma. To take care of its guest, the bird cooked and offered fish to Gautama and fanned him with its feathers. But who was his guest, Raajadharma wished to know. Gautama gave his name, that he was a brahmana, and stopped. When Raajadharma asked him why he had come to the ocean, Gautama replied that he had come in search of wealth. Gautama had left his village where the bandit had given him enough wealth to last a year, and yet he was now in search of more wealth. He left this bit out. The crane replied that Gautama's wish would come true, for there were four ways of obtaining wealth—inherit it, obtain it through fate, through hard work, or from friends. Which one would Gautama resort to?

> It is Brihaspati's view that there are four means of obtaining riches—inheritance, fate, deeds and friends.[9]

Gautama was, after all, both a friend and well-wisher, the trusting Rajadharma said. Gautama nodded. All he wished for was to make a meal of the bird.

When dawn came, Rajadharma told Gautam to travel along the path for three yojanas when he would come to Meruvraja, the capital city of a kingdom ruled by Virupaksha, a raakshasa with great wealth. Virupaksha and Rajadharma were friends. Through a friend of a friend would Gautama get rich.

All Gautama had to do was to travel to Meruvraja, meet Virupaksha, and tell the king that he was a friend of Raajadharma. Wealth would be his. Gautama's eyes lit up with visions of wealth untold.

Filled with anticipation and excitement, Gautama departed post haste for Meruvraja. When he reached the city, he was confronted by ramparts made of stone, a mechanical gate that controlled ingress and egress into the town, and fierce guards at the entrance. He approached the guards. They took his message to the king. The moment the raakshasa king, Virupaksha, learned that Gautama was a friend of Raajadharma, he ordered his guards to let him in without delay. A wide-eyed Gautama entered the city, marvelling at the sights of the wondrous town he was in.

As had Raajadharma, Virupaksha also asked Gautama his gotra,[10] his studies, his behaviour, and the nature of his brahmacharya. As he had answered Rajadharma, Gautama gave Virupaksha also cryptic answers—just his name and gotra. What he couldn't say, he didn't—that he no longer followed the dharma of a brahmana, that he no longer studied, that he no longer observed the vow of brahmacharya. Virupaksha repeated his question.

Seeing Gautama's hesitation, Virupaksha assured him that he had nothing to fear. Gautama opened up, but even then, shared only that he had married a shudra woman who had married earlier, and that he no longer followed the conduct of a brahmana. Virupaksha was now in a quandary. It was clear that Gautama was a non-practicing brahmana. But he also Raajadharma's friend. How could he best serve his friend and relative.[11]

Virupaksha decided that since this was the month of Kaartika, he would feed a thousand brahmans, including Gautama, and give them wealth as dakshina. Gautama got what he had coveted—wealth. Virupaksha gave him, and other brahmanas, gold, silver, gems, pearls, and deer and antelope skin to use as a seat. Today was one day when they would have no fear of the raakshasas stealing their wealth or taking their lives, Virupaksha assured them. They could traverse dense forests and tread lonely paths. No one would accost them.

Gautama took as much as he could and then some more. Straggling, struggling, he staggered to the tree he had started his journey from, where Raajadharma lived. The crane welcomed him, gave him food, fanned him with its wings. Gautama closed his eyes, fed, but neither sated nor satisfied. The wealth Virupaksha had given him had only aroused more greed. He wanted more, and more, and more.

> 'All this wealth that I have got from Virupaksha, I have to carry back to my village. Yes, I can manage that,' he thought.
> But what about food? There is none on the way.
> Yes, that is more than an inconvenience. What use is this wealth if I cannot get it back to my home.
> But food is here. The bird. It will sustain me for the duration of my journey back.
> But the bird has been good to me.
> Of what use is a friend if it cannot be of help in my time of need? Do I not need food on my journey back home? Of what use is this wealth if I die of hunger?
> Yes, so it shall be, so it must be. A friend when I am in need, and food when I am in need."

Gautama waited; his eyes closed. Soon enough, Raajadharma slept off. The moment it had, Gautama sprang up, killed the crane, cooked it in the fire that Raajadharma had kindled to feed Gautama. His vile deed done, Gautama departed.

Virupaksha, meanwhile, was a worried king. He had not heard from his friend, the bird, for two days. He asked his son to go find out where Raajadharma was and whether he was well. Somewhere in his mind, a suspicion gnawed that perhaps, just perhaps, Gautama may have had something to do with his friend's disappearance, for Gautama lacked the virtues associated with brahmanas. He hoped his fears were unfounded.

Virupaksha's son went with some other raakshasas to the banyan tree that they knew was Raajadharma's abode. A ghastly site awaited them. Under the tree they saw a burned-out fire. Bones were strewn about. They started tracking the path and soon caught up with Gautama, who had made slow progress because of the wealth and Rajadharma's cooked flesh that he had to lug with him. Furious, but still cognizant that only Virupaksha could determine a punishment appropriate for this gory crime, they brought Gautama back to Meruvraja.

After much lamentation over the dastardly murder of his friend, Virupaksha decreed that Gautama be killed. His flesh would be eaten by the raakshasas. The punishment fitted the crime. But there was a hitch.

Even the raakshasas wanted to have nothing to do with Gautama's flesh. They debated the matter and decided that Gautama be given to bandits. After all, he had taken the favours of a bandit and become one like them. Gautama was executed. His body was chopped into little pieces. The raakshasas took those pieces to the forest and offered them to bandits. Even the bandits wanted nothing to do with an ingrate like Gautama. Even predatory animals refused to touch Gautama's pieces.

Virupaksha meanwhile had a grand funeral pyre prepared for his departed friend, Raajadharma. At that occasion, the goddess Dakshayaani Surabhi appeared, and from the milk that poured from her mouth onto the pyre, Rajadharma was revived. The king of the gods, Indra, also manifested himself before Virupaksha. Rajadharma's death was the result of a curse Brahma had pronounced on the bird a long time back. But all was well now.

Raajadharma, on coming back to life, requested Indra that his friend Gautama also be brought back to life. Indra acquiesced and brought Gautama back to life. Even if Gautama had abandoned his dharma, Raajadharma could not forego his swadharma. Raajadharma returned to his abode.

> How can an ungrateful person obtain fame? What is his status? Where is his happiness?[12]

As for Gautama, he returned to his wife. Over the years they had several children. But nothing good could come from nothing good. They turned out to be no different from Gautama. All were cursed by the gods to go to hell.

Bheeshma concluded his answer to Yudhishthira.

> If someone kills a brahmana, if someone is a drunkard, if someone is a thief, if someone has broken his vows-there are indicated means of atonement. O King! But there is no salvation for someone who is ungrateful.[13]

With this upakhyaana, the Apad-dharma upa parva also came to an end.

50
JAAPAKA

A Question of Give and Take

Parva: Shanti (12)	Upa parva: Moksha-dharma (86)
Chapters: 189-193	Shlokas: 204

Thus far Bheeshma had answered Yudhishthira's questions about the four ashrams—brahmacharya, gaarhasthya, vanaaprastha, and vanavaas. He had counselled Yudhishthira on rajadharma—the duties of a king. Yudhishthira's question this time to Bheeshma was simple—what were the fruits that accrued to jaapakas?[1] He wanted to know the rules laid down for jaapakas in saankhya and yoga.

Bheeshma recounted an ancient account of a conversation between Yama, Kaala,[2] and a brahmana. He said that the choice to follow or not follow the path of saankhya or yoga was an individual's, but he would tell the reasons for following them.

As far as the path of abstention was concerned, a celibate was supposed to immerse himself in japa and renounce rituals. Before renouncing all material objects, he should bow down one last time before these material objects. After that he should focus his mind on his mind, with no further thoughts about those material objects. He would eventually free himself from all attachments, confusion, sorrow, and even happiness.

> He will be without attachment and confusion. He will not sorrow. Nor will he be delighted. He does not think of himself as the doer, nor as the one who enjoys from this action. Nor does he suffer from the action.[3]

While the doer does not seek anything for himself, that sense of detachment does not stop him from action. As he engages himself in meditation, eventually he enters a state of samaadhi where he obtains the bliss of having renounced everything, uniting with brahman. A jaapaka could also then choose a path to be forever free from the cycle of rebirth.

Having heard this, Yudhishthira wanted Bheeshma to clarify whether this was the only end possible for a jaapaka, or whether some other state was also possible.

Bheeshma replied that if a jaapaka did not properly follow the rites prescribed, or was disrespectful in nature, or who started japa but failed to complete it, then a descent into hell awaited such a jaapaka. Well-begun may be half done, but not fully completing the task was not without consequences.

If a jaapaka performed japa properly, why did he have to take birth again, Yudhishthira wanted to know. This was because either they lacked wisdom or had faults in their aatmas.

For those who were based on dharma, as Yudhishthira was, born as he was from Dharma, there were regions of the gods that were open to such people, and where the gods, Shukra, Brihaspati, Marutas, Vishwadevas, Ashwins, Rudras, and the Adityas and Vasus resided. On the other hand, there were hells where nothing happened, and which were free from both,[4] the three,[5] the four,[6] and the eight.[7]

Bheeshma had begun by referring to a dispute between Yama, Kaala, and a brahmana, but he had not elaborated. Yudhishthira reminded Bheeshma, who now recounted that history.[8]

There was once a dharmic jaapaka brahmana who was Pippalaada's son, descended from Kushika, and who lived on the slopes of the Himalayas. Immersed in austerities and in japa, he was unaware of the passage of time. Pleased with his devotion, the goddess Gaayatri[9] manifested herself before him. The brahmana did not look up or speak to her, immersed as he was still in japa. When his japa was over, he bowed before the goddess. She granted him a boon. He asked for only one thing—that his mind always be immersed in japa.

Goddess Saraswati blessed him that he would not only be spared of all the hells but he would go to heaven. All that he had asked for would come true. However, before leaving, she told him that a time would come when there would be a dispute between him and Ikshvaaku, Surya's son, and where Kaala,[10] Mrityu,[11] and Yama would also be involved. The question would be on dharma. The brahmana bowed. What had to be would be.

Time passed by. The brahmana remained immersed in japa. This time it was Dharma,[12] pleased with the brahmana, who manifested himself and told him that he had obtained what he had wished for, and that it was therefore time for him to give up his body and go to the worlds he desired. The brahmana replied that he had already obtained all those worlds here itself. Yes, the body gave him joy as well as sorrow, but he did not wish to give up his body. Dharma insisted. The brahmana remained steadfast.

Unable to convince the brahmana, Dharma summoned Yama, Kaala, and Mrityu, who all manifested themselves before the brahmana. They took turns to tell, persuade, and convince the brahmana that his austerities, his japa, had borne fruit. It was time for him to go to heaven. The brahmana welcomed all three, offered them water to wash their feet, and an offering meant for guests.

> Know me to be death. I have shown my own form to you. O Brahmana! I have been urged by Time and have come to take you away.[13]

As it happened, Ikshvaaku, Surya's son, also happened to be arrive there, on his way to a teertha. The brahmana welcomed him also.

> You are content in your own dharma and in a similar way, so am I with mine.[14]

'O King, please tell me what it is you desire. If it is within my mean, I shall surely do that,' the brahmana said.

"O Brahmana, you are engaged in the difficult task of austerities. I wish to give you some wealth,' Ikshvaaku bowed before the brahmana.

'I have withdrawn from desires and wants. I do not need anything. What you have and wish to give me, give to others instead. Tell me, what can I give you,' the brahmana replied.

'O Brahmana,' Ikshvaaku straightened up. 'I am a kshatriya. I do not know how to ask. I give. If there is one thing we kshatriyas know to ask for, it is battle.'

'Well, I do not indulge in battles.' the brahmana shrugged, 'You are content in your dharma; I am in mine.'

'Fine, if that is what you insist on,' Ikshvaaku said, 'then give me the fruits of your japa.'

'Well, why are you asking for something now, O Ikshvaaku? If there is something you want from me, even if that is the fruits of my japa, why don't you take them in a fight?'

'Aren't we already fighting, O Brahmana? The difference is that we are using words instead of weapons. Give me the fruits of your japa if you want to.'

'I would give them to you if I knew what those fruits were, O King. I performed my penances without attachment to, or desire for, any fruits. What I have got, I neither asked for, nor do I know what they are. How, then, can I give you those fruits?'

'That is a fine situation, then, isn't it?' Ikshvaaku smiled. 'If you don't even know what you possess, what will I do with that? Keep them; I do not want them.'

'No, O Ikshvaaku, this cannot be,' the brahmana replied.

'Why?'

'I have already given you the fruits of my japa. You had asked for them. Do not commit a falsehood by not taking them now, nor let adharma descend on me by causing my words to come false,' the brahmana reasoned. 'I am being honest when I tell you I don't know what those fruits are,' the brahmana concluded, 'but they must be of some value, else Kaala, Yama, and Mrityu all would not have come here. They are my witnesses to the fact.'

Where there is dharma, truth is there.[15]

Dharma had been watching the discussion, debate, and argument brew between the brahmana and Ikshvaaku. He decided to intercede. He asked the two to stop squabbling, and that each adhere to their respective dharmas—the brahmana of giving, the king of adhering to the truth. Ikshvaaku found that acceptable. He suggested that if the brahmana insisted on giving him the fruits of his japa, then he should take some of what the king gave, and thus reach a middle path.

If there wasn't enough confusion, even as the discussion stewed between the brahmana and Ikshvaaku, two deformed men came to the spot. One was named Vikrita, appropriately enough; the other Viroopa, aptly. Each was telling the other that he didn't owe him anything. They saw Ikshvaaku, recognized him to be a king, and stopped. Since they now had a king present, he could adjudicate their dispute, they decided.

Viroopa explained their squabble. Vikrita had once donated a cow to a brahmana. Viroopa had gone to Vikrita and asked him for the fruits of his good deed. Vikrita agreed. Viroopa then went and bought two milch cows and calves. He then donated these cows to another brahmana who practiced unchhavritti.[16] Having earned some fruits on his own, Viroopa now wanted to give back to Vikrita twice the fruits he had taken from him initially. Vikrita, however, refused. Viroopa asked Ikshvaaku to decide.

Ikshvaaku thought that it was not proper that Vikrita should refuse to accept what Viroopa was giving him. Vikrita replied that the cow was given as a gift. Nothing was expected in return. Once given, he could not take a gift back. Ikshvaau told Vikrita and Viroopa to leave. This row between Vikrita and Viroopa had one unintended effect. Ikshvaaku had an epiphany. He realized that he was the king, and in him vested the responsibility of upholding raja-dharma. He relented and accepted what the brahmana was offering. The brahmana offered the fruits of his japa to Ikshvaaku. The king asked the brahmana to accept the drops of water that had fallen on his hand. The exchange was now equal. The king had now also given.

Seeing this, Viroopa spoke. He said he was Kaama[17] and Vikrita was Krodha[18] personified. Together, the two had provoked the brahmana and Ikshvaaku into this debate. Kaala, Mrityu, and Dharma had also taken part in this examination. What Saraswati had prophesied had come true.

51

CHIRAKAARI

Think First, Think Hard, Think Long, Think Again

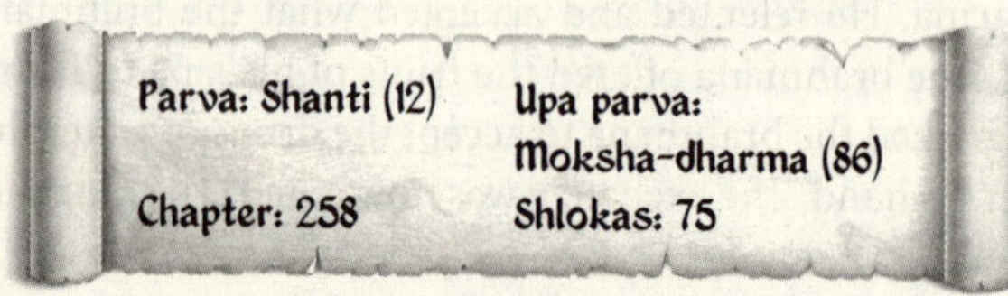

The fifteenth-century saint and poet, Kabir, had penned a famous couplet about the perils of procrastination.

> Not tomorrow, today; not today, now. If the world ends in a trice, then will you do it how?[1]

Injunctions against sloth have been around for millennia. On the other hand, was anything to be gained through dawdling, hesitating, lingering? Prompt action had its undeniable virtues, but was deferring a task necessarily a vice? This was Yudhishthira's question to Bheeshma.

Delays were not dreadful. It all depended. Dharma was subtle. In the lineage of Sage Angiras was a sage named Gautama, Bheeshma began. He had a son named Chirakaari. Chirakaari was a person who liked to weigh the pros and cons of every action, debating the need to act, or not, and only then make up his mind. Any task assigned to him, therefore, took a long, long time. This earned him the sobriquet of being lazy; some even called him a fool.

> A person who acts after a long time is fortunate. A fortunate person is one who acts after a long time. A person who acts after a long time is intelligent and does not commit a sin in his acts.[2]

Once it so happened that his father, Gautama, suspected his wife, Ahalya, of infidelity.[3] The sage flew into a fit of rage and on the spur of the moment, decided that the punishment for adultery was death. He ordered his son to behead her—his wife and Chirakaari's mother. Passing his injunction, he walked off in a huff.

Chirakaari agreed to his father's command, for that was his dharma. But Chirakaari pondered over his father's command, as was his nature. On the one hand, obeying his father was dharma; but on the other hand, protecting his mother was also dharma. Dharma that went against dharma could not be dharma. But what did dharma dictate in such a situation?

How could he, Chirakaari wondered, ever be happy by killing a mother and a woman? Would defying his father's decree bring him joy, on the other hand?

Hadn't he been born from a part of his father? Hadn't his father given him education? Wasn't it but natural for the son to follow and obey his father? Certainly, it was, of that there was no question. But what about the mother, Chirakaari thought.

> The father is heaven. The father is dharma. The father is the supreme of austerities.[4]

Didn't the mother bind the five elements[5] together to create the son? Wasn't she the originator of his life? Didn't the mother bear him in her womb? Wasn't she, therefore Dhaatri?[6] Didn't the mother give birth? Wasn't she, therefore, Janani?[7] Wasn't she also Ambaa,[8] Virasu,[9] and Sushru?[10] To kill one's mother was a senseless act, Chirakaari reasoned.

> Even if a person has many sons and grandsons, even if he is one hundred years old, when he approaches his mother, he behaves like a two-year-old[11].... There is no shelter that is equal to a mother. There is no objective that is equal to a mother. There is no sanctuary equal to a mother. There is no protection equal to a mother.[12]

Chirakaari pondered over the matter more.

> The mother's pleasure comes from nurturing alone. The father's affection is from a desire to have offspring.[13]

A husband, known as a Bharta and a Pati, ceased to be either if he neither sustained nor protected his wife. While the status of the father could not be disputed, Chirakaari was veering towards the conclusion that the status of the mother was higher.

> It is known that the father is alone a collection of all the gods. But because of her affection, the mother is a collection of all mortal beings and the gods.[14]

Chirakaari went on and on, reasoning, rationalizing, ruminating. He meditated, pondered, and debated the matter and his father's injunction. Even as he was cogitating thus, his father returned. Gautama, unlike his son, had issued his instructions in haste, and had had the time to repent. He had had second thoughts. But was it too late? Perhaps not, for Gautama knew who he had given his instructions to—Chirakaari. A glimmer of hope still flickered in Gautama. Knowing his son's nature, there was a chance, a better than even chance, that perhaps his son had not yet acted on his orders. Perhaps this would be that occasion where his son, acting true to his name, would bring joy.

Full of apprehension and anticipation, Gautama entered the hermitage. He saw his son, and he also saw his wife, Ahalya. His son had been debating, and was still debating, whether to carry out his father's instructions or not. Gautama was delighted, for a terrible calamity that would otherwise have befallen him had passed. He praised his son and the virtues of patient men.

> One should take a long time before making a friend.[15]

> One should take a long time before severing a friendship.[16]

Bheeshma concluded that a long enough period deserved to be spent on contemplating a course of action, whether it was plotting revenge or serving the aged and learned. All these were the secret to being respected for a long time.

52

KUNDADHAARA

Getting What You Need; Not What You Want

Parva: Shanti (12) | Upa parva: Moksha-dharma (86)
Chapter: 263 | Shlokas: 55

A balance between the pursuit of dharma, artha, and kaama would lead to moksha. All three were praised by the Vedas, but was there one among the three which provided the most benefit? Yudhishthira asked Bheeshma.

A long time ago, there was once a poor brahman. He didn't have any wealth, but he wanted some so that he could use it to perform sacrifices. He set about worshipping the gods. Severe were his austerities and single-minded was his penance. Neither brought him what he had been praying for—wealth. The brahmana pondered over the matter, thinking of what he could do different. Perhaps, he thought, there was a god that he could worship and who was easier to please. As he sat thinking, he saw Kundadhaara, a follower of the gods, standing near him. Kundadhaara was neither a man nor a god. He was a concentration of energy in the form of a cloud.

Seeing Kundadhaara's gentle and divine form, the brahmana decided that he would pray to him. Kundadhaara was close to the gods, and he was someone men didn't worship, and hence would be easier to please, thus went the brahmana's reasoning. He was likelier to get wealth from Kundadhaara. The brahmana decided thus and set about worshipping him. Kundadhaara, pleased, spoke words of wisdom to the brahmana.

> Desire has a son named adharma. Anger is said to be the son of jealousy. Greed is the son of deceit. But ungratefulness has no offspring.[1]

Kundadhaara's energy pervaded the brahmana that night. In the light of that energy, the brahmana saw the world of gods, and among them, a yaksha named Manibhadra. Also present there was Kundadhaara, who had prostrated himself before the gods. Manibhadra spoke up, asking why Kundadhaara had prostrated himself for.

Kundadhaara replied that he was praying on behalf of the brahmana and requested that he be given whatever the brahmana desired. Manibhadra, on the instructions of the gods, replied that it would be so because the brahmana was a friend of Kundadhaara. The brahmana's thinking was paying off dividends.

Kundadhaara was pleased but was worried too. With wealth would come temptations and the likelihood of straying. He didn't want wealth to corrupt the honest brahmana. Kundadhaara modified his request. In place of wealth, the brahmana instead be blessed so he stayed steadfast to dharma, Kundadhaara asked the gods. If he wanted to earn a living, Kundadhaara wished that the brahmana do that via only dharmic means, and that dharma stay at the top of his mind. The gods listened and they accepted Kundadhaara's entreaties. This is how it would be, Manibhadra replied on behalf of the gods.

After all this had been done, Kundadhaara saw that while there were many expensive items of clothing scattered around the brahmana, he was indifferent to them. The brahmana, however, thought that Kundadhaara had failed to get him riches and therefore resolved to retire to the forest to pursue austerities.

The brahmana had prayed to Kundadhaara, and Kundadhaara had interceded on behalf of the brahmana to get him what would be best for him—steadfastness to dharma. The brahmana resumed his austerities, thoughts of dharma in his mind. The penances brought him divine sight.

The brahmana's penances had endowed him with powers not available to the ordinary. If someone desired wealth and the brahmana blessed the person with wealth, the person would gain wealth. The same went for kings—if the brahmana blessed him with a kingdom, then the king would gain a kingdom. His words would not come false.

As the brahmana sat one day, Kundadhaara appeared before him. The brahmana received him with due honours. Kundadhaara knew what the brahmana had been thinking. He himself had not gained wealth and the riches he had hoped for a long time back, but his penances had given him the power to grant wealth and power to others.

Kundadhaara asked the brahmana to use his newly acquired divine sight to see for himself the ends that kings came to. Intrigued, the brahmana did so. He saw those kings—all in hell. The brahmana was taken aback. Kundadhaara shed light on the situation. He told the brahmana that had he asked for wealth from the gods on behalf of the brahmana, which is what the brahmana had wanted, then the same fate would have awaited him too.

Kundadhaara said that men were bound by desire, anger, greed, fear, intoxication, sleep, laziness, and procrastination. None of these traits were befitting one who was devoted to dharma. Men with these traits would never attain heaven. Only gods' favours could grant one with the wisdom and fortitude to follow dharma.

The brahmana realized that had he obtained what he had once desired—wealth, he would have lost his focus on dharma and descended into the hell of indolence and greed. He sought Kundadhaara's forgiveness.

Bheeshma said that while wealth brought fleeting happiness, the happiness that dharma brought was everlasting.

53

HAYASHEERA

Appropriate Avatars for Asuras

Parva: Shanti (12)	Upa parva: Moksha-dharma (86)
Chapter: 335	Shlokas: 89

Sage Naarada had on Shvetadeepa recited a stotra in Narayana's praise,[1] invoking several of his names. One such name he had used was Hayasheera.[2] In this form, with the head of a horse, Vishnu had killed the asura Hayagreeva. Janamejaya's questions to Sage Vaishampaayana were basic, and obvious—why had Vishnu created this form of his, and since he had created this form, what attributes and qualities did this form possess that were unique and special?

It turned out that this question, or these questions, had been posed many years back by Yudhishthira. He had asked this question of Vyaasa, and now Vaishampaayana would repeat to Janamejaya what Vyaasa had told Yudhishthira.

To understand this avatara of Vishnu, one had to go back to a time when the entire world had been immersed in water. Water had merged into light; light had merged into the wind; wind had merged into space; space had merged into the mind; the mind with the manifest;[3] the manifest into the unmanifest;[4] the unmanifest had merged into Purusha; and Purusha had into the paramaatman.

There was all-pervading darkness. From this darkness arose brahman. Brahman created Purusha, a form also known as Aniruddha or Pradhaan. As he lay on the waters, he became aware of his qualities, and thus consciousness was generated in the form of Brahma, who appeared seated on a thousand-petalled lotus.

Wishing to create the world, Hari placed two drops of water on the petals of the lotus. One of those drops looked like honey, and from this was created Madhu, with tamasic qualities. From the other drop was created Kaitabha, with rajasic qualities. Once created, however, the first thing these two did was to seize the Vedas from Brahma and vanish into the nether regions.[5]

With the Vedas stolen, Brahma was inconsolable. Without the Vedas he was unable to continue in his task of creation. Only Vishnu could help him now. Brahma composed and sang verses in praise of Hari.[6] Hari was roused from his sleep. He assumed the form of Hayasheera. But this was no ordinary being with no ordinary head of a horse. Each part was made of and symbolized something divine.

> The firmament, with its nakshatras and stars, became his head. His long and flowing hair was as radiant as the rays of the sun. The sky and the nether regions constituted his ears. The earth was his forehead. The sacred and great rivers, Ganga and Sarasvati, were his eyebrows. The sun and the moon were his eyes. The evening was said to be his nose. The syllable 'Om' was his mind and the lightning was his tongue.[7]

With this form, Hayasheera entered the nether regions and uttered the syllable, 'Om'. This was perhaps the first time that this primal sound of creation had been heard in rasaatala. This sound pervaded the entire nether regions and the daanavas, Madhu and Kaitabha, mistook them for the Vedas. Perhaps this was a more complete form of the Vedas, they thought. Leaving behind the Vedas that they already had, Madhu and Kaitahba made way for where the sound of 'Om' originated.

Hari, still in the form of Hayasheera, took this opportunity and rushed to where the Vedas were, and retrieving them, he took them back to Brahma. His task complete, Hari assumed his original form and went back to sleep on the infinite serpent.[8]

Meanwhile, Madhu and Kaitabha could find neither any person nor the Vedas. They returned and found that the Vedas that they had snatched from Brahma were also gone. Furious, they raised themselves from rasaatala in search of the one who had purloined their Vedas.

When they emerged from the nether region they looked around. They saw only Hari, asleep on Sesha. If someone had stolen their Vedas, and if there was only one person they could spot, Madhu and Kaitabha concluded that it was Hari who had decamped with the Vedas. They resolved that they would fight and defeat this person. Hari meanwhile awoke from his sleep, saw Madhu and Kaitabha ready to do battle. He too roused himself. A great battle ensued between the three. Eventually, Madhusoodana[9] slew them.

> To accomplish different kinds of tasks, the god assumes different kinds of forms. Using his atman, the god creates himself and performs those different tasks.[10]

Different tasks required Narayana to assume different forms, Vyaasa elaborated. Such was Narayana's greatness. Vyaasa then described the qualities of Narayana to Yudhishthira.[11]

> The supreme Narayana is the deities of Kirti, Shri and Lakshmi.[12]

54

UNCHAVRITTI

The Wealth the Serpent Revealed

Parva: Shanti (12) | Upa parva: Moksha-dharma (86)

Chapters: 340-353 | Shlokas: 175

There was raj-dharma, the dharma to be followed by a king in normal times; there was apad-dharma, the dharma to be followed by a king in times of adversity; there was moksha-dharma, which would lead to moksha—the liberation of the soul from the cycle of birth and rebirth; there was daana-dharma, the dharma of giving. Then there was a dharma according to the stage of life one was in, from brahmacharya to sanyaasa. Which dharma was the best—this is what Yudhishthira wanted to know from Bheeshma.

> There are many doors to dharma and no rites in the world are fruitless.[1]

Bheeshma recalled an account between Sage Naarada and Indra. Naarada, the celestial sage who travelled around the worlds, once went to Indra's court. After greeting Naarada with the customary honours, Indra asked Naarada if he had seen anything interesting or noteworthy from his travels around the worlds.

Yes, Naarada said, he had. By the banks of the river Ganga was a city called Mahaapadme. In that city lived a noble brahmana named Dharmaaranya. The brahmana lived a virtuous life, adhered to the truth, and was, expectedly, respected by others.

Dharmaaranya often had thoughts on what kind of tasks he could perform that would be most in consonance with dharma.

Much as he pondered, he could never arrive at a definitive answer. One day, as he pondered over the three kinds of dharma,[2] a brahmana visitor came knocking.

Dharmaaranya welcomed his guest and the two started talking. He was impressed by his visitor's knowledge and erudition. He, therefore, thought it best to pose his quandary to his guest; the same question that had been nagging him for some time. He had, the brahmana began, spent a part of his life to obtain a son, and having now handed over the duties of gaarhasthya aashram to his son, his mind was now focused on what would help him navigate the next world.

The guest confessed that he too was confused about which path to choose since different people chose different dharmas. Some chose vaanaprastha, some followed moksha-dharma, some gaarhasthya, some raja-dharma, some attained heaven by telling the truth, some by getting martyred on the battlefield, while some praised unchhavritti[3]—the practice of subsisting on grains that have been left over in a field after harvesting. In other words, the paths to attaining heaven were many. No one path could be called an exclusive path to liberation.

> There are many doors to heaven.[4]

During their conversation, the guest told Dharmaaranya about a city of serpents. Located by the banks of the Gomati River, in the Naimisha forest, in that city of serpents there lived a naaga named Padmanaabha. Like the city's king, Padmanaabha was also just and knowledgeable. He was sure to know more about dharma and could answer Dharamaaranya's queries, suggested the brahmana. That goaded the brahmana into deciding to journey to the city. Once night had passed and the guest had taken his leave, he set out for this city by the Gomati river. He would get his answers there.

After a long journey, Dharmaaranya reached his destination. He entered the city of serpents and went around asking for directions to Padmanaabha's house. Eventually he found his way to his house and knocked on the door. Padmanaabha's wife opened the door and welcomed the guest. When she asked Dharmaaranya why he had come, he replied that he wanted to meet the wise serpent. Padmanaabha's wife informed him that he was away. He would be back only after fifteen days, for he had gone to bear Surya's chariot. If that was the case, Dharmaaranya decided he would wait. He told Padmanaabha's wife that he would reside by the banks of the Gomati river. He requested her to inform him as soon as the serpent was back.

By the riverbank, Dharmaaranya sat under a tree and meditated. He would wait till Padmanaabha returned. He also decided to fast till Padmanaabha returned. This caused no little distress to the resident serpents of the city. Dharamaaranya was a guest in their city. Dharma required that they extend all hospitality to him. And yet, here was Dharamaaranya sitting under a tree without taking any food.

Padmanaabha's family, his wife, his brother, and others went to Dharmaaranya and requested him to partake some food. Neither was it proper that he reside without any food, nor were they people who had committed any act that would render them unfit to offer food to the brahmana.

The brahmana was honoured and told them their very act of offering him food was as good as him having eaten. However, six days had already passed, and once eight more nights passed, Padmanaabha would return. He could go for a few more days without food; he would wait. The residents returned.

The fortnight over, Padmanaabha took Surya's permission and returned to his town and to his house and wife. She informed him about Dharmaaranya the brahmana, who had come to the town to meet him and who now waited by the banks of the Gomati river.

> If a king or a prince does not wipe away the tears of someone who has come with hope, he commits the sin of having killed a foetus.[5]

The brahmana was not a god, nor was he someone after his wealth. This was also something Padmanaabha was wary about, for it was well known that serpents were wealthy. Had the brahmana come with the ulterior motive of stealing his wealth? No, Padmanaabha's wife allayed those fears that her husband had. Dharmaaranya was not such a person. However, she did harbour some misgivings. Not about the brahmana, but about her husband and what may happen when he met the brahmana.

Why? It was known that serpents were prone to anger. It was equally well known that while kshatriyas used their sword to kill, brahmanas used their words to curse if angered. No, Padmanaabha assured his wife; he would go without delay to meet the brahmana, but also that he would go without any of the anger that was the nature of serpents. Yes, it was the nature of his species to be wrathful, but that anger had been burned by his wife's wise words, he assured her. The brahmana had come to meet him with some objective; he would ensure that the brahmana did not depart unsuccessful. Great fruits accrued to those who gave; those who gave never went to hell. Padmanaabha had no intentions of going to hell, or doing anything that would take him there. He set out for the banks of the Gomati.

> I am indeed praiseworthy, since I have someone like you as my wife.[6]

Padmanaabha reached the riverbank. He found Dharmaaranya seated under a tree by the river. He approached the brahmana and asked him his reason for coming to the town. Dharmaaranya replied that he had come to meet the serpent named Padmanaabha. Padmanaabha replied that he was indeed who the brahmana was looking for.

Yes, Dharmaaranya did have a question for Padmanaabha. He had had that since he had set out for the city of serpents. But when Padmanaabha's wife told him that he had gone to draw Surya's chariot, another, more immediate question arose in Dharmaaranya's mind. What were all the fascinating things that Padmanaabha had witnessed when he had gone to Surya?

Of course, there had been many sights and experiences that exceeded the most wondrous things one could imagine, Padmanaabha told Dharmaaranya. There was the marvellous sight of the solar wind that emerged from the sun's rays. Equally fascinating was to witness the sun drink water through its rays from the oceans for eight months and then rain for four. But the most wondrous sight he had witnessed was even more astounding than all of this.

Once it so happened that when the sun was at its peak at midday, another entity, equally radiant and resplendent, was seen approaching the sun. The sun seemingly stretched out its hand, as did the entity, and both merged into themselves.

There could not be two suns, and yet the other entity had been as brilliant as the sun. Who, what was it? Intrigued, the serpent had asked the sun. Surya had replied that this was a sage who had lived his entire life following the conduct of unchavritti and had now attained heaven. Dharmaaranya smiled. The serpent had answered both his questions. He didn't need to ask any other. He got up to take leave and depart for his village.

Padmanaabha asked him what task he had come to fulfil, and to leave only after completing that task. The brahmana replied that he had now learned the way to obtain merit and had resolved to follow unchavritti.

Though Dharmaaranya wished to leave, Padmanaabha would have none of it. After all, he had come to the city to meet him with a specific purpose in mind. He had to give the serpent a chance to fulfil it. He was Padmanaabha's guest, after all.

No, Padmanaabha had answered his unasked question and cleared his doubts, Dharmaaranya thanked the serpent. The path he had been searching for, pondering over, and to seek an answer from the serpent had been laid clear. He took leave and set out for Sage Chyavana's hermitage and performed penances there.

This account, Bheeshma said, had been recounted by Sage Bhaargava to King Janaka, who had told this to Naarada, who then recounted this to Indra. Indra had then repeated this story to the Vasus, and the Vasus had told this to Bheeshma when he had fought Parashuraama. Bheeshma was, after all, the eldest of the Vasus who still lived on earth, for the curse that the other Vasus had been freed from still lived in Bheeshma. He had lived a long life, and that had been his curse. As the last days of his life counted down to Uttarayaana, Bheeshma completed recounting this story to Yudhishthira. This story about the merits of unchavritti now travelled from Bheeshma to Yudhishthira.

With this upakhyaana ends the Moksha-dharma upa parva and also the major parva, Shaanti.

55

SUDARSHANA

Refuge in Dharma

Parva: Anushaasana (13) Upa parva: Daana-dharma (87)

Chapter: 2 Shlokas: 95

The dharma prescribed for different ashramas differed. Was there any person who had escaped death by following the dharma of gaarhasthya ashrama, asked Yudhishthira of Bheeshma, the lifelong celibate who now possessed knowledge of all there was because of Krishna's blessings.

Yes, there had been one such instance, Bheeshma replied. A long time ago, Bheeshma began, King Ikshvaaku reigned. He had a hundred sons. The tenth son was named Dashaashva. This tenth son of Ikshvaaku became the king of Mahishmati. Dashaashva's descendants, in order, were Madiraashva, Dyutimat, Suveera, Durjaya, and Duryodhana.[1] This Duryodhana, unlike his later namesake, was a dharmic king and had, through the river goddess Narmada, a daughter named Sudarshanaa.

When Princess Sudarshanaa grew up, Agni wished to marry her. Taking the form of a brahmana, he went to Duryodhana's court and asked the king for his daughter's hand in marriage. Duryodhana was now in a quandary. He was unwilling to accede to the brahmana's request. The brahmana and the king were of different varnas. The brahmana was poor. The king didn't want to refuse the brahmana, either. He was in a fix.

Agni, still in the guise of a brahmana, saw the king's reluctance. He exited the sacrificial fire that burned in the king's palace. The fire was extinguished. The king was anguished. What sins had he committed, he lamented, for him to suffer a fate reserved for the wicked. He instructed his brahmanas to get to the root of this calamity.

Since Agni had extinguished itself from the king's sacrificial fire; to Agni therefore the brahmanas in the kingdom prayed. Agni assumed his true form[2] and manifested himself before the brahmanas. He told them that he had sought Sudarshanaa's hand in marriage. But the king had been reluctant. The brahmanas rushed to the king and reported this matter to Duryodhana.

Alright, the king acquiesced. He would marry his daughter to Agni. But he had a condition. Agni would have to pay a bride-price. Having lost Agni from his sacrificial fires once, Duryodhana didn't want to suffer the adharma of its recurrence. He asked that Agni always reside in his kingdom. Agni agreed. The marriage was solemnized, and Agni married Sudarshanaa. In due course, they had a son named Sudarshana.

But what had all this to do with gaarhasthya aashrama and death? Bheeshma was leading to that. In another kingdom there was a king named Oghavat. He gave his daughter, Oghavati, in marriage to Sudarshana. The couple resided in Kurukshetra. Here, Sudarshana took a vow that he would conquer death in his gaarhasthya ashrama itself. To achieve that end, he told his wife, Oghavati, to always honour and serve guests. Oghavati agreed.

Mrityu[3] heard about this vow, resolve, of Sudarshana and decided to test both husband and wife. He followed Sudarshana, waiting for an opportunity and weakness. If he faltered, Mrityu would be there, ready to strike Sudarshana down.

One day, when Sudarshana had gone to the forest in search of firewood, a brahmana came knocking on Oghavati's house. She welcomed the brahmana and asked him his reason for coming there. This was no ordinary brahmana.

Yes, he would now find out how steadfast the wife was to the husband's advice. The brahmana came straight to the point and said he had come there for her, and she, and nothing else, would have to give herself to him to prove that she truly followed gaarhasthya ashram and her husband's counsel of satisfying guests. Oghavati tried to dissuade the brahmana, to no avail, and finally, after thinking over her husband's words, agreed.

Meanwhile, Sudarshana returned after collecting firewood, but found no answer when he called out Oghavati's name. Mrityu, still by Sudarshana's side, watched. Oghavati did not answer, but the brahmana did. He told Sudarshana[4] why Oghavati was not in a position to answer, or perhaps she was too mortified to. He asked Sudarshana to respond. Mrityu raised his club of death, ready to strike Sudarshana if he was found deviating from the vow of gaarhasthya ashrama. If he had been lying, if he now deviated from the oath he had taken of following the dharma of a householder, Mrityu would strike.

Sudarshana, instead, responded that his wife was only following the dharma of gaarhasthya and was faithful to the vow he had taken. The ten gunas[5] were witness to his words and the gods were free to act as they pleased.

At this, the brahmana emerged from the hut, and rising into the sky, took on a form that pervaded the skies and earth. He said he was Dharma and he had come to test Sudarshana. Had he failed, Mrityu would have struck him down. Instead, it was Sudarshana who had ended up conquering Mrityu. As for his wife, Oghavati, she was untouched, her chastity protected by her husband's and her own qualities.

Such was the purity inherent in Oghavati that she would become a river that would purify people. Since Sudarshana and Oghavati lived in Kurukshetra, the riverine half of Oghavati would flow through Kurukshetra. The other half of her would stay as her own body. Both Sudarshana and the human half of Oghavati would ascend to heaven, having scrupulously followed gaarhasthya aashrama, having conquered Mrityu.

Yes, thus had Sudarshana and his wife Oghavati, following gaarhasthya aashrama, conquered death, Bheeshma concluded.

56

VISHWAAMITRA

Consequences Unintended

Parva: Anushaasana (13) Upa parva: Daana-dharma (87)

Chapters: 3-4 Shlokas: 80

The Bharata lineage had begun in Sage Kanva's hermitage when his adopted daughter, Shakuntala, had married King Dushyanta. Shakuntala had been Sage Vishwaamitra's daughter, and it was unsurprising that mentions of the sage were frequent in the Mahabharata. Janamejaya had already learned how Indra's insecurities had given rise to the Bharata lineage.[1] He had learned of the conflict with Sage Vasishtha that had driven King Kaushika to become Vishwaamitra the brahmarshi.[2] Arjuna had learned more about the ghastly consequences of the feud between the two sages from the gandharva, Chitraratha.[3]

The Parashuraama upakhyaana had also shed light on how a mix-up had caused Vishwaamitra to be born as a kshatriya but with the attributes of a brahmana. This was something that Janamejaya wanted to learn more about. Vishwaamitra had been a kshatriya, and yet ended up becoming a brahmana. This was notable for at least three reasons. It was not an easy matter becoming a brahmana; yet Vishwaamitra had done so. Often enough, when this did happen, it took several births; yet Vishwaamitra had become one in the same life. Not just a rajarshi or a maharshi, Vishwaamitra had become a brahmarshi. How had that happened, Yudhishthira asked Bheeshma.

In the lineage of Bharata there was once a king named Ajameedha. Ajameedha's descendants were Jahnu, Sindhudveepa, Balaakaashva, Vallabha, Kushika, and Gaadhi. To Gaadhi was born a daughter named Satyavati.[4]

Meanwhile Sage Chayvana had a son named Richika, and he sought to marry his son to Satyavati. Just as Duryodhana had initially balked at marrying his daughter, Sudarshanaa, to Agni who had approached the king for her hand in marriage in the guise of a poor brahmana, Gaadhi also refused.[5]

However, Gaadhi provided a compromise. If the poor Richika were to somehow obtain one thousand swift horses that were white but with one black ear, he would marry his daughter to Richika. Not one, but two difficult tasks. Richika decided that as a brahmana he could ask the gods to help him; and off Richika went to Varuna, the god of the waters, to ask for alms. The alms he wanted were the kinds of horses that Gaadhi had specified. Varuna agreed without hesitation. As soon as Richika thought of the horses, one thousand white horses arose from the waters of the Ganga.[6]

Richika went with the horses to present them before the king. When Gaadhi saw Richika return with the horses, he was amazed. A promise was a promise. Furthermore, Gaadhi was also apprehensive of what may happen if he went back on his word to Richika. If there was one calamity that turned the bravest of kings pale, it was a sage's curse. Gaadhi married Satyavati to Richika. Satyavati didn't share any of her father's hesitations. She couldn't be happier at having obtained a pious husband.

Richika and Satyavati, now married, lived in bliss. One day, Richika wished to grant his wife a boon. Satyavati went to her mother for advice. A son would be the best boon to have, Satyavati's mother told her daughter. But she also told Satyavati to ask Richika to bestow a son on her too! Satyavati dutifully conveyed both wishes to her husband. Richika granted both the mother's and daughter's wishes. Events would not unfold in a straightforward manner, however.

Richika told Satyavati to embrace a fig tree and her mother to embrace an ashwattha tree. He then gave two bowls of a pudding. Richika pointed out one bowl to Satyavati—she was to take that one; her mother the other one.

When Satyavati took these bowls to her mother, she asked her daughter to exchange them—her mother would take the bowl intended for Satyavati. She also asked Satyavati to embrace the ashwattha tree instead. The daughter agreed, for she saw no harm. After all, both would still get sons.

When Richika came to know of this, he was saddened. He told Satyavati that he had endowed her pudding bowl with the energy of the brahman and the bowl intended for her mother with the energy of a kshatriya. After all, she was now the wife of a sage, whereas her mother was a queen to King Gaadhi. The implications were clear—Satyavati would have a son with the nature of a kshatriya, while her mother's son would have the attributes of a brahmana.

Satyavati was appalled. No, this was not what she wanted her son to be like. She wanted a son with the qualities of a brahmana. She beseeched her husband to undo the damage done. No, what had been done would have to now run its course, Richika replied. If it could not be undone, then couldn't it be delayed by a generation, implored Satyavati? Could it be her grandson who became a kshatriya, asked Satyavati? Richika agreed.

Satyavati's son thus born was Jamadagni, whose son would be the fearsome Parashuraama. Gaadhi's wife gave birth to Vishwaamitra, born a kshatriya to a king but endowed with the qualities of a brahmana. Vishwaamitra would remain a king till that fateful day when he would meet Sage Vasishtha. Humbled by the might of a brahmana against the armies of the king, Vishwaamitra would embark on a lifelong quest to acquire the austerities of a brahmana.

Thus, in the same life, Vishwaamitra would transition from a king to a brahmana, attaining the status of a brahmarshi. In the same life, Parashuraama would transform from a brahmana into a fierce warrior.

57

BHANGAASHWANA

A Question of Pleasure

Parva: Anushaasana (13) Upa parva: Daana-dharma (87)

Chapter: 12 Shlokas: 49

What should one's conduct be in each stage of life; what kinds of donations bring the most benefit; what kinds of people should one associate with—Yudhishthira had asked Bheeshma questions on the duties of a king, of the dharma to be followed in times of crises, of the dharma of donations, and much more. Each new day would dawn with a fresh set of questions from the Paandava, and each day Bheeshma, the lifelong celibate, lying on a bed of arrows, would counsel Yudhishthira.

Was Bheeshma expecting this next question that Yudhishthira posed? One can only speculate, and most would answer in the negative. The question: 'In a union between a man and woman, who feels the greater pleasure?'

Bheeshma, the lifelong celibate, pondered the question. His thoughts went back to Ambaa, the eldest princess of Kashi. He recalled the terrible battle he had fought with Parashuraama over Ambaa. He remembered his stepmother, Satyavati, for whose sake he had taken a lifelong vow of celibacy so that her father would consent to her marriage with Shaantanu.

Did a wry smile escape the aged patriarch's lips? The question had been asked, and Bheeshma had an answer. His was not an equivocal reply, either. Bheeshma had an unambiguous opinion on the matter; and he used an incident involving Indra and King Bhangaashwana to elucidate.

Bhangaashwana was a great king with just one problem—he and Indra didn't get along, and Indra harboured a deep animosity towards the king. Enmity with the king of the gods was always fraught with danger, and this situation was no different. Indra was not one to let bygones be bygones. He wanted to exact retribution. Bhangaashwana, meanwhile, wanted to extend his lineage by having a son. To that end, he performed a sacrifice known as Agnishtu, and a hundred sons were born to his wives. This sacrifice angered Indra even more, for reasons that Indra would reveal much later. Indra was very good at stalking his foe, lurking, waiting for a moment of weakness when he could strike. After all, this is what he had done in the case of Gautama and Ahalya, and what he had attempted to do in the case of Devasharma and Ruchi.[1]

In search of an opportunity to wreak vengeance on Bhangaashwana, Indra started following the king.

One day, Bhangaashwana went out on a hunt, a favourite pastime of kings. Events had a way of happening when kings went out on hunts—whether it was Dushyanta, or his descendant Pareekshit, or, in this case, Bhangaashwana. Dushyanta had come deep in the forest, found his way to Sage Kanva's hermitage, and met Shakuntala. Pareekshit had found his way to Sage Shamika's hermitage, and ended up getting cursed by Shringi, the sage's son. In this case, Indra sowed confusion in Bhangaashwana's mind, and consequently the king lost his way. Wandering, trying to find his way back, getting lost deeper and deeper in the forest, hungry, thirsty, exhausted, Bhangaashwana stumbled around, till he chanced upon a lake.

Bhangaashwana got off his horse and entered the lake to bathe and refresh himself. Unlike the Paandavas during their exile, there was no invisible yaksha[2] waiting to question the king here, but a very unexpected turn of events nonetheless awaited the king. His thirst quenched, his body refreshed after a bath in the lake's waters, the king emerged—as a woman. Bhangaashwana was appalled, astonished, nonplussed. He could not figure out why this had happened. How could he, a man, have turned into a woman? It was unheard of. He had to return to the kingdom, which he couldn't in this altered state. He felt ashamed.

After much deliberation, Bhangaashwana decided he would return to his capital. Man or woman, it was irrelevant. He, now a she, got back on his horse and rode back to the capital, a woman now. He told his family what had happened, and blamed himself for what had happened, for he was sure there must have been some diktat of destiny or some discontent on his part that had led to this pass. He handed over the reins of his kingdom to his sons and left for the forest.

Bhangaashwana, now a woman, went to an ascetic's hermitage in the forest and resided there. Over a period of time, she gave birth to a hundred sons, fathered by the ascetic there. She took her hundred sons to the kingdom and introduced them over to her earlier hundred sons, counselled them to live together as brothers and in peace. The two-hundred sons all agreed. Content, she then left for the forest. The hundred sons from Bhangaashwana the man and hundred sons from Bhangaashwana the woman lived together in peace and harmony. Indra had been watching all this unfold.

Indra's revenge was only just beginning. This harmony among the sons of his enemy didn't sit well with the king of the gods.

Sage Kashyapa had several sons—the adityas, the daanavas, the daityas, all were his sons from different wives. The adityas from Aditi, daanavas from Daanu, and daityas from Diti. None of them lived in harmony. They were forever locked in acrimony. If the sons of a sage like Kashyapa could not co-exist peacefully, how could the sons of a mere king like Bhangaashwana do so?

Indra took it upon himself to sow discord among Bhangaashwana's sons. He took the form of a brahmana and went to Bhangaashwana's kingdom. There he began his task of sowing dissension and discord among Bhangaashwana's two hundred sons. Sons from different mothers were not supposed to live in harmony; they never had, they never could, Indra reminded the two hundred. One would have to conquer the other, lest they perish to the other.

Indra, disguised as a brahmana, gathered together the hundred sons of Bhangaashwana the king and sat talking. How could they, the hundred princes, even think of sharing this grand kingdom with them—the hundred sons of the destitute ascetic? Surely, they had more self-respect than that, Indra goaded them. Indra's words had the desired effect. Clamour replaced calm, friction replaced filial love, and the sons fought among themselves. They fought till they had killed each other—to the last one of the two hundred sons. Indra sat back, pleased. But there was one last task still left to perform.

Yes, the hundred sons of Bhangaashwana the king and the hundred sons of Bhangaashwana the woman were dead. His revenge wreaked; Indra now wanted to tell Bhangaashwana why all this had happened. Only then would Bhangaashwana realize the folly of crossing the king of the gods. Indra marched to the forest, disguised as a brahmana. There he found a disconsolate Bhangaashwana, weeping for the deaths of her sons. She told Indra, who was still disguised as a brahmana, what had transpired since his journey to the forest, his transformation into a woman, and the deaths of her sons. She unburdened her woes.

A beaten, broken, and bereaved Bhangaashwana wept, the tears flowing freely, the grief would not lessen, however. Indra's revenge was complete. He transformed into his true form as the king of the gods and told Bhangaashwana that this misfortune was of her own doing. When he had been a king, he had performed the Agnishtu sacrifice, but he had not invoked the king of the gods. The offerings were for the gods, and he, as the king of the gods, had not been given his due. For this reason alone, Indra had unleashed his retribution on Bhangaashwana. Yes, what had happened had been an oversight. A penitent Bhangaashwana prostrated herself before Indra, asking for his forgiveness.

Indra forgave Bhangaashwana. He then asked her to choose which of her two hundred sons be brought back to life—those hundred when he had been a man or those hundred after he had turned into a woman. She asked that her hundred sons, born to her as a woman, be brought back to life.

Indra was taken aback. Why did she not want the sons fathered by Bhangaashwana the king to be brought back to life? Bhangaashwana replied that she had chosen her sons to be brought back to life because the affections of a woman, the mother, were greater than that of a man, the father.

> Rishis who have seen the truth about dharma have said that mildness, gentleness and timidity are the qualities of women. The attributes of men are exertion, harshness and valour.[3]

Pleased with the answer, Indra brought back to life not just a hundred, but all two hundred of her sons. He gave her a second boon where she could choose to retain her present form of a woman or return to her original state of a man. Bhangaashwana surprised Indra a second time—she chose to remain a woman, for that was the form she now preferred. Why? She answered Indra that during the act of a union, she had, as a woman, more pleasure from the act than a man, and hence she wished to remain a woman.

> O Supreme among Gods! Truthfully, there is greater pleasure in being a woman.[4]

Thus, Bheeshma, the lifelong celibate, lying on a bed of arrows that were the doing of Ambaa reborn as Shikhandi, concluded his answer—it was a woman who derived the greater pleasure from a union between a man and a woman.

58

UPAMANYU

A Thousand Names and a Boon

Parva: Anushaasana (13) **Upa parva: Daana-dharma (87)**

Chapters: 14-18 **Shlokas: 455**

The days were counting down to Uttarayaana. Bheeshma was keeping count. Not much time was left. When the sun started its northward journey, Bheeshma would also return to where he had come from, bidding farewell to the earth. But Yudhishthira was still not done with his questions. Every day he would ask questions; every day Bheeshma would answer. Yudhishthira had asked Bheeshma about the different names of Shiva. For this answer, Bheeshma directed him to Krishna, saying that only Vishnu could do justice to the thousand names of Shiva. Sage Tandi had recited the thousand names of Shiva in front of Brahma and which were heard by Vyasa and other sages. Krishna would now recite those names.

Later, the Vishnu-sahasranaam stotra—the thousand names of Vishnu—would also be recited in the Anushaasan Parva.[1]

One day, Krishna's wife, Jaambavati,[2] approached Krishna and asked for a son. She said that Rukmini had eight sons through Krishna—Charudeshna, Sucharu, Charuvesha, Yasodhara, Charushrava, Charuyasha, Pradyumna, and Shambhu. She too wished to become mother to Krishna's son.

Krishna agreed to Jaambavati's prayer and took her leave. He went to meet Vasudeva (his father), his mother, King Ugrasena, and Ahuka,[3] and then his elder brother, Balaraama. The blessings of the wise would yield a blessed son. Krishna had Garuda take him to the Himalayas where he saw Upamanyu's[4] hermitage. The place was a verdant heaven, with multitudes of trees, flowers, animals, and the waters of the Ganga flowing by. There, in the middle of the circle of hermitages, Krishna saw Upamanyu seated, surrounded by many other sages.

Krishna bowed before Upamanyu, who told him that he would have a son just like himself. Upamanyu said that Shiva was also there, along with his wife. Shiva, Upamanyu said, had given several boons earlier to those who had prayed to him for a son. The asura Hiranyakashyipu had obtained a son named Mandaara through Shiva's boon; the Valkhilyas were given a boon by Shiva that their austerities would result in the birth of Garuda, who would grow to challenge Indra; Anusuya left Atri and by praying to Shiva obtained a son named Dattatreya; another asura Vidyutprabha had a million sons through Shiva's boon. There was no doubt in Upamnayu's mind that he would bless Krishna too with a son.

Upamanyu told Krishna that he was Vyaaghrapaada's son and Sage Dhaumya was his younger brother. Once, when they were children, Upamanyu and Dhaumya had gone to a hermitage where they saw a cow being milked. Used to eating cakes boiled in water, the milk tasted like nectar to them. Coming back home, Upamanyu asked for milk. His mother told him that sages who lived in the forest subsisted on fruits and roots and didn't have milk. Only through Shiva's grace could they have milk.

Upmanyu started austerities to worship Shiva from that day onwards. Shiva, pleased with Upamanyu's devotion, took on Indra's form and manifested himself before him. Upamanyu told him he wanted no boon from him or any other god other than Shiva. If Shiva so instructed, Upamanyu said, he was ready to become an inanimate object, an insect, a tree, anything. But if granted by Indra, he didn't want even the three worlds. As Upamanyu said these words, Airaavata, Indra's celestial elephant, transformed itself into a bull with Shiva[5] seated on it along with Uma. This was no ordinary vision of Shiva that Upamanyu witnessed.

Shiva had manifested with eighteen arms, was dressed in white, with a white sacred thread, a crescent moon as his diadem, three eyes, a golden garland strung with lotuses, his Pinaaka bow in an embodied form of a snake, and his trident. Seated to the left of Shiva, on an airborne chariot, was Brahma; also on the left side was Vishnu, seated atop Garuda and with his chakra, conch, and shell; next to Parvati was Skanda atop his peacock. Sage Bhrigu,

Indra, and others were also present there. Upamanyu watched, speechless, taking in the divine sight.

Finally, Shiva spoke to Upamanyu and praised his devotion, telling him that by appearing first as Indra, he had wished to test his devotion. When Shiva offered a boon to Upamanyu, he wished for unending devotion towards Shiva, for intelligence to know the past, present, and future; and for a supply of food cooked with milk. Shiva granted these boons. He also said that Upamanyu would be without death and old age.

Worshipping Shiva was the path, Upamanyu said. He initiated Krishna into the worship of Shiva, giving him the mantra that would help him see Shiva. Krishna shaved his head and received the staff and dressed himself in appropriate clothes. After a long period of devotion, Krishna finally saw Shiva in his divine form, and sang verses in praise of Shiva.[6]

Shiva told Krishna to ask for eight boons. Krishna asked, and Shiva blessed it to be so.

> Firmness in dharma, the ability to destroy enemies in battle, fame, ferocity, supreme strength, devotion to yoga, your proximity and hundreds and hundreds of sons—these are the boons I seek.[7]

Now Uma, Shiva's consort, also asked Krishna to ask for eight boons. Krishna did so.

> Lack of anger towards brahmanas, the favours of my father, hundreds of sons, supreme objects of pleasure, affection towards my family, the favours of my mother, the attainment of tranquility and skill—these are the boons I seek.[8]

After Shiva and Uma left, Krishna recounted this to Upamanyu. He, in turn, told Krishna about Sage Tandi[9] who had worshipped Shiva and finally received the blessings to be with divine energy, famous, and without misery.

Brahma had first recited these thousand names of Shiva. Indra received them from Brahma and recounted them to Mrityu, who recounted them to the Rudras, and the Rudras passed them to Tandi. Tandi received these names and brought them from heaven to earth. He recounted them to Shukra, who recounted them to Gautama, who passed them to Vaivasvata Manu, who instructed Narayana and the Sadhyas; from them it was recounted to Yama; then to Naachiketa, then to Maarkandeya, and finally to Upamanyu, who then repeated them to Krishna.[10]

A host of sages spoke then, each describing how praises of Shiva had resulted in boons being bestowed on them. These included Vyaasa; Chaturshira, who performed austerities in Gokarna and was blessed with a hundred sons; Valmiki,[11] who was cleansed of the sin of having killed a brahmana; Parashuraama; Asita-Devala, whose dharma was restored by Shiva after having been cursed by Indra; Gritsamada, who was cursed by Vasishtha for pronouncing verses incorrectly and who was saved by Shiva; Jaigishavya, who was bestowed with the eight powers of yoga by Shiva; Gargya, who was given the knowledge of astronomy by Shiva; Paraashara,[12] who said that it was because of Shiva's boon that Vyaasa was born and blessed to be immortal; Maandavya,[13] who was freed from pain after being impaled; and Gaalava, whose father was brought back to life by Shiva.

Such was the power of worshipping and praising Shiva, Vyaasa concluded.

59

MATANGA

Becoming a Brahmana, Again

Parva: Anushaasana (13) | **Upa parva:** Daana-dharma (87)
Chapters: 28-30 | **Shlokas:** 60

One could be born a brahmana, and if one performed the duties of a brahmana, then one stayed a brahmana. The hunter of Mithila[1] had told the brahmana as much, and this is also what Yudhishthira had replied to Nahusha, his ancestor.[2] Conduct defined who a brahmana was. Nevertheless, Yudhishthira wanted to hear from Bheeshma how one could become a brahmana.

Bheeshma answered by recounting an old discussion between Sage Matanga and a she-ass. Matanga was born to a brahmana. Once his father sent him on an errand to collect some material for a sacrifice. Matanga departed on a wagon driven by an ass. The young donkey drove the wagon straight to his mother instead. Angered, Matanga hit the donkey on his nose. Seeing the wounds on her son, the mother said that these could not be the acts of a brahmana, but of that a chandaala. These were strong words, indeed. Matanga was cut to the quick. But they also rang true.

Mataga got down and approached the donkey's mother and asked her what she knew about his birth. The donkey's mother replied that Matanga had been born as an illegitimate union between a lustful brahmana woman and a barber. Shattered, Matanga returned home. When his father asked him why he had not got the material for the sacrifice, Matanga replied that when his entire existence had been thrown into turmoil, he could scarcely think about anything else. Saying thus, he left for the forest.

Matanga sat in the forest, meditating. His penances were rewarded. Indra manifested himself. He granted Matanga a boon. Matanga wanted the status of a brahmana. However, Indra replied that this status was not attainable for someone whose soul was not cleansed and it was beyond the reach of a chandala like Matanga.

Undeterred, Matanga continued his austerities for a long time. Yet again, Indra appeared before him and gave him the same message. Indra also told him that it would be after thousands and thousands of births that he would progress to becoming a brahmana.

Disappointed, Matanga left and went to Gaya, where he continued his penances, reducing himself to mere bones. As he fell due to weakness, Indra caught and held him up. Indra again gave the same message to Matanga.

If the status of a brahmana is so difficult to obtain, why do men who have obtained it deviate?[3]

Matanga said he was not addicted to desire, he was non-violent; why didn't he deserve to become a brahmana, he asked Indra. Indra finally relented and granted Matanga the status of a brahmana.

Yavakreeta, on the other hand, had wanted knowledge of the Vedas without expending the effort needed. Matanga had performed severe penances for a long duration. Both had wanted a boon from Indra, but both had gone about it in different ways. The results were also different.

60

VEETAHAVYA

The Path to a Brahmana

Parva: Anushaasana (13)	Upa parva: Daana-dharma (87)
Chapter: 31	Shlokas: 64

The path to becoming a brahmana was neither an easy nor a straightforward one. Bheeshma had told Yudhishthira how Matanga had acquired the status of a brahmana. There was also one king who had become a brahmana. No, this was not Vishwaamitra, but a rajarshi named Veetahavya.[1]

In Manu's lineage, Bheeshma began, two kings were born to King Vatsa—Haihaya and Taalajangha. Haihaya was also known as Veetahavya. He had a hundred brave sons. They fought a battle with Haryashva, the king of Kashi, in which the king died. Triumphant, the hundred sons returned to their kingdom. In Kashi, Haryashva's son, Sudeva, ascended the throne after his father's death. Hardly had Sudeva become king than Haihaya's sons again laid siege to Kashi. Despite Sudeva's best efforts, Haihaya's sons were again triumphant. Divodaasa, Sudeva's son, now became king of Kashi.

Divodaasa decided that matters could not continue as before. If the Haihayas attacked again, and it was certain they would, the town had to be fortified better than it had been. He ordered the town's ramparts and fortifications to be enhanced. As expected, the Haihayas attacked Kashi, but this time the battle raged for a long time. The Haihayas could not breach the town's defences. The faceoff turned into a long-drawn siege. No one could get in; no one could get out.

As time went by, however, the town's supplies dwindled. The king's soldiers succumbed in greater numbers. A decision loomed over Divodaasa. Continue the siege and see his soldiers and citizens fall to starvation. Or…

Divodaasa conceded defeat. He abandoned Kashi and escaped. He took refuge in Sage Bharadwaaja's hermitage. There he lamented to the sage that Veetahavya's sons had killed off his lineage and he was left without an heir. Bharadwaaja consoled him. While what had happened could not be changed, he could alleviate the king's sorrow on account of being heirless. He performed a sacrifice for the king. A son named Pratardana was born and immediately after birth took on the form of a teenager. Bharadwaaja used his yogic powers to infuse Pratardana with immense energy.

Divodaasa appointed Pratardana his heir. His father instructed him to go wreak havoc on Veetahavya's sons, the Haihayas. Pratardana amassed an army and crossed the Ganga. This time the tables had turned. The Haihayas found their capital besieged by Pratardana. A fierce battle was fought. Every single of Veetahavya's sons were slain in that encounter. Veetahavya himself fled and took refuge in Sage Bhrigu's hermitage. Pratardana was close behind, in hot pursuit. Pratardana reached Bhrigu's hermitage and stopped. He was armed and he would not enter the sage's hermitage without first disarming himself, which he was unwilling to. Inside the sage's hermitage was hidden his prey, King Veetahavya.

'Yes, O King, what brings you to my hermitage,' Bhrigu asked.

'I am in pursuit of a kshatriya who has hidden himself in your hermitage, O Sage,' Pratardana replied.

'A kshatriya, you say?' asked Bhrigu.

'Yes, King Veetahavya has taken refuge here. For two generations he and his sons have destroyed my city and killed my ancestors. This time I have been victorious. I will destroy him today. As he has done to me, I will do to him.'

'I see,' Brigu replied.

'O Sage, what is the matter?' Pratardana grew impatient.

'There is only one problem, O King.'

'What is that, O Sage?'

'There is no kshatriya here in my hermitage.'

'I don't understand, O Sage. What are you saying?'

'Yes, there are only brahmanas in this hermitage.'

Pratardana looked at the sage. Bhrigu was not joking, nor was he taunting the king. 'Thank you, O Sage,' Pratardana bowed before Bhrigu, a smile on his lips.

'I don't understand, O King,' it was Bhrigu's turn to be nonplussed.

'Yes, O Sage. If there is no kshatriya in this hermitage, then my work is done. I have destroyed Veetahavya the kshatriya.'

Pratardana took leave of the sage and departed.

Veetahavya the kshatriya thus became Veetahavya the brahmana in a most curious way imaginable.

This account doesn't quite end here. Bheeshma went on to list Veetahavya's descendants—Gritsamada, Suteja, Varcha, Vihavya, Vitatya, Satya, Santa, Shravaas, Tama, Prakaash, Vagindra, Pramati, Ruru, Shunaka, and finally Shaunaka.

Who was Shaunaka? Shaunaka was a venerable sage. It was in this Sage Shaunaka's hermitage that the bard Ugrashrava now sat, reciting the Mahabharata to the sages assembled there.

VIPULA

They Who Always Watch

Parva: Anushaasana (13) Upa parva: Daana-dharma (87)

Chapters: 39–43 Shlokas: 165

Yudhishthira posed a most unusual question to Bheeshma, the lifelong celibate. A question even more unusual than when he had asked, 'In a union between a man and woman, who feels the greater pleasure?'[1] Yudhishthira asked Bheeshma what was it about women that attracted men?

> The intelligence of a woman is superior to the sacred texts that Ushanas[2] and Brihaspati know.[3]

Bheeshma didn't disagree with whatever Yudhishthira had opined about women and recounted the example of Vipula to elaborate.

Once upon a time people were devoted to dharma. So devoted were they that their conduct alone was sufficient for them to attain divinity. This distressed the gods. Heaven was not meant to be attainable for everyone. If every human attained heaven upon death, then heaven would be overrun with humans. They approached Brahma for a solution.

Brahma solved the gods' problem. He created women, but with a wicked disposition, and who fought with men. When even Brahma couldn't restrain them, how could mere mortal men?

There was once a sage named Devasharma who had a beautiful wife named Ruchi. Knowing that Indra, the gods, and gandharvas coveted her, he did his best to protect her from their prying eyes. Once, when he decided to conduct a sacrifice, he enlisted the help of his disciple, Vipula, to stand guard over his wife while he was away at the sacrifice. When the sage was away, the gods would make a play for his wife, Devasharma feared. To protect the sage's wife from Indra, Vipula wanted to know what forms the king of the gods could assume. The sage replied that Indra could take any number of forms, from appearing like a god to a chandaala, a fat or a thin person, dark or fair, intelligent or dumb, and even take non-human forms, and so on. The only way to identify Indra was through the sight of knowledge. In other words, Vipula would have to be on guard against everyone. It would fall on his own intelligence to save the day.

Once Devasharma had departed, Vipula began to think how best he may protect Ruchi. He would have to protect her from not ordinary mortals, nor even the gods, but the king of the gods. Ordinary efforts would be futile against someone like Indra. He resolved to use his yogic powers to enter the sage's wife and protect her. This obviously meant risking Devasharma's curse and wrath. After much deliberation, Vipula decided that it was a risk he would have to take.

> On his journey, a traveller seeks shelter in a deserted house....[4] A drop of water moves, but does not touch the lotus leaf that it is on.[5]

Vipula seated himself next to Ruchi and using his yogic powers, immersed himself into her, his attributes mingling with hers, subtly, imperceptibly, such that even she didn't realize it. Vipula stayed there for the duration of Devasharma's sacrifice.

Expectedly, soon enough, Indra assumed a different form, young and handsome, and came by the hermitage. His intentions were to unite with the sage's beautiful wife. When he reached the hermitage, he saw Vipula and Ruchi seated. While Vipula was immobile, his eyes closed, Ruchi saw the young man and wished to get up and greet him. Perhaps desire had risen in the sage's wife. However, Vipula, inside Ruchi, held her back, restrained her senses, rendering her incapable of even speech. When Indra made known his desire for her, Ruchi could neither speak nor move.

Seeing her indifference, a puzzled Indra again told her who he was—the king of the gods—and why he had come there and praised her beauty to the skies. Sage Gautama's wife, Ahalya, had been unable to resist Indra's charms. Why was Ruchi not yielding to his charms? Indra sensed that something was amiss. He used his divine sight and saw Vipula immersed inside Ruchi. Vipula's store of austerities was immense, and the sight of the sage terrified Indra.

Vipula momentarily exited Ruchi and re-entered his own body. He warned Indra to control his senses and reminded him of Gautama's curse when he had taken advantage of the sage's wife, Ahalya. He asked Indra to begone lest his curse burn down the king of the gods. A mortified Indra left.

A short while later, Devasharma returned to the hermitage. When Vipula told Devasharma of Indra's arrival and what had transpired, the sage was pleased. He blessed Vipula. Had Vipula told the sage everything?

Ruchi's sister, Prabhavati, was married to Chitraratha, the King of Anga. Once, some flowers on an apsaraa, who happened to be traveling in the skies, fell down to earth, and were picked up by Ruchi. She took those flowers when she went to meet her sister in Anga. Prabhavati saw those flowers and expressed a desire for similar flowers. Ruchi told Devasharma, her husband, how she had come by those flowers.

Devasharma summoned Vipula and asked him to go find the same flowers. Vipula went to the place where the flowers had fallen and saw some on the ground that were still fresh. He picked them up and started on his way back to Anga.

On the way he came across a couple dancing in a bleak forest. One took one step too fast and a squabble broke out between the two. While quarrelling each uttered an unspoken oath that if they were lying, they would suffer a fate as terrible as what was reserved for Vipula.

Vipula was stunned at hearing this. He had lived a life of austerities, committed no sin, no act of adharma, and yet a terrible fate awaited him according to the couple. Advancing, he came across six gamblers engrossed in a game of dice. Vipula heard each gambler taking a similar oath—that if they were cheating, the too would suffer the same fate as was going to be Vipula's.

After much thought Vipula could think of only act of transgression that he had committed—when telling his guru, Devasharma, about how he had protected Ruchi from Indra, he had omitted telling him the part where he had also permeated her being, her sight and senses, with his. But what had happened had happened. He proceeded to Anga and handed over the flowers to Devasharma.

Vipula's surprises did not end there, for Devasharma asked him whether he had seen the couple and the gamblers who knew the truth about him and Ruchi. On Vipula's asking, the sage replied that the couple were night and day; the gamblers were the seasons, and they had witnessed Vipula's transgressions.

> Even if a man performs a wicked deed secretly, the seasons, night and day are witness to this.[6]

Logic and calm were called for when protecting women, for there was no other way, Bheeshma concluded.

62

CHYAVANA

Beyond Price

Parva: Anushaasan (13)	Upa parva: Daana-dharma (87)
Chapters: 50-51	Shlokas: 74

Sage Chyavana once observed a fast at the confluence of the Ganga and Yamuna.[1] He stood in the water for twelve long years. Once some fishermen came there to catch fish. They cast out their nets and when they pulled them in, along with a great number of fishes, Chyavana was also ensnared and dragged along. This made for a very strange sight to the fishermen. Along with the fishes they had netted, the fishermen saw a sage with matted hair, long beard, his body covered in moss, and conches attached to his body.

The fishermen were aghast at their act, even if performed inadvertently. They had ill-treated a venerable sage. They bowed before the sage and asked for his forgiveness. Chyavana, on the other hand, had spent many years in the water where these fishes had been his companions. He saw the fishes ensnared in the fishermen's nets, many still thrashing around, many now dead. He sat down, sighing, sorrowful.

Chyavana told them that all he wished for was to stay with the fishes. The fishermen could take him along with the fishes and sell both. Or they could leave the fishes here, along with him. The fishermen were at their wits' end. Clueless on how to resolve this dilemma, they went to King Nahusha and told him what had happened.

Nahusha arrived where Chyavana was and paid his respects. He asked the sage to command him—only the sage could suggest a way out of this dilemma. The fishermen earned a living by catching and then selling fish, Chyavana reasoned. Along with the fish, they had caught him too. It was only proper that the king pay the fishermen a price for both him and the fish. This was easier than Nahusha had feared, he thought. Or not.

Nahusha commanded his men that one thousand coins be given to the kaivartas (fishermen) for the sage. No, Chyavana replied that he was worth more. Nahusha offered one hundred thousand coins, one crore coins, and then half of his kingdom, and then his entire kingdom. To each offer, the sage refused. Nahusha stood there, not knowing what more he could offer that would be an appropriate price for the sage. Chyavana advised Nahusha to go consult his sages and ministers. They would be able to suggest an appropriate price for him. A confused and dejected king returned to consult with his sages and ministers.

As these deliberations were going on, a sage who dwelled in the forest chanced by. He saw the king and his ministers locked in deliberations. He offered to come up with a price that would be agreeable to Chyavana. The kind took the sage up on his offer. The price for Chyavana? One cow—the forest dwelling sage replied. Of course, the answer had been obvious. But how had he come up with this solution, Nahusha asked the sage.

Brahmanas were priceless, but so were cows. Something priceless could be purchased only with something invaluable.

The king went back to Chyavana and made this offer. The sage agreed. He told the king the qualities of cow, that they cleansed one of sins, were the foundation of prosperity, they represented the ladder to heaven.

The fishermen bowed before Chyavana. They reminded the sage, just as Saavitri had told Yama,[2] that seven steps taken together constituted friendship. The sage was, therefore, a friend of the fishermen. They requested Chyavana to take the cow back from them. Chyavana agreed. He also blessed them, freeing them from all and any sins they may have committed. They were blessed by the sage to ascend to heaven along with all the fish they had caught.

63

NRIGA

Accidental Adharma

Parva: Anushaasan (13) Upa parva: Daana-dharma (87)
Chapter: 69 Shlokas: 33

An act of cruelty, even if committed unintentionally, had consequences. Sage Maandavya had found that out.[1] Giving was praised; taking away frowned upon. An act of taking away, even if done unintentionally, would have consequences. Yes, what had happened to King Nriga was a cautionary tale, Bheeshma remembered.

Some travellers, thirsty after a long journey, entered the city of Dwaaravati.[2] Trudging along, they came across a well in the distance. Happy to have found a source of clean, cool water, they approached it with much anticipation. Their hopes were dimmed a little when they saw it covered with grass and creepers. The travellers needed water and there was no other well in sight. They set about clearing the grass and creepers from the well. When all that had been done, they couldn't spot any water. They peered some more and drew back in horror.

No water, or trace of water, but at the bottom of the well was a giant lizard covering the entire opening of the well. Perhaps there was water beneath the lizard. Still thirsty, they tried and tried and tried to move the lizard, but it wouldn't budge. Despairing, they went to Krishna.[3] Krishna accompanied the travellers back to the well. Yes, there was a giant lizard there. He was able to remove the lizard.

Once it was out of the well, Krishna asked the lizard who it was and, well, how it had come about in the bottom of the well.

The lizard replied it was King Nriga. He was a king who had performed a thousand sacrifices. Yes, Krishna had heard of King Nriga. He was the king who had given brahmans countless cows. He was the king who had performed good deeds, not wicked ones. How had he taken rebirth as a lizard, Krishna wanted to know. Every deed had its consequences, even unintended deeds. Nriga began his story.

> We have heard that in ancient times, you repeatedly gave brahmanas hundreds of thousands of cows one hundred times. Then you again gave hundred and eight thousand of cows a hundred thousand times.[4]

Once a brahmana's cow wandered off and ended up mixed with the king's herd of thousands of cows. When the king gave away thousands of cows, in those thousands of cows was that one cow that belonged not to the king but to the brahmana. One day, the cow's original owner saw that his cow was in another brahmana's house. He went to retrieve it. The cow's new owner would have nothing of it. The cow was his, given rightfully by none other than King Nriga. A dispute arose between the two. Neither could arrive at a consensus. The dispute eventually reached the king.

Nriga heard both brahmanas. He realized the mistake had been his. The cow belonged to the first brahmana and it would have to be returned. But what about the second brahmana? He would have to be compensated. Since the lapse had been on his part, the king offered a large number of cows in exchange for that one cow. No, the brahmana refused. That particular cow had proven beneficial to him. Its milk was sweet, and his son, weak, had been nourished by the cow's milk. Saying this, rebuffing the king's offers, the brahmana left.

There was now the first brahmana in the court, whose cow had been given away accidentally. The king made the same offer to this brahmana—take one cow, take a hundred cows, take gold, take silver, take chariots for that one cow of his that had been accidentally given away. No, the brahmana wanted not one, not ten, not a hundred cows; he wanted no gold, no silver, no chariots. He wanted only his cow. There the matter rested, that one inadvertent sin waited to be accounted for. The day of reckoning would come, and Yama would adjudicate the dispute the king had been unable to resolve.

As with every mortal, Nriga died and went to Yama. Yes, Nriga had led a virtuous life and his good deeds were countless. On the other hand, there was this tiny matter of a sin committed, albeit inadvertently, that would need to be accounted for. Nriga had been a virtuous king. Yama gave Nriga a choice—suffer for the sin now or later.

> You promised that you would protect. You took a false pledge. You seized the possession of a brahmana. These are the three aspects to the sin you committed.[5]

Nriga chose to suffer for the sins first and enjoy the fruits of his good deeds later. He displayed better impulse control than most. Yama accepted Nriga's decision. Nriga fell back to earth, into the well, waiting for Vaasudeva to save him. And Vaasudeva had now freed him, Nriga said. He had paid for the sin he had committed in ignorance. He was now free to ascend to heaven to enjoy the fruits of his good deeds.

64

NAACHIKETA

An Appointment with Yama

Parva: Anushaasan (13)	Upa parva: Daana-dharma (87)
Chapter: 70	Shlokas: 56

Donating something that didn't belong to you could have serious consequences, even if they were in the afterlife, as Nriga found out. But what was the fruit one obtained from donating cattle—was Yudhishthira's next question to Bheeshma. The patriarch could think of no better incident than what had happened between Uddaaliki and Naachiketa[1] to highlight his answer.

Once Sage Uddaaliki[2] asked his son, Naachiketa, to fetch firewood, darbha grass, and a pot of water kept at the riverbank. However, when Naachiketa got there, the river's current had washed all those away. Naachiketa returned empty-handed. When his father asked, he told him he had not seen any firewood, darbha grass, and no pot. Uddaaliki, overcome with exhaustion and hunger, cursed his son in a fit of anger that he would see Yama instead. No sooner than he had uttered these words than Naachiketa fell to the ground.

A grief-stricken Uddaaliki could do no more than place his son's body on a mat of grass and shed tears. A most unexpected and delightful surprise awaited Uddaaliki. His tears revived Naachiketa. He got up, still weak. His father embraced his son and asked if he knew how he had come back to life. Naachiketa recounted what had happened.

A curse was a curse. Cursed by his father, Naachiketa had fallen dead. Once dead, he found himself in Yama's abode, as cursed by his father. There Vaivasvata offered a seat to Naachiketa and told him that he was not dead. Yes, he was in Yamaloka, but merely because he had to fulfil his father's curse, whose words could not come false. Now that he had seen him, Yama told Naachiketa, he could return to his father.

Naachiketa asked Yama to show him the worlds that were meant for those who performed good deeds. Yama took Naachiketa on his chariot where he saw resplendent residences of such persons. Houses with countless jewels, mountains of ghee and food to eat, trees that granted wishes, and more. Yama explained that these were for those who donated milk and cows. He also elaborated the dos-and-don'ts of donating cows.

Donating cows rescued from distress was good but keeping cows where they suffered from the sun was not, Yama explained. A bull, if donated, had to be controllable, young, and strong. Those who did not have cows to donate could donate ghee; if they didn't have ghee, they could donate sesamum seeds; and if they didn't have even sesamum seeds, they could donate water. Sometimes the greatest of sacrifices required the least amount of donations. Cows produced the food that sustained the world, and hell awaited the tormentor of cows. Dharmaraja advised Naachiketa to follow his own dharma (svadharma) and to be pure when pursuing artha.

> Knowing about what cattle do, if a person oppresses them,
> he is evil in his consciousness and goes to hell.[3]

Naachiketa completed his account and thanked his father. The curse had turned into a boon. Saavitri had walked with Yama and brought back Satyavaan back from Yama's grip. But Naachiketa had met and conversed with Yama, the god of death, and come back alive to tell the tale. It also allowed him to hear all that was possible through donations.

65

KEETA

As Was the Karma, so Was the Rebirth

Parva: Anushaasan (13)	Upa parva: Daana-dharma (87)
Chapters: 118-120	Shlokas: 65

Not everyone who had died at Kurukshetra would go to heaven. Nor would everyone who had perished would be reborn as a human. The cycle of rebirth would be determined by one's karma. Yudhishthira wanted to know from Bheeshma what species would those who had died in the battle be born as. Bheeshma recounted a conversation that Vyaasa—Krishna Dvaipaayana—once had with a worm he had seen moving rapidly on a road.

Vyaasa asked why the worm was scurrying about on the road.

'Why am I frightened, you ask, O Sage? I will tell you why—it is because I am scared. I am terrified,' the worm replied.

'Why is that?' Vyaasa asked.

'You hear these sounds of the carts, do you? Do you hear the roar they make? The sounds of the wheels as they roll towards me; the hoofs of these countless bulls as they clip-clop? These sounds scare me.'

'I see,' Vyaasa replied. 'In your state, in the life form you have been born, wouldn't death be a happier state for you?'

'Why? Why should I desire death?'

'Look at you. You can neither smell, nor taste, nor can you experience the joys of all the beautiful sounds in this world. You cannot even converse with anyone except me.'

> 'This is the body I have been born in. This is what I am, who I am. This is what I like, this is what brings me happiness. But I wasn't always like this. Once I too was a human,' the worm replied.

The worm elaborated on his prior life. He had been a human, a rich shudra who had the luxury of a good house, many servants, and more. However, he was neither honest in how he earned his living, nor was he soft in speech. Guests he did not care about, servants he didn't treat well. He donated neither money nor food. To the gods he didn't offer anything. What he was, however, was envious of those who had more than him. His jealousy didn't stop there; he wished ill of those who had more than him.

His next life, as a worm, would have been worse, but for the fact that he still remembered his previous life. For that he had to thank perhaps the one good deed he had done in his entire previous life—he had once worshipped his mother and a noble brahmana who had come to his house. He now wanted to know from Vyaasa the best course for itself.

Vyaasa assured the worm that it was on account of his one good deed that he had met him. On the strength of the austerities he possessed, Vyaasa said he would confer on the worm the status of a brahmana. The worm gave up its life under the wheels of an oncoming cart and was born, after many cycles, as a kshatriya. He went and met Vyaasa and asked his advice on the best course of action for him now.

Vyaasa told him that he would die on the battlefield and be born as a brahmana. Bheeshma concluded this account by telling Yudhishthira not to worry about those who had died on the battlefield, for they had followed their respective natures. Hadn't Vyaasa warned Dhritaraashtra against letting his sons go to the forest to kill the Paandavas, telling him that a person's nature didn't abandon him before his death?[1] As a person acted, so would they become, and so would be their end in the present life and state in the next life.

66

UTTANKA

When Seeing Was Not Believing

Parva:	Upa parva:
Ashwamedhika (14)	Ashwamedhika (89)
Chapters: 52–57	Shlokas: 202

After Bheeshma had left his mortal coil and ascended to heaven, after the funeral rites for the Kurus killed in the war had been completed, and after Yudhishthira had entered Hastinapura,[1] Krishna expressed his desire to leave for Dwaarka. A reluctant Arjuna agreed.

On Krishna's instructions, his charioteer, Daruka, yoked the horses. Krishna took Dhritaraashtra's and Yudhishthira's approval, met his aunt, Kunti, and then left for Dwaarka. Arjuna would leave soon thereafter with the Ashwamedhika horse to ensure that it had an unhindered passage. Arjuna would return to Hastinapura once the horse had completed its journey around the land.

As Krishna's chariot proceeded towards Dwaarka, they entered a desert that was known to be Sage Uttanka's abode.[2] Sure enough, soon enough, Krishna saw the sage and stopped his chariot. They paid their respects to each other. Living in the desert, far from people and habitations, immersed in his penances, Uttanka was not abreast of developments at Hastinapura. The last he had heard was that Krishna had been on his way to Hastinapura to bring about peace between the Paandavas and Kauravas. Krishna was now returning to Dwaarka. The question on Uttanka's mind was the obvious one—had Krishna succeeded in bringing about reconciliation between the cousins?

Yes, Krishna started, he had been to Hastinapura. Yes, he had tried to bring about a reconciliation between the Paandavas and Kauravas. No, his peace mission had been unsuccessful. No, the Kauravas had not paid heed to his peace overtures. Nor had Duruyodhana listened to Bheeshma and Vidura's counsel. A war had ensued in Kurukshetra between the cousins where all the Kauravas and their relatives had been killed. The Paandavas too had lost their relatives and friends. Of those who fought on the Paandava side, only the five Paandavas remained alive from the Kuru clan.

Uttanka flew into a rage on hearing this news.

'You could have stopped this, but you didn't!' Uttanka rasped.

'O Sage,' Krishna spoke. 'What had to happen had to happen. It could not have been otherwise.'

'These are excuses. You had the power to stop this bloodshed. Yet you let it happen.'

'Peace could not be had if it meant the victory of adharma, O Sage,' Krishna replied.

'I am going to curse you, O Krishna. What you allowed to happen is inexcusable,' Uttanka was adamant.

'Don't lose your temper, O Sage,' Krishna counselled.

'Why shouldn't I?'

'First, anger depletes the store of austerities of sages. I wouldn't want that to happen to you. Second, I will share some thoughts on adhyaatma with you; perhaps you will not curse me then. And third…,' Krishna paused.

'And what else, O Keshava, and what else?' Uttanka demanded.

'Your austerities, great or little though they may be, are not going to overwhelm me. Yours, or anyone else's, for that matter,' Krishna smiled. 'What has to happen will happen only if I wish it so, O Sage.'

Not too long back Gandhaari had cursed him. The destruction of his clan was certain thirty-six years from now.

'Speak, O Keshava. Only after hearing you will I decide whether to curse you or not,' Uttanka fell silent.

No man is capable of overwhelming me with a little bit of austerities.[3]

Krishna gave a short discourse, telling Uttanka that everything had originated from him—the Rudras and Vasus; the daityas, yakshas, raakshasas, serpents, apsaraas, and gandharvas. Everything existed in him—the manifest, the unmanifest, and that while both existence and non-existence was within him, he himself was beyond both. When he took birth in a womb, he took on the behaviour of that womb—whether it was a god, a gandharva, a serpent, or a human. As a human, he had beseeched the Kauravas to desist from adharma, to no avail. That the Kauravas had been destroyed had been entirely because of their own acts.

Krishna's words had the desired effect; Uttanka's rage subsided. He now wished to see Krishna's divine form, the same form he had revealed in the assembly hall at Hastinapura, the same form he had shown Arjuna on the battlefield at Kurukshetra. Krishna obliged and Uttanka glimpsed Krishna's universal form.[4]

Krishna then granted Uttanka a boon. Uttanka hesitated, for the very sight of Krishna's universal form was boon enough. Krishna persisted. Uttanka relented. He lived in a desert, where water was scarce. He, therefore, asked for the boon of water. Krishna granted the boon. All Uttanka had to do when thirsty was to think of Krishna. Their meeting over, Krishna continued to Dwaarka.

> This must be done, since the sight of me cannot be in vain.[5]

Time passed. One day, as Uttanka wandered in the desert, he felt thirsty. Of course, this was a desert; water was not to be found anywhere close by. Of course, Uttanka had Krishna's boon. He thought of Krishna. No sooner had he thought of water than he saw a man walking towards him. Yes, Krishna himself had come to give him water and quench his thirst. No, it was not Krishna. Was this even a person? Yes, but one surrounded by dogs. Yes, this was a chandaala! A sword dangled from his waist, his body caked with mud, and he had no clothes on. Uttanka was repulsed. Where was his water? Where was Krishna? What had happened to the boon he had bestowed on him? Could things get any worse? Yes, they could. And they did.

Uttanka could not believe what his eyes saw. The chandaala was urinating. He then offered that urine to Uttanka, a grotesque grin on his face. Uttanka shrank in horror and disgust. Had his entire life and its austerities come to this, to be offered urine instead of water from a chandaala? The man persisted. Uttanka flew into a rage. He would rather die of thirst than accept what that man was offering. The chandaala vanished.

> I gave it to you in the form in which it should have been given.[6]

Where the chandaala had stood a moment ago now stood Krishna. It took Uttanka a moment to realize what had happened.

> 'This is not fair, O Purushottama. I did not deserve this, to be given water in the form of urine from a chandaala,' Uttanka remonstrated.
> 'It was as it had to be, O Uttanka,' Krishna replied.
> 'Is this how it had to be? I can't believe what I am hearing, and that too from you. Urine?' Uttanka said.
> 'Yes, what you had been offered was not water.'
> 'Yes, I know that; it was urine.'
> 'It was amrita, the nectar of immortality.'
> 'What?' Uttanka was shocked a second time.
> 'Yes. I was with Indra when you thought of me. It was my wish that you be given amrita. Indra demurred. I insisted. He believed mortals should not be given amrita. When I persisted, he said he would take amrita to you, and if you accepted, it would be yours.'
> 'Oh.'
> 'Yes, you refused amrita from the king of the gods.'
> 'What a sin I committed,' Uttanka lamented.
> 'Yes, you did. But what had to happen, happened, didn't it?'
> 'Yes, it did,' a disconsolate Uttanka concurred.
> 'But I did give you a boon, didn't I? While amrita was not to be yours, and never will be now, water still will be. Whenever you are thirsty, rain-bearing clouds will shower water over the desert. These clouds will become famous as Uttanka clouds,' Krishna concluded.

Uttanka was a great sage, of that Janamejaya had no doubt. Not everyone got to witness Krishna's universal form; not everyone was granted a boon from Krishna; not everyone was considered worthy enough to be offered nectar. But how had he acquired such great powers of austerities to be able to even think of cursing Krishna, of cursing one from whom everything originated? Janamejaya asked Vaishampaayana.

As a student, Uttanka had been a devoted disciple of Sage Gautama and a role model to the other disciples in the hermitage. Over time, other disciples completed their education and with Gautama's permission, departed the hermitage. All but Uttanka, for Gautama loved his disciple too much to let him leave. Time passed, the years passed, and Uttanka grew old.

With old age came infirmities and weakness. One day, overwhelmed while carrying a load of wood, Uttanka flung it to the ground out of exhaustion and frustration. A strand of his now silver hair broke off and fell to the ground. Uttanka saw the hair. He had aged. He sat there, shedding silent tears of sorrow. Gautama saw Uttanka. He walked over and asked him why he was sad.

Was Uttanka sad at staying in the hermitage for as long as he had? No, he was not; but he had missed out on the other joys of life. Yes, his affection for his favourite student had come in the way of doing what was proper, Gautama realized. Gautama made amends immediately. He gave Uttanka permission to leave.

Uttanka could leave, but he would not do so without first giving his guru dakshina. Gautama replied that Uttanka's devotion had been dakshina. Had he been younger, he would have given his daughter in marriage to Uttanka. That was something that was still in Gautama's powers. He turned Uttanka into a young man again. As for the guru dakshina, while the sage did not want anything from Uttanka, if his student still insisted, perhaps there was something his wife wanted, Gautama said.

The young Uttanka went to Gautama's wife, Ahalya. She also didn't want anything from Uttanka. Uttanka persisted. Ahalya relented and asked Uttanka to get her the divine earrings of Madayanti, King Saudasa's[7] wife. Uttanka nodded and set out immediately.

Later that day when Gautama did not see Uttanka he asked Ahalya. She told him that Uttanka had set out to get Saudasa's wife's earrings for her. The sage grew pensive on hearing this. King Saudasa was now a man-eater.[8] Uttanka was a human. If the twain met, there could be but one outcome, Gautama feared. Ahalya, however, remained confident that Gautama's blessings would protect him. The sage waited, hoped.

Saudasa was as frightful as maneaters went. His long, unkempt beard was stained with human blood. As fate would have it, Uttanka's and Saudasa's paths crossed. Saudasa welcomed Uttanka as food sent at the right time. If that was how it was supposed to be, Uttanka would accept what destiny had in store for him. However, he was here on a mission. He had a duty to complete, he told Saudasa—he needed to get the queen's earrings and take them to Ahalya, his guru's wife. To stop him, therefore, would be most inappropriate, Uttanka reasoned with Saudasa the maneater.

Saudasa would not relent. Food was food. Uttanka proposed a compromise. If Saudasa allowed him to leave and complete his task of getting earrings for his guru's wife's, he would return and submit himself to Saudasa's control, free for him to make a meal of Uttanka.

Saudasa relented and Uttanka made his way to the queen's palace. There he presented himself before Madayanti, Saudasa's wife. Here another hurdle presented itself. The queen had no hesitation in handing over her earrings if the sage's wife, Ahalya, had asked for them. However, what proof was there that Uttanka had indeed come at the instructions of her husband? The earrings were no ordinary ones—they were divine and the gods, serpents, and yakshas were waiting for an opportunity to steal them. A momentary lapse, a moment of carelessness and they would be stolen. If left on the ground, serpents would purloin them. If the wearer ate leftovers, yakshas would take off with them. If the wearer dozed off, the gods would be waiting to make off with them.

Uttanka returned to Saudasa and presented his new problem before him. Saudasa told him to tell Madayanti that Saudasa's condition is a terrible one, but one from which there was no escape either. This was not very clear to Uttanka, but he nonetheless went back to Madayanti and repeated Saudasa's words. Madayanti understood that these words were truly coming from her husband, for no one else knew that the king had turned into a maneater. It was her husband who was asking her to hand over the earrings to Uttanka. Madayanti gave Uttanka the earrings. Uttanka now set out to the forest, to Saudasa. That had been their pact. Once he got the earrings, he would return to become Saudasa's meal.

Standing in front of the king, Uttanka now asked Saudasa to explain the meaning of his cryptic words. Saudasa replied that his current state was because of a brahmana's curse, for which none but he was responsible. By doing this favour to Uttanka, Saudasa hoped for some favour in return from the brahmana.

> Those who are learned and accomplished in their insight about the dharma to be followed vis-à-vis friends say that one who behaves unfairly towards friends is like a thief.[9]

Uttanka now posed a question to Saudasa. Before placing himself under Saudasa's control, he wished the king to answer a question truthfully. Given that Saudasa was a maneater, should Uttanka have come back or not.

Saudasa wished that Uttanka had not asked this question. However, his truthful answer was that Uttanka should not, never ever, return to Saudasa. Uttanka smiled, thanked the king for his honesty, took his leave and proceeded to his hermitage to hand over Madayanti's earrings to Ahalya.

He carried the earrings in a bag made of black antelope skin. Along the way, he got hungry. He espied a tree nearby laden with fruit. To climb the tree, he would have to put the bag down, which he could not, because serpents would steal the earrings if he did. Uttanka therefore first secured the bag by tying it to a branch and then climbed up the fruit-laden tree. However, the knot loosened and the pouch fell down. No sooner than it fell to the ground than a serpent grabbed the earrings and escaped underground via a termite hill. What Madayanti had warned him about, what Uttanka had taken care to avoid, had come to pass.

A furious Uttanka set about digging up the termite hill. As it happened, Indra happened to pass by and saw the brahmana digging away with his stick. When he learned from Uttanka what had transpired, Indra advised him to give up the search, for the world of serpents was a long distance away. Uttanka would end up digging his entire life and still not make much headway. Uttanka replied that he was willing to give up his life than give up the search for the earrings. Those earrings were for his guru's wife. He would return only with those earrings. Seeing his determination, Indra pervaded the energy of his vajra weapon into the stick.

Uttanka pounded away with the stick. The vajra's energy did the job. The earth gave way and a path to the world of the serpents opened up. Uttanka stepped in and proceeded down. Reaching the world, he saw it wide and big, and his hopes receded, for he had no idea how he was going to find the earrings in a place so vast.

Just as he was about to give up hope, a dark horse with a white tail arrived there and asked Uttanka to blow into its rear. Seeing Uttanka's obvious surprise, the horse replied that it was none other than Jatadeva, the fire god, and this blowing into the fire was what Uttanka would do back at his guru's hermitage.

Uttanka did as told. Flames emerged from every pore of the horse, and thick smoke billowed, causing havoc everywhere. The world of the serpents was immersed in confusion. There was only one way out of this predicament. They gathered and humbly returned the earrings to Uttanka. The brahmana circumambulated the fire and departed.

Once back at the hermitage, Uttanka handed over the earrings to Ahalya. Uttanka had been a devoted pupil of a great sage; he had collected over the years a great deal of austerities through his penances, including the power to curse Krishna.

67

NAKULA

When Only Adharma Could Set One Free

Parva:	Upa parva:
Ashwamedhika (14)	Ashwamedhika (89)
Chapters: 92–96	Shlokas: 200

After Uttaryaana had started, in the month of Maagha, with only a few days remaining in shuklapaksha, fifty-eight nights after he had been felled and had spent on the bed of arrows, Bheeshma took Krishna's approval and cast aside his life; blessed by Krishna to again become a Vasu.[1]

With Vyaasa's permission and counsel, Yudhishthira had started preparations for the Ashwamedha sacrifice. The rituals would be performed by Vyaasa himself, along with sages Paila and Yajnavalkya. But a grand sacrifice needed wealth. A sacrifice as great as the Ashwamedha needed even more wealth. Where the wealth was going to come from, Yudhishthira didn't know. The treasury was empty after the war. Kings that acknowledged suzerainty to the Paandavas and who could have given wealth to Yudhishthira had all perished in the war. Yudhishthira neither wanted to ask the princes who had succeeded those kings for wealth, nor did he wish to perform the sacrifice without giving away wealth, even though such a course of action was approved of in difficult times.[2]

Every problem had a solution. To this hurdle also there existed a way out. There was a store of wealth that was available to use for such times, Vyaasa confided in Yudhishthira. A long time ago, in King Marutta's sacrifice, so great had been the wealth given away that brahmans had been unable to carry all of that back. What they could, they took with them; what they couldn't, they had left behind in the Himalayas. That wealth, Vyaasa told Yudhishthira, could be used.[3]

The Paandavas retrieved the wealth and there was great celebration in Hastinapura. The Ashwamedha sacrifice could finally commence. The first step was the release of the sacrificial horse. Where the horse went, the kingdoms had two choices—to either accept Yudhishthira's suzerainty and allow the horse to pass through their kingdom unhindered; or obstruct the horse's path. If the king chose the latter option, they would have to fight and defeat the retinue that accompanied the horse. In this case, the Paandava they would have to fight was Arjuna, for he followed the horse. Most kingdoms allowed the horse to pass through; some didn't.

Trigarta was one of the few kingdoms that chose to challenge the horse's passage. Though the king had fallen in the war at Kurukshetra, his sons tried to seize the horse. A battle with Arjuna ensued with the Trigarta princes, Suryavarma, Ketuvarma, and Dhritavarma. They were brave and even managed to injure Arjuna, but this was destined to be a short battle.[4] Arjuna still possessed the Gandeeva bow, and he still had the strength and dexterity to counter any warrior he faced in battle.

The horse then trotted into Pragjyotisha, where King Bhagadatta's son, King Vajradatta, took it upon himself to stop the horse and challenge Arjuna. This was a tougher battle and it lasted for three days, but the result was the same as the battle with the Trigartas—Arjuna's victory.[5]

There was a brief skirmish with another recalcitrant king, the Saindhavas, who had succeeded Jayadratha and where the battle stopped only when Duhshala, Dhritaraashtra's daughter and Jayadratha's wife, approached Arjuna with her grandson, Suratha's son. It turned out that Suratha, Duhshala's son, had died of fright on the battlefield on seeing Arjuna, and the queen mother did not want to lose even her grandson. She needn't have had cause for worry had she known that Yudhishthira had cautioned Arjuna against killing any of these kings. Arjuna's aim in this expedition was to only vanquish the kings if they resisted.

One kingdom where Arjuna did not face hostility was the kingdom of Manipura, ruled by King Babruvaahana, Arjuna and Chitrangada's son.[6] Babruvaahana didn't wish to fight his father,

Arjuna. Kshatriya dharma demanded otherwise and Babruvaahana was reprimanded by his father for forgetting kshatriya dharma. Uloopi,[7] Arjuna's wife and therefore, stepmother to Babruvaahana, advised him to pick up arms. A battle commenced between father and son. This was one combat in which Babruvaahana got the better of Arjuna. The Paandava fell to the ground.

Seeing the great Arjuna felled in battle, Uloopi, Chitraangada, and Babruvaahana all lamented. Babruvaahana had intended to defeat his father in battle, for that was what the dharma of kshatriyas called. But having killed him, or so he thought, Babruvaahana decided to fast to death. Just when it appeared that all was lost, Uloopi, who had been grieving, remembered that she had the samjeevanam jewel that could revive the dead. Thus, Arjuna came to life. Arjuna's fall in battle, a first for him, had also been for a reason. On the battlefield at Kurukshetra, on the tenth day, Arjuna had brought down Bheeshma through an act of deceit. Shikhandi had engaged Bheeshma in a duel, and Arjuna had used Shikhandi as a cover to bring the Kuru warrior down. To atone for that sin, the gods had decreed that the mighty Arjuna too would have to fall in battle.[8]

The horse eventually returned to Hastinapura. Kings arrived, as did the Vrishnis along with Balaraama and Krishna. The great Ashwamedha yagna[9] commenced. Vyaasa's instructions on giving out three times the norm as dakshina were followed. Donations, food, and more were given out. Sixteen priests presided over the ceremony. All sections of society were given wealth. What Vyaasa got, he handed over to his daughter-in-law, Kunti.[10] Unlike the Rajsuya sacrifice[11] many years ago that had ended in acrimony, much envy, Shishupaala's death at Krishna's hands, and the start of a chain of events that resulted in that fateful game of dice, there were no such unpleasant events at the Ashwamedhika sacrifice, much to Yudhishthira's relief.[12] Or perhaps, not quite.

As Vaishampaayana finished this account, Janamejaya asked the sage if anything extraordinary had happened during the sacrifice. Both auspicious and inauspicious events could be extraordinary, and Janamejaya was a perceptive king. Vaishampaayana smiled.

The appearance of a mongoose[13] at the sacrifice would not have been an extraordinary event, had it not been for the fact that one half of the mongoose's body was golden. Oh, and the mongoose spoke. As the sacrifice drew to a close, the mongoose emerged from its burrow and, in a thunderous voice, addressed the gathering. This sacrifice, it declared, was not equal to even a tenth of the coarse ground meal that a brahman residing in Kurukshetra, and following unchavritti, had given away.

All gathered around the mongoose, gazing at the small mammal as it sniffed around. This was a sacrifice that was grander than even the Rajsuya yagna, where thrice the prescribed donations had been handed out, where everyone had gone back satisfied, where not a single step out of place had taken place, and all rites followed. Who was this mongoose to dismiss this yagna so disdainfully, and in such strong, painful, and hurtful words, the brahmanas demanded?

Everyone had been gratified with appropriate gifts, oblations had been poured into the fire, mantras had been chanted, what the sacred texts prescribed had been followed, maintained the brahmanas. The mongoose stuck to its opinion. The mongoose looked up at all. It started speaking again.

> Hunger destroys wisdom and drives away dharma and intelligence. Hunger overcomes knowledge and destroys fortitude.[14]

Once upon a time, in the holy land of Kurukshetra, there lived a poor brahmana with his family. Poor, but devoted to, and knowledgeable about, dharma, he lived with his wife, son, and daughter-in-law. Life was not easy for one devoted to dharma and devoted to the practice of unchavritti. Such was their penurious state that sometimes they had to forego eating on a day.

> The bar to heaven has greed as its seed. That bar is kept protected by attachment, which is extremely difficult to overcome.[15]

As if this was not a difficult enough life, the region got afflicted by a great famine. What little they had for food, even that supply dwindled. Their survival became an even greater daily struggle. One day the brahmana had managed to collect a small amount of barley. He ground it and mixed it up with water to make a meal for the four of them. As they sat down to eat, a guest came knocking. They all received him with customary honours and then offered him all that a guest be offered—arghya as a ceremonial gift, padya for washing his feet, kusha grass for seating, and one portion of the saktu they had prepared from the barley.

> A person who is capable of giving away a thousand, but gives away a hundred; a person who is capable of giving away a hundred, but gives away ten; and a person who has nothing, but is only capable of giving away water—it has been said in the sacred texts that the fruits obtained by all these are equal.[16]

The guest accepted and ate the offering. Having finished the barley offering, he still looked hungry. Seeing this, the brahmana's wife, thin, hungry, emaciated, and reduced to skin and bones, offered her share of the barley meal to the guest. The brahmana did not approve of this and the two debated this for some time. Sustaining and protecting the wife was the dharma of the husband; he could not approve of his wife giving the guest her share of the meal. The husband protected, which is why he was called a pati; the husband sustained, which is why he was called a bhartri; in the husband's dharma lay the wife's dharma. The brahmana finally relented and offered this second portion of the barley meal to the guest. The guest ate the portion and still looked hungry.

> Riches obtained through greed may be given away in sacrifices. However, it is extremely difficult for those deeds to lead to any success.[17]

The son now stepped up and offered his meal. The guest still showed signs of hunger. The daughter-in-law now stepped up with her portion of the meal. The brahmana wrangled with his son and then daughter-in-law, but in each case, relented.

The guest, having eaten the fourth portion, finally looked sated. Who was he? He, the guest, was Dharma[18] himself. He was not only very happy with the conduct of the family, despite their poverty and state of deprivation, the entire family had earned a place in heaven. A celestial chariot appeared, the gods showered flowers on the family, and the four ascended for heaven.

> Dharma is not pleased with the fruits from giving a large amount of donations. He is instead satisfied with a little bit that has been obtained through lawful means and is given with faith and purity.[19]

When the four had departed for heaven, the mongoose continued, it emerged from its burrow. There was some leftover food on the ground along with flowers showered from the heavens on the brahmana's family. Contact with these turned the mongoose's head and one-half of his body golden.

What other offering existed in this world that would turn the other half of his body also golden, the mongoose wondered. Driven by this quest, the mongoose went to one sacrifice after the other. No sacrifice sufficed—the other half of his body stayed unchanged. Even Yudhishthira's Ashwamedhika. This great, grand sacrifice was not equal to the barley meal offered by the brahmana and his family. Saying this, the mongoose disappeared.

This did not appear fair; it was inexplicable, Janamejaya stated. A sacrifice as lavish, grand, and which adhered to all prescribed rites and texts, could not be so easily dismissed as the mongoose had.

Once Indra himself performed a great sacrifice, Vaishampaayana said. The learned priests performed it with diligence. Soon enough, the time came to offer the sacrifice. A large number of animals had been collected, all of whom would be sacrificed. The sages assembled there saw the animals, waiting to be slaughtered. Compassion overtook them. They felt it wrong to commit such a great slaughter of innocent animals. When the time came to sacrifice the animals, the great sages approached Indra and suggested alternatives. Couldn't seeds stored for three years be used instead for the sacrifice? Wouldn't that also be acceptable, they asked Indra. No, Indra proclaimed. The sages disagreed. They debated and they argued. Who would adjudicate, since clearly neither side was willing to concede the other's point? They conferred and decided that King Vasu[20] would be the one they would approach.

> A learned person who desires dharma should not perform a sacrifice with an object that has been obtained unlawfully.[21]

The sages and Indra went to Vasu. The question posed before him was simple—what was the right way to conduct a sacrifice—with or without the slaughter of animals?

Vasu probably didn't think the question over carefully, or perhaps he didn't know enough, or perhaps he was hasty in his reply. Pat came his answer—a sacrifice could be conducted with whatever was available. Vasu had spoken in haste; he would repent in leisure. The moment he uttered these words, Vasu was dispatched to hell.[22] Why, people wondered. Because what he had said was not true. A sacrifice could not be performed with just anything that was available. Certainly, a sacrifice could not be performed with something obtained by wrong means. Vasu had been in the wrong; he had to suffer the consequences, and he did.

Fruits of dharma could not be obtained by brahmanas overcome by greed and evil deeds, by donations made by the evil, by those who indulged in wanton violence, or by giving away wealth obtained through greed.

> Brahmanas, kshatriyas, vaishyas and shudras who resort to austerities and purify themselves in the fire of dharma and donations, go to heaven.[23]

Once sage Agastya had performed a sacrifice that lasted twelve years, Vaishampaayana continued. Several hotras[24] participated in the sacrifice. However, while the sacrifice went on, Indra didn't shower rains. The priests discussed this among themselves and concluded that Agastya's food offerings were tinged with malice—this is why Indra[25] was not showering rains. If the sacrifice went on for twelve years, Indra would not shower rains for twelve years. They presented their views to Agastya.

Agastya was not going to take this lying down. If Indra would not rain, he would become an Indra and ensure that rains fell. He would perform the sacrifice without anyone interrupting it. He would use the power of his austerities to bring there all the wealth and gold that existed. He asked all the divine beings to assemble there.

The sages assembled there, however, requested Agastya not to use his powers, for that would diminish his own store of austerities. While they were discussing this matter, Indra had also been observing the proceedings. He too saw that Agastya possessed the strength of austerities to do what he had proclaimed he would. Indra relented; he showered rains. The rains continued till the sacrifice was completed.

Having listened to this account, Janamejaya returned to the question of the mongoose. Who was he? Why had he come there? How could he have spoken in a human voice?

To understand who the mongoose was, where he had come from, why he had spoken what he did, and what he had hoped to accomplish through his words, Vaishampaayana told Janamejaya about a time when Sage Jamadagni had once milked a cow for the purposes of a funeral ceremony.[26] He kept the milk in a pot. Along came Krodha,[27] wishing to test how the sage, famous for his anger, would react at an act very odious. How odius? He entered the pot, contaminating and corrupting the milk, rendering it unfit for the ceremony. Would Jamadagni fly into a rage? No, he didn't. He knew this was Krodha's act. Yet he remained calm.

Krodha was now terrified. He had not only performed an act of adharma, but he was now at the mercy of Jamadagni, a sage known for his temper. He appeared before the sage, hands folded. Jamadagni, however, replied that this milk had been kept for his ancestors, and it was those ancestors that Krodha would have to go for forgiveness. The ancestors cursed Krodha, turning him into a mongoose. His redemption from the curse would happen only when Krodha would speak ill of dharma.

Time went by, Krodha kept on going to sacrifices, hoping for redemption. Till one day he came by Yudhishthira's Ashwamedhika sacrifice. He belittled this too by comparing it unfavourably to the brahmana's meal of barley. The brahmana's act of giving away what little they had been a great act of dharma, but where Krodha had transgressed dharma was to belittle Yudhishthira's Ashwamedhika sacrifice. He had to commit this deliberate act of adharma to be freed from the curse. Krodha did just that, spoke ill of dharma in front of Dharma's son.

Speaking ill of your elders was also a transgression of dharma. Arjuna had done just that when he had criticized Yudhishthira. Praising oneself was also a transgression of dharma. Arjuna had also done just that. But that transgression was a minor one compared to the alternative of Arjuna killing his brother and then taking his own life.[28]

Dharma is indeed subtle.

> Remember dharma. The course of dharma needs to be reflected about. It is subtle and difficult to follow.[29]

This upakhyaana also concluded the Ashwamedhika Parva.

Endnotes

Foreword

1. *The Mahabharata: Its Genesis and Growth (A Statistical Study)*, M.R. Yardi, Bhandarkar Oriental Research Institute, Poona, 1986.

Introduction

1. *Not Without Subtales: Telling Laws and Truths in the Sanskrit Epics*, Alf Hiltebeitel.
2. Ibid.

1. Shakuntala

1. An akshauhini was a division of an army. The second upa parva, Parvasamgraha; Chapter 2 of Adi Parva tells us more details. Shlokas 1.2.19–21 tell us one akshauhini comprised 21,870 chariots, 21,870 elephants, 1,09,350 foot soldiers, and 65,610 horses. Eleven such akshauninis fought on the Kaurava side and seven on the Paandava side in the Kurukshetra battle.
2. In 11.26.9 Yudhishthira answers Dhritaraashtra's question on the fatality count in the Kurukshetra war. The number of fatalities is one billion, twenty thousand and sixty-six crore.
3. The sages' curse is pronounced in 16.2.8 and is described in the ninety-third upa parva, Musala; Chapter 2 of Musala Parva.
4. Descendants of Yadu were called Yaadavas. We will read about Yadu in the upakhyaana on Yayaati.
5. A famous king in the Yadu dynasty. His descendants were also called Vrishnis.
6. Also, a famous king in the Yadu dynasty. His descendants were called Andhakas.
7. This is described in Vishnu Parva; Chapter 86 of Harivamsha.
8. [16.9.31] Vyaasa to Arjuna.
9. Uttanka's story is recounted in a later upakhyaana.
10. [1.51.11] Janamejaya to the officiating priests at the *sarpa-satra*.
11. This is described in the third upa parva, Paushya; Chapter 3 of Adi Parva.
12. The mongoose's story is recounted in the Nakula upakhyaana.
13. Aasteeka was the son of Jaratkaaru the ascetic and Jaratkaaru the serpent. Jaratkaaru was the daughter of Sage Kashyapa and Kadru. Kadru had cursed her serpent children to be destroyed in the fires of a sacrifice. One of her sons was Takshaka. This is described in the fifth upa parva, Aasteeka; Chapter 13 of Adi Parva.

14. Pareekshit was Arjuna's grandson and Abhimanyu's son. Born after the war had ended, he was killed by Takshaka because of Sage Shringi's curse.
15. Vaishampaayana was a disciple of Sage Ved Vyaasa, and one of five people to whom Vyaasa taught the Mahabharata after composing it—his son Shuka, and his four disciples, Sumantu, Jaimini, Paila, and Vaishampaayana [1.57.74]. It was Vaishampaayana who recited the Mahabharata at King Janamejaya's snake sacrifice.
16. He was called Krishna because he was dark in colour; Dvaipaayana because he was born on an island; and Ved Vyaasa was a title given to him because he divided the Vedas.
17. Vaishampayaana gives this summary in the sixth upa parva, Adi-vamshavatarana; Chapter 55 of Adi Parva.
18. [1.56.33] Vaishampaayana to Janamejaya, and again in 18.5.38.
19. A very famous rishi who finds mention in the Rig Veda. He was born in Sage Kashyapa's lineage, and therefore, sometimes also referred to as Kaashyapa.
20. [1.65.11] Description of Shakuntala.
21. The story of Vishwaamitra and Vasishtha is recounted in the Vasishtha upakhyaana.
22. A celestial nymph; she and other apsaraas were born during the churning of the ocean.
23. Known as Koushiki.
24. Another name for Kaama, the god of love.
25. Another name for Vaayu, the wind god.
26. This incident is described in the Valmiki Ramayana; Chapter 23 of Baala Kaanda.
27. Vultures or kites.
28. The eight forms of marriage listed are—*brahma*, *daiva*, *arsha*, *prajapatya*, *asura*, *gandharva*, *raakshasa*, and *paishacha*.
29. [1.67.18] Dushyanta's promise to Shakuntala.
30. Subhadra's abduction by Arjuna is described in the seventeenth upa parva, Subhadra-harana; Chapter 212 of Adi Parva. Krishna's defence of Arjuna is described in the eighteenth upa parva, Harana-harika; Chapter 213 of Adi Parva.
31. So named because he could subdue (*damana*) everyone (*sarva*).
32. [1.69.29] Shakuntala to Dushyanta.
33. [1.68.19] Dushyanta's reply to Shakuntala.
34. One meaning of the word *jaya* is wife. Other meanings include glory, victory, to conquer.
35. A daughter is, by extension, called a *putri*. Both sons and daughters save their ancestors from the hell named *put*.
36. [1.68.40] Shakuntala to Dushyanta.
37. [1.68.46] Shakuntala to Dushyanta.
38. The six apsaraas mentioned are Urvashi, Purvachitti, Sahajanya, Menaka, Vishvachi and Ghritachi.
39. [1.68.51] Shakuntala to Dushyanta.
40. [1.69.2–3] Shakuntala to Dushyanta.
41. [1.69.6] Shakuntala telling Dushyanta a popular saying.
42. [1.69.9–10] Shakuntala to Dushyanta.
43. The curse is pronounced in 16.2.8. The episode is described in the ninety-third upa parva, Musala; Chapter 2 of Musala Parva.

2. Yayaati

1. This lineage is described in the seventh upa parva, Sambhava; Chapter 7 of Adi Parva.
2. Daakshaayani is also sometimes used to refer to any of Daksha's daughters. In this case, it refers to the one who married Kashyapa.
3. Vivasvat is considered one of the Adityas.
4. Surya. Sometimes Vivasvat and Maartanda are both used to refer to the sun god.
5. Sometimes also called Vaivasvata Manu since he was descended from Vivasvata.
6. Ikshvaaku was one of Vaivasvata Manu's sons. His descendants were called as belonging to the Solar dynasty (Suryavansh) because Manu was Vivasvaan's (Sun god) son. Some illustrious descendants in this lineage were Maandhaata (his story is recounted in the Maandhaata upakhyaana), Ambareesha, Kaakutstha, Harishchandra, Saagara, Bhagirath (his story is recounted in the Agastya upakhyaana), Raghu, Dasharatha, and Raama (his story is recounted in the Raama upakhyaana).
7. Ila was born a female, and later turned into a man.
8. The son of Sage Angirasa
9. The son of Kavi, who was one of the Prajapatis. Shukra was also known as Kaavya and Ushanaas.
10. [1.71.12] The Gods speaking to Kacha. The Sanskrit line reads thus—रक्षते दानवांस्तत्र न स रक्षत्यदानवान् ।
11. [1.71.14] The Gods speaking to Kacha.
12. [1.71.44] Shukra to Devayaani.
13. [1.71.47] Shukra to Kacha.
14. [1.72.16] Devayaani to Kacha.
15. Kacha was a sage's son.
16. Some of the names used for Indra here are Shatakratu, Purandara, and Maghavan.
17. One of the sons of Daanu and Sage Kashyapa.
18. [1.73.11] Sharmishtha to Devayaani.
19. This is described in the Shakuntala upakhyaana.
20. Pareekshit, in a fit of anger, garlanded Sage Shamika with a dead snake, and was cursed by the sage's son, Shringi. This is described in the fifth upa parva, Aasteeka; Chapter 38 of Adi Parva.
21. This is described in the Bhangaashwana upakhyaana.
22. This is described in the Ambaa upakhyaana.
23. Not to be confused with Pareekshit, who was the son of Abhimanyu and Uttaraa, and the father of Janamejaya.
24. This is described in the Manduka upakhyaana.
25. Shaantanu's encounter with Satyavati is described in the seventh upa parva, Sambhava; Chapter 94 of Adi Parva.
26. This is described in the seventh upa parva, Sambhava; Chapter 109 of Adi Parva.
27. This is described in the Tapati upakhyaana.
28. [1.73.29] Shukra to Devayaani.
29. Another name for Shukracharya.
30. [1.74.2] Shukra to Devayaani.
31. [1.74.4] Shukra to Devayaani.
32. [1.74.7] Shukra to Devayaani.

33. [1.74.11] Devayaani to Shukra.
34. This is described in the forty-fifth upa parva, Vairata; part of the Virata Parva. The events there take place in the thirteenth year of exile of the Paandavas.
35. This is described in the Nala-Damayanti upakhyaana.
36. [1.76.24] Yayaati telling Devayaani why he would not marry her without obtaining her father's approval first.
37. [1.77.14] Yayaati to Sharmishtha.
38. [1.77.16] Sharmishtha to Yayaati.
39. [1.77.19] Sharmishtha to Yayaati.
40. [1.78.20] Sharmishtha to Devayaani.
41. Shukra.
42. [1.79.5–6] Yadu to Yayaati.
43. [13.7.24] Bheeshma to Yudhishthira, in the Anushaasana Parva. जीर्यन्ति जीर्यतः केशा दन्ता जीर्यन्ति जीर्यतः चक्षुःश्रोत्रे च जीर्येते तृष्णैका तु न जीर्यते
44. [1.80.17] Yayaati to the people.

3. Mahaabheesha

1. Janamejaya's sons were Shataneeka and Shanku. This is not to be confused with another Paurava named Shataneeka, who was Draupadi and Nakula's son. Janamejaya's son, Shataneeka, had a son named Ashvamedhadatta. This listing of Janamejaya's sons and grandsons was more for the benefit of those hearing the account. Janamejaya would have obviously known this.
2. Shaantanu's elder brother was called Devapi, but he retired to the forest and therefore Shaantanu became king. This is described in the fourth sarga of Vishnu Purana.
3. This is described in the seventh upa parva, Sambhava; Chapter 89 of Adi Parva.
4. Samvarana and Tapati's story is recounted in the Tapati upakhyaana.
5. Not to be confused with Janamejaya, the son of Pareekshit and the grandson of Abhimanyu.
6. Not to be confused with Pareekshit, son of Abhimanyu and the grandson of Arjuna.
7. Not to be confused with Dhritaraashtra, Duryodhana's father.
8. Not to be confused with Paandu, who was Kunti and Maadri's husband, and the father of Yudhishthira and the other Paandavas.
9. The eight vasus were the sons of Manu. Their names were Dhara, Dhruva, Soma, Aha, Anila, Anala, Pratyusha and Prabhasa. This is listed in the fourth upa parva, Sambhava; Chapter 60 of Adi Parva.
10. Dhara and Dyou have almost the same meaning and can be used interchangeably. The list of eight vasus varies slightly from text to text.

4. Animaandavya

1. Because King Ajameedha was one of Yudhishthira's ancestors.
2. Son of Prithaa (Kunti). (Chapter 8 of Sabha Parva). Being the sons of Prithaa, all the Paandavas were called Paartha. In the ninth upa parva, Hidimba-vadha; Chapter 143 of Adi Parva, Arjuna himself refers to Bheema as Paartha.

3. One without enemies (Chapter 183 of Adi Parva).
4. The son of Dharma. Dharma in this case referred to Yama.
5. A maun-vrat.
6. The tip of the stake was called 'ani'; since the tip still stayed embedded in Maandavya, he came to be called Animaandavya.
7. This is described in the ninetieth upa parva, Ashrama-vaasika; Chapter 33 of Ashram-vaasika Parva. 15.33.26 tells us that Vidura used yoga to merge with Yudhishthira, leaving behind his mortal self, which the heavens told Yudhishthira not to cremate.

5. Vyushitashva

1. The events leading to the Vyushitashva upakhyaana are described in Chapters 109–111 of Adi Parva.
2. [1.109.13] Paandu to Kimdama.
3. [1.109.17] Paandu to Kimdama.
4. [1.109.28] Sage Kimdana's curse.
5. Paandu's mother, Ambalika, was married to Vichitravirya, who was Satyavati's son.
6. Chapter 96 of Adi Parva describes how Vichitravirya died.
7. [1.110.10] Paandu speaking.
8. [1.111.12–15] Paandu speaking with ascetics at Shatashringa.
9. [1.111.27–29] Paandu speaking.
10. The story of Ashmaka's birth is recounted later, in Vasishtha's upakhyaana.
11. Karna's birth is described in the seventh upa parva, Sambhava; Chapter 104 of Adi Parva, and again, in more detail, in the forty-third upa parva, Kundala-harana; Chapters 290 and 291 of Aranyaka Parva.

6. Tapati

1. Paandu's and Maadri's deaths are recounted in the seventh upa parva, Sambhava; Chapter 116 of Adi Parva.
2. Ambaalika is called Kaushalya here, since she had been the princess of Kashi.
3. [1.119.6] Vyaasa to Satyavati.
4. [1.119.8] Vyaasa to Satyavati.
5. This is recounted in the seventh upa parva, Sambhava; Chapter 119 of Adi Parva.
6. Karna's entry into the tournament is described in the eighth upa parva, Jatugriha-daha; Chapter 125 of Adi Parva.
7. This incident is described in the eighth upa parva, Jatugriha-daha; Chapter 126 of Adi Parva.
8. [1.130.5] Dhritaraashtra to Duryodhana.
9. Duryodhana's confabulations with Purochana are described in the eighth upa parva, Jatugriha-daha; Chapter 132 of Adi Parva.
10. Vidura's counsel to Yudhishthira is described in the eighth upa parva, Jatugriha-daha; Chapter 133 of Adi Parva.
11. [1.130.9] Duryodhana to Dhritaraashtra.
12. This is recounted in the ninth upa-parva, Hidimba-vadha.
13. This is recounted in the tenth upa parva, Baka-vadha Parva.

14. [1.158.15] Arjuna responding to Chitraratha.
15. [1.159.10]
16. [1.159.12] Tapati is another name for the sun god.
17. Saavitri is also the personification of the Saavitri mantra. Princess Saavitri was named for this goddess. Her story is recounted in the Saavitri upakhyaana.
18. The lineage and Riksha are mentioned in the Mahabheesha upakhyaana.
19. Another name for the sun god.
20. The word used for the sun god here is Anshuman.
21. The word used for the sun god here is Vibhavasu.
22. The word used for the sun god here is Gopati.

7. Vasishtha

1. Vishwamitra and his sons.
2. Nandini was a kamadhenu—a cow that had the power to grant its owner whatever it wished.
3. [1.165.38] The state of Vishwaamitra's army.
4. A king in the Ikshvaaku lineage. He was the son of Sudaasa and was also known as Mitrasaha and Saudaasa.
5. [1.166.35] Kalmaashapaada to Shakti.
6. Vasishtha gave the river the name, Vipaasha.
7. Also known as modern day Sutlej.
8. Madayanti. She is the same queen who handed over her earrings to Sage Uttanka, who also encountered Kalmaashpaada in the forest. This is recounted in the Uttanka upakhyaana. Madayanti's example is also recounted by Paandu in the Vyushitashva upakhyaana.
9. Also called Mitrasaha.
10. The brahmana's wife.
11. This is recounted in the Vyushitashva upakhyaana.

8. Aurva

1. So named after the founder of the lineage, King Haihaya.
2. Descendants of Sage Bhrigu.
3. Descended from the Bhrigu lineage, the child was thus a Bhaargava.
4. Literally, the limbs of the Vedas. These six disciplines are Chanda (prosody), Jyotisha (astronomy), Kalpa (rituals), Nirukta (etymology), Shikshaa (phonetics), and Vyaakrana (grammar).
5. [1.171.3] Aurva to his ancestors.
6. Sacrifice.
7. [1.171.10–11]

9. Panchendra

1. Dhaumya was the younger brother of Devala. Devala was a very learned sage and present at the sarpa satra of Janamejaya (this is mentioned in fifth upa parva, Aasteeka; Chapter 48 of Adi Parva). Devala also recited the Mahabhaarata to the gods (this is mentioned in the very first chapter of the text).

2. This is recounted in the twelfth upa parva, Draupadi-swayamvara; Chapter 174 of Adi Parva.
3. South of the Bhagirathi is where Drupada had moved his capital after his defeat at the hands of the Paandavas, after which Drona had taken the northern half of the kingdom. This is recounted in the eighth upa parva, Jatugriha-daha; Chapter 128 of Adi Parva.
4. Kaampilya was the capital of Drupada's new kingdom, while Drona's capital was Ahichhatra.
5. Drupada is called Yagnasena here, since he was the one who had organized the yagna (sacrifice) from which Draupadi and Dhrishtadyumna had been born; therefore Draupadi was also called Yaagnaseni, one who had emerged from the yagna.
6. Amba's story, reborn as Shikhandi, is recounted in the sixtieth upa parva, Ambopakhyaana. Her story here is recounted in the Amba upakhyaana.
7. [1.178.12] State of the Paandavas on seeing Draupadi.
8. Described in Chapter 178 of Adi Parva. Among the gods were Yama, Kubera, and the Ashwin twins.
9. Dhrishtadyumna lists all the kings who had come in Chapter 177 of Adi Parva.
10. This is described in Chapter 177 of Adi Parva.
11. [1.182.11] The state of the Paandavas as they looked at Draupadi.
12. That Karna also took part, and failed, in the swayamvara is described in Chapter 179 of Adi Parva. Shloka 1.179.4 specifically names Karna and Shalya as two accomplished archers who tried and failed.
13. [1.178.3] The assembled kings at Draupadi's swayamvara.
14. [1.188.11] Dhrishtadyumna to Vyaasa.
15. [1.192.3]
16. [1.192.4]
17. [1.181.21] Karna withdraws from fighting Arjuna.
18. [1.182.11] The state of the Paandavas on seeing Draupadi.
19. [1.190.2] Drupada to Vyaasa.
20. Born in the Gautama lineage, she was also called Gautami.
21. The name used for Shiva is Shankara.
22. [1.189.44]
23. [1.189.46]
24. [1.190.4] Drupada to Vyaasa.

10. Sunda and Upasunda

1. [1.192.17]
2. [1.192.22] Dhritaraashtra to Vidura.
3. [1.194.7] Karna's reply to Duryodhana on his suggestion of sowing dissension between the Paandavas and Draupadi. Draupadi here is called Krishnaa.
4. [1.195.4] Bheeshma's advice to Dhritaraashtra.
5. [1.196.2] Drona's concurrence with Bheeshma.
6. Archaeological excavations have identified Khaandavprastha as Purana Qila in New Delhi.
7. The sons of Diti were called daityas.
8. This is mentioned in the seventh upa parva, Sambhava; Chapter 59 of Adi Parva.

9. This is recounted in the Raama upakhyaana.
10. [1.202.22–23]
11. Even the smallest part (tila) of her being was perfect (uttama).
12. [1.204.16–17] Sunda and Upasunda fighting with each other over Tilottama.

11. Shaarangakas

1. This is recounted in the sixteenth upa parva, Arjuna-vanvaasa; Chapter 205 of Adi Parva.
2. This is recounted in the sixteenth upa parva, Arjuna-vanvaasa; Chapter 206 of Adi Parva.
3. This is recounted in the sixteenth upa parva, Arjuna-vanvaasa; Chapter 207 of Adi Parva. The kingdom mentioned in that upakhyaana is Manipur.
4. This is recounted in the Nakula upakhyaana.
5. This is recounted in Chapters 208–209 of Adi Parva.
6. This is recounted in the seventeenth upa parva, Subhadra-harana.
7. [1.213.15] Draupadi to Arjuna.
8. This is described in the seventy-third upa parva, Karna-vadha; Chapter 66 of Karna Parva.
9. Maaya was a daanava and the architect of the asuras and devas.
10. This is recounted in the Vyushitasvha upakhyaana.
11. [1.220.11] The gods to Mandapaala.
12. Not to be confused with Drona, son of Sage Bharadwaaja and teacher to the Kuru princes.
13. [1.133.20] Vidura to Yudhishthira. This exchange takes place in the eighth upa parva, Jatugriha-daha; Chapter 133 of Adi Parva.
14. [1.222.4] Shaarangakas to their mother, Jarita.
15. The word used is Jatadeva, another name for Agni.
16. [1.224.15] Mandapaala to Lapita.
17. [2.45.38] Shakuni to Dhritaraashtra. This exchange takes place in the twenty-seventh upa parva, Dyuta, in Chapter 45 of Sabha Parva.
18. [2.46.18–19] Duryodhana to Shakuni.

12. Shaalva-vadha

1. [2.3.7]
2. [2.3.6]
3. [2.3.34]
4. This discourse, sometimes also known as Naarada Neeti, is recounted in the twentieth upa parva, Sabha; Chapter 5 of Sabha Parva.
5. [2.12.35] Yudhishthira to Krishna.
6. [2.19.49] Krishna to Jarasandha.
7. This is recounted in the seventy-sixth upa parva, Teertha-yatra; Chapter 31 of Shalya Parva.
8. This is recounted in the twenty-sixth upa parva, Shishupaala-vadha; in Sabha Parva.
9. This is recounted in the initial chapters of the twenty-seventh upa parva, Dyuta; in Sabha Parva.
10. [2.66.8] Duryodhana repeating Brihaspati's words to Dhritaraashtra.
11. [2.53.25]

12. [2.54.3]
13. [2.54.7]
14. [2.54.11]
15. [2.54.15]
16. [2.54.18]
17. [2.54.21]
18. [2.54.23]
19. Arjuna is called Gandeevadhanva; the one with the Gandeeva as a bow.
20. [2.54.27]
21. [2.54.29]
22. [2.58.6]
23. [2.58.8]
24. [2.58.10]
25. [2.58.28]
26. [2.58.43]
27. [2.61.35–36] Karna to the Kuru assembly.
28. The state of the Paandavas and their anger is described in the first chapter (this is Chapter 66 of Sabha Parva) of the twenty-eighth upa parva, Anudyuta.
29. [3.2.60] Sage Shaunaka to Yudhishthira.
30. [2.71.3–6] Vidura describing to Dhritaraashtra the Paandavas and Draupadi as they left Hastinapura.
31. [2.73.19–20] Vidura repeating Draupadi's words, as she departed, to Dhritaraashtra.
32. A sage descended from Atri.
33. Kirmira's death at the hands of Bheema is recounted in the thirtieth upa parva, Kirmira-vadha.
34. [3.9.11] Vyaasa warning Dhritaraashtra against letting his sons go to the forest to kill the Paandavas.
35. [3.13.61] Draupadi to Krishna.
36. Shaalva was the king of Marttikavata.
37. Soubha was a city that could fly in the skies.
38. Krishna and Rukmini's son.
39. Krishna and Jambavati's son.
40. Krishna and Rukmini's son.
41. Makara is one of the names of Shiva. It is also the name of a formation. In this case, it refers to a mythical creature that most resembles a crocodile. Pradyumna was sometimes also referred to as Makaradhwaja—one whose banner was the makara.
42. Pradyumna's charioteer. He was the son of Krishna's charioteer, Daruka.
43. Ugrasena.
44. He blew his conch, Panchajanya.
45. Shaalva's kingdom.
46. Fired from his bow, Shaarnga.
47. [3.23.23] Daruka to Krishna.

13. Nala Damayanti

1. [3.31.7] Draupadi to Yudhishthira. The Sanskrit shloka reads: राजानं धर्मगोप्तारं धर्मो रक्षति रक्षितः इति मे श्रुतमार्याणां त्वां तु मन्ये न रक्षति
2. [3.29.6] Draupadi recounting Prahlada's words to Bali.

3. [3.30.37] Yudhishthira to Draupadi, recounting Kashyapa's hymn.
4. This is recounted in the seventy-sixth upa parva, Teertha-yaatra; Chapter 30 of Shalya Parva.
5. [9.30.64] Yudhishthira to Duryodhana.
6. [2.5.38] Naarada to Yudhishthira.
7. [3.37.14] Yudhishthira to Bheema.
8. [6.41.36–37] Bheeshma to Yudhishthira, on the eve of the start of the battle at Kurukshetra.
9. [3.38.4] Yudhishthira to Arjuna.
10. This is described in the Shaarangakas upakhyaana.
11. [3.49.34] Yudhishthira lamenting.
12. Also called Punyashloka sometimes.
13. Nishadhas were forest dwellers. Their origin is described more fully in the first part of Vishnu Purana. In the Bibek Debroy translation, this is in Chapter 13.
14. Not to be confused with Bheema, son of Kunti.
15. [3.50.28] Swan telling Damayanti about Nala.
16. Parvata was a devarshi and son of Narada's sister. There is more about the two in the Naarada-Parvata upakhyaana.
17. [3.52.12] Nala sees Damayanti.
18. [3.53.4] Damayanti to Nala.
19. The personifications of the two yugas—*Dwaapara* and *Kali*. *Dwaapara yuga* is when dharma stands on two legs, while in *Kali yuga* it stands on only one leg. By contrast, dharma stands on all four legs in *Krita yuga*, and on three legs in *Treta yuga*.
20. [3.55.9] Gods telling Kali about Nala.
21. Nala's charioteer.
22. Nala and Damayanti had two children, twins.
23. He was the king of Ayodhya at the time.
24. [3.58.3] Pushkara to Nala.
25. [3.58.15] Birds to Nala.
26. Ancient path, like the Uttarapath, that went in a north-south direction.
27. [3.58.27] Damayanti to Nala.
28. [3.59.22–23] Nala's state when leaving Damayanti.
29. [3.60.7–8] Damayanti lamenting after Nala abandons her.
30. The word used is ajagara (अजगर).
31. [3.60.36] '*Damayanti cursed in her anger, since the time of using words had passed.*'
32. Ashoka means without grief, and the tree is said to remove the sorrow of anyone who looks at it.
33. This is recounted in Chapter 58 of the third kaanda of Valmiki Ramayana, Sundara.
34. A person named Shuchi.
35. [3.61.118] Damayanti to the caravan's travellers.
36. [3.62.23] The mother of King Subahu to Damayanti.
37. A descendant of the Ikshvaaku lineage.
38. Varshneya was the charioteer who Damayanti had asked to take her twins—Indrasenaa and Indrasena—to their grandfather, king Bheema, and who had then gone to King Rituparna for employment.
39. [3.64.10] Nala pining for Damayanti.
40. The king's mother and Damayanti's mother were both daughters of Sudamna, king of Dasharna.

41. Mother's sister is often called a mausi or maasi, literally meaning 'like a mother'.
42. The name used is Bhangasvari, another name for Rituparna.
43. Sudeva was the same brahmana who had been sent out by King Bheema to search out his daughter, Damayanti, and who had identified her in the king of Chedi's palace.
44. [3.68.21] Damayanti's message that Sudeva was to deliver to Rituparna at Ayodhya.
45. Varshneya had been Nala's charioteer when he was king.
46. [3.69.6] Nala to himself.
47. Shaalihotra was a sage who wrote principally on the care of horses and is considered the founder of veterinary sciences.
48. Indra's charioteer.
49. A Vibhītaka tree refers to *Terminalia bellirica*, a deciduous tree that can grow to a hundred feet or more in height.
50. [3.71.10] Damayanti to herself.
51. Damayanti had asked her mother to send Sudeva to Ayodhya without letting her father, King Bheema, know about it.
52. Rituparna is referred to as the lord of Koushala.
53. [3.74.8] Damayanti to Nala.
54. [3.75.1] Damayanti to Nala.
55. Varshneya was Nala's charioteer and he stayed back with Nala.
56. [3.77.9] Nala to Pushkara.
57. [1.61.80] Duryodhana was born from a part of Kali.
58. [3.78.14] Brihadashva to Yudhishthira.
59. This is described in the sixty-fifth upa parva, Drona-abhisheka; Chapter 11 of Drona Parva. The reason Duryodhana didn't want Drona to capture and then kill Yudhishthira was because he feared the surviving Paandava brothers would wreak vengeance on him and kill him. If, on the other hand, Yudhishthira lost yet another gambling match, with the same stakes, the other brothers would have no option to follow Yudhishthira into exile.
60. [7.62.2] Sanjaya to Dhritaraashtra.
61. [8.52.13] Arjuna to Krishna.

14. Agastya

1. This is described in the thirty-third upa parva, Teertha-yaatra; Chapters 80–83 of Aranyaka Parva.
2. [3.92.8] Lomasha's reply to Yudhishthira's question why he was facing great tribulations. The asuras had followed neither dharma nor done pilgrimages to sacred sites.
3. In the fortieth upa parva, Mriga svapna bhaya; Chapter 44 of Aranyaka parva, deer appeared in Yudhishthira's dream and lamented that overhunting had drastically thinned their herd. Moved by their plight, the Paandavas left Dvaitavana and moved to the Kaamyaka forest.
4. Not to be confused with the daanava, Durjaya, or with one of the hundred sons of Dhritaraashtra. Durjaya is a truncation of Durjayamanimatinagara, believed to be modern day Ellora caves.
5. Gone to Yama's abode.

6. An offspring saves ancestors from the hell known as put. Hence a son is called put-ra, a daughter put=ri.
7. This is described in the Vyushitashva upakhyaana.
8. [1.111.27–29] Paandu mentions these four debts in the Vyushitashva upakhyaana. The debt to ancestors was to be repaid by having offspring.
9. [3.95.3] Lopamudra's father's state of mind on hearing Agastya's proposal.
10. Agastya and Vasishtha both were born in a pot.
11. The text says that the sound of wind emanated from Agastya [3.97.7]; the implication being that he broke wind!
12. Vijaya and Suvaja were the two horses.
13. He was sometimes also called Idhmavaha.
14. Called Paramesthi here.
15. Also called Tvashtra (त्वष्ट्र)
16. This story is recounted in the Sunda-Upasunda upakhyaana.
17. Indra's story is recounted in greater detail in the Victory of Indra upakhyaana.
18. [3.99.20] Danavas discussing among themselves.
19. The names for Vishnu used are Vaikuntha Narayan, Madhusoodana, along with references to his Varaaha, Narasimha, and Vaamana avatars.
20. [3.101.4] Gods to Vishnu.
21. Agastya was the son of Mitra and Varuna and also called Mitravaruni and Kumbhayoni.
22. This is recounted in The Victory of Indra upakhyaana.
23. The ocean.
24. [3.104.2] Brahma to the gods.
25. One wife was from Vidarbha, the other from Shibi.
26. Here, Shiva is referred to by several different names—Tryaksha (the one with three eyes), Tripura-mardana (the destroyer of Tripura), Shankara, Bhava, Ishaana, Shulapani, Pinaki, Tryambaka, Shiva, Ugresha, the one with many forms, and as Uma's husband.
27. The word used is Hara, another name for Shiva.
28. The word used is muhurata.
29. Neelkantha Maheshwara is the name used for Shiva.
30. Shankara Mahaadeva, Sharva, Hara, and Ishaana are the names used for Shiva here.

15. Rishyashringa

1. Kashyapa was also known as Vibhaandaka.
2. So named because he was born with a horn on his head.
3. This is recounted in the sixth upa parva, Adi-Vamshavatarana; Chapter 57 of Adi Parva.
4. Indra is called Sahasraaksha here—the one with a thousand eyes.
5. The names used for Indra are Sahasraaksha (the one with thousand eyes) and Parjanya (rain, and also Indra's name as the god of rain).
6. [3.112.8] Rishyashringa describing the courtesan's daughter to his father, Kashyapa Vibhaandaka.

16. Kaartavirya, Jamadagni, Raama

1. A sage who had been witness to all of Parashurama's deeds. We will read more about Akritvrana in the Ambaa upakhyaana.
2. Parashuraama is called Raama.
3. Parashuraama was the son of Sage Jamadagni.
4. Not to be confused with Satyavati, the mother of Krishna Dvaipaayana and the wife of King Shaantanu.
5. The story of this mix-up is recounted slightly differently in the Raama upakhyaana.
6. This is described in the seventh upa parva, Sambhava; Chapter 121 of Adi Parva.
7. Raama, while not explicitly vanquished by Bheeshma, still admitted defeat in that encounter. This is recounted in the Ambaa upakhyaana.
8. The Brahmaanda Purana tells us that Sage Dattraatreya had granted Kaartavirya Arjuna the boon of a thousand arms. It was Sage Aapava (not to be confused with Sage Vasishtha, who was also called Aapava) who cursed him that a brahmana would slice off the arrogant king's thousand arms. This is recounted in the Raja-dharma upa parva; Chapter 49 of Shanti Parva.

17. Sukanya

1. The time they spent in Dvaitavana resulted in overhunting and a thinning of the deer in the forest. This is recounted in the fortieth upa parva, Mriga svapna bhaya; Chapter 44 of Aranyaka parva.
2. Balaraama is referred here as Vanamaali Raama.
3. [3.119.5] Balaraama to Krishna, referring to Yudhishthira's plight. Balaraama uses the name Partha to refer to Yudhishthira.
4. [3.119.8] Balaraama to Yudhishthira.
5. [3.31.7] Draupadi to Yudhishthira. धर्मो रक्षति रक्षितः
6. Saatyaki was a Yaadava warrior and a friend of Krishna. He was descended from Kaartavirya Arjuna. He was also a descendant of Vrishni, and thus also known as a Vrishni. He was Satyaka's son and Shini's grandson. He was also known as Yuyudhaana. He was one of the few warriors from the Paandava side that survived the Kurukshetra war.
7. Dhritaraashtra's sons were also called Dhaartaraashtras.
8. Sharyaati was a king, the seventh son of Manu Vaivasvata, and the father of Sukanya.
9. A descendant of Bhrigu was called Bhaargava.
10. The Devi Bhaagavatam has more details. When the three emerged from the lake, they looked identical. Sukanya prayed to the Devi, who appeared before Sukanya and told her how to identify the real Chyavana.
11. The nectar of immortality that arose at the churning of the ocean.
12. The word used is yajna.
13. Indra's thunderbolt, made from the bones of sage Dadhichi. This is described in Agastya upakhyana.
14. Indra is referred to as Shakra and Purandara.

18. Maandhaataa

1. Saudyumni is another name for Yuvanaashva.
2. [3.126.28] Derived from *mam dhata*, '*the nurse will be me*,' as explained in footnote #556 of Vol. 3 of Bibek Debroy's translation.

19. Jantu

1. In popular perception it is believed that Dhritaraashtra had a hundred sons. However, he was also the father of one daughter, Duhshala, who was married to Jayadratha. Dhritaraashtra was also the father of another son named Yuyutsu through a maid. He was thus the father of a hundred and two children.
2. [3.127.12] King Somaka to his priests and advisers.
3. Naraka.
4. Yama, the god of death
5. [3.128.13] Yama to Somaka.

20. Shibi

1. The seventh of Brahma's spiritual sons.
2. This is also taken as a reference to the gradual drying up of the Saraswati River and the belief that it started to flow underground. This reference is also used to arrive at an approximate period for when the Mahabharata was composed and when the events described may have occurred. This has led to an estimate that the events in the Mahabharata may be at least 3500 years old.
3. [3.130.10]
4. [3.130.2] Lomasha repeating Daksha's words about Kurukshetra.
5. He was the son of Ushinara and Maadhavi, and sometimes also called Ushinara.
6. A hawk is called shyena, and a dove a kapota in Sanskrit. This upakhyaana is also called Shyena-Kapotiya.
7. [3.131.10] Indra, in the form of a hawk, to Shibi. धर्मं यो बाधते धर्मो न स धर्मः कुधर्म तत्
8. [3.131.19] Hawk to Shibi.

21. Ashtavakra

1. Ashtavakra means eight *(ashta)* and deformed *(vakra)*. He was born deformed in eight places, and thus his name.
2. The story of Dhruva is recounted in the eleventh chapter of the first part of Vishnu Purana.
3. This is recounted in the Vasishtha upakhyaana.
4. [3.133.1] Ashtavakra to King Janaka.
5. [3.133.4] Ashtavakra to the doorkeeper.
6. The implication being that someone who was learned, knew the Vedas, was knowledgeable, and in control of their senses was like the aged, and therefore an adult.

7. [3.133.12] Ashtavakra to the doorkeeper.
8. This is recounted in the Ambaa upakhyaana.
9. [3.133.20] Ashtavakra to Janaka.
10. [3.134.4] Bandi to Ashtavakra.
11. [3.134.34] Kahoda to Janaka.

22. Yavakreeta

1. [3.136.13]. Sages mourning Medhaavi's death.
2. A krityaa—a sorceress.
3. Daksha was Brahma's son, Sati's father, and Shiva's father-in-law.
4. This episode is described in various Puranas.
5. This is described in Chapter 155 of Adi Parva, in the Chaitraratha upa parva.
6. Presumably because Yavakreeta was unclean.
7. The word used in 3.138.6 is मन्दचेतन, which means someone of slow intelligence.
8. [3.138.16] Bharadwaaja grieving over his son, Yavakreeta.

23. Vainya

1. This is recounted in the thirty-third upa parva, Tirtha-yatra; Chapters 146–150 of Aranyaka Parva.
2. [3.149.9] Hanuman to Bheema.
3. Recounted in the thirty-fourth upa parva, Jatasura Vadha; Chapter 154 of Aranyaka Parva.
4. Recounted in the thirty-fifth upa parva, Yaksha-yuddha; part of Aranyaka Parva.
5. Recounted in the thirty-fifth upa parva, Yaksha-yuddha; Chapter 157 of Aranyaka Parva.
6. Arjuna returns to earth in Chapter 162 of the Aranyaka Parva.
7. [3.159.1] Kubera (Vaishraavana) to Yudhishthira.
8. [3.172.18] Naarada to Arjuna.
9. This is recounted in the thirty-sixth upa parva, Ajagara Parva, part of the Aranyaka Parva. Nahusha's story is recounted in The Victory of Indra upakhyaana.
10. This is recounted in the Yaksha Prashna upakhyaana.
11. [3.177.18] Nahusha to Yudhishthira.
12. [3.177.20] Yudhishthira to Nahusha.
13. This marks the beginning of the thirty-seventh upa parva, Maarkandeya Samasya, part of Aranyaka Parva.
14. [3.181.7–8] Yudhishthira to Maarkandeya.
15. The Vainya upakhyaana begins here, with the start of Chapter 183 of Aranyaka Parva.
16. Vainya was another name for King Prithu. Since he was the son of King Venu, he was also called Vainya.
17. Called an aśvamedha yagna.
18. One of Brahma's spiritual sons. Also, one of the six maharshis, the other five being Angiras, Kratu, Marichi, Pulaha, and Pulastya.
19. Sanatakumara was one of the four sages known as Sanakaadis; the mental sons of Brahma. There were also the same sages who had cursed the gatekeepers of Vaikuntha, Jaya and Vijaya, to be reborn thrice on earth.

24. Matsya

1. This is recounted in the thirty-seventh upa parva, Maarkandeya Samasya; Chapter 184 of Aranyaka Parva.
2. Sun god.
3. Jujube tree.
4. [3.185.8] दुर्बलं बलवन्तो हि मत्स्यं मत्स्या विशेषतः
5. The list of seven sages is different for each cycle of creation (Manvantara).
6. In some accounts, this fish is revealed to be the Matsya avatara of Vishnu.

25. Manduka

1. [3.186.11] Yudhishtira to Maarkandeya.
2. The word used is sandhya.
3. The Bhagavata Purana, Skandha 1, Chapter 17, tells us that these four legs represented austerities, compassion, truth, and purity.
4. [3.188.10–12] The analogy of yugas and the decay of dharma with the legs of a bull is described in these shlokas.
5. [3.186.47] Maarkandeya to Yudhishthira.
6. [3.188.70] Maarkandeya to Yudhishthira.
7. The Manduka upakhyaana begins here, with the start of Chapter 190 of the Aranyaka Parva.
8. Not to be confused with Pareekshit, who was the son of Abhimanyu and Uttaraa, and the father of Janamejaya.
9. It is not clear whether the king of frogs too brought a dead frog as tribute before being allowed to meet the king. Presumably this rule did not apply to brahmanas.
10. A sage who is said to have composed parts of the Rig Veda.
11. [3.190.62] Vaamadeva to King Shala.
12. The word used is Yatudhana. Yatudhanas were a family of raakshasas descended from Kashyapa and Surasaa.

26. Indradyumna

1. नाडीजङ्घो
2. [3.191.21] Heavenly voice about King Indradyumna.

27. Dhundhumaara

1. Yuvanaashva's story has been recounted in the Maandhaata upakhyaana.
2. The story of Madhu and Kaitabha, two asuras born from the earwax of Narayana, is recounted in the Maarkandeya Purana.
3. There is more about Uttanka in the Uttanka upakhyaana.
4. Uttanka's stuti in praise of Vishnu can be found from 3.192.11–19.
5. [3.193.13] Uttanka to Brihadasvha.
6. Vishnu is referred to by his many names—Keshava, Madhusoodana, Hrishikesh, Govinda.
7. When the sage burned down Sagar's sixty thousand sons.

28. Vyaadh Gita

1. This is recounted in the Vipula upakhyaana.
2. This upakhyaana is also called *Pativrata* (devotion to husbands); but for reasons that will become clear soon enough, we've decided to name it *Vyaadh* (hunter) Gita.
3. [3.196.15] Markandeya to Yudhishthira.
4. [3.196.17] Markandeya to Yudhishthira.
5. [3.197.33] Householder's wife to Kaushika.
6. [3.197.40] Householder's wife to Kaushika.
7. This is recounted by the lady from 3.197.31–36.
8. [3.198.22] Hunter to Kaushika.
9. [3.198.53] Hunter to Kaushika.
10. [3.198.57] Hunter to Kaushika.
11. [3.198.70] Hunter to Kaushika.
12. An ancient king who employed 2 lakh cooks in his kitchen. The river Chambal is said to have formed from the secretions of the skins of the animals sacrificed.
13. Saudasa was also known as Kalmaashpaada; his story has been recounted in the Vasishtha upakhyaana and also mentioned in the Uttanka upakhyaana.
14. [3.199.15] Hunter to Kaushika.
15. [3.199.31–32] Hunter to Kaushika.
16. [3.199.34] Hunter to Koushika.
17. [3.200.11–13] Hunter to Koushika.
18. This topic is covered in the Keeta upakhyaana.
19. [3.200.2] Hunter to Koushika.
20. [3.206.20] Hunter to Koushika.
21. व्यक्त—vyakta
22. अव्यक्त—avyakta
23. [3.202.21] Hunter to Koushika.
24. [3.203.40] Hunter to Koushika.
25. [3.204.26] Hunter to Koushika.
26. [3.206.21] Hunter to brahmana.
27. Vedangas are the six ancillary disciplines of the Vedas. They are shiksha (articulation and pronunciation), chhanda (prosody), vyakarana (grammar and linguistics), nirukta (etymology), jyotisha (astronomy and astrology) and kalpa (rituals and instructions).
28. [3.206.12] Brahmana to hunter.

29. Mudgala

1. This is recounted in Chapters 206–212 of Aranyaka Parva.
2. This is recounted in Chapters 213–221 of Aranyaka Parva. Maarkandeya-samasya upa parva ends with this account.
3. This is recounted in the thirty-eighth upa parva, Droupadi-Satyabhaama-samvaada, part of Aranyaka Parva.
4. This is recounted in the thirty-ninth parva, Ghosha Yatra, part of Aranyaka Parva.
5. [3.226.13–14] Karna to Duryodhana.
6. [3.226.18] Karna to Duryodhana.

7. This is described in Chapter 229 of Aranyaka Parva.
8. Described in verse 3.230.31.
9. [3.242.14] Bheema to Duhshaasana's messenger.
10. This is recounted in the fortieth upa parva, Mriga svapna bhaya; Chapter 44 of Aranyaka parva.
11. The Mudgala upa parva begins here, from the 246th chapter of Aranyaka parva.
12. The upa parva is called Vreehi-Drounika Parva. Vreehi means rice, while drona is a pot or vessel. Drona is also the name of the guru of the Kuru princes because he was born in a pot.
13. [3.245.27]
14. [3.246.24] Durvaasa to Mudgala.
15. Trishanku was a king who Vasishtha, his guru, refused to elevate to heaven in his mortal body. When Vishwaamitra attempted to do so, Indra hurled Trishanku back to earth. Vishwamitra arrested his fall and Trishanku was left suspended between the earth and heaven. Ascending heaven in one's mortal body was reserved only for those with great powers of austerities. One such instance is recounted in the Unchavritti upakhyaana.
16. [3.246.26] Durvaasa to Mudgala.
17. [3.247.35] Messenger of the gods to Mudgala.
18. [3.247.45] Vyaasa to Yudhishthira.

30. Raama

1. [3.251.3] Jayadratha to King Kotikashya; Draupadi is the 'lady' being referred to.
2. [3.251.16] Jayadratha to Draupadi.
3. This incident is described at the start of Draupadi-harana upa parva, in Chapters 248–256 of Aranyaka parva.
4. Yudhishthira had said the same, in verse 3.49.34, at the start of the Nala Damayanti upakhyaana.
5. [3.257.10] Yudhishthira to Maarkandeya.
6. The Bhagavata Purana (Chapter 1 of the Seventh Skandha) tells us that the doorkeepers of Vishnu, Jaya and Vijaya, were cursed by Brahma's sons, Sanandana and others, to be born thrice on earth. Hiranyaksha and Hiranyakashipu were killed by Vishnu's Varaha and Narasimha avataras, respectively; Raavana and Kumbhakarna by Vishnu's Rama avatara; Shishupaala and Dantavakra by Vishnu's Krishna avatara.
7. The lineage described here differs from the Valmiki Ramayana. Chapters 3–9 of Uttara Kanda of the Valmiki Ramayana tell us that Pulastya was one of Brahma's sons. Pulastya's son was Vishrava. Vishrava was married to sage Bharadwaaja's daughter, Devavarnini. Their son was named Vaishraavana (Kubera). He got a boon from Brahma to be the fourth lokpala (guardian) of the world, after Indra, Yama, and Varuna, and was named Dhanesha (god of wealth). The raakshasa Sumali had four daughters—Raka, Pushpotkata, Kaikasi, and Kumbhinasi. Kaikasi approached Vishrava to be her husband, but at an inauspicious time. Vishrava told her that the sons born to her would be raakshasas, all except the last one. The children thus born were Raavana, Kumbhakarna, Shoorpnakha, and Vibheeshana. Both Raavana and Kubera were also called Vaishraavana.

8. Also known as Dashagreeva.
9. Chapter 10 of Uttara Kanda of the Valmiki Ramayana tells us that Raavana offered one head every thousand years as a sacrifice. He had sacrificed nine heads before Brahma manifested.
10. This is described in the Sunda-Upasunda upakhyaana.
11. This is recounted in the Yavakreeta upakhyaana.
12. Chapter 10 of Uttara Kanda of the Valmiki Ramayana tells us that the gods implored Brahma to not grant Kumbhakarna any boon. He had devoured apsaraas, sages, and humans. Brahma asked Saraswati, the goddess of learning, to manifest on Kumbhakarna's speech and make him ask a boon that would be beneficial to the gods. Kumbhakarna ended up asking for a boon to enable him to sleep for many, many years.
13. [3.259.35] Vaishraavana to Raavana.
14. Raavana.
15. The word used is Vibhaavasu, another name for Agni.
16. Mareecha was the son of the asuri Taadakaa. In an earlier battle, his brother, Subaahu, had been killed by Raama. Mareecha himself was flung far out into the ocean. Swearing off all violence, terrified of Raama's prowess, Mareecha retired to Gokarna to live the life of an ascetic.
17. The word used for Raama is Kaakutstha, since one of Raama's ancestors was Kakutstha.
18. [3.262.9] Mareecha's thoughts.
19. A three-poled staff, called a tridaṇḍ (त्रिदण्ड)
20. [3.262.26] Seeta to Lakshmana.
21. [3.262.34] Raavana to Seeta.
22. Aruna was Garuda's brother and Surya's, the Sun-god's, charioteer. Aruna's story is recounted in the Aasteeka upa parva, in Chapter 13 of Adi Parva.
23. [3.262.37–38] Seeta to Raavana.
24. The word used is Vaidehi, another name for Seeta.
25. The region Pampa is identified with modern-day Hampi, by the river Tungabhadra, 350 kilometres north of Bengaluru.
26. The word used for Raama is Kaakutstha, since he had descended from Kakutstha.
27. The word used for Lakshmana is Saumitri, son of Sumitra.
28. Mainda, Dvivida, Jaambavan, and Hanuman were Sugreeva's four advisors.
29. Vaali was Sugreeva's brother and had exiled Sugreeva from the kingdom. He had also taken Sugreeva's wife, Taara, as his own consort.
30. Avindhya was a giant raakshasa who was trusted by Raavana.
31. Nalakubera was Kubera's son. Raavana had violated his wife, Rambha, after which Nalakubera had cursed Raavana that if he attempted to force himself on another unwilling woman, his head would split into seven fragments. This is recounted in Chapter 26 of Uttara Kaanda of the Valmiki Ramayana.
32. [3.265.24] Seeta, when Raavana came to meet her.
33. Raama refers to Lakshmana as Kaakuktstha.
34. Angad was Vaali's son.
35. [3.266.33] Raama to Hanuman.
36. Gandhamaadana was a monkey who was thus named because he lived on the Gandhamaadana mountain.
37. These were raakshasas and pishaachas—Aruja, Hari, Jambha, Khara, Krodhavasha, Parvana, Pootana, Praghhasa, Praruja, and others.

38. Raavana's son.
39. A yaksha who was part of the group of yakshas who were in Kubera's court.
40. This is described in the Yavakreeta upakhyaana.
41. [3.273.29–30] Avindhya to Raavana.
42. [3.274.31] Raavana's end.
43. [3.275.15] Seeta, upon hearing Raama's words.
44. [3.275.22] Seeta to Raama.
45. [3.276.5] Maarkandeya to Yudhishthira.

31. Saavitri

1. [2.61.35] Karna's statement in the Kuru assembly.
2. [2.61.36] Karna's statement in the Kuru assembly.
3. The word used in the shloka is महाभागा, which can mean highly fortunate.
4. [2.60.7] Draupadi to the Kuru attendant.
5. [2.64.1]
6. [3.277.3] Yudhishthira to Maarkandeya.
7. Saavitri is the principal deity addressed in the Gaayatri mantra. She is also Brahma's consort.
8. [3.277.13] Goddess Saavitri to Ashvapati.
9. [3.278.11] Naarada to Ashvapati.
10. Shibi's story has been recounted in an earlier upakhyaana.
11. Brihaspati was the preceptor of the gods.
12. Rantideva's generosity is mentioned in the Vyaadh-gita upakhyaana.
13. [3.278.25] Saavitri to her father.
14. An offering of water made to a guest.
15. A muhurta is 48 minutes long; a day is divided into 30 muhurtas.
16. A unit of time equal to 4/5th of a second.
17. [3.281.19] Yama to Saavitri.
18. [3.281.22] Saavitri to Yama.
19. [3.281.25] Yama to Saavitri.
20. [3.281.28] Saavitri to Yama.
21. [3.281.29] Saavitri to Yama.
22. [3.281.30] Yama to Saavitri.
23. [3.281.39] Saavitri to Yama.
24. [3.281.43] Yama to Saavitri.
25. [3.281.50] Yama to Saavitri.
26. [3.281.51] Saavitri to Yama.
27. Sage Maandavya's story has been recounted in the Animaandavya upakhyaana.

32. Yaksha Prashna

1. Arjuna and Karna had a brief skirmish after Draupadi's swayamvara and Karna withdrew from the battle. This is described in the Draupadi swayamvara Parva. Specifically, 1.181.21 says, '*Radheya Karna withdrew from the battle, because the maharatha thought that Brahmana strength was invincible.*'
2. In the battle of Viraata between Arjuna and the Kaurava army, Karna had to flee after an encounter with Arjuna. This is described in the forty-seventh

parva, Go-Grahana Parva. Specifically, 4.49.23 says, '*Thus wounded by the arrows shot by Partha, and scorched by Pandava's arrows, like a swift elephant that has been defeated by another elephant, Vaikartana fled from the forefront of the battle.*'

3. [12.138.58] Bheeshma to Yudhishthira.
4. [3.294.20] Karna tells Indra, '*O Vasava! In exchange for my armour and earrings, give me the invincible shakti that kills large numbers of enemies on the field of battle.*'
5. Name of a forest; also the name of a lake in the same forest.
6. [3.296.01] Yudhishthira to Nakula.
7. [3.297.40] Yaksha's question to Yudhishthira.
8. [3.297.41] Yudhishthira's answer to the Yaksha.
9. [3.297.44] Yaksha's question to Yudhishthira.
10. [3.297.45] Yudhishthira's answer to the Yaksha.
11. [3.297.48] Yaksha's question to Yudhishthira.
12. [3.297.49] Yudhishthira's answer to the Yaksha.
13. [3.297.56] Yaksha's question to Yudhishthira.
14. [3.297.57] Yudhishthira's answer to the Yaksha.
15. [3.297.58] Yaksha's question to Yudhishthira.
16. [3.297.59] Yudhishthira's answer to the Yaksha.
17. [3.297.60] Yaksha's question to Yudhishthira.
18. [3.297.61] Yudhishthira to Yaksha.
19. Also known as Yama.
20. In Bibek Debroy's translation, he has a footnote explaining this—'Hunger, thirst, sorrow, delusion, fear and death. Hunger and thirst occur early in life, sorrow and delusion later and fear and death right at the end.'
21. [3.298.9] Dharma to Yudhishthira.

33. Victory of Indra

1. [4.1.9] The kingdoms that the Paandavas had considered were Chedi, Dasharna, Malla, Matsya, Navarashtra, Panchala, Patachchara, Shaalva, Shurasena, and Yugandhara.
2. This is described in the Yaksha-prashna upakhyaana.
3. Yudhishthira had learned to be skilful in dice from Sage Brihadashva. This is recounted in the Nala-Damayanti upakhyaana.
4. Meaning, 'big stick', as both an ironical and somewhat risqué allusion.
5. This is described in the Nala upakhyaana.
6. [4.4.10] Dhaumya's advice to Yudhishthira.
7. [4.4.21] Dhaumya's advice to Yudhishthira.
8. [4.4.24] Dhaumya's advice to Yudhishthira.
9. Described in 4.12.24.
10. [4.8.26] Queen Sudeshna to Draupadi.
11. [4.13.6] Keechaka to Sudeshna.
12. [4.17.1] Draupadi to Bheema.
13. Described in 4.21.59.
14. Described in 4.22.25.
15. [4.21.46] A disguised Bheema to Keechaka.

16. This is described in the forty-seventh parva, Go-grahana.
17. This is described in the forty-eighth parva, Vaivaahika.
18. There is a long list of kings and kingdoms that Drupada enumerates who could be approached for help. Some of those names are Shalya, Bhagadatta, Ugra, Hardikya, Malla, Brihanta, Chitravarma, Bahlika, etc.
19. [5.4.1] Drupada to the Paandavas.
20. This is described in Chapter 6 of Udyoga Parva, where Drupada briefs the priest before his departure for Hastinapura.
21. [5.125.26] Duryodhana to Krishna.
22. The Paandavas were also sometimes called Kauravas since they too had descended from Kuru.
23. This is described in Chapter 7 of Udyoga Parva.
24. [5.8.30] Shalya to Yudhishthira.
25. Tvashta finds a mention in the Rig Veda. He was a Prajapati, but also the son of an asura. He is said to have had a hatred for Indra.
26. [5.9.21] Indra rationalizing his decision to kill Trishiras.
27. This is a reference to Vishnu's Vaamana avatara.
28. [5.10.23] Sages to Vritra.
29. [5.11.6] Gods and rishis to Nahusha.
30. In personified form.
31. [5.11.7]
32. Brihaspati was the son of Sage Angiras and the preceptor of the gods.
33. [5.12.8] Nahusha to the gods.
34. [5.12.19] Brihaspati recounting Brahma's words to the gods.
35. [5.12.26] Brihaspati to the gods.
36. Ashwamedha yagna.
37. Goddess Night.
38. The patron goddess of Uttarayaana.
39. Chapter 9 of the first part of Vishnu Purana tells us that Durvaasa had cursed Indra to be bereft of Shri. The loss of prosperity and the resulting decay in dharma eventually led to the churning of the ocean (samudra-manthan).
40. Another name for Shachi, Indra's wife.
41. The list of seven sages varies slightly from text to text, but one commonly accepted list, is Agastya, Atri, Bharadwaaja, Gautama, Jamadagni, Vasistha, and Vishwaamitra.
42. [5.15.16–17] Nahusha boasting to Shachi.
43. Agni—fire is said to have been created from water.
44. In other retellings there is a slight difference in this account. Nahusha kicks Agastya, the shortest of the seven sages, to move faster, shouting, 'Sarpa, sarpa (faster)'. Agastya curses Nahusha to become a sarpa (serpent).
45. This encounter takes place in the thirty-sixth upa parva, Ajagara Parva, part of the Aranyaka Parva, when the Paandavas spent twelve years in exile, in the forest.
46. Celestial elephant.
47. [5.18.16]. Shalya speaking to Yudhishthira. In the same shloka, Shalya also describes this as the upakhyaana of Indra's victory.
48. One such incident is recounted in the Hansa-Kaak upakhyaana.
49. [9.16.55] Shalya's death at Yudhishthira's hands.
50. [9.16.54] Shalya falls, having been pierced by Yudhishthira's javelin.

34. Dambhodbhava

1. Upaplavya was a town situated near the capital of the Matsya kingdom, Viraata, and this is where the Paandavas stationed themselves after the thirteenth year of exile.
2. This is recounted in Chapter 20 of Udyoga parva.
3. This is recounted in Chapter 21 of Udyoga parva.
4. [5.21.16] Bheeshma to Karna.
5. [5.22.39] Dhritaraashtra to Sanjay.
6. [5.31.23] Krishna to Sanjaya.
7. Vidura's discourse to Dhritaraashtra is recounted in the fifty-first upa parva, Prajagara; Chapters 33 through 41 of Udyoga Parva. This is sometimes also known as Vidura Niti.
8. Sage Sanatsujata's discourse is contained in the fifty-second upa parva, Sanatsujata; Chapters 42 through 45 of Udyoga Parva.
9. [5.42.4] Sanatsujata to Dhritaraashtra.
10. The word used for Balaraama is Sankarshana.
11. [5.70.29] Yudhishthira to Krishna.
12. [5.70.19] Yudhishthira to Krishna.
13. [5.70.23] Yudhishthira to Krishna.
14. [5.70.30] Yudhishthira to Krishna.
15. [12.8.11] Arjuna to Yudhishthira, quoting Nahusha.
16. [12.8.17] Arjuna to Yudhishthira.
17. [12.8.19] Arjuna to Yudhishthira.
18. The 18 kings are listed from 5.72.11–17, and are Bali, Udavarta, Janamejaya (not to be confused with the great-grandson of Arjuna), Bahula, Vasu, Ajabindu, Kusharddhika, Arkaja, Dhoutamulaka, Hayagriva, Varapra, Bahu, Pururava, Sahaja, Brihadbada, Dharana, Vigahana, Shama.
19. Another name for Draupadi since she was dark.
20. Vasudeva and Pritha were King Shurasena's children. Pritha was adopted by King Kuntibhoja and thus also became known as Kunti. Krishna was Vasudeva's son. That made Kunti Krishna's bua—paternal aunt.
21. In 5.88.71, Kunti tell Krishna that her sons are dead to her, and she to them, if they don't act. In 5.88.74 she says that this is the time for which kshatriya mothers give birth to sons.
22. [5.89.25] Krishna to Duryodhana.
23. Chapter 94 of Udyoga Parva begins here. This is the start of this upakhyaana.
24. 5.94.38 lists the eight weapons—Kakudiya, Shuka, Naka, Akshisamtarjana, Santana, Nartana, Ghora, and Ajyamodaka.

35. Ambaa

1. Recounted in the fifty-fifth upa parva, Karna-upanivada.
2. Recounted in the fifty-sixth upa parva, Abhiniryaana.
3. Recounted in the fifty-seventh upa parva, Bheeshma-abhishechana.
4. Recounted in the fifty-eighth upa parva, Ulooka-yaana.
5. [5.157.15] Duryodhana's message to Ulooka for Arjuna.
6. [5.157.17] Duryodhana's message to Ulooka for Bheema.
7. [5.169.20]

8. [5.169.16] Bheeshma to Duryodhana.
9. Described in 5.168.1.
10. [5.169.20]
11. This is described in Chapter 8 of Soutpika parva.
12. Bheeshma was Shaantanu's son through Gangaa. Chitraangada and Vichitravirya were Shaantanu's sons through Satyavati.
13. This is described in Chapter 95 of Adi Parva.
14. Veeryashulka is also used to describe the event. Veeryashulka refers to a ceremony where the warrior who displays the greatest show of valour is given the bride.
15. [5.172.15] Ambaa to Shaalva.
16. [5.172.20] Ambaa to Shaalva. तत्र मे सन्तु गतयः सन्तः सत्यं यथाब्रुवम्
17. [5.174.7] Ascetics to Ambaa.
18. Parashuraama's story has been recounted in the 'Kaartavirya, Jamadagni, Raama' upakhyaana.
19. [5.176.13] Ambaa to Akritavrana.
20. Parashuraama was descended from sage Bhrigu, and thus he is referred to as Bhaargava here.
21. [5.177.20] Parashuraama telling Akritvrana of his prowess.
22. [5.178.11] Bheeshma to Raama.
23. [5.178.19] Bheeshma to Raama.
24. [5.178.24] Bheeshma to Raama, quoting a shloka by Marutta (मरुत्त).
25. [5.178.36–37] Bheeshma addressing Raama.
26. [5.180.4] Raama to Bheeshma.
27. [6.41.32] Yudhishthira removes his armour, takes off his weapons, approaches Bheeshma on foot, and asks for his permission and blessings—'*We are inviting you to fight with us. O Father! Grant us the permission. Give us the blessings.*'
28. [6.41.36–37] Bheeshma confesses to Yudhishthira, '*A man is the servant of wealth. But wealth is never anyone's servant. ... I am tied to the Kouravas because of wealth. ... The Kouravyas have robbed me through wealth.*'
29. [5.180.24–25] Bheeshma to Raama.
30. Bheeshma used the vayavya and agneya weapons, while Raama used the guhyaka and varuna weapons.
31. Stated in [5.183.27].
32. Just as Shachi had prayed to Night (Raatri). This is described in the Victory of Indra upakhyaana.
33. Many, many years later, in the battle at Viraata, Arjuna would fire a similar weapon—sammohan—that put almost all the Kuru warriors assembled to sleep; all but Bheeshma. This is described in the forty-seventh upa parva, Go-grahana; Chapter 61 of Viraata Parva.
34. [5.184.16] Brahmanas to Bheeshma.
35. Jamadagni, Richika, and Aurva appeared before Raama; his father, grandfather, and great-grandfather, respectively.
36. [5.186.21] Raama to his forefathers.
37. [5.186.25] Bheeshma to Narada.
38. The name used for Shiva is Mahaadeva Kapardi Vrishadhvaja. Mahaadeva means great god; Kapardi means one with matted hair; and Vrishadhvaja means one who has a bull on his banner.
39. [5.188.17–18]

40. Through his spy and through Naarada.
41. Hiranyavarma was sometimes also called Kanchanavarma, since both hiranya and kanchan are synonymous.
42. [5.191.1] Drupada on hearing Hiranyavarma's messenger.
43. Kubera is described here as Naravaahana Kubera, since his mount is a man.
44. [5.193.59] Bheeshma talking to Duryodhana.
45. [5.193.62–63] Bheeshma talking to Duryodhana.

36. Vishwa

1. The Bhagavada Geeta upa parva is the sixty-third parva, and a part of the Bheeshma parva. While the entire upa parva is twenty-seven chapters long, the eighteen chapters of the Bhagavada Geeta are contained within the tenth through twenty-seventh chapters of this upa parva.
2. [6.44.45–46] Sanjaya describing the war to Dhritaraashtra.
3. Uttara's death is described in Chapter 45 of Bheeshma Parva.
4. Bheeshma was Arjuna's grand uncle. Arjuna's father was Paandu; Paandu's father was Vichitraveerya (though fathered on Ambika by Vyaasa); and Vichitraveerya was Bheeshma's stepbrother (Bheeshma's mother was Gangaa, while Vichitraveerya's mother was Satyavati).
5. This is described in Chapter 55 of Bheeshma Parva.
6. This is described in Chapter 60 of Bheeshma Parva. The fourteen sons killed by Bheema are listed as—Senapati, Sushena, Jalasandha, Sulochana, Ugra, Bheemaratha, Bheema (not to be confused with Kunti's son), Bheemabahu, Alolupa, Durmukha, Dushpradharsha, Vivitsu, Vikata, and Soma.
7. [6.60.67] Bheeshma to Drona.
8. [6.61.14] Sanjaya to Dhritaraashtra.
9. [6.61.16] Sanjaya to Dhritaraashtra. The phrase uttered by Sanjaya is—यतो धर्मस्ततो जयः
10. [6.61.42] Brahma to Narayana.
11. Parashurama, Jamadagni's son.
12. [6.62.34] Bheeshma to Duryodhana. The phrase is यतः कृष्णस्ततो धर्मो यतो धर्मस्ततो जयः।
13. Some of the names that Vasudeva is referred to as are Pundarikaksha, Purushottama, Govinda, Janaardana, Madhusoodana, Keshava, and Hrishikesha.
14. [6.63.5] Bheeshma describing Vasudeva's greatness to Duryodhana.
15. The word used is स्तवम्, which means a song of praise. This is contained in shlokas 6.64.2–6.64.9.

37. Tripuraa Vadh

1. This is described in the sixty-fourth upa parva, Bheeshma-vadha; Chapter 114 of Bheeshma parva.
2. Summer solstice.
3. This is described in the Mahabheesha upakhyaana.
4. This is described in the sixty-fourth upa parva, Bheeshma-vadha; Chapter 117 of Bheeshma parva.

5. This is described in the sixty-fifth upa parva, Dronabhisheka; Chapter 5 of Drona parva.
6. [7.5.14] Karna responds to Duryodhana's request for a recommendation on who should be the next commander of the Kaurava army.
7. [7.5.16] Karna recommends that Drona be appointed the commander of the Kaurava army.
8. Abhimanyu's death is described in the sixty-seventh upa parva, Abhimanyu-vadha.
9. After abducting Draupadi, Jayadratha was defeated by Arjuna and Bheema. His head shaved, his life spared by Yudhishthira, a humiliated Jayadratha prayed to Shiva (also called Sharva, Hara, Rudra) and got a boon that in one battle he would be able to withstand the combined assault of all the Paandavas except Arjuna. Draupadi's abduction by Jayadratha is described in the forty-second upa parva, Draupadi-harana; Chapter 42 of Aranyaka parva. Jayadratha's boon is described in the sixty-seventh upa parva, Abhimanyu-vadha; Chapter 41 of Drona parva.
10. In 7.47.28–29, Drona advises Karna and others to slice Abhimanyu's bowstring, cut the reins of his horses, and kill his horses and charioteers. This is described in the sixty-seventh upa parva, Abhimanyu-vadha; Chapter 47 of Drona parva.
11. Arjuna's oath is described in the sixty-seventh upa parva, Abhimanyu-vadha; Chapter 51 of Drona parva.
12. This is described in the sixty-ninth upa parva, Jaydratha-vadha; Chapter 121 of Drona parva.
13. [7.126.38] Drona to Duryodhana.
14. This is described in the seventieth upa parva, Ghatotakacha-vadha; Chapter 154 of Drona Parva.
15. This is described in the seventy-first upa parva, Drona-vadha; Chapter 155 of Drona Parva.
16. Yudhishthira says these words in 7.164.105.
17. [8.49.29–30] Krishna to Arjuna.
18. This is described in the seventy-first upa parva, Drona-vadha; Chapter 165 of Drona Parva.
19. This is described in the seventy-second upa parva, Narayana-astra Moksha; Chapter 166 of Drona Parva.
20. This is described in the seventy-second upa parva, Narayana-astra Moksha; Chapter 172 of Drona Parva.
21. This is recounted in the Victory of Indra upakhyaana.
22. This is described in the forty-third upa parva, Kundala-aharana; Chapter 294 of Aranyaka Parva.
23. This is described in the fifty-fifth upa parva, Karna-upanivaada; Chapter 144 of Udyoga Parva.
24. [8.23.48] Duryodhana to Shalya.
25. Taarakmaya was an asura who had got a boon from Shiva that none other than a son born to Shiva would be able to kill him. Subrahmanya (also called Kaartikeye) was born as a son to Shiva and who killed Taarakmaya in a great battle. Kaartikeya's birth is described in the thirty-seventh upa parva, Maarkandeya-samasya; Chapters 213–221 of Aranyaka Parva.
26. [8.24.35] Brahma to the gods. Brahma refers to Shiva as Sthaanu, Ishaan, and Jishnu. Sthaanu means one who is stationary, immoveable, motionless. Ishaan

means the splendid lord. Jishnu means the victorious one and is also one of Arjuna's names.

27. The stuti runs from shlokas 8.24.44–51.
28. Brahma calls Shiva Kapardin (कपर्दिन) here—one with matted hair.

38. Hansa-Kaak

1. [8.28.23] Crow to the swans.
2. [8.28.49] Crow to swan.

39. Indra-Namuchi

1. This is described in the fifty-fifth upa parva, Karna-upanivaada; Chapter 144 of Udyoga Parva.
2. This is described in the seventy-third upa parva, Karna-vadha; Chapter 33 of Karna Parva.
3. [8.33.37–39] Karna to Yudhishthira.
4. This is described in the sixty-ninth upa parva, Jayadratha-vadha; Chapter 114 of Drona Parva.
5. [7.114.67] Karna remembers his promise to Kunti.
6. [7.114.69] Karna to Bheema.
7. This is described in the seventy-third upa parva, Karna-vadha; Chapter 17 of Karna Parva.
8. [8.17.94–95] Karna to Nakula.
9. This is described in the seventieth upa parva, Ghatotakacha-vadha; Chapter 142 of Drona Parva.
10. [7.142.14] Karna to Sahadeva.
11. [7.142.14]
12. Shalya's battle with the Paandava army and his death at the hands of Yudhishthira is described in the seventy-fourth upa parva, Shalya-vadha; Chapter 16 of Shalya Parva.
13. Shakuni's death at the hands of Sahadeva is described in the seventy-fifth upa parva, Hraada-pravesh; Chapter 27 of Shalya Parva. Sahadeva's vow to kill Shakuni is described in the twenty-eighth upa parva, Anudyita; Chapter 68 of Sabha Parva.
14. Bheema's vow to kill Duryodhana is described in the twenty-eighth upa parva, Anudyita; Chapter 68 of Sabha Parva.
15. [9.16.55] Shalya falls to Yudhishthira, who was Dharma's (Yama) son.
16. Duryodhana's entry into the lake is described in the seventy-fifth upa parva, Hraada-pravesh; Chapter 28 of Shalya Parva.
17. Duryodhana falls to Bheema. This is described in the seventy-fifth upa parva, Gada-yuddha; Chapter 57 of Shalya Parva.
18. [9.30.64] Yudhishthira to Duryodhana.
19. Rukmi, proud, even vain, about his prowess, was rebuffed by both the Paandavas and Kauravas. This is described in the fifty-seventh upa parva, Bheeshma—Abhishechana; Chapter 155 of Udyoga Parva.
20. 9.34.11 tells us that Balaraama had wanted Krishna to help the Kauravas. Krishna refused. That was also one reason why Balaraama went on a pilgrimage—to calm himself down.

21. Soma's story is described in the seventy-sixth upa parva, Teertha-yatra; Chapter 34 of Shalya Parva.
22. Trita's story is described in the seventy-sixth upa parva, Teertha-yatra; Chapter 35 of Shalya Parva.
23. This is described in the seventy-sixth upa parva, Teertha-yatra; Chapter 36 of Shalya Parva.
24. This is described in the seventy-sixth upa parva, Teertha-yatra; Chapter 37 of Shalya Parva.
25. This is King Dashratha's son.
26. This is described in the seventy-sixth upa parva, Teertha-yatra; Chapter 38 of Shalya Parva.
27. This is described in the seventy-sixth upa parva, Teertha-yatra; Chapter 39 of Shalya Parva.
28. Sthaanu is another name for Shiva.
29. [9.42.18] Raakshasas to sages.
30. [9.42.21–22] Brahmanas to the raakshasas.
31. Namuchi was the son of Prajapati Kashyapa and Danu and who invaded Indra's kingdom with a large army of raakshasas.
32. [9.42.30] Indra to Namuchi.
33. The mist meant it was neither day nor night; the foam was neither wet nor dry.

40. Vriddha Kumari

1. This is described in the seventy-sixth upa parva, Teertha-yaatra; Chapter 52 of Shalya Parva.

41. Srinjaya

1. These events are described in the seventy-ninth upa parva, Sauptika; part of Sauptika Parva.
2. These events are described in the eightieth upa parva, Aishika; part of Sauptika Parva.
3. These events are described in the eightieth upa parva, Vishoka; Chapter 11 of Stri Parva.
4. This is described in the eighty-first upa parva, Stri; Chapter 13 of Stri Parva.
5. [11.13.9] Vyaasa reminding Gandhaari of her blessings to Duryodhana.
6. This is described in the eighty-first upa parva, Stri; Chapter 15 of Stri Parva.
7. These events are described in the eighty-first upa parva, Stri.
8. [11.25.40–41] Gandhaari curses Krishna.
9. These events are described in the eighty-second upa parva, Shraddha; part of Stree Parva.
10. This is described in the Agastya upakhyaana.
11. These events are described in the eighty-third upa parva, Jala-pradaanika; part of Stree Parva.
12. Krishna is referred to here as Hrishikesha, Maadhava, Janaardana, Govinda, and Achyuta.
13. [12.29.8] Krishna to Yudhishthira.

14. Samvarta was the third of Angiras' eight sons, and the younger brother of Brihaspati.
15. Shibi's story has been recounted in an earlier upakhyaana.
16. [12.29.58–60] Naarada telling Srinjaya about Bhagiratha.
17. Bhagiratha's father.
18. A king in the Ikshavaaku dynasty. This story has been recounted in the Maandhaataa upakhyaana.
19. Ikshavaaku's brother.
20. [12.29.99] Naarada telling Srinjaya about Shashabindu and his sons.
21. Srinjaya's son is called Swarnashtheevi, Hiranyanaabha, and Kanchanashtheevi, all meaning the same.

42. Naarada-Parvata

1. Parvata had prophesized that Srinjaya's son's excreta would be golden, and hence be known as Swarnashtheevi.

43. Parashuraama

1. [11.26.9] Yudhishthira answers Dhritaraashtra's question on the fatality count in the Kurukshetra war. The word used is daśāyutānām ayutaṁ. Aayut is ten-thousand. The count is therefore ten times ten-thousand times ten-thousand, which gives one billion.
2. [12.48.4–6] The battlefield of Kurukshetra after the war.
3. Usually referred to as Raama.
4. A famous king in the Puru dynasty.
5. Not to be confused with Vyaasa's mother and Shaantanu's wife, Satyavati.
6. A famous sage descended from Bhrigu.
7. Richika tells Satyavati that this mix-up was on account of her mother, and a deliberate deception.
8. Agni is referred to as Chitrabhaanu.
9. [12.49.62] The state of the earth after no kshatriyas were left.
10. Rasaatala—one of the seven hells.
11. Uru and urvi both mean thigh. Bhaasa was an Indian playright who wrote the Sanskrit play, *Urubhanga—The Breaking of the Thighs*, based on the breaking of Duryodhana's thighs in the Mahabharata.

44. Muchkunda

1. [12.50.6] Vaishampaayana describing Bheeshma lying on a bed of arrows.
2. [12.51.14] Krishna to Bheeshma.

45. Ushtragreeva

1. [12.113.16] Bheeshma talking about the lazy camel.

46. Danda Utpatti

1. 5.57, Ramcharitmanas. The Avadhi couplet reads:
   बिनय न मानत जलधि जड़ गए तीन दिन बीति।
   बोले राम सकोप तब भय बिनु होइ न प्रीति॥
2. [12.121.13]
3. These names are mentioned in shlokas 12.121.19–21.
4. [12.121.33] Bheeshma to Yudhishthira.
5. Bheeshma quotes Manu, Vasishtha, and Brahma to tell Yudhishthira that judgment is vyavhaara, and vyavhaara is dharma.
6. [12.121.54] Bheeshma to Yudhishthira.
7. Maandhaata was a king in the Ikshvaaku dynasty and the son of Yuvanaashva. His story is recounted in an earlier upakhyaana.
8. [12.122.20–21]
9. Death.
10. The name used for Shiva here is Ishaana.
11. This is detailed in shlokas 12.122.27–34.

47. Rishabha Gita

1. [12.125.31] Sumitra's question to the sages.
2. Drona's meeting with Drupada is recounted in the seventh upa parva, Sambhava; Chapter 122 of Adi Parva.
3. [12.126.35] Tanu to Viradyumna.
4. [12.126.39] Tanu to Viradyumna.
5. Yama.

48. Kapota

1. The burning of the Khaandava forest is described in the nineteenth upa parva, Khaandava-daha. Arjuna's saving of Maaya's life is described in the Khaandava-daha upa parva; Chapter 221 of Adi Parva. This is also mentioned in the Shaarangakas upakhyaana.
2. Jayadratha's kidnapping of Druapadi is described in the forty-second upa parva, Draupadi-harana; part of Araynaka Parva. This is also briefly recounted in the Raama upakhyaana.
3. [12.142.8] Bird thinking about its wife.

49. Kritaghna

1. [12.162.6] Bheeshma to Yudhishthira.
2. [12.162.7] Bheeshma to Yudhishthira.
3. [12.162.9] Bheeshma to Yudhishthira.
4. [12.162.26] Bheeshma to Yudhishthira.
5. [12.162.16] Bheeshma to Yudhishthira on the kinds of men to avoid.
6. The bird mentioned in 12.163.9 is the bhaarunda; a mythical bird with two heads. This bird was the emblem of the princely state of Mysore and later became the emblem of the state of Karnataka.

7. The king of cranes, also known as Raajadharma.
8. A name used for the daughters of Daksha, who was one of Brahma's sons.
9. [12.164.12] Rajadharma speaking to Gautama.
10. Gotra here refers to one's line of descendants. Among brahmanas, a gotra is used to trace one's lineage back to one of the seven sages.
11. Raakshasas were also descended from Sage Kashyapa. Rajadharma was also a descendant of Kashyapa.
12. [12.167.19] Bheeshma to Yudhishthira. कुतः कृतघ्नस्य यशः कुतः स्थानं कुतः सुखम्
13. [12.166.24] Bheeshma to Yudhishthira.

50. Jaapaka

1. A jaapaka is someone who recites mantras.
2. Though Yama is also called Kaala, here the reference is to time.
3. [12.189.16]
4. Bibek Debroy's translation informs us this refers to the agreeable and the disagreeable.
5. Bibek Debroy's translation informs us this refers to sattva, tamas, and rajas. It also refers to distinctions between the knower, the object of knowing, and the act of knowing.
6. Bibek Debroy's translation informs us this refers to the four seasons, and also to seeing, thinking, hearing, knowing, and the reasons behind these.
7. Bibek Debroy's translation informs us this refers to the five elements, the senses, mind, and intelligence.
8. Yudhishthira reminds Bheeshma at the start of Chapter 192 of the twelfth parva, Shanti.
9. She is also the goddess of the Vedas, sometimes also known as Saavitri.
10. Personification of time.
11. Personification of death.
12. Sometimes also called Yama, the god of death and justice.
13. [12.192.31] Mrityu to the brahmana.
14. [12.192.42] Brahmana to Ikshvaaku.
15. [12.192.69] यतो धर्मस्ततः सत्यं Brahmana to Ikshvaaku.
16. Unchhavritti is described in detail in another upakhyaana.
17. Desire.
18. Anger.

51. Chirakaari

1. The couplet reads thus: काल करे सो आज कर, आज करे सो अब । पल में परलय होएगी, बहुरि करेगा कब ॥
2. [12.258.3] Bheeshma to Yudhishthira, in reference to Chirakaari.
3. The episode, where Indra seduces Ahalya, is mentioned in several texts, including the Baala kaanda of the Ramayana, Padma Purana, Brahma Purana, and others.
4. [12.258.20] पिता स्वर्गः पिता धर्मः पिता परमकं तपः Chirakaari thinking about his father.

5. The five elements are earth, fire, wind, water, and space. These are referred to as the *pancha-tattva*.
6. [12.258.30] Because the mother bears the child in the womb.
7. [12.258.30] Because the mother gives birth.
8. [12.258.30] Because the mother nurtures the child's limbs.
9. [12.258.30] Because the mother gives birth to a brave son.
10. [12.258.31] Because the mother nurtures the child.
11. [12.258.26] Chirakaari thinking about his mother.
12. [12.258.29] Chirakaari thinking about his mother.
13. [12.258.33] Chirakaari's thoughts.
14. [12.258.40] Chirakaari reflecting on the mother and father.
15. [12.258.66] Gautama to Chirakaari.
16. [12.258.66] Gautama to Chirakaari.

52. Kundadhaara

1. [12.263.12] Kundadhaara to the brahmana. The subject of ungratefulness has been touched upon in more detail in the Kritaghna upakhyaana.

53. Hayasheera

1. This stotra can be found in the Moksha-dharma upa parva; Chapter 325 of Shanti Parva.
2. Hayasheera is also referred to as Hayagreeva, and can refer to one of several asuras, or also to an avatara of Vishnu.
3. Consciousness.
4. Praakriti—that which existed even before creation.
5. Rasaatala, one of the nether regions.
6. The stuti in praise of Hari runs from 12.335.34–42.
7. [12.335.45–47] The description of Hayasheera.
8. Ananta, the serpent.
9. Madhusoodana is another name for Vishnu and means the destroyer of Madhu.
10. [12.335.73] Vyaasa talking to Yudhishthira.
11. This stuti in praise of Narayana runs from 12.335.74–89.
12. [12.335.81]

54. Unchavritti

1. [12.340.2] Bheeshma to Yudhishthira.
2. The dharma written in the Vedas, the sacred texts, and the dharma followed by people.
3. This is a practice and also the name of a brahmana.
4. [12.342.9] Guest to Dharmaaranya.
5. [12.348.9] Padmanaabha's wife to the serpent.
6. [12.348.19] Padmanaabha to his wife.

55. Sudarshana

1. This is not the same Duryodhana as Dhritaraashtra's son.
2. Agni is called Havyavaahana—the bearer of offerings.
3. God of death, though Mrityu has been referred to as both a god and goddess.
4. Sudarshana is called Paavaka's son. Paavaka is another name for Agni, and Sudarshana had descended from Agni.
5. Ten qualities being the five elements—earth, wind, water, space, and light—and intelligence, atman, mind, time, and the directions.

56. Vishwaamitra

1. This is described in the Shakuntala upakhyaana.
2. This is described in the Vasishtha upakhyaana.
3. This is described in the Vasishtha upakhyaana.
4. Not to be confused with Satyavati who was Shaantanu's wife and Vyaasa's mother.
5. This is described in the Sudarshana upakhyaana.
6. Ganga here refers to the Gautami Ganga, or the Godavari. The place where the horses emerged from the waters is known as Ashwateertha.

57. Bhangaashwana

1. This incident is described in the Vipula upakhyaana.
2. This incident is described in the Yaksha prashna upakhyaana.
3. [13.12.13] Bhangaashwana's thoughts.
4. [13.12.48] Bhangaashwana to Indra.

58. Upamanyu

1. The thousand names of Vishnu are recited in the eighty-seventh upa parva, Daana-dharma; Chapter 135 of Anushaasana Parva.
2. Jaambavati was Jaambavan's daughter, the king of bears.
3. Ahuka was Ugrasena's father.
4. Also known as Vaiyaaghrapadya, he was the son of Sage Vyaaghrapaada.
5. Some of the names of Shiva used here are Mahaadeva, Pashupati, Rudra, Isha, Maheshwara, Sthaanu, Sthaanu Maheshwara, Neelkantha.
6. There is a stuti that Krishna sings in praise of Shiva here, from 13.15.29 to 13.15.45.
7. [13.16.2] Krishna asking Shiva as a boon.
8. [13.16.6] The eight boons Krishna asks from Uma.
9. Tandi's stuti runs from 13.16.13–65.
10. Shiva's names are recited from 13.17.30–150.
11. A sage who was mistakenly castigated for having killed a brahmana.
12. Krishna Dvaipaayana's father.
13. His story is told in the Animaandavya upakhyaana.

59. Matanga

1. In 3.206.12, the brahmana tells the hunter of Mithila, '*I think him to be a brahmana who becomes a brahmana because of his conduct.*' This is described in the Vyaadh-geeta upakhyaana.
2. In 3.177.16, Yudhishthira tells Nahusha, '*It is said that a brahmana is one in whom truthfulness, charity, forgiveness, good conduct, lack of cruelty, self-control and compassion can be seen.*' In 3.177.32 he again tells Nahusha, '*I have earlier defined as a brahmana one in whom the principles of good conduct are seen.*'
3. [13.30.9] Matanga's question to Indra.

60. Veetahavya

1. Also known as Haihaya, or King Ekveera. Descended from Yayaati, he was the founder of the Haihaya dynasty.

61. Vipula

1. This episode is recounted in the Bhangaashvana upakhyaana.
2. Ushanas is another name for Shukra, the preceptor of the asuras.
3. [13.39.7] Yudhishthira speaking.
4. [13.40.51] Vipula's thoughts.
5. [13.40.52] Vipula's thoughts.
6. [13.43.7] Devasharma to Vipula.

62. Chyavana

1. This incident is not described in the Sukanya upakhyaana.
2. Saavitri says this in [3.281.22] and this incident is recounted in the Saavitri upakhyaana.

63. Nriga

1. This is recounted in the Animaandavya upakhyaana.
2. Another name for Dwaarka.
3. Janaardana, Vasudeva, and Maadhava are Krishna's names used here.
4. [13.69.9] Krishna to Nriga. If we take one hundred thousand cows a hundred times, we get a figure of ten million. The figure of 108 thousand cows multiplied 100 thousand times gives us ten billion, eight hundred million cows. In essence, King Nriga was abundantly generous when it came to giving.
5. [13.69.23] Yama to King Nriga.

64. Naachiketa

1. Naachiketa's story, found in the Kathopanishad, is different from the account in the Mahabharata in several respects. The only common point in the two accounts is Uddaaliki cursing his son. Naachikta waits for three days for Yama, nor does Yama offer him rewards other than wisdom that Naachiketa asks for.
2. Sage Uddaaliki was also called Uddaalaka. There was another sage by the same name. He was a disciple of Sage Aayodhadhaumya. He was called Aruni and later acquired the name Uddaalaka. His story is recounted in the third upa parva, Paushya; Chapter 3 of Adi Parva.
3. [13.70.51] Naachiketa telling his father, Uddaaliki, what Yama told him.

65. Keeta

1. [3.9.11] Vyaasa to Dhritaraashtra. This incident is recounted in the Shaalva-vadha upakhyaana.

66. Uttanka

1. Some names used for Hastinapura are Nagapura, Varanasahvya, and Gajasahvya.
2. The Dhundumaara upakhyaana also talks about Sage Uttanka.
3. [14.52.24–25] Vasudeva Krishna to Uttanka.
4. [14.54.5] Krishna's vishwaroopa.
5. [14.54.11] Krishna urging Uttanka to ask for a boon.
6. [14.54.25] Krishna to Uttanka.
7. A famous king in the Ikshvaaku lineage. He was also known as Kalmaashpaada, and his story is described in the Vasishtha upakhyaana.
8. Saudasa had been cursed by Shakti, Sage Vasishtha's son, to become a maneater. He had then also been cursed by a brahmana to become a maneater. This is described in the Vasishtha upakhyaana.
9. [14.57.11] Uttanka addressing Saudasa.

67. Nakula

1. Bheeshma's journey heavenwards is described in the eighty-eighth upa parva, Bheeshma-swargaarohana; Chapter 153–154 of Anushaasana Parva.
2. This is described in the eighty-ninth upa parva, Ashwamedhika; Chapter 3 of Ashwamedhika Parva.
3. The story of King Marutta is described in the eighty-ninth upa parva, Ashwamedhika; Chapters 4–10 of Ashwamedhika Parva.
4. This battle is described in the eighty-ninth upa parva, Ashwamedhika; Chapter 73 of Ashwamedhika Parva.

5. This battle is described in the eighty-ninth upa parva, Ashwamedhika; Chapters 74–75 of Ashwamedhika Parva.
6. Arjuna's marriage with Chitraangada is described in the Arjuna-vanvaasa upa parva; Chapter 207 of Adi Parva. Babruvaahana's birth is also mentioned in the same chapter.
7. Uloopi was the daughter of the king of the Nagas and her marriage to Arjuna described in the Arjuna-vanvaasa upa parva; Chapter 206 of Adi Parva.
8. This battle between Arjuna and Babruvaahana is described in the eighty-ninth upa parva, Ashwamedhika; Chapters 78–83 of Ashwamedhika Parva.
9. Horse sacrifice.
10. Paandu was Vyaasa's son through Ambaalika, and Kunti was Paandu's wife.
11. The events of the Rajasuya yagna are described in the twenty-fourth upa parva, Rajasuya; part of Sabha Parva.
12. Yudhishthira expressed his apprehensions in Chapter 88 of the Ashwamedhika Parva.
13. A mongoose is called a nakula in Sanskrit; hence the name of this upakhyaana.
14. [14.93.65] Dharma addressing the brahmana and his family.
15. [14.93.69] Dharma to the brahmana and his family.
16. [14.93.70–71] Dharma to the brahmana and his family.
17. [14.94.29] Dharma to the brahmana and his family.
18. Another name for Yama, the god of death and justice.
19. [14.93.73] Dharma to the brahmana and his family.
20. King of the Chedis.
21. [14.94.23] Vaishampaayana to Janamejaya.
22. Rasaatala, one level of hell.
23. [14.94.34] Vaishampaayana to Janamejaya.
24. A class of priests who participated in Vedic sacrifices and chanted verses from the Rig Veda.
25. Indra's names used here are Sahastraaksha, the one with a thousand eyes; Parjanya, the god of rain; Vaasava, chief of the Vasus.
26. A shraadh ceremony is held for the honour and benefit of one's dead relatives.
27. Personification of anger.
28. These events are described in the seventy-third upa parva, Karna Vadha; Chapter 49 of Karna Parva.
29. [8.49.24] Krishna to Arjuna.

Bibliography

Adluri, Vishwa, and Joydeep Bagchee, ed. *Argument and Design: The Unity of the Mahabharata*. Brill, 2016.

Adluri, Vishwa, and Joydeep Bagchee, ed. *Philology and Criticism*. Anthem Press, 2018.

Adluri, Vishwa, and Joydeep Bagchee, ed. *Reading the Fifth Veda: Studies on the Mahabharata-Essays by Alf Hiltebeitel*. Brill, 2011.

Adluri, Vishwa, ed. *Ways and Reasons for Thinking about the Mahbhrata as a Whole*. Bhandarkar Oriental Research Institute, 013.

Adluri, Vishwa. 2022. *Frame Narratives and Forked Beginnings: Or, How to Read the Adiparvan*. Journal of Vaishnava Studies. 19 (2). https://www.ivsjournal.com/index.php/jvs/article/view/221.

Debroy, Bibek, tr. *The Bhagavata Purana, Vol. 1*. Penguin, 2018.

Debroy, Bibek, tr. *The Mahabharata, Vol. 1*. Penguin, 2010.

Debroy, Bibek, tr. *The Mahabharata, Vol. 2*. Penguin, 2010.

Debroy, Bibek, tr. *The Mahabharata, Vol. 3*. Penguin, 2011.

Debroy, Bibek, tr. *The Mahabharata, Vol. 4*. Penguin, 2011.

Debroy, Bibek, tr. *The Mahabharata, Vol. 5*. Penguin, 2012.

Debroy, Bibek, tr. *The Mahabharata, Vol. 6*. Penguin, 2012.

Debroy, Bibek, tr. *The Mahabharata, Vol. 7*. Penguin, 2013.

Debroy, Bibek, tr. *The Mahabharata, Vol. 8*. Penguin, 2013.

Debroy, Bibek, tr. *The Mahabharata, Vol. 9*. Penguin, 2014.

Debroy, Bibek, tr. *The Mahabharata, Vol. 10*. Penguin, 2014.

Debroy, Bibek, tr. *Harivamsha*. Penguin, 2015.

Debroy, Bibek, tr. *The Valmiki Ramayana, Vol. 1*. Penguin, 2016.

Debroy, Bibek, tr. *The Valmiki Ramayana, Vol. 3*. Penguin, 2016.

Debroy, Bibek, tr. *Vishnu Purana*. Penguin, 2022.

Hiltebeitel, Alf. *Rethinking the Mahabharata*. The University of Chicago Press, 2001.

Smith, John, tr. *Electronic text of the critical edition of the Mahabharata*. https://bombay.indology.info, 1999. Last accessed 21st May 2023.

Mani, Vettam. *Puranic Encyclopaedia*. Motilal Banarsidas, 2021.

Sorensen, S, tr. *An Index to The Names In the Mahabharata*. Motilal Banarsidas, 1978.

Wisdom lib. https://www.wisdomlib.org/ last accessed 28 May, 2023.

Ambuda. *Mahabharata*. https://www.ambuda.org/texts/mahabharatam/3.277, last accessed 28 May, 2023.

ABOUT THE AUTHOR

Abhinav Agarwal holds a bachelor's degree in computer engineering from Mumbai University and is a gold medallist from the Indian Institute of Management, Bangalore. He is the author of a fiction thriller, *Predators and Prey. Completing Vyasa's Mahabharata* is his second book. Abhinav lives in Bangalore with his wife and two children.

He can be reached at aa@abhinavagarwal.net, twitter.com/AbhinavAgarwal, instagram.com/writeAbhinav, and fb.com/AbhinavAuthor